Texts in Philosophy
Volume 25

# Karl Popper

A Centenary Assessment

Volume II

Metaphysics and Epistemology

Texts in Philosophy Series Editors
Vincent F. Hendriks                          vincent@hum.ku.dk
John Symons                                  jsymons@utep.edu
Dov Gabbay                                   dov.gabbay@kcl.ac.uk

# Karl Popper

## A Centenary Assessment
## Volume II
## Metaphysics and Epistemology

Edited by

## Ian Jarvie
## Karl Milford

and

## David Miller

This edition is a reprint of the Ashgate edition of 2006.

ISBN 978-1-84890-191-9


College Publications
Scientific Director: Dov Gabbay
Managing Director: Jane Spurr


http://www.collegepublications.co.uk


Original cover design by Laraine Welch


Printed by Lightning Source, Milton Keynes, UK

---

# Contents

# Preface

For five warm summer days (3-7 July 2002), more than 300 people from more than 50 countries attended KARL POPPER 2002, a congress held in Vienna to commemorate the 100th anniversary of Popper's birth (28 July 1902). The principal activity at the meetings held in the main building of the University of Vienna, his alma mater, was, in keeping with Popper's outlook, critical engagement with his intellectual achievement in the many fields to which he contributed. Besides the investigation, development, and critical assessment of Popper's ideas, participants were able to enjoy a walking tour of Vienna sites relevant to Popper's early career, a recital of his organ fugue at the church of St Michael in Heiligenstadt, an exhibition at the Palais Palffy of his life and work, the unveiling of a bronze bust in the *Arkadenhof* in the University main building, and the opening ceremony at the City Hall (*Rathaus*) at which the Honorary President of the Congress, Professor Dr Hans Albert, gave the Inaugural Address. There was also an excursion after the congress to the University at Klagenfurt, where Popper's working library is housed.

The three volumes are a selection from more than 200 invited lectures and contributed papers presented at Vienna. The cull was made as follows. Chairs of sessions and members of the programme committee made an initial selection based upon what they had heard and read. Contributions planned for publication elsewhere were excluded. Every selected paper was sent to two referees. Authors made their final revisions in the light of the referees' reports. We are grateful to those who shortened their papers on request.

The present volume contains papers on Popper's metaphysics and epistemology, with special emphasis on the empirical basis of science, and on induction. Volume I contains papers on Popper's life and influence, and on democracy and the open society. Volume III is devoted to papers on the various sciences to which Popper contributed.

The notes on the contributors and editors have been revised for this edition. The text of the volume is otherwise identical with that of the Ashgate edition of 2006, except for the correction of a few typographical and linguistic errors, some amendments to the index, and some inconsequential formatting changes.

KARL POPPER 2002 was more than six years in the planning. Many were involved in its organization, but it would not have taken place without the heroic efforts of Heidi König in Vienna. The editors should like to thank, in addition, the speakers, chairs, and referees, and Mrs Melitta Mew and the Karl Popper Charitable Trust. All royalties earned by these three volumes will go to the Trust.

Ian Jarvie
Karl Milford
David Miller

# Notes on the Contributors

(*revised 2016*)

**Joseph Agassi** has an MSc in physics, Hebrew University of Jerusalem, 1951 and a PhD in General Science (Logic and Scientific Method), University of London (London School of Economics), 1956. He is Professor Emeritus, Tel Aviv University and York University, Toronto. He has produced over 400 contributions to the learned press, over a dozen monographs, and a few edited volumes. E-mail: `agass@post.tau.ac.il`

**Gunnar Andersson** is Emeritus Professor of Philosophy of Science at the University of Umeå. E-mail: `gunnar.andersson@philos.umu.se`

**Hubert Cambier** studied philosophy at the University of Paris X Nanterre, and devoted his PhD dissertation to the study of the philosophy of Karl Popper (2001). The thesis has since been published by the Editions Universitaires Européennes, Saarbrücken in two volumes: *La philosophie de Karl R. Popper. 1. La théorie de la connaissance*; 2. *Philosophie pratique et métaphysique* (2012). His current researches focus on a pragmatic approach in the philosophy of language. E-mail: `hubert.cambier@skynet.be`

**Antoni Diller** studied philosophy at the Universities of Cambridge and Leeds, and computer science at the University of Oxford. He taught at the University of Birmingham for almost 26 years until he retired in 2013. He continues to study testimony, anti-justificationism, the Angry Young Men of the 1950s, and the philosophical implications of artificial intelligence. E-mail: `antoni.diller@cantab.net`

**Volker Gadenne** is Professor of Philosophy and Theory of Science at the University of Linz. His main interests are methodology, philosophy of the social sciences, the mind-body problem, consciousness. His publications include: *Kritischer Rationalismus und Pragmatismus* (editor), Rodopi 1998; *Philosophie der Psychologie*, Hans Huber 2004. E-mail: `Volker.Gadenne@jku.at`

**Stefano Gattei** graduated in philosophy from the University of Milan in 2003 and was awarded a PhD in philosophy of science at the University of Bristol in 2004. He is currently a research fellow at the Chemical Heritage Foundation in Philadelphia. He is the author of several articles and a few books in both history and philosophy of science, among them, *Thomas Kuhn's 'Linguistic Turn' and the Legacy of Logical Positivism* (Ashgate 2008) and *Karl Popper's Philosophy of Science: Rationality without Foundations* (Routledge 2009). Most recently, he has edited (with Joseph Agassi), the fourth volume of Paul Feyerabend's collected papers, *Physics and Philosophy* (Cambridge University Press, 2015). E-mail: `stefano.gattei@gmail.com`

**Shereen Hassanein**'s research focuses on philosophy of language and philosophy of mind, with an emphasis on cognitive and linguistic development in both typical children and children with developmental and learning delays. E-mail: `Shereen.Hassanein@senecacollege.ca`

**Toby E. Huff** is Chancellor Professor Emeritus in the Department of Policy Studies at the University of Massachusetts Dartmouth and Research Associate at Harvard University in the Department of Astronomy. He is the author of *The Rise of Early Modern Science: Islam, China and the West* (Cambridge 1993, 3rd edition 2016), and *Intellectual Curiosity: The Scientific Revolution in Global Perspective* (Cambridge 2011). E-mail: `thuff@fas.harvard.edu`

**Herbert Keuth**, born 1940, who has a master's degree in economics, and a PhD in philosophy, is Professor of Philosophy of Science at Eberhard Karls University, Tübingen. He is author of *The Philosophy of Karl Popper*, Cambridge 2005. E-mail: `Herbert.Keuth@t-online.de`

**Artur Koterski** teaches at Maria Curie-Skłodowska University, Lublin. He is a historian of the philosophy of science, and author of *Verificational Criteria of Demarcation in the Vienna Circle's Philosophy of Science*, 2002, and *Falsificational Criteria of Demarcation in 20th Philosophy of Science*, 2004 (both in Polish). He has translated and edited several books and papers by members of the Vienna Circle. E-mail: `Artur.Koterski@umcs.lublin.pl`

**Ilkka Niiniluoto** has made his career at the University of Helsinki: PhD in 1973, Professor of Theoretical Philosophy from 1977 to 2014, Rector from 2003 to 2008, and Chancellor from 2008 to 2013. He has defended scientific realism by a novel explication of Popper's notion of verisimilitude. His main works are *Is Science Progressive?*, Reidel 1984, *Truthlikeness*, Reidel 1987, and *Critical Scientific Realism*, Oxford 1999. E-mail: `ilkka.niiniluoto@helsinki.fi`

**Jonas Nilsson** is Head of the Department of Historical, Philosophical, and Religious Studies and Programme Coordinator, Philosophy at Umeå University. His *Rationality in Inquiry: On the Revisability of Cognitive Standards* was published in 2001. He works on the dynamics of rationality and methodological change in science. E-mail: `jonas.nilsson@philos.umu.se`

**Robert Nola** is Professor of Philosophy at the University of Auckland. His area of research is in philosophy of science, metaphysics, epistemology as well as the sociology of science and science education. His books include: *Rescuing Reason*, Kluwer 2003; (with G. Irzik) *Science, Philosophy, Education and Culture*, Springer 2006; and (edited with Howard Sankey) *After Popper, Kuhn and Feyerabend: Recent Issues in the Theory of Scientific Method*, Kluwer 2000. E-mail: `r.nola@auckland.ac.nz`

**Ingemar Nordin** is Professor, at tema Health and Society, Linköping University. He did graduate studies in mathematics, physics, and philosophy, and was awarded a PhD in philosophy in 1980. He has taught at the University of Lund and the University of Umeå. His fields of research are philosophy of science and technology, political philosophy, especially human rights, and philosophy of medicine, especially problems of knowledge within medical research and practice. E-mail: `ingemar.nordin@liu.se`

**Herman Philipse** studied at Leyden, Oxford, Paris IV, and Cologne, and has taught at Louvain (Husserl Archives) and at Leyden (PhD on Husserl's philosophy of logic, 1983). At present he is University Professor at the University of Utrecht. He writes on modern philosophy and epistemology. His most recent books are *God in the Age of Science? A Critique of Religious Reason*, Oxford 2011; *Atheïstisch manifest*, Prometheus 1995, 1998; new edition in one volume with *De onredelijkheid van religie*, Bert Bakker 2004; and *Heidegger's Philosophy of Being. A Critical Interpretation*, Princeton 1998. E-mail: `H.Philipse@uu.nl`

**Kurt Salamun** is Professor Emeritus at the Institute of Philosophy, University of Graz. He has written articles (in German) on Popper's conception of Man, his ethos of Enlightenment, and the relevance of his philosophy to the critique of fundamentalist ideologies. He is Founder and Co-Editor of the SERIES IN THE PHILOSOPHY OF KARL R. POPPER AND CRITICAL RATIONALISM (Rodopi, Brill), 21st volume in preparation. E-mail: `kurt.salamun@uni-graz.at`

**Alfred Schramm**, Professor (University of Graz), retired since 2009; visiting scholar at LSE, 1976-1978; President of the Austrian Philosophical Society, 1994-1996; President of the Research Center for Austrian Philosophy 1999-2009; Founder (2004) and Chairman (2004-2009) of the Alexius-Meinong-Institute at the University of Graz. Publications in epistemology, philosophy of science, rationality theory, history of Austrian philosophy. E-mail: `alfred.schramm@uni-graz.at`

**Jonathan P. Seldin** is Emeritus Professor of Mathematics and Computer Science at the University of Lethbridge, Alberta. His main areas of research are lambda-calculus, combinatory logic, and proof theory. He is interested also in the history and philosophy of mathematics and the philosophy of science. E-mail: `jonathan.seldin@uleth.ca`

**Jeremy Shearmur** is Emeritus Fellow in the School of Philosophy, RSSS, CASS, Australian National University. He is the author of *The Political Thought of Karl Popper*, Routledge 1996, and of *Hayek and After*, Routledge 1996, and is joint editor, with Piers Norris Turner, of Karl Popper's *After the Open Society*, Routledge 2008, and, with Geoffrey Stokes, of *The Cambridge Companion to Popper*, Cambridge 2016. E-mail: `Jeremy.Shearmur@anu.edu.au`

**Guglielmo Tamburrini** is Professor of Logic and Philosophy of Science in the School of Sciences at University of Naples Federico II. His research interests include the methodology of the cognitive (neuro-)sciences, robotics, and artificial intelligence. E-mail: `tamburrini@na.infn.it`

**Karsten Weber** is Chair for General Science of Technology at the Brandenburg University of Technology in Cottbus-Senftenberg, Germany, and Co-Head of the Center of Competence, Institute for Social Research and Technology Assessment (IST) at the Ostbayerische Technische Hochschule Regensburg. His research interests include technology assessment, philosophy of science, and applied ethics. E-mail: `Karsten.Weber@b-tu.de`; `Karsten.Weber@oth-regensburg.de`

# Notes on the Editors

*(revised 2016)*

**Ian Jarvie** (editor in chief) is Distinguished Research Professor in Philosophy (Emeritus) at York University, Toronto, and Managing Editor of the journal *Philosophy of the Social Sciences*. His books include *The Revolution in Anthropology*, Routledge 1964; *Philosophy of the Film*, Routledge 1987; and *The Republic of Science*, Rodopi 2001. E-mail: `jarvie@yorku.ca`

**Karl Milford** is Associate Professor of Economics at the University of Vienna. He has written extensively on the epistemological views of Carl Menger, for example in *Zu den Lösungsversuchen des Induktions und Abgrenzungsproblems bei Carl Menger*, Verlag der Österreichischen Akademie der Wissenschaften 1989. E-mail: `karl.milford@univie.ac.at`

**David Miller** is Emeritus Reader in Philosophy at the University of Warwick, where he taught logic (and some other things) from 1969 until 2007. He is the editor of *Popper Selections*, Princeton 1985, and author of *Critical Rationalism. A Restatement and Defence*, Open Court 1994, and of *Out of Error. Further Essays on Critical Rationalism*, Ashgate 2006. Web site: `http://www.warwick.ac.uk/go/dwmiller`; E-mail: `dwmiller57@yahoo.com`

# PART 3
# Metaphysics and Epistemology

## A: The Constitution of the World

# Metaphysics and the Growth of Scientific Knowledge

Joseph Agassi

When a philosophical problem vanishes, according to Ludwig Wittgenstein, everything goes back to normal.[1] This claim is sophomoric, since, obviously, the philosophically normal is problem-ridden: the vanishing of one philosophical problem gives rise to a better one. The problem of the characterization or demarcation of science is an example of this. Wittgenstein shared the standard philosophical view of science as authoritative because inductive. By announcing that it was meaningless, he decreed the problem of induction to vanish.[2] He thus made this disappearance give rise to the problem of meaning.[3] When Karl Popper tried to dispense with the problem of the basis of the authority of science, he gave rise to the problem, why do we prefer scientific theories or at least find them preferable? The problem of the characterization or demarcation of science remains, and Popper's solution to it is a major contribution to contemporary philosophy in general.

The concern of rationalist philosophers with this problem is traditional — both theoretical and practical. The theoretical concern is still valid: even if we do not find science authoritative, we continue to find interesting and significant the question, what makes science so special? (It is, said Popper, the question of the limits of the possibility of knowledge, which, he added, is the deepest problem of epistemology. He found the problem of induction subsidiary to

---

[1] Wittgenstein (1922), § 4.003: 'Most propositions and questions, that have been written about philosophical matters, are not false but senseless.' § 4.11 'The totality of true propositions is the total natural science.' § 4.112: 'The result of philosophy is not a number of "philosophical propositions", but to make propositions clear.'
Wittgenstein (1953), § 109: 'We must do away with all *explanation*, and description alone must take place.' § 123: 'A philosophical problem has the form; "I do not know my way about." ' § 133: '...philosophical problems should completely disappear.' § 255: 'The [Wittgensteinian] philosopher's treatment of a question is like the treatment of an illness.'

[2] Wittgenstein (1922), §§ 6.31, 6.32., and elsewhere. His argument for this decree is that the rule for inductive inferences (just like the rule for deductive ones) is metalinguistic, and the metalanguage does not exist. It does, as even his followers admit. See, for example, Hintikka (1996), Introduction.

[3] The problem of meaning is metalinguistic and so, by the rules fixed by Wittgenstein (see previous note) he should have decreed it meaningless too. Yet it has been the daily bread of the analytic school of philosophy for generations, although a few leading members of this school have silently given it up.

it.[4]) The practical concern with the problem of the demarcation of science requires a modification of the problem. The second scientific revolution of the early twentieth century upset the absolute authority of science — apparently for good. Nonetheless, in practice science still has some kind of authority. This is an observed general fact. We want to explain this fact and alter it if need be. The continuation of authority is not its own justification, and there is no need for one. As a general principle, we should view as imperfect whatever any authority does. Hence, its output is always open to tests and at efforts at improving it. Justifying it by no matter what means, would block progress (Lord Acton). Whichever way we characterize an authority, the people in authority will see to it that our characterization fits them (Robert Boyle[5]). Therefore, it is better to ask, what arrangement will help us free ourselves of an unbecoming authority and how can we improve the output of others (Popper[6]).

Most of twentieth-century philosophy of science begs to differ; it lags behind. In the received philosophy of science, science is authoritative, and it gets its authority from the available scientific evidence by means of what philosophers of science are pleased to call inductive logic, namely, the received view of probability as surrogate certitude. Inductive logic, being logic, gives to science a supreme and unchallengeable authority. As researchers regularly challenge scientific theories, inductive logicians see this not as a challenge to science but as a challenge to the ascription of scientific status to the theory under challenge. The challenge to any scientific theory, then, shows that the application of inductive logic is not as simple a procedure as the application of deductive logic. Yet its adherents allege that it is an algorithm for the selection of hypotheses. Hence, on the face of it, the received view of science is absurd. How is this possible? The answer is that inductive logic is but a pious hope. Why do they not say so? They say, we are working on it, and this should do. But what if this is a wild goose chase? They say, this cannot be, since common sense supports science. In response Popper said,[7] common sense might err. In other words, whereas the commonsense authority of science is fallible, the inductive authority is not. Hence, inductive logic is contrary to common sense.

Inductive logic assumes the following:

(1) A fund of hypotheses and of information is given and the algorithm should assign each hypothesis a probability given that information.

(2) More precisely, the set of hypotheses is partitioned into sets of competing alternatives, where in each of the subsets at most one is true; regrettably, no further characterization of this partitioning is available.

---

[4]Popper (1959), § 4, fourth paragraph.
[5]Boyle (1665).
[6]Popper (1945), Chapter 7.
[7]Popper (1935) Preface, 1934.

(3) Further, the algorithm is for the choice of one hypothesis out of a set of competing ones; inductive logic recommends that we should believe in it.

(4) Still further, the recommendation should coincide with received scientific opinion and reinforce it.

Regrettably, the programme of inductive logic, the search for such an algorithm, is still popular, despite Popper's half-a-century of effort at mounting arguments against it, arguments of such cogency that continuing to advocate it is downright irrational. Popper's arguments are not really necessary. Hume's critique of induction was already sufficient. He argued that inductive logic is impossible. Popper's main addition to Hume's arguments is his many proofs that whatever the rules are for resting the choice of hypothesis on some given evidence, and whatever that choice exactly is, these rules conflict with the rules of the calculus of probability. Armies of philosophers who call themselves Bayesians (in injustice to Bayes[8]) are busy with this matter.[9] They claim that they are offering the most promising alternative to Popper's methodology, or perhaps an addition to it, as they wish to handle the problem of rational belief that he has wisely shunned. He was not concerned with belief, as it is a matter for psychology. After a delay of decades, his criticism forced some advocates of inductive logic to retreat. They offer now a new idea: the theory of inference to the best explanation.[10] They hardly explain. Possibly, they refrain from explaining as they too wish to present Popper's view under a new guise. Otherwise, one can easily refute their view by contrasting it with Popper's. The contrast should open easy ways to construct test cases. Test cases should prove the difference and elucidate it. Every obvious test case goes Popper's way.[11] This is hardly surprising, for the simple reason that the new theory is not well thought-out. Of course, the new theory may still win. If it does, its success will comprise great progress. Therefore, it is worthwhile for

---

[8]The philosophy of science known as Bayesianism rests loosely on a theorem of Thomas Bayes that belongs to the calculus of probability. Their system does not. His theorem applies to any pair of sets, one of which is the set of all possible outcomes and the other is the set of all conditions under which they may occur. Given the probability of each of these outcomes given any of these conditions, Bayes's theorem concludes the probability of a condition given an outcome. Self-styled Bayesians offer nothing like it, since they cannot possibly offer any complete list of possible outcomes or of possible conditions for them.

[9]See Howson & Urbach (1989/1993).

[10]See Thagard (1978), Lipton (1991).

[11]The simplest test case is when none of the extant explanations is good enough. If they recommend the best among these, then they advocate faith in a false hypothesis. (This is the demand for constructive criticism advocated by Lenin. It is a licence to ignore critics who do not have an alternative offer, or to ignore their criticism and criticize their offer, as attack is the best defence.) Otherwise, the new theory does not say which hypothesis is best; Popper does. Finally, they do not prescribe a course of action. Popper did. He said, the question is not what to believe but what to do, and he recommended the search for a new explanation, but without offering any heuristic. He entered the field of heuristic in a later stage of his career. The reason for this is that his critique of induction came first, and traditionally the advocates of induction justified whatever conclusions they reached by reference to the way they had reached them.

its advocates to offer the new theory in some well-thought out exact wording and to scrutinize it carefully. We must wait for its advocates to show that they are serious by discussing its rationale and its wording, and by comparing it with Popper's views. In the meanwhile, we should proceed, although it is harder to proceed in the absence of a worthy opponent.

As tradition deems the problem of the demarcation of science both theoretical and practical, it solves them together, but it offers two solutions. One characterized science by its *a priori* presuppositions — such as mechanism — that express the scientific world view or the scientific attitude or the scientific ethos. The other characterized science by its empirical character. Let me consider each of these ideas before discussing their combination.

What is empirical character? It is what makes science an experimental philosophy, to use the original term of the seventeenth-century fathers of the first scientific revolution. The general expectation from individuals interested in science was then that they would create laboratories, use them, and thereby add to the stock of scientific knowledge. This last statement is phenomenological and commonsense. Its phenomenological character is as obvious as possible. Its common sense is fragile. Anything that goes beyond the very basic information mentioned thus far threatens it. And much goes beyond the basic information and covers a vast field, as Hume showed in detail. To speak practically, we know that only a relatively small number of extant laboratories are sources of valuable new information that merits the title 'scientific', since valuable new information is still very hard to come by.

Two facts cover this vast field. First, only repeatable observations count as scientific. Repeatability is problematic. Very few philosophers have ever discussed it. The first was Boyle, who instituted the rule (that Galileo had implied and Descartes had stated tersely) that observations should be granted scientific status only if they are repeated (by independent observers) and claim the status of repeatability. Boyle noted that this was highly problematic. The second was Kant, who claimed that mathematical wording renders observations scientific.[12] This claim conflicts with Boyle's rule. (Kant denied chemistry scientific status as it is not mathematical, even though its facts are repeatable.) Let me ignore it. Next came Karl Popper and Mario Bunge, who justified the demand for repeatability by the demand for testability, and thus by reference to human fallibility.

This fully covers the case of observations. It shows how problematic it is and so how remote from common sense it is. The case of theory is naturally even more problematic. Tradition views a theory as scientific if and only if it emerges from empirical information. This is too vague. An alternative traditional answer is, a theory becomes empirical after it has gained empirical verification. A still later alternative replaced verification with support. This is common sense, but not all the way. Common sense views it at times as

---

[12]Kant said repetition of a test is always advisable; it is, however, unimportant as a mode of proof. See his first *Critique*, Kant (1781/1787), A702/B820.

(practically) stable and at times as precarious:[13] common sense is pragmatic without supporting pragmatism or any other version of relativism.

Two things that Popper did are repeatedly (con)fused in many if not most commentaries on his work. First, he replaced support by supportability, and, second, he identified supportability with refutability. Not with refutation or with its absence but with its sheer possibility: with its refutability: a theory is empirical if and only if it is capable of undergoing empirical tests that may lead to its refutation. (This possibility is not the mere logical possibility that always exists; it is the ability to describe an experiment that one may perform, whose outcome may refute the theory in case it is false.) This fully answers the question, what theory is scientific. Another question remains: what is empirical support? It is important, since it signifies for practice.

And so we move from the theoretical aspect of the problem of demarcation to its practical aspect. Popper did two things here: first, he dismissed the practical aspect as irrelevant to the problem of demarcation, since the problem is theoretical. Second, he answered the irrelevant question anyway. Popper's theory of empirical support is the same as that of Whewell (though he could put it much more crisply than Whewell could). It is this. Empirical support is failed refutation. Regrettably, Popper did not explain his interest in it beyond the fact that the examples of known empirical support conflict with the received views and conform to his.[14]

Before addressing the question of Popper's interest, let me state my own opinion on the matter. I place it here for four reasons. First, my idea is simple. Second, to show that it is more Popperian than what Popper has suggested. Third, to show that my admiration for Popper's ideas is not uncritical. Fourth, to show the tremendous practical power of Popper's methodology. The idea is this. Popper's negativism clashes with the fact that science is a positive guide for action. Inductive logic comes to fill this gap. It fails to do so. The fact is that in the modern world support for hypotheses is a requirement for their legitimate application. Now every modern democracy anchors this legitimacy in its legal system. Licensing the application of a new idea in the market depends on its passing certain specified tests for possible side effects. This is not a matter of inductive logic or philosophy, as it is imperfect and in need of corrections that legislation repeatedly applies to it. But the tests that the law requires differ from those that science applies for intellectual ends. Moreover, the rationality of the whole procedure does not relate to beliefs and is not in any way obligatory; rather, it is a matter of licence. In any case, Popper's interest in tests and in the support that they may lend a theory was rightly more theoretical than practical.

---

[13]Common sense offers no criterion of repeatability or of openness to generalization or of the claim for lawlike character. But it helps to decide with ease whether we should judge an event repeatable or not. This is a commonsense intuition that is clear and unproblematic. But it does not stay unaltered. To explain this fact one has to refer to the change of received intellectual frameworks, so-called, that is, of the metaphysical systems that researchers endorse as a matter of course.

[14]Popper (1959), Appendix *ix.

There are several items concerning empirical support that exhibit this theoretical interest in it. First, as at times evidence does support a hypothesis, whatever precisely this support is, we may want to know what it is — for theoretical as well as for practical reasons. Second, some people want it — for practical reasons or for self-satisfaction — and Popper has shown them how to try to obtain it. Third, a critic may suggest that Popper's theory is unsatisfactory, since it cannot describe the facts of empirical support of hypotheses. So, he showed that it can. Indeed, he showed that his theory accounts for the empirical facts of empirical support of hypotheses better than any of his opponents ever did, since their theories are hit by the paradoxes of confirmation that are deadly whereas his is immune to them. (Moreover, the claim that most writers on empirical support make is that empirical support conforms to the mathematical theory of probability, and this claim always mattered to Popper: it was his pet aversion. The fusion of empirical support and probability clashes with his theory of empirical support, which spawns countless deadly arguments against it.)

Popper did not explain his interest in the theory of empirical support. Consequently, he was repeatedly saddled with the traditional view that to become empirical a theory must gain empirical support. He vehemently denied this, all to no avail. As far as I know, he never withdrew his replacement of the traditional identification of the empirical characterization of science as empirical support of hypotheses by his novel characterization of it as their refutability. This remained to the last his criterion of demarcation of the empirical character of science and of its hypotheses or theories. It is a wonderfully simple and ingenious idea. If ever someone criticizes it effectively, the result should be very exciting and deep. So far, there is nothing at all in this direction; not even a hint.

Let me mention my qualifications to my total endorsement of Popper's idea so as to avoid misreading. First, Popper has also discussed degrees of refutability. This idea is very interesting and intriguing. We cannot leave it as it stands, nor did Popper consider it this way. (He said so emphatically.) Second, he characterized as refutability not only empirical character but also scientific character. This is an error that he corrected, but not with his usual exemplary clarity. He said, especially in his lecture courses for over two decades, that a theory is scientific if and only if it is a satisfactory explanation. I consider this idea to be true. No doubt I could be mistaken, but that is my opinion for what it is worth. What then is a satisfactory explanation? Popper's answer is brilliant. An explanation is satisfactory if, and only to the extent that, it is not ad hoc. (Ad hoc explanations are often verbal or metaphorical sleight of hand, and they are always defensive and distasteful unless they have empirical support, in which case they are still unsatisfactory but not easy to replace by better alternatives.) And in order to show that an explanation is not ad hoc, we may try to show that it is independently testable. And testability, Popper always said, equals refutability.

Even regarding refutability, new ground was thereby covered. A testable explanation that has been tested and has passed its tests certainly does not lose its empirical character, yet it gets stale and becomes increasingly unsatisfactory. This explains the erroneous view of Newtonian mechanics as a mere mathematical system in which to store information. Popper's conclusion from it that the demand for explanation sustains the demand for testability (refutability) is from his lecture courses. Let me observe that the discussion of these ideas about the problem of demarcation is remote from the practical aspect of the problem.

Traditionally, to be scientific, or satisfactory, a theory has to be more than empirical. It has to comply with the scientific world view or the scientific attitude or the scientific ethos. What is this? Is it of any practical value?

The most popular and most important answer to this question is positivism. It has a classical variant and a new, twentieth-century variant, due to Wittgenstein. He denied the very existence of metaphysics, and on the grounds of sheer grammar: the very rules of grammar, he said, render metaphysics impossible. This new variant is so substandard that those who stick to it are not likely to pay attention to any new argument against it. And, indeed, its adherents usually ignored Popper's criticism of it and his alternative to it. And when they did mention him, they ignored and distorted both.[15] Therefore, I ignore them.

Classical positivism is different. It identified the scientific attitude or ethos with a total disregard for all alternatives to science. Traditionally, there was one alternative: religion. Under the influence of the leading early twentieth-century anthropologist, Sir James Frazer, positivists see two alternatives to science: magic and religion. (Frazer put them in an ascending order: magic is more remote from science as it is a pseudo-science. Otto Neurath reversed this order and said, as pseudo-science, and more so as an ineffective technology, magic is nearer to science than religion is.) All this sounds odd: where did metaphysics disappear? The answer is that all positivists were fighting religion more than metaphysics, and so in a pinch they simply identified the two.

---

[15]The distortion was the assertion that Popper's demarcation of science is a demarcation of meaning or of language, which makes him an adherent of a variant of the philosophy of Wittgenstein, of course. It appears in Carnap (1936-1937). See also Ayer (1959) for Ayer's distortion (pp. 14, 229) and for Hempel's distortion (pp. 113f.). Ayer says (p. 14), 'But Popper's criterion has demerits of its own. Thus, for instance, as he himself recognizes, it allows one to deny an indefinite existential statement but not to affirm it.' This is Wittgenstein-style talk. Popper offered a proposal as to which theory has empirical character, or, what makes a theory empirical. Unlike Wittgenstein, he never forbade making any assertion, no matter how non-empirical it may be. Ayer also said more clearly (ibidem, p. 229 and note) that the asymmetry between verification and refutation 'has led some philosophers', including Popper, 'notably', 'to adopt the possibility of falsification rather than that of verification as their criterion of empirical significance'.

Hempel ascribes to Popper the meaning criterion of refutability (p. 113, note), adding (p. 114, note) 'Whether Popper would subscribe to the proposed restatement [of Hempel] ...I do not know.' Once in a public lecture he did ascribe it to Popper, and when I objected he refused to correct his statement. (See Agassi 1993, p. 98.)

While Popper offered deadly criticism of the new, Wittgenstein-style positivism, he endorses the older positivism of Ernst Mach. Two significant additions to positivism are due to Mach. The first concerns the value of metaphysics as a general view of the world or as a world view. He had no need for it, he said, as his world view comprises the sum total of all extant scientific theories. This is brilliant, but hopelessly defective. In particular, it refers to science as it is now, ignoring its growth. Moreover, even when we restrict our considerations to extant scientific theories, we cannot avoid noticing that they do not fall into place all by themselves: they need some unifying idea. That idea, whatever it may be, is metaphysical.

Mach's second contribution to classical positivism is the idea that since metaphysics is unscientific it is inherently controversial: metaphysical controversies are not capable of resolution. Engaging in them, then, is wasting time: we should not take part in any metaphysical controversy. Popper accepted this demand of Mach's, but with a proviso: he was a realist in his personal disposition; but in his methodology he tried to stay out of such controversies. The most important one is, of course, that between realism and idealism, and Popper claimed that his methodology stays clear of it.[16] This was his attitude to all extant metaphysical controversies. Another important controversy that he avoided concerns the nature of truth (though not the falsity of contradictions: that is incontestable).[17] In short, he endorsed Mach's view that the scientific attitude or ethos requires only a stringent empiricism that stays aloof from all metaphysical controversy.

As Popper refused then to partake in any metaphysical controversy, he ignored the fact that metaphysical controversies may become scientific, even though he made this point at the very end of his *Logik der Forschung*. He did so at least twice, when he argued from it against the new positivist doctrine that such controversies are nonexistent, and earlier there, in his criticism of Heisenberg's reading of his own inequality. Popper wanted empiricism stringent: he wanted testability maximal. This was an error. He did not uphold this stringency systematically: he upheld it only regarding the status of given theories. He did not support it when he discussed the growth of knowledge. At the end of this book, to repeat, he noted that metaphysical ideas had contributed to the growth of science. Nevertheless, even there he discouraged the use of metaphysical ideas in research.

This was inconsistent with his own viewpoint, and he finally gave it up. The damage due to the error is not limited, however, to its having prevented him from examining more fully certain heuristic problems that he touched upon (with valuable results). The most important damage it did to his *Logik*

---

[16]Popper (1959), end of § 27.

[17]Popper (1959), opening of § 84. Of course, Hegel asserted that some contradictions are true, and some have followed him in this. Popper never took Hegel seriously, and he proved that the willingness to endorse contradictions renders rationality impossible. See his (1940), now Chapter 15 of his (1963). The essay did have some impact. Nevertheless, some orthodox Hegelians still openly adhere to this folly.

*der Forschung* appears in his theory of explanation. It is hard to discuss this, as it is a minor blemish. And before discussing it, we had better glance at the design of the book as a whole. It is clear what its first two chapters do: they discuss two problems announced in its opening. This is not true for the rest of the book. My conjecture is that this is the result of the fact that the version of the book in our hands is greatly abridged: he abridged it in order to render it acceptable to his publisher.[18] (The book's full version is lost.) Any answer to my question, what do the last eight chapters of the book do, must remain a conjecture. My suggestion is that Popper discusses there some possible criticisms of his theories and some possible alternatives to them. His strategy was forceful. He first tried to show of an alternative to his view that it is a variant of it. Barring that, he criticized the alternative effectively. Thus, the idea that empirical character is probability in the light of extant evidence is false. And simplicity is either refutability and respectable, or not and then not.

The case of explanations is the same: they are testable or else unempirical. And to be testable they should be deductive nomological, to use the expression of Hans Reichenbach. To this end, Popper added, they must be universal. At least ever since Descartes everybody took this idea for granted. Yet, Descartes demanded that a deductive explanation fit his mechanical philosophy: he deemed nomological only mechanical hypotheses. Not so Popper: he deemed testability sufficient. Here he was closer to Boyle than to Descartes, and rightly so. But both parties went too far.

The mechanical philosophy enjoyed the status of the scientific world view or attitude or ethos. This persisted until the second scientific revolution.[19] Old and new positivists endorsed it. For example, Freud found clairvoyance fascinating, and suspected that it may be possible. He feared that this would destroy the scientific outlook. When certain (allegedly) successful experiments in parapsychology came to the attention of Reichenbach, he saw in them a threat to his whole philosophy. This is amusing.

Positivists eagerly endorse materialism, preferably Cartesian. Already a generation after Descartes, Boyle issued a warning against dogmatic adherence to it.[20] He reported that researchers ignore empirical information that does not seem to tally with it. He gave an example from his own study of the elasticity of air. Descartes, we remember, viewed matter as utterly inelastic. But, said Boyle, it is incumbent upon Cartesians to explain elasticity — that of metal springs, for example. So, when he considered air elastic, he assumed that when they could cope with the challenge of elastic springs, his theory of the elasticity of air will thereby also become Cartesian. Boyle's warning rested

---

[18] See Popper's 'Intellectual Autobiography' (1974/1976), § 16.

[19] The popularity of Descartes's view as the ethos of science remained for surprisingly long. Kant unnoticingly adhered to Cartesian physics (see his first *Critique*, (1781/1787), A770-1/B798-9) and to the Cartesian demand to explain the unknown by the known (ibidem, A772; B800). Whittaker (1949) still exhibits admiration for Descartes as the author of the scientific ethos and contempt for him as a metaphysician.

[20] See my (1997).

on the idea that one can use unscientific theories as challenges for boosting research but not as excuses for blocking it.

Is disregard for some information always harmful? Much information regularly goes unnoticed. This is unavoidable. Even some seemingly refuting evidence is not noticed. Thomas S. Kuhn, Paul Feyerabend, and Imre Lakatos all said that this amounts to a refutation of Popper's whole philosophy. By their own lights they are in error, but they simply did not like Popper's stringency. The question is not of temperament, however: a stringent attitude leads to the search for a better alternative.[21] The assumption that some empirical information is false may cause trouble. Many assumptions are troublesome, and science is both a trouble maker and a troubleshooter. Its task is to explain, not to overlook. So all oversights are always defects, and it behooves researchers to admit this and acknowledge that some time or another, before their views become serious putative truths, before they take them to task and test them as severely as possible, they should prevent all oversight. (This is a variant of Descartes's fourth rule of method.)

Much of the criticism of Popper's view as it appears in his *Logik der Forschung* is that it lacks a discussion of heuristic. This is no criticism, since it was his right to refuse to discuss heuristic. And he insisted that this renders his view of science incomplete. Still, he did not discuss the import of the scientific ethos, including atomism and mechanism and even plain old materialism, and the heuristic role that the ethos has played throughout history. He said to the last that his methodology is both prescriptive and descriptive. He noted that this raises certain problems. He could not go further: his major contributions are not yet absorbed, and so the field is much too poor as yet to cope with the tremendous and exciting problems that his methodology raises.

Adding the heuristic component to Popper's views — as he did in his later phases — improves them. But he could not go over old ground to iron out some older ideas, especially since regrettably he remained busy in seeking ever newer refutations of the worthless ideas of his old Viennese peers who kept — and still keep — the reputation that he wrongly envied them. Let me mention but one instance. Popper said, when a theory and experiment clash, the default choice should be to consider true the empirical evidence not the hypothesis, unless it is possible to replace it with newer empirical evidence that refutes it. This seems to be common sense. He would have done better had he observed that clinging to the default option too closely might be too dogmatic. This, however, is scarcely criticism.

This is not to detract from the qualifications made here earlier. Popper made it clear that he did not discuss heuristic in his *Logik der Forschung*.

---

[21]The paradigm case is the very powerful Charles law for the ideal gas: for a container of one moll of any gas the product of its volume and its pressure is proportional to its temperature with a universal factor of proportionality. Powerful as it is, the efforts of Johannes Diderik van der Waals to improve upon it led to a better and more interesting result (van der Waals's law), which nonetheless did not quite satisfy its originator, who tried to improve it further all his life.

Nor did he have to, of course. But he occasionally did discuss it. He used it against the theory of inductive inference, stressing that hypotheses are inspired and that the question is not where they comes from but, how do researchers render the fruit of inspiration empirical? At times, contrary to the inductivist lore, they come from metaphysical visions of the world. Perhaps this point is still not sufficiently clear to all. Inductive logic is still rampant. This explains the reasonableness of Popper's decision to leave heuristic aside. Under the influence of Mach, however, he did speak at the end of his *Logik der Forschung* against the use of metaphysical systems as heuristic. He did not also discuss beliefs there. He did speak of acceptance, though, and it is clear that acceptance in his sense differs form the one common at the time. He said, to accept a hypothesis is to accept seriously the challenge to test it (not to believe it).

The authoritative physicist-philosopher-publicist Moritz Schlick maligned Popper[22] and declared him a self-aggrandizer.[23] He said that Popper was trying to present his views as more unusual than they really were. Carnap, and then Stegmüller, repeated this charge. Schlick also said, Popper's philosophy is masochistic: who wants to be in the wrong? These two personal attacks clash with each other, but let this ride. Is Popper's view masochistic? In his seminar, Popper repeatedly answered this charge. Of course, I want to be in

---

[22]Schlick said that, according to Popper the choice as to which statement to view as conveying information is utterly arbitrary (Ayer 1959, p. 231). Ayer softened this verdict considerably when he repeated it (ibidem, p. 236).

Popper was sufficiently irate about this story to allot it a detailed discussion. He called it 'the Popper legend'. See his (1974), § 17 and notes 113 and 113a, and his 'Replies', § 2, 'The Popper Legend', and § 3, 'The Background of the Legend'.

[23]Schlick's verdict that Popper was guilty of self-aggrandizement stuck. Carnap and Hempel repeated it in their friendly reviews of Popper's first book, cited in Popper's 'Replies to My Critics' (Popper 1974, p. 971). Ayer then said (ibidem, p. 6), 'Popper ... would at no time have wished to be classed as a [logical] positivist, but the affinities between him and the positivists whom he criticized appear more striking than the divergencies.' Wolfgang Stegmüller has repeated this senselessness in his obituary on Carnap and elsewhere (Hintikka 1975, p. lxv). So did Hempel. (Hempel 2000, p. 269). I am afraid it still is a part of the lore of the 'Vienna Circle' (Stadler 2001, pp. 176, 448).

Stadler is the latest. He admits that the major difference between Popper and the 'Vienna Circle' is his dismissal of their equation of the demarcation of science with that of sense. And he admits that this was their specific characteristic and their debt to Wittgenstein. Yet he insists that the disagreement was minor. Common sense says, a disagreement is major if the differing parties deem it a matter of principle. Yet they may differ about this very point: what is a principle may be under dispute. Here, however, there is no dispute: the change that Wittgenstein advocated concerned principles: nothing could be more fundamental than the idea that there are no (articulated) philosophical principles. Popper could not possibly differ from them more when he dismissed this idea. Schlick, Carnap, Ayer, Hempel, Stadler, and others gloss over this fact; what they say is pathetic.

Arne Naess has stated and Popper has cited him (in his autobiography 1974/1976, note 114) that this kind of distortion was no accident. As a systematic policy, especially of Neurath, the 'Vienna Circle' took regularly all basic criticism as if it was marginal. It seems to me that it was Schlick who adopted this policy. The philosophical community should take it for what it is: sheer evasion.

the right, he said. But we all err. And as I err, I want to find my error first. I want to correct it as soon as I possibly can.

This is satisfactory as an answer to Schlick. But it is not satisfactory as a philosophy. Much better is Popper's view of objective knowledge, which deserves to attract more scholarly attention than it does at present. Individual views, beliefs, attitudes, play a role in science, as in all social affairs, and more. But they are never substitutes for social institutions. Science is a social institution. And so is the growth of science. Objectively, science is institutions in which people pose questions, offer possible solutions to them, and discuss them critically. Thus, said Popper, science as a whole is an institution, and we should portray it as it is, significant errors and all.

This leaves open the question, is there a scientific world view (as an institution)? Popper spoke of World 3 as the world of extant ideas, of ideas publicly available namely as institutional. Now only a part of World 3 is empirical. Does the scientific part amount to the empirical part? Does the other part play a role in the growth of science? In my view some empirical research is not science — such as market research — and some science is not empirical — any scientific ethos, egalitarianism, and metaphysics.

What I have just said is all too obvious. Science is specifically western. Empirical knowledge is ubiquitous. So the two cannot be equal. The view that science is common sense refined is very appealing and quite often advocated (including by Einstein). What is this refinement? The same goes for questions and for answers. Even lower animals, Popper has observed, solve problems. But only humans articulate them. And not all articulated problems and solutions are scientific.

This leads to the hypothesis that science depends on presuppositions, on the scientific world view. The attitude of backing it is the scientific attitude or ethos. What is it? Frazer said, it is the denial of the supernatural. What is the supernatural? The obvious answer is, 'Open Sesame!' Yet, science-based technology performs many tasks that are much more miraculous in this sense. The second obvious answer is, magic and religion are spiritual. This leads to coarse materialism. All his life Popper fought against it. He said, we do not argue with a machine, and if we do and then realize it, we stop. And we do in fact care for our souls and for the souls of our friends.[24] Hence, we assume that human souls are special. In addition, we ought to prevent human suffering, and to some extent also animal suffering, not computer suffering. This is empirical information. It is easily available. It invites explanation.

This shows how some difficult philosophical questions may seek solutions on relatively obvious matters by the application of Popper's inherently methodological approach. So, it is very important to notice that there is a limit to that, and that beyond this limit there is a need for additional tools — for powerful metaphysics and heuristic.

---

[24]Popper (1945), Chapter 10, note 44.

This clearly is no criticism. The criticism of Euclidean geometry may be empirical. But it is not possible to criticize it validly for the absence from it of discussions of tools more powerful than the ruler and the compass. Writers have the right to decide what problems to attack, and with what tools. And we can only hope that they will try to stand by their promises.[25] Popper did not promise to discuss heuristic. Still, what he did say is a proper subject for criticism. He said that an explanation that is more easily testable should take precedence over one that is more satisfactory from the viewpoint of a given world view. Another error: were it followed through, it would force all researchers into one mould, and then their output may all too easily become a kind of 'normal science' (in Kuhn's sense) the increasing prevalence of which Popper has rightly deemed a danger to the growth of science.[26] In his early work Popper suggested that we should not emulate the atomists, who devised a new world view that was so helpful for the growth of science. He feared that this would cause stagnation. He observed that science grows in the inductive direction (but not inductively), from empirical observations to increasingly higher abstractions. This is only a part of the story. Science grows in a two-prong movement, bottom-up as well as top-down. The top-down direction emerges as people develop views of the universe and try to increase their content so as to render parts of them testable. This leads to progress in metaphysics. In the meantime, researchers may develop less specific theories in the light of general visions — or (*pace* Lakatos[27]) they may develop theories that are independent of any metaphysics in some other way. The trouble with attacks on a problem in different ways is that this invites clashes between competing theories, especially between those reached by the top-down method and those reached by the bottom-up one. This is why the advocates of moves in the top-down direction insisted that results of a priori reasoning are superior to empirical data. This also why empiricists hate metaphysics. For Popper's philosophy this is no problem at all: clashes of opinion may lead to critical discussions, with luck to crucial tests, and thus to the growth of empirical science.

Intellectualists rejected empirical foundations and empiricists rejected metaphysical foundations. Empiricists even rejected metaphysics as such — for fear of clashes. Popper's methodology eschews question of foundations and welcomes clashes that lead to the development of testable ideas. So it need

---

[25] In addition to discussing critically Euclidean geometry on its own terms, we may discuss these terms themselves and their merits and defects. Popper has discussed magnificently the metaphysical reasoning behind Euclid's choice of confining his system to the use of the ruler and the compass alone. See Popper (1945), Chapter 6, note 9.

[26] Popper (1970).

[27] Lakatos said that the measure of the success or the value of a theory is by its conformity to an extended research programme that conforms to some metaphysical or non-empirical or untestable idea. A theory that comes with no supporting programme then does not count. Alternatively, we may invent metaphysics to legitimize it. These are two very different readings of Lakatos. He was not aware of it all, as he took seriously not his philosophy of science but his philosophy of mathematics.

not side with either traditional party — not for fear of partaking in any old metaphysical controversy but due to its rejection of the ground for this controversy.

Again, Popper's methodology proves a powerful incentive for exciting research. Metaphysics is thus not the queen of science and not an outcast. At least metaphysics can be a handmaid of science. In a more egalitarian description, science and metaphysics may cooperate; often they do. But still science has the edge: metaphysics without science stagnates; science without metaphysics is not quite blind: it can follow technological ends and it can grow bottom-up without the help of any top-down assistance. This seems unnecessary, though, as the fear of the dogmatism of metaphysics is by now reduced, at least by comparison with the fear of the dogmatism of some researchers and of some pro-science philosophers. Science is free to employ interesting metaphysical ideas and to explore them, as metaphysics is free to employ some scientific research to develop.

# Bibliography

Agassi, J. (1993). *A Philosopher's Apprentice*. Amsterdam: Rodopi.

——— (1997). 'Truth, Trust and Gentlemen'. *Philosophy of the Social Sciences* **27**, pp. 219-237.

Ayer, A. J., editor (1959). *Logical Positivism*. Glencoe IL: The Free Press.

Boyle, R. (1665). *Occasional Reflections upon several svbiects, whereto is premis'd a discourse about such kind of thoughts*. London: Printed by W. Wilson for H. Herringman.

Carnap, R. (1936-1937). 'Testability and Meaning'. *Philosophy of Science* **3**, pp. 419-471; **4**, pp. 1-40. Reprinted with corrigenda as a booklet. New Haven: Yale University Graduate Philosophy Club, 1950.

Hempel, C. G. (2000). *Selected Philosophical Essays*. Edited by R. C. Jeffrey. Cambridge: Cambridge University Press.

Hintikka, K. J. J. (1996). *Ludwig Wittgenstein: Half Truths and One-and-a-Half Truths*. Dordrecht: Kluwer.

———, editor, (1975). *Rudolf Carnap: Logical Empiricist*. Dordrecht: Reidel.

Howson, C. & Urbach, P. (1989). *Scientific Reasoning: The Bayesian Approach*. La Salle IL: Open Court. 2nd edition 1993, Chicago: Open Court.

Kant, I. (1781). *Kritik der reinen Vernunft*. Riga: Verlag Johann Friedrich Hartknoch. 2nd edition 1787. English translation by N. Kemp Smith 1929. *Immanuel Kant's Critique of Pure Reason*. London & elsewhere: Macmillan.

Lipton, P. (1991). *Inference to the Best Explanation*. New York: Routledge.

Popper, K. R. (1935). *Logik der Forschung*. Vienna: Julius Springer Verlag. English translation, Popper (1959).

——— (1940). 'What is Dialectic?' *Mind* **49**, pp. 403-426. Reprinted as Chapter 15 of Popper (1963).

——— (1945). *The Open Society and Its Enemies*. London: George Routledge & Sons Ltd. 5th edition 1966. London: Routledge & Kegan Paul.

——— (1959). *The Logic of Scientific Discovery*. London: Hutchinson.

——— (1963). *Conjectures and Refutations*. London: Routledge & Kegan Paul. 5th edition 1989. London: Routledge.

——— (1970). 'Normal Science and Its Dangers'. In I. Lakatos & A. E. Musgrave, editors, *Criticism and the Growth of Knowledge*. Cambridge: Cambridge University Press, pp. 51-58.

——— (1974). 'Intellectual Autobiography'. In P. A. Schilpp, editor (1974), pp. 1-181. *The Philosophy of Karl Popper*. La Salle IL: Open Court. Reprinted as *Unended Quest* (1976). London & Glasgow: Fontana/Collins.

Stadler, F. (2001). *The Vienna Circle: Studies in the Origins, Development, and Influence of Logical Empiricism*. Vienna: Springer.

Thagard, P. (1978). 'The Best Explanation: Criteria for Theory Choice'. *Journal of Philosophy* **75**, pp. 76-92.

Whittaker, E. T. (1949). *From Euclid to Eddington: A Study of Conceptions of the External World*. Cambridge: Cambridge University Press. Reprinted 1958. New York: Dover.

Wittgenstein, L. J. J. (1922). *Tractatus Logico-Philosophicus*. London: Routledge & Kegan Paul.

——— (1953). *Philosophical Investigations*. Oxford: Blackwell.

# The Open Society, Metaphysical Beliefs, and Platonic Sources of Reason and Rationality

## Toby E. Huff

Karl Popper's classic study, *The Open Society and Its Enemies* (Popper 1945), was a pioneering endeavour, one filled with novel insights and a useful framework of analysis. His creation of the ideal types of 'open' and 'closed' societies was a useful starting point. Today, of course, we recognize a greater complexity of modes of communication and of state formation, requiring a far more fine-grained analysis. Nevertheless, for certain broad scale comparative purposes, Popper's study contains enduring insights. Indeed it contains critical insights about the nature of human dialogue and communication that apply with vivid power to contemporary situations. I am thinking in particular of the current situation in large parts of the Muslim world, a very large part of the human community that is going through a wrenching period of simultaneous stagnation and development, about which I will elaborate a comparative framework.

As we know, in the *Open Society and Its Enemies* Popper was at pains to show that the crisis of political life and the continuing progress of Western civilization could be resolved and advanced only by adopting the attitude of *critical rationalism*. This entailed giving up both the myth of inevitable progress and the myth of inevitable decline, while replacing such closed idea systems with *rational* argument. For Popper, 'rationalism' meant that ongoing attempt 'to solve as many problems as possible by an appeal to reason, [that is, by using] clear thought and experience, rather than by an appeal to emotions and passions' (Popper 1945, Chapter 24, §I). For Popper, controlled experiment and observation were also part of critical rationalism. Adopting this strategy along with the principle of democratic participation would create the 'open society'. Moreover, Popper's 'critical rationalism' entailed what he called 'the rational unity of mankind', the notion that 'we must recognize everybody with whom we communicate as a potential source of argument and of reasonable information' (ibidem). But it is just that principle — of accepting criticism and new information from any source — that has often and recently been rejected by some Muslims. For example, in Malaysia, a country for which I have only fondness and the greatest respect, the Ministry of

Religious Affairs (ABIM — a semi-autonomous state agency), issued an edict in the Spring of 2002 preventing those 'with no in-depth knowledge' of Islam from publicly expressing their views (*Malaysiakini*, 19 April 2002; see Kar Yen 2002). Among the targets of this edict (which included some Muslims) was a first rate Islamic scholar — a non-Muslim — but one with impeccable credentials, including mastery of Arabic and the classical sources.

The idea that non-Muslims should not comment on anything having to do with the Islamic faith, and even that Muslims should not be taught by non-Muslims, has a very long history, though in recent years the prohibition has generally fallen by the wayside. Nevertheless that sentiment remains strong in many sections of the Muslim world. And while we recognize the existence of both progressive as well as reactionary forces in the Muslim world today, it must be said that excessive restrictions on freedom of discussion, on debate, and even on the ordinary reporting of vital public information, are widely in place in the Muslim world. There are numerous cases of individuals who have reported on corruption, on public malfeasance, and so on, in Tunisia, Morocco, Egypt, and Saudi Arabia, among other countries, who have been sent to jail for such candour. The recent report by Lawrence Wright (2003) on the state of the press in Saudi Arabia can be summed up as 'see no harm, hear no harm, and report no harm'. One of the more poignant recent summations of such restrictions on the public sphere has been expressed by the Muslim activist, Zainah Anwar, the Executive Director of Sisters in Islam. On 17 May 2003 she gave an invited lecture at the *Center for the Study of Islam and Democracy* in Washington DC. At the heart of her speech was a plea for 'the expansion of the public space for debate', the opening of discussion to the many contrasting points of view that exist *within* the Muslim community. But she lamented the fact that there is very little room for such discussion and debate today. 'Unfortunately', she said (Anwar 2003),[1]

> in many Muslim societies today, this public space does not exist, not just to talk about Islam, but to talk on other issues that are deemed sensitive by the power elite, such as democracy, human rights, politics, freedom, [or] fundamental liberties.

But let us return to Karl Popper and his great effort to understand how civilizational conflicts could be resolved through peaceful means. It is to be understood that even when those devices facilitating public discussion are available, they do not always work (as the two world wars of the twentieth century show). My comparative analysis, however, places somewhat different stresses on aspects of Plato's writings than did Sir Karl. In addition, my focus is on the comparative trajectories of science in the three religions of Islam, Christianity, and Judaism, and the underlying support for unfettered reason in those religious communities.

---

[1] I have discussed these issues further in Huff (2005). For an additional analysis of censorship in the Muslim world, see Mostyn (2002).

Popper found his starting point in Greek philosophy and above all in Plato's philosophy. He found it to contain a number of repugnant ideas, including an apparent effort to halt social and political change, the rejection of democratic principles, and the search for 'essences' in intellectual thought. In a word, Popper tagged Plato with establishing a number of detrimental ideas that seemed to plague Western Europe in the second quarter of the twentieth century. At the same time, Popper acknowledged that Plato was a great philosopher who had important contributions to make.

However, as Popper dug into his problem of how to get people to adopt the rational attitude and create the 'open society', he discovered that this critical attitude itself was dependent on an 'irrational *faith in reason*' (Popper 1945, Chapter 24, § II). He admitted that people cannot generally be persuaded by logical argument to adopt 'reason' rather than 'passion' or 'emotion'. Instead it seems that this is a choice that must be made without sufficient argument. If this is so, then it must be a shock for all of us to realize the fact that in the Western world large numbers of people did indeed opt for this 'faith in reason', which as we like to believe, is inextricably tied to the pursuit of science, especially modern science. This provokes us to ask, what historical sources must there have been that led Europeans to adopt reason and rational criticism as tools for the advancement of human knowledge?

In the following account I propose to lay out a triadic comparison of intellectual developments in Judaism, Islam, and Christianity (which were all exposed to Plato's thought) in order to conduct a sort of thought experiment. I want to highlight the centrality of three powerful metaphysical beliefs, without which I believe (and I believe Popper would have agreed) modern science would not be possible. In the process of laying out this comparison I will suggest that Popper may have been mistaken to criticize Plato so severely and for suggesting that Plato's elitism was mainly a source of authoritarianism.

## 1 Reason, science, and metaphysical beliefs

Let me now recast our problem in the following manner. Popper was fully aware that he (and other 'rationalists') had in fact adopted an 'irrational faith in reason', but he did not attempt to explore how this faith in reason might have, historically speaking, come about. Accordingly, I shall sketch an outline of how certain metaphysical beliefs may have arisen and subsequently have given humans the belief and the confidence that they were in possession of reason, and that with this faculty they might unravel the mysteries of nature and the universe. Stated differently I propose that the path toward modern science — which many would say was the chief exhibit of our progress toward the liberation of reason and rationality (in Popper's sense) — could be successfully trodden only if the following three metaphysical assumptions came into play. Moreover, I suggest that it is the existence of these assumptions that empowers human beings to adopt Popper's thesis of the 'rational unity of mankind', and allows us to overcome what I shall call 'textual literalism', or simply 'textualism'.

The following metaphysical beliefs, in my view, are indispensable for the rise of modern science. Only through the gradual and increasingly articulate evolution of the following three metaphysical assumptions was modern science possible:

First, *it had to be believed that nature is a rational order, that is to say, an all-encompassing, coherent, orderly, and predictable domain.* Without this axiomatic belief concerning the natural world, we could neither understand it nor explain it scientifically.

Second, *scientific reasoning is predicated on the belief that human beings are endowed with reason and have the intellectual capacity to understand the workings of nature.* Of course, particular theories may be wrong at any moment in time, but the assumption is that gradually over time nature will yield up its secrets to rational inquiry.

Thirdly, *it has to be taken for granted that it is permissible, and even mandatory, for men and women, using their powers of reason, to question all forms of truth claims, including religious, political, ethical, and even science's own claims.* This is a very important consideration because it is by no means assured that the political and intellectual elite of any particular society or civilization will agree that it is permissible for ordinary mortals — especially lay persons — to speak out, to challenge and upset traditional understandings, based on scientific findings, and above all, to disturb revealed truths stated in sacred texts. It is not even certain today in many parts of the globe that public information that describes the collective state of well-being (or ill-health) can be publicly viewed or discussed. In many societies today all sorts of social statistics, economic results, and public health reports, are classified as state secrets, and cannot be published or discussed without obtaining official permission, at the risk of criminal sanctions, especially in Asia and the Middle East.[2]

From this point of view, the rise of early modern science concerns the rise and institutionalization of these three enormously empowering principles. In the present discussion I shall focus mainly on the first two assumptions — that nature is a rational, coherent, and orderly domain, and that human beings have the capacity to understand that order, unaided by scripture. The question then becomes one of identifying some of the early manifestations of these metaphysical assumptions and how they were received by the three religions of the book. Although I focus here on *metaphysical beliefs*, nothing I say in this essay is meant to exclude the broader *cultural, economic, legal,* and *institutional* factors that should be considered while investigating the reasons

---

[2]This is not the place to discuss the recent impositions of restrictions on access to public documents by the Bush Administration. Clearly such restrictions, however dubious they are, put in place in reaction to actual terrorist attacks, are not equivalent to state policies that on moral or religious grounds simply forbid public discussion of a broad range of subjects.

for the rise of modern science in any cultural setting, as I have done elsewhere (Huff 1993/2003).

## 2 The Greek and Hellenic heritage

As we know, the period leading up to the beginnings of Christianity was one in which Hellenic culture reigned supreme throughout the settled communities surrounding the Mediterranean. Alexander the Great's conquest in the fourth century BC resulted in the sudden spread of Hellenic culture over a vast region of Asia and the Middle East. At the centre of that culture we find not only Aristotle's great organon of natural philosophy, but also the equally persuasive works of Plato (died 347 BC).

So I remind the reader that before there were Christians or Muslims, and perhaps before there were Jews, there were Greeks. The New Testament of the Christian Bible says, 'In the beginning was the Logos' (the Greek term for 'word', 'reason', or 'indwelling spirit'). So it is fitting for our context to say, 'in the beginning were the Greeks'. Of course archaeological remains would probably give priority to the Jews, but that is another story.

As a result of Alexander's expansion of the Greek *oecumene*, it is said that seventy new Greek cities were founded across the Middle East and elsewhere in the path of his conquest (Chamberlain & Feldman 1961, p. 732). Undoubtedly the most significant of the new Greek cities was Alexandria, founded in 332 BC on the coast of Egypt. Indeed Alexandria's cultural life, based on the language, law, and philosophical culture of Greece during the last two centuries before Christ, rivalled that of Athens. During this period the Greek language had in fact become the 'lingua franca' throughout this vast stretch of what was called the 'inhabited world'. As two classical scholars put it, 'Greek might take a man from Marseilles to India, from the Caspian to the Cataracts.' (Tarn & Griffith 1966, p. 3). Hence the schools and academies of that time were wholly framed by Greek learning, and deeply embedded in the works of Plato and Aristotle, their followers and commentators: Stoics, Sceptics, Cynics, Neoplatonists, and many others. What developed out of this was not always a literal restatement of what Plato and Aristotle taught; nevertheless, it represented in some ways a radical departure from the various indigenous cultures, especially Semitic, that had flourished outside the Greek cultural ambience. In the end, the intellectual idioms of Plato and Aristotle became the conceptual hinges on which the Western scientific tradition turned thereafter.

It has been recognized for some time that Plato's little classic, the *Timaeus* (Cornford 1959), is not only one of his most influential books, but also one of the most concise statements of the classical Greek scientific heritage, above all, as an exposition of cosmology, physics, physiology, and the idea of cosmic creation (Morrow 1965). At the centre of Plato's dialogue is the notion that the cosmos and the world in which we dwell were created by design, through the persuasion of 'intelligence', shaping the material of the world. In Plato's words (*Timaeus* 48A),

> The generation of this cosmos came about through a combination of necessity and
> intelligence, the two commingled. Intelligence controlling necessity persuaded her
> to lead towards the best the greater part of the things coming into being; and
> in this way this universe was constructed from the beginning, through necessity
> yielding to intelligent persuasion.

There is embedded in this powerful extract from the *Timaeus* an enormous
amount of metaphysical presupposition. The whole cosmic creation (and the
smaller world in which we dwell) is said to be the product of (a) creation,
(b) by a (divine) intelligence or Demiurge, and (c) necessity. Throughout
this creation 'necessity' and 'causation' are at work, making the whole into
a balanced unity. In other places Plato speaks of 'Reason' as the guiding
principle. However, the text also says, 'If, then, we are really to tell how it
came into being on this principle, we must bring in also the Errant Cause —
in what manner its nature is to cause motions' (48b).

Thus, the purposeful designer of the cosmos also had to deal with chance
and fortuitous circumstance. Nevertheless, throughout the discussion reference is made to 'rational design' and purposefully rational motivation behind
the creation of this universe and all the acts of the creatures in it. It is a
creation with purpose and hence design. Likewise, man is said to be part of
this rational creation. The creator bestowed upon man the faculty of sight
and this in turn allowed him to observe and study the workings of nature,
especially the movements of the sun, moon, and celestial bodies. This in turn
led man to discover the concepts of time as well as number. From all this we
get philosophy, that blessing 'than which no greater boon has ever come or
shall come to mortal man as a gift from heaven' (*Timaeus* 47B). Furthermore,
by observing the more perfect motions of the heavens we, like them, may so
order our own existence into a more perfect pattern of life (47B-C). In other
words, man is given the gifts of sight and intelligence that allow him to understand the workings of the natural world in all its manifestations, giving us
philosophy, perhaps even divine wisdom. This very contemplation of nature
(philosophy), is the greatest good that heaven could bestow on humankind.

In this discourse Plato has created the image of a rationally ordered world,
an organic living whole, which was later interpreted as a 'world machine' (by
European medievals), regulated by reason and necessity, though as noted,
Plato allows for chance, which is the outcome of those fortuitous combinations
of the workings of the separate 'powers'. The study and contemplation of this
whole is not only permissible, it is the highest form of human activity that
the world intelligence has created, and through us this rational contemplation
is carried on.

This bare-bones sketch of Plato's great work reveals the presence of nearly
all of the metaphysical elements that I suggested earlier must be present if
modern science is to rise and flourish: an orderly world, governed by chance
and law in precarious balance, and the encouragement of man to study it.
Yet from a sociological point of view, such ideas as these, which lie at the

heart of natural science, have not been universally accepted. But if modern science is to flourish, then some version of such ideas must be institutionally available. So let us turn to the encounter of Judaism and Hellenism and to the reception and transformation of these ideas in the other two Abrahamic religious traditions.

## 3  Athens versus Jerusalem

When Hellenism began its spread across the Middle East in the time of Alexander, Judaism was full blown, though it was still evolving. During the Hellenistic phase of Greek cultural expansion in the last three centuries before Christ, the Greek language, as noted earlier, became dominant throughout the region. Accordingly, the Jewish sacred scriptures (the Torah) were translated into Greek, from which we get the Pentateuch — the so-called Five Books of Moses in Greek translation. This was the edition of the Bible that was most commonly studied and read around the time of the birth of Christ.

Given this cultural situation, it should not be surprising to find a powerful encounter between the metaphysical presuppositions of Greek philosophy and the theological ones of Judaism of this period. In fact we find just such an encounter in the life and writings of Philo of Alexandria, also known as Philo the Jew.

Remarkably, Philo lived at the very moment of the birth of Christianity, from about 15 BC to 50 AD. What is interesting for us is the use that Philo made of Greek modes of thought in his interpretation of the Books of Moses — the Torah for Jews and the Pentateuch for Christians. What classical scholars have long known is that Philo created a synthesis of Greek philosophy and Judaism, producing what some would call 'Jewish philosophy'. But more importantly Philo fused the ideas of Judaic law and natural law into one entity. This claim of a new synthesis has been the subject of some controversy. Some scholars have said that the articulation of the idea of natural law was a Stoic idea (found already in the writings of Cicero and Antiochus of Ascalon) more than a generation before Philo, while others claim that Philo produced an original fusion of the Greek concepts of *nomos* and *physis* (Troeltsch 1960, I, pp. 150f.; Wolfson 1948, II, pp. 180-87; Koester 1968, pp. 521-541; Horsley 1978, pp. 35-59).

At this point in time, however, it is fair to say that while there are earlier formulations of the natural law theory, especially among the Stoics, Philo's writings do indeed achieve the fusion of Mosaic law and the law of nature by means of allegory. For example, Philo writes (Jos. 29-31 [Opifex: 143f.]; as cited in Horsley 1978, pp. 137f.):

> This world is the great city and it has a single constitution and law, which is the reason in nature. [Jos. 29-31] Since every well ordered state has a constitution, the world-citizen enjoyed the same constitution as did the whole world... this constitution is the right reason of nature more properly called an ordinance seeing that it is divine law.

Central to this understanding is the idea that a single universal law governs the universe and that this law or reason is inherent in nature (cp. Wolfson 1948, pp. 11, 183). Thus nature (man, animals, and the cosmos itself) is regulated by the Logos, by right reason, which is the divine indwelling in nature.[3] Furthermore, scholars agree that in his exegetical studies of the Mosaic scriptures Philo used the *Timaeus* of Plato as the framework of his enterprise, thereby rising to an allegorical and philosophical form of interpretation very different from the exegetical work of Talmudic scholars (see Runia 1986). Philo incorporates Plato's arguments that I set out above: that the world is regulated by natural law, that there is virtue in studying nature, and the idea that philosophy is not only good, but is the rightful gift of God to man.

In a word, Philo approached the sacred Jewish scriptures as a believing Jew but at the same time he used the philosophical apparatus of Plato and the *Timaeus*, to elucidate the scriptures, thereby fusing Judaic belief with an implicit permission, even injunction, to undertake philosophical exegesis. According to Philo's account, philosophy as understood by Plato and Aristotle had really been invented by God through Moses, and therefore, there was no reason to deprive Jews of this great intellectual blessing. But neither Philo's contemporary co-religionists in Alexandria or Palestine, nor later generations of Jews, were receptive to his innovation. Rabbis remained wary of the dangers of indulging in philosophical speculation. Had this not been so, Maimonides, twelve centuries later, would not have adopted such a cryptic and convoluted style of exposition when he wrote the *Guide of the Perplexed*, nor would his writings have provoked such controversy.

Put in slightly different terms, Judaic thought was to remain transfixed by the Torah, the oral tradition of the Mishnah, and the great compilations of commentaries known as the Talmud. Accordingly, theology as an enterprise in its own right, and natural philosophy, were considered (throughout the period we are dealing with) as extraneous additions that bordered on the impious. Within the Jewish community philosophical speculation remained dangerous until modern times.

On another level, one can see the split between Judaism and Christianity as the difference between those God-fearing individuals who preferred the letter of the law and those who looked to the spirit of the law. As was to be the case later in Islam, the sacred law — the Halakhah in Judaism and the Sharia in Islam — was to be the controlling intellectual centre of Jewish thought.[4] Indeed, the tension between the particularism of Jewish law versus the norms of the larger society was to be the defining problem of the Judaic community for the next millennium and a half of the Christian era. Jews were

---

[3] It has been pointed out by Biblical scholars that the word Logos appears more than thirteen hundred times in Philo's allegorical interpretations of Old Testament passages; see *Interpreter's Bible* vol. 7, p. 442a.

[4] On the lack of Jewish philosophy in the Greek mould until the medieval period, see Cohn-Sherbok (1996) and Frank (1997), pp. 1-10; and the essays in Hyman & Walsh (1973), pp. 337ff.

forced to ask themselves why they were chosen to receive the Torah, and then on the other hand, if, out of a spirit of ecumenism, they neglected to follow the law but instead joined the universal community, how could they still be called Jews?

Seen in this light the Christians truly had a new message (Gospel): they were released from strict observance of the law, and were told to substitute universal love, not an eye for an eye, but a brotherly ethic of turning the other cheek.

In the end Philo's influence was primarily felt by Christians, especially the early Church Fathers who preserved his writings. Apparently they had greater freedom for philosophical speculation since they were bound not by the literalism of legislation in the Holy Book, but by the spirit of their New Gospel.

In the meantime, Philo's work became unknown in the Jewish community, not to be recovered until the sixteenth century (Winston 1981, p. 36; and Sterling 1995, p. 17). In a word, the attempt to fuse traditional Jewish thought with metaphysical speculation derived from Athens during this period, was a failure. This brings us to the advent of Christianity.

## 4  Christianity and Greek philosophy

Given the preceding excursion into Greek philosophy and the Hellenistic modes of thought, it requires a considerable transposition of mind to enter into the simple, non-Greek mindset of the Jewish carpenter's son who came to be known as Jesus Christ. For it is quite certain that Jesus himself was a person deeply immersed in local Hebraic culture, not Greek learning. Furthermore, by the time of Christ, the Romans had taken over the Holy Land and begun the great transformation to Roman cultural patterns.

Yet, as we know, the Gospel record of the life and times of Christ was written in Greek, and contains an abundance of Greek metaphysical concepts. The earliest extant records of the life and religious message of the Jewish cum Christian prophet from Nazareth were given to posterity first in Greek, later in Latin, and then after fierce battles, translated into English and other vernacular languages. Those whom we may call the 'mediatorial elite' of Christianity were Greek speakers struggling to capture the message of a religious leader who spoke another tongue. The important point, however, is that they were fully shaped by Greek philosophical habits of thought.

In the classic nineteenth-century study by Edwin Hatch (1888), *The Influence of Greek Ideas on Christianity*, we hear the lament that from the beginning Christian intellectuals, due to their exposure to Greek thought, increasingly applied Greek philosophical forms to Christian thought and sentiments. This entailed the formal use of *definitions*, the effort to create *universal statements*, and the attempt to cast the whole complex of definitions and propositions into a *formal system of ideas*, something that seems unlikely to have been uppermost in the mind of the historical Jesus and his immediate followers.

Furthermore, Hatch argues, these Christian formalizers wanted to create a uniform system of beliefs shared by all members of the community, wherever it might be located. And while we can see that this encouraged a universalizing impulse within the Christian community, it also led to the production of universally proclaimed creeds and officially mandated statements of belief (dogmas), such as the Nicean Creed. It also took the form of replacing untutored faith by a set of abstract propositions, which were then taught by a method that emphasized rote learning, as in catechism. In the long run, the simple faith of the life and message of Christ was replaced by formal dogma, and the very reading of the scriptures was put exclusively in the hands of the clergy. However, revolts against this priestly monopoly began in the Middle Ages, reaching a culmination in the sixteenth century with the Reformation. In addition, in the late nineteenth century, German scholars, among others, began a search for both 'the historical Jesus' and a more authentic description of the so-called 'Primitive Church'. This is seen in the writings of Harnack (1897) and his followers, as well as Ernst Troeltsch (1960).

Thus from the outset the Christian world view was deeply impregnated by Greek philosophical assumptions. In general (but not without exception), the Patristic Fathers had a high regard for the idea of natural law (R. M. Grant 1952; Hatch 1888; and Runia 1986). At the same time, just as they adhered to the creation story of Genesis, they tended to infuse it with Platonic ideas that filtered through from the *Timaeus* as well as from Philo. The creator/Demiurge of Plato was replaced by the Judeo-Christian God, but the ubiquitous Logos (indwelling reason) was ever present. The Christian fathers appeared to be prepared to accept the philosophical principle of natural necessity, but they had to work out the problem of free will and God's omnipotence. Christian thinkers insisted both that men have free will and that God transcends nature, even controlling it. But taking up these questions served to push Christian theologians deeper into the Greek philosophical literature in search of defensive ideas supplied by Greek philosophers (R. M. Grant 1952).

In sum, the world view of early Christianity is so infused with Greek habits of thought that it is fair to say that it was unusually well prepared to entertain the idea of cosmic self-regulation governed by the laws of nature. It took until the middle ages for all of these elements supportive of scientific thought to come together, not least because the Hellenistic world was in a great transition from the Greek language and modes of thought to those of the Romans, which were then to be displaced by Islamic culture in the seventh century. From then onwards the Biblical lands and much of the formerly Hellenic world were transformed into an Arabic speaking civilization committed to a new religious orientation. Consequently, from the ninth until the twelfth century, the only work of Plato available in Latin translation and commentary was the *Timaeus*. But before tracing that development, I turn to the case of Islam.

## 5 Islam and the straight path

The prophet Mohammad was born in 570 AD in Mecca, at a time when the Roman Empire was in decline. It is highly significant that the Arabian peninsula had remained virtually untouched by either Hellenic or Roman culture during the preceding centuries. Mecca was an important urban trading centre halfway down the peninsula, and thus was not totally isolated from outside currents. Still the Arabic language was little known outside the Arabian peninsula, though it is close to Hebrew in its basic structure.

The holy book of Islam, the Qur'an, is frequently characterized by Muslims as the final and complete revelation of the word of God, bringing to completion the Abrahamic prophetic tradition. Furthermore, the Qur'an is described even by Muslims today as a complete book of *truth*, a copy of the heavenly speech of God, beyond comparison with any other source of knowledge. Thus the Qur'an contains many reminders that it is 'a detailed exposition of all things' (Sura 12:111), that the new revelation 'is the Truth' (Sura 41:53); and that God 'taught man what he did not know' (Sura 96:5).[5] The many 'signs' (*ayat*) of the Qur'an (see Watt 1970, pp. 121-127), which many Muslim exegetes say reveal the scientific character of the Qur'an, actually tell the believer to recognize that all of the movements of the natural world are signs of God's omnipotence, of his control over nature. Thus Sura 3:190: 'Verily in the creation of the Heavens and the earth, and in the succession of night and day, there are indeed signs for all who are endowed with sight.' The highly acclaimed Swiss Muslim, Tariq Ramadan, added to his discussion of this passage, that the Prophet was visibly moved by this revelation, which clearly announced the 'total submission to God' of the whole of creation (Ramadan 1999, p. 16). In a word, Muslims are enjoined, very much like the ancient Jewish tradition, to 'ponder' or 'reflect on' the natural world in order to appreciate the majesty and omnipotence of God, *not* to develop scientific explanations. This stress on religious 'reflection' is similar to the Judaic view (see Ruderman 1995, pp. 33, 160, and passim).

If we look for metaphysical images and presuppositions in the Qur'an that might guide scientific inquiry, they would be entirely different from the images of those accustomed to Greek philosophy. They tend to be concrete images rather than generalized propositions. The idea of the Logos as creative intelligence embedded in the structure of the universe or in the human actor, is absent. While God is said to have created the world in six days following the Genesis story, the world continues, as noted, to be governed by God's uninterrupted control of all events. Secondly, God and man are utterly different from each other. The Judeo-Christian idea that God created man in his own image is replaced by the belief that man and God share no qualities or attributes. God is all powerful, all knowing, and actively creative, but humankind shares none of these attributes. Indeed, it is a form of blasphemy for anyone to claim

---

[5]I have primarily used the translation of Abdullah Yusuf Ali (1934/1987) but also consulted the translations of N. J. Dawood, M. H. Shakir, and Zafrullah Khan for all of these passages.

any of God's attributes, and it is heresy (*shirk*) to 'associate' anything with God, or to imagine God as having a peer. This declaration, that 'God has no partners', in fact became a matter of formal dogma in later centuries reflected in various Islamic creeds (Wensinck 1932; and Watt 1994). In short, the creative spark, that is, reason or inner light, that Christian theology invested in mankind, no doubt influenced by Plato, is absent from Islamic thought.[6]

Likewise the idea of natural necessity or laws of nature governing either the human realm or the natural world is rejected. For example, the Qur'an says (Sura 14:32):

> It was Allah who made the heavens and the earth. He sends down the rain from the sky with which He brings forth fruits for your sustenance. He drives the ships which by His leave sail the ocean in your service.

Thus God's agency is a constant, ongoing controlling force in nature (Sura 7: 54):

> Your Lord is Allah, and who in six days created the heavens and the earth and then ascended His Throne. He throws the veil of night over the day.

In the context of scientific inquiry and the possibilities of natural necessity, there are numerous verses that clearly reserve to God all the powers that would otherwise belong to natural processes in and of themselves. Thus another Sura affirms that if God but wished it, it would be done, as in Sura 40:68: 'When He wills a thing He simply says to it, "Be" and it is.' Likewise Sura 34:9 reads:

> We could if We please, cause the earth to swallow them up, or cause clouds to fall upon them a deluge. In that, verily, is a sign for every servant of Ours who turns to Us.

This line of thought seems to be inhibitive with regard to the possibility of a natural world governed by autonomous forces of nature. Indeed, over the course of time, this issue of natural causation versus God's complete omnipotence developed into a major confrontation between Greek-inspired Muslim philosophers and those who took a more literalist view of the powers of God. Thus the great al-Ghazzālī (died 1111) argued that (see Watt 1953, p. 37)

> the natural sciences are objectionable because they do not recognize that nature is in subjection to God most high, not acting of itself but serving as an instrument in the hands of the creator. Sun, moon, stars and elements are in subjection to His command. There is none of them whose activity is produced by or proceeds from its own essence.

---

[6]This a complex subject, on which see Falzur Rahman (1958); and the discussion in the Introduction to Maimonides, *The Guide of the Perplexed*, volume 1, by Shlomo Pines (1963).

Before taking up that controversy let me note also the numerous Qur'anic passages that warn against *conjecture* and *speculation*, and could be taken as a repudiation of philosophical inquiry in the Aristotelian mode. For example, Sura 6:116 asserts: 'They follow nothing but conjecture: they do nothing but lie.' Likewise Sura 53:28:

> But they have no knowledge therein. They follow nothing but conjecture; and conjecture avails nothing against Truth.

To this passage, Yusuf Ali adds the commentary, 'Conjecture is a dangerous thing in speaking of divine things' (Ali 1987, p. 1446, note 5098). These passages seem to warn against the philosophical life that is so vividly affirmed by Plato and adopted by Philo of Alexandria as a gift of God.

Accordingly, when Islam spread out of the Arabian peninsula (in both directions across the Middle East), it encountered a radically different cultural ambience. Finding themselves in a vastly richer cultural setting than that of Mecca, the intellectual leaders of the expanding Islamic civilization encouraged the translation into Arabic of the great corpus of the so-called 'foreign' or 'ancient' sciences that existed in libraries and private collections throughout the region. In addition, efforts where made to assimilate the store of scientific works from India.

But this appropriation of foreign cultural capital was also selective, as should be expected. For example, Philo of Alexandria was not translated, and though Galen's epitome of the *Timaeus* was rendered into Arabic, the actual *Timaeus* itself, as well as discussion of its rational image of the cosmos and man's place in it, are unknown among Muslim philosophers and theologians.[7]

Nevertheless, Islamic followers of Aristotle did emerge in the person of such formidable intellects as al-Kindi (c. 800-870), al-Farabi (died 950), al-Razi (died 923 or 932), Ibn Sina (died 1037), and al-Biruni (died 1048). The importing of Hellenistic thought appears to have occurred in two waves, the first taking place in the mid-eighth century, and the second in the mid-tenth century. The earlier phase of assimilation was one largely of translation and one in which Neo-Platonic thought was very strong. Later the individuals named above became active and aggressive champions of Aristotle.

It must be said, however, that the guardians of orthodoxy within Islam strenuously opposed Aristotelian philosophy and its metaphysics of natural necessity. From the ninth century onwards, the *mutakallimun* (Muslim theologians) became committed to what has been called Islamic occasionalism (cp. Fakhry 1958; Pines 1936/1977; Watt 1974). According to this view, the basic building blocks of nature are indivisible 'atoms', and no atoms can subsist for more than 'two moments' without God's power.

---

[7]In his study of Ibn Sina, Lenn Goodman discusses an argument regarding creation and causality that appears to be grounded in the causal logic of the *Timaeus*. But it could as easily be grounded in Aristotle, and no evidence is presented that Avicenna (or al-Ghazzālī) actually studied or discussed the *Timaeus* or its Galenic epitome. See Goodman (1992), pp. 49f.

This doctrine had been in gestation from Islam's beginnings in the seventh and eighth centuries (the first two of the Islamic era). In later phases it was used to counteract the writings of Islamic philosophers who adopted the naturalistic view according to which the domains of nature function according to their own essential nature. It was the ninth-century theologian al-Ash'ari (873-935) who solidified the atomist/occasionalist view in which all existence is composed of 'atoms' and 'accidents', each of which lasts only a moment, and then disappears.

By the tenth century Ash'ari's atomism had become the dominant orthodoxy and those free-thinking philosophers who seemed to oppose it — such al-Farabi and Ibn Sina — came under suspicion of religious deviation by the *mutakallimun*. This unfolding conflict between Greek modes of philosophizing and Muslim orthodoxy came to a head in the twelfth century with the work of al-Ghazzālī, that philosophically inclined devout believer who flourished in Baghdad at the time when Peter Abelard was taking a different path in Paris.

Al-Ghazzâlî's motivation for attacking the philosophers was no doubt complex. On one level, he sought to protect ordinary believers from the corrosive effects of philosophical speculation, which was something that Ibn Sina had also been concerned with. On another, al-Ghazzālī was driven by a strong desire to achieve a level of religious certainty within which there could be no doubt or uncertainty. He had been smitten by the allures of demonstrative argument, and when he elevated such logical-rhetorical skills to the position of final arbiter of all claims to knowledge, it did not leave much to believe in. That is to say, from a strictly logical point of view, the proof of any argument is always in doubt unless the syllogism is a strictly deductive claim, as in: 'All men are mortal, Aristotle is a man, therefore Aristotle is mortal.' Inductive arguments, on the other hand, which use empirical observation, rely on the 'inductive leap' in order to get from particulars to the general, and hence cannot claim apodeictic truth. This outcome drove al-Ghazzālī into fideism, the position according to which one believes solely on the basis of faith, without rational argument. Unsurprisingly, al-Ghazzālī's fideism led directly to his efforts to strengthen his position by adopting the mysticism of the sufis (see Watt 1953, p. 37).

Al-Ghazzâlî's anti-naturalistic views became deeply ingrained in Islamic thought and continue to surface in contemporary discussions among some segments of the Muslim world. His famous book condemning philosophers was a wide-ranging inquiry that drew upon logic and mathematics as it considered the fundamental issues of natural causation (see Marmura 1997). But it was no 'mere' philosophical exercise. As al-Ghazzālī wrote in his autobiographical *Deliverance from Error*, the errors of the philosophers 'are combined under twenty heads, on three of which they must be reckoned infidels and on seventeen heretics' (Watt 1953, p. 37). Al-Ghazzâlî's ringing rebuttal of natural causality reads as follows (as cited in van den Berg 1954, p. 170):

> According to us the connection between what is usually believed to be a cause and what is believed to be an effect is not a necessary connection; each of the

two things has its own individuality and is not the other, and neither the affirmation nor the negation, neither the existence nor the non-existence of the one is implied in the affirmation, negation, existence, and non-existence of the other, for example, the satisfaction of thirst does not imply drinking, nor satiety eating, nor burning contact with fire, nor light sunrise, nor decapitation death, nor recovery the drinking of medicine, nor evacuation the taking of purgative, and so on for all the empirical connections existing in medicine, astronomy, the sciences, and the crafts. For the connection of these things is based on a prior power of God to create them in successive order, though not because this connection is necessary in itself and cannot be disjointed — on the contrary, it is in God's power to create satiety without eating, and death without decapitation, and to let life persist notwithstanding the decapitation, and so on with respect to all connections.

By this means al-Ghazzālī dealt a severe blow to the study of philosophy and the natural sciences in the Islamic world. As a recent translator of the Persian version of al-Ghazzālī's *Revivification of the Religious Sciences* put it, 'there is little doubt in the court of Muslim popular opinion that [al-Ghazzālī's critique of the philosophers] prevailed, forever altering the intellectual climate of the Islamic world' (Daniel 1991, p. xxv).

Nevertheless, al-Ghazzālī's attack on philosophy had a paradoxical effect. On one side, his condemnation of natural philosophy entailed a legal condemnation of those philosophers who held various naturalistic views. His wide-ranging arguments were 'not [mere] rhetorical utterances, but a legal pronouncement' punishable by death (Marmura 1996, p. 280). Consequently those who espoused al-Ghazzālī's condemned theses were condemned as heretics with the legal consequence that their lives were in danger and their houses and property could be confiscated — though this is not known to have happened. On the other side, al-Ghazzālī's clarity of exposition of Aristotelian modes of philosophy led later theologians (*mutakallimun*) to adopt the tools of logic, albeit for the purpose of denying philosophy's claims. In the end, al-Ghazzālī's argument prevailed while the rebuttal by Ibn Rushd (Averroes, died 1198) a generation later fell entirely on deaf ears in the Muslim world, while medieval Christians embraced it.

Given the limitations of this presentation, I must forgo an adequate discussion of the many epistemological ramifications of this line of thought within Islam. But it is important to say that during the period from the ninth century until about the thirteenth century, scientific creativity within the Islamic world did occur, though the innovations for which Muslims are known did not encroach on basic metaphysical assumptions of the Muslim world view. Apart from assuming the uniformity of nature and its patterned regularity, none of the advances in mathematics, astronomy, optics, and medicine entailed metaphysical assumptions counter to the Islamic world view. Still it should be remembered that the writings of gifted Muslim scientists and philosophers such as al-Farabi, Ibn Sina and al-Biruni, give ample evidence of their commitment to Islam. Some of them, for example, al-Biruni, were explicit in linking their scientific work with Qur'anic injunctions, and the Qur'anic 'sign passages' mentioned earlier. But by casting doubt on certain fundamental tenets of Islam, such as the divine creation and the resurrection of the dead, their writings were called into question, above all by al-Ghazzālī. Thus those Muslim scholars of jurisprudence who took a literalist view of the Qur'an aligned themselves with the scientific folklore evolving from pre-Islamic times, and consequently ignored the real advances being made in astronomy, time-keeping, and planetary topography (for instance, the direction of the *qibla*). For example, the Qur'an refers to the movements of the moon as a time keeping sign and thus the scripturalists insisted on preserving the lunar calendar and visual sighting of the moon for ritual purposes, when those based on modern astronomy would be far more satisfactory.[8]

In short, by the fourteenth century, Islamic intellectual culture had lost its curiosity, and a reactionary attitude came to dominate virtually all fields. From then onwards, all innovations had to be filtered through the excessively conservative views of the religious scholars. Moreover, the ban on Arabic printing, except for a brief respite between 1728 and 1745, continued into the early nineteenth century. In the area of medicine, the Ottoman Turks began to develop a modern medical vocabulary in Turkish only in about 1826 when scholars set about translating European medical treatises into Turkish for the first time (Lewis 1965, pp. 84f; and Russell 1992; Huff 1993/2003, pp. 364-373). Likewise, adoption of the Copernican world view was delayed until the end of the nineteenth century.

## 6 Europe on the eve of modernity

I come now to another major shift in the civilizational ascendancies of the Middle East and Europe. By the twelfth century the metaphysical call encouraging natural philosophy within the Muslim world had been neutralized. The religious and legal scholars had thoroughly routed the Greek idea of an autonomous world system governed by natural law. Likewise, the idea that man possesses that spark of divine intelligence enabling him to decipher the mysteries of nature had been denied. According to Islamic orthodoxy, God is the only creator. Furthermore, as we saw in al-Ghazzālī's attack on Greek natural philosophy that blessing, in Plato's words, 'than which no greater boon has ever come or shall come to mortal man as a gift from heaven' was dismissed. As A. I. Sabra has shown, by the fourteenth century, *kalam* (Islamic theology) had indeed overcome philosophy and the latter was disparaged while Islamic occasionalism remained intact (Sabra 1994).

In Western Europe, however, a new surge of creativity burst forth. Beginning with the religious scholars of Chartres and then enveloping all of

---

[8]Those who suggest that a lunar calendar is just as 'precise' as a solar calendar neglect to mention that a lunar calendar displaces all holidays as well as monthly intervals marking seasonal change from the natural growing cycles that are aligned with the movements of the sun, or rather the earth's position with respect to the sun.

Western Europe, these scholars saw ubiquitous signs of reason and rationality, of orderly nature, of harmonious divine creation, everywhere. The message of cosmic unity and orderly intelligent creation made available by Chalcidius's translation of the *Timaeus* was now fully incorporated into Christian thought. People such as Hugh of St Victor (died 1141), William of Conches (died 1154), Thierry of Chartres (died 1148), and many others saw evidences of God's harmonious creation fully in line with Plato's system of nature, indeed saw nature as a system of causal necessity. As William of Conches's commentary on the *Timaeus* reads (cited in Chenu 1968, p. 41):

> Having shown that nothing exists without a cause, Plato now narrows the discussion to the derivation of effect from efficient cause. It must be recognized that every work is the work of the Creator or of Nature, or the work of a human artisan imitating nature. The work of the Creator is the first creation without pre-existing material, for example, the creation of the elements or spirits, or it is the things we see happen contrary to the accustomed course of nature, as the virgin birth, and the like. The work of nature is to bring forth like things from like through seeds or offshoots, for nature is an energy inherent in things and making like from like.

From top to bottom the world system was seen as a fully articulated mechanism willed by God. The metaphor of a world machine (*machina mundi*), is found in the writings of a great variety of twelfth- and thirteenth-century scholars. For example, Robert Grosseteste asserted that, 'The world machine most evidently speaks of the eternal art by which it has been made' (cited in Gieben 1964, p. 144). In his work on *The Sphere*, Grosseteste used this metaphor three times in the first thirteen lines of his treatise (White 1962, p. 174, note 5). Similarly the metaphor of the world machine is found in the writings of Alan of Lille, Hugh of St Victor, Bernard Sylvester, Sacrobosco, and no doubt others. For them, there were two 'books of nature' — a visible and an invisible one — and whether one was referring to the visible or invisible world, there seems to be significant order, a universal machine (cited in Chenu 1968, p. 7, note 10):

> The ordered disposition of things from top to bottom in the network of this universe ... is so arranged that, among all the things that exist, nothing is unconnected or separable by nature, or external. ... [t]he visible world is this machine, this universe, that we see with our bodily eyes.

Likewise Sacrobosco cites with approval a passage from Dionysius the Areopagite: 'Either the God of nature suffers, or the mechanism of the universe is dissolved' (as cited in E. Grant 1974, p. 451).

While this enthusiasm for naturalistic images cropped up in many places, some did take objection to it. But defenders of the naturalistic view among the clergy were well represented and even made a distinction between the *natural* and the *supernatural*. A certain Andrew of St Victor argued that in the interpretation of scripture one should first consider all naturalistic possibilities before offering miracles as explanations. The interpreter, he wrote, 'should realize this: in expounding Scripture, when the event described admits of no naturalistic explanation, then and only then should we have recourse to miracles' (in Chenu 1968, p. 17, note 35). In this Andrew was apparently following St Augustine.

In this manner the Christian medievals reclaimed the Old Testament notion that humankind was created in the image of God. But now that image was reinforced with the Greek idea that man and nature were fully rational orders of existence. Not only was nature a fully rational unity, but man as a part of it was a fully rational creature. Both continentals and Englishmen such as Adelard of Bath (fl. 1116-1142) put forth optimistic paeans extolling the rationality of mankind (cited in Stiefel 1976, p. 3):

> Although man is not armed by nature nor is [he] naturally swiftest in flight, yet he has that which is better by far and worth more — that is, reason. For by possession of this function he exceeds the beasts to such a degree that he subdues them. ... You see, therefore, how much the gift of reason surpasses mere physical equipment.

With the arrival of the newly translated 'natural books' of Aristotle, this neo-Platonic enthusiasm for naturalistic inquiry was given another powerful boost. Soon they were put at the centre of the university curriculum, in Paris formally by statute in 1255. From there they reigned supreme for the next 400 years. Moreover, the teachings of Aristotle were linked to the so-called *questio* literature. That is, philosophy was taught in a format that began by asking a question: 'let us inquire whether'. For example, 'let us inquire whether the world is round ... whether the earth moves ... whether it is possible that other worlds exist, ... whether the existence of a vacuum is possible', and so on (see Grant 1974, pp. 127ff). These inquiries took the form of arguing, in Abelard's memorable phrase, *Sic et Non* [Yes and No], for and against various answers to puzzling questions. While they did not often arrive at novel conclusions, they did proclaim the acceptability of publicly asking such questions and engaging in formal controversy. In that regard they *institutionalized* a form of public inquiry that lies at the heart of the scientific enterprise from that day to this.

In the area of cosmology alone, E. Grant has catalogued 400 questions that were raised regarding the celestial bodies, their composition and motions. This generated 1,176 known responses, and these were by no means slavish replies, by 52 or more investigators (1994, p. 681).

In short, the medieval universities *institutionalized* a mode of philosophical inquiry that laid the foundations for the emergence of modern science (cp. Huff 1993/2003, and E. Grant 1996, 2001). The curriculum was a unique fusion of Christian theology and Greek metaphysics, and it was just this educational foundation that was experienced in the universities by Copernicus and Galileo a century or two later. Just as William of Conches in the twelfth century affirmed that it is not the task of the Bible to teach us about nature, so too, Galileo wrote about four and half centuries later, 'the intention of the Holy

Spirit is to teach us how one goes to heaven, not how the heavens go' (in Finocchiaro 1989, p. 96).

## 7 Faith and reason

But let me add a few additional words regarding the fate of philosophy and science in Judaism during this period. The battle between faith and reason clearly has a long history and has taken many forms. If we look back to Philo of Alexandria, with whom I began this discussion, we see a prescient vision of the unity of reason and religion. For Philo the revealed law of Moses was in harmony with natural law and universal principles. The five books of Moses revealed to Philo not just the sacred word, but the superiority of Moses as a philosopher. This theme — that Judaism was the superior religion and perfect philosophy — became a major theme in Jewish circles throughout all succeeding centuries, even into the eighteenth century. Had Philo's synthesis been taken up by the Judaic community following his death, no doubt scientific history would have been different, as it accepted philosophy as a legitimate enterprise fully consistent with scripture. As it is, the Jewish community was to engage in periodic internal conflicts for the next seventeen hundred years over the appropriate role of reason in religious affairs. Every rationalist attempt at fusing philosophy and scripture was met by an equally strong anti-rationalist parry that virtually deadlocked the community. Only with the emancipation of Jews in Europe — in Germany in particular in the late eighteenth century — was the struggle to achieve an acceptable balance between the claims of reason and those of revealed law able to reach acceptable fusion.

In the meantime, during the period I have been discussing there was only one truly outstanding Jewish scientist, namely, Levi ben Gerson (Gersonides) who lived in Southern France in Provence, and died in 1344. Gersonides contributed a variety of innovations in astronomy, including unique astronomical instruments. He proposed a realist theory of astronomy, which is to say he believed that physical observations ought to correspond to mathematical models and worked toward that goal. At the same time Gersonides composed commentaries on the Bible and related discussions of religious topics (see Goldstein 1985, 1997; and Feldman 1997). Nevertheless, Gersonides stands as a lone exception during the whole intervening period of Arabic-Islamic ascendancy up to the fourteenth century. As one scholar put it, 'there are no Jewish counterparts to such scientific geniuses as ... al-Biruni, Ibn al-Haytham, and Thabit Ibn Qurra in the Arabic culture, or Robert Grosseteste, Roger Bacon, and Nicole Oresme in the Latin [culture]' (Freudenthal 1995, p. 29). There were, of course, scientists and notable intellectuals in the Jewish community spread out as it was during this time, but they were not able to make contributions to scientific progress equivalent to those mentioned. This was largely because the Jewish community was unable to resolve the conflict between religious authority and naturalistic inquiry. Stated differently, it stemmed from the strongly held view within the Jewish community that natural philosophy served strictly as a handmaiden to religion, and otherwise had no independent function. Reason as the exercise of the critical faculties could undercut traditional religious views and thus was severely curtailed (Freudenthal 1995, pp. 46f.).

While it is commonplace to mention the name of the great Maimonides, it must be said that the writings of Maimonides served more to split the Jewish community than to energize it for scientific inquiry. One result of his writings was an attempt in the Jewish communities in southern France and Spain to restrict the study and teaching of philosophy and the natural sciences until the age of 25 (Dobbs-Weinstein 1997, p. 333; Silver 1965, pp. 148ff.). While Maimonides encouraged the study of the natural sciences, some have criticized him for intimately linking this with the achievement of religious piety, for it suggested that philosophy had no independent role to play. Furthermore, Maimonides, following ancient tradition, treated the study of the sciences as an esoteric enterprise reserved for the privileged few and transmitted only through private instruction.

As late as the fourteenth century observers in the Jewish community noted how different the educational practices were in the Christian and Jewish communities. A late fourteenth century physician from Provence, Leon Joseph of Carcassone, lamented that in comparison to the Jewish community (cited in Freudenthal ibidem, pp. 46f):

> [the Christians'] exchanges on these sciences [are] unceasing, and they miss nothing of what is worth investigating. Instead, they leave out nothing when it is a question of debating the truth and even the falsehood of a [proposition]. Through their vigorous scrutinizing questions and answers by way of disputation ... and by explaining everything through two contrary [opinions] they have the truth emerge from the center [of the contradiction] as a lily among the thorns.

Thus the unresolved conflicts between faith and reason in the Jewish community persisted. By the mid fifteenth century the scholastic question-and-answer method of presenting arguments had been adopted by leading Jewish scholars (Tirosh-Rothschild 1997, p. 505), but they had not devised a policy compromise that would allow the public teaching of philosophy and the natural sciences in Jewish schools, unfettered by traditional Jewish presuppositions. David Ruderman, in his study (1995) of Jewish scientific thought in early modern Europe, is forced to concede that there were no pioneering scientific innovations produced by Jewish scholars during this period. Indeed, it was not until after the assimilation of the Jews in Europe — due to Moses Mendelssohn's translation of the Torah into German — that European Jews became fully assimilated, and from that point onward excelled in science.

Defenders of Jewish scientific prowess during the medieval and early modern period often point to the existence of Jewish physicians and their noteworthy service to the gentile community. But the problem with that thesis is that the major agenda of scientific medicine — and the primary site of new

discoveries — from the twelfth to the seventeenth century, was in anatomy.
To engage in anatomy required the use of dissection — something that was
forbidden to both Jews and Muslims, especially dissection of the bodies of
their co-religionists except under very extreme situations — until the 1940s
(see Huff 2002, 1993/2003, Chapter 5; and Huff 2006).[9]

On the other hand, Christian Europeans had engaged in human dissection
since the thirteenth century, and with the blessing of religious authorities.
This research enterprise culminated in the fabulous anatomical sketches of
Vesalius in 1543 — the same year as the publication of Copernicus's famous
book, *The Revolution of the Heavenly Spheres*. It appears to have been in
the mid sixteenth century that Jewish students were first admitted to European medical schools, where they did indeed have to witness and participate
in dissections, yet so far as we know no Jewish students made outstanding
contributions in this field until much later.

## 8 Conclusion

In summation let me add the following thoughts. From a historical point
of view, Plato's powerful cosmological work published under the title of the
*Timaeus* was one of those extraordinary seminal sources of metaphysical ideas
that informed Europeans and others for millennia. Its powerful metaphysical
claim that the world is a rationally ordered place, governed by law and chance,
and with humans also endowed with reason and rationality, inspired numerous generations. It led them to believe that the human species does indeed
possess reason and that it can use this faculty to unravel the mysteries of
nature, unaided by scripture. No doubt many other philosophical strands —
some from Aristotle —entered into this image. Nevertheless, the European
medievals took up this rationalist image of man and nature with utmost seri-
ousness, leading them to subject *both* nature and scripture to rational inquiry.
Hence it looks as if this strand of Plato's thought supplied a crucial element
for the construction of the Open Society.

On the other hand, we saw that both the Jewish community and the
Muslims resisted this metaphysical impulse and subsequently their philosophical commitments remained tied to legalistic and scripturalist approaches. In
the case of the Jews, the dominance of Talmudic commentary resulted in an
aborted commitment to unfettered scientific inquiry — especially in Europe
— until the point when Jewish intellectual leaders forged a bridge between
Jewish identity and full participation in European scientific culture. Thereafter Jewish intellectuals have been seen as virtual scientific supermen.

In the case of the Muslim world, the effort to embrace fully the rationalist
image of man and nature — and the impulse to subject the sacred scriptures to
open-ended scientific inquiry — has been delayed till the twenty-first century.

---

[9]It turns out that there was not even a Jewish medical literature before the middle ages,
that even in the Hellenic period, Jews apparently were not drawn to the study or practice
of medicine; cp. Joseph Shatzmiller (1994) and John M. Efron (2001).

Muslims today are quick to say that there is no conflict between Islam and science, but they would not be willing to allow the unrestrained use of the instruments of scientific inquiry on the sacred text of the Qur'an. Indeed, in many quarters nothing critical of Islam is permitted at all. Nevertheless, there are signs today that many Muslims realize the need to examine critically the various strands of the Muslim past and to fashion an educational policy that is more tolerant, humane, and progressive.

# Bibliography

Ali, Y. A., editor/translator (1934/1987). *The Qur'an*. Text, Translation & Commentary. Elmhurst NY: Tahrike Tarsile Qur'an, Inc. Page references are to the 1987 edition.

Anwar, Z. (2003). 'Islamisation and Its Impact on Democratic Governance and Women's Rights in Islam: A Feminist Perspective'. www.islamdemocracy.org/4th_Annual_Conference-Anwar_address.asp/.

Berg, S. van den, translator (1954). *The Incoherence of the Incoherence [Tahafat al-Tahafah]* by Averroes (Ibn Rushd). London: Luzac.

Chamberlain, R., & Feldman, H. (1961). *The Dartmouth Bible*. An Abridgment of the King James Version, with Aids to Its Understanding as History, Literature and as a Source of Religious Experience. 2nd revised edition. Boston MA: Houghton-Mifflin.

Chenu, M.-D. (1968). *Nature, Man, and Society in the Twelfth Century*. Boston MA: Little Brown.

Cohn-Sherbok, D. (1996). *Jewish Philosophy*. Richmond, Surrey: Curzon Press.

Cornford, F. M. translator (1959). *Plato's Timaeus*. Indianopolis IN: Bobbs-Merrill.

Daniel, E. L. (1991). 'Preface' to *The Alchemy of Happiness*. English translation of Abu Hamid Muhammad al-Ghazzālī by C. Field. Revised and annotated by E. L. Daniel. Armonk, New York: M. E. Sharpe.

Dobbs-Weinstein, I. (1997). 'The Maimonidean Controversy'. In Frank & Leaman (1997), pp. 331-349.

Efron, J. M. (2001). *Medicine and the German Jews. A History*. New Haven: Yale University Press.

Fakhry, M. (1958). *Islamic Occasionalism, and its Critique by Averroes and Aquinas*. London: Allen & Unwin.

Feldman, S. (1997). 'Levi ben Gershom (Gersonides)'. In Frank & Leaman (1997), pp. 379-398. New York: Routledge.

Finocchiaro, M., editor (1989). *The Galileo Affair*. Berkeley: University of California Press.

Frank, D. (1997). 'What is Jewish Philosophy?' In Frank & Leaman (1997), pp. 1-10.

Frank, D. & Leaman, O., editors (1997). *History of Jewish Philosophy*. New York: Routledge.

Freudenthal, G. (1995). 'Science in the Medieval Jewish Culture of Southern France'. *History of Science* **33**, pp. 23-58.

Gieben, S. (1964). 'Traces of Word in Nature According to Robert Grosseteste'. *Franciscan Studies* **24**, pp. 144-158.

Goldstein, B. (1985). *The Astronomy of Levi Ben Gerson (1288-1344)*. A Critical Edition of Chapters 1-20 with Translation & Commentary. New York: Springer Verlag.

——— (1997). 'The Physical Astronomy of Levi Ben Gerson'. *Perspectives on Science* 5, pp. 1-30.

Goodman, L. E. (1992). *Avicenna*. New York: Routledge.

Grant, E. (1974). *A Source Book In Medieval Science*. Cambridge MA: Harvard University Press.

——— (1994). *Planets, Stars, and Orbs. The Medieval Cosmos, 1200-1687*. New York: Cambridge University Press.

——— (1996). *The Foundations of Modern Science in the Middle Ages*. New York: Cambridge University Press.

——— (2001). *God and Reason in the Middle Ages*. New York: Cambridge University Press.

Grant, R. M. (1952). *Miracles and Natural Law in Graeco-Roman and Early Christian Thought*. Amsterdam: North-Holland Publishing Company.

Harnack, A. von (1897). *History of Dogma*. Translated from the 3rd German edition. Boston MA: Roberts Brothers.

Hatch, E. (1888). *The Influence of Greek Ideas on Christianity*. Gloucester MA: Peter Smith. Reprinted 1970.

Hourani, G., editor & translator (1976). *Averroes on the Harmony of Religion and Philosophy*. London: Luzac.

Horsley, R. A. (1978). 'The Law of Nature in Philo and Cicero'. *Harvard Theological Review* 7, pp. 35-59.

Huff, T. E. (1993). *The Rise of Early Modern Science: Islam, China and the West*. New York: Cambridge University Press. 2nd edition 2003.

——— (2002). 'Attitudes Towards Dissection in the History of European and Arabic Medicine'. In Bennacer el-Bouazzati, editor (2002), pp. 61-88. *Science: Locality and Universality*. Rabat, Morocco: Mohammad V University.

——— (2005). 'Freedom versus Restrictions in the Public Sphere in the Arab-Muslim World'. Presented at the International Conference on Muslims and Islam in the 21st Century: Image and Reality', at The International Islamic University Malaysia, Kuala Lumpur, Malaysia, 4-6 August.

——— (2006). 'Dissection and Autopsy'. In G. Laderman and A. Eisen, editors (2006), forthcoming. *Science, Religion, and Society: History, Culture and Controversy*. Armonk NY: M. E. Sharpe.

Hyman, A. & Walsh, J. J. (1973). *Philosophy of the Middle Ages*. 2nd edition. Indianapolis IN: Hackett Publishing Company.

*Interpreter's Bible* (1995). 8 volumes. Nashville TN: Abingdon Press.

Kar Yen, L. (2002). 'Banning Public Views on Islam a Sign of Theocratic Dictatorship: SIS [Sisters in Islam]'. *Malaysiakini*, 19 April 2002.

Koester, H. (1968). 'Nomos and Physeos: The Concept of Natural Law in Greek Thought'. In J. Neusner, editor (1968), pp. 521-541. *Religions in Antiquity: Essays in Memory of E. R. Goodenough*. Leiden: E. J. Brill.

Lewis, B. (1965). *The Emergence of Modern Turkey*. London: Oxford University Press.

*Malaysiakini* (2002). 'No More Articles on Islamic Tenets and the Prophet, media told', 12 April 2002.

Marmura, M. (1996). 'Some Remarks on Averroes's Statements on the Soul'. In M. Wahba & M. Abousenna, editors (1996), pp. 279-288. *Averroes and the Enlightenment*. Amherst NY: Prometheus Books.

———, translator (1997). *The Incoherence of the Philosophers* by Abu Hamid Muhammad al-Ghazālī. Provo UT: Brigham Young Press.

Morrow, G. R. (1965). 'Necessity and Persuasion in Plato's TIMAEUS', in R. E. Allen, editor (1965), pp. 421-437. *Studies in Plato's Metaphysics*. London: Routledge & Kegan Paul.

Mostyn, T. (2002). *Censorship in Islamic Societies*. London: Saqi Books.

Pines, S. (1936). *Studies in Islamic Atomism*. Translated by M. Schwarz. Jerusalem: Magnes Press. Reprinted 1977.

——— (1963). 'Introduction'. In Maimonides (1963), pp. lvii- cxxxiv. Chicago: University of Chicago Press.

Plato. *Timaeus*.

Popper, K. R. (1945). *The Open Society and Its Enemies*. London: George Routledge & Sons. 5th edition 1966. London: Routledge & Kegan Paul.

Rahman, F. (1958). *Prophecy in Islam*. Leiden: E. J. Brill.

Ramadan, T. (1999). *To Be A European Muslim*. London: Islamic Foundation.

Ruderman, D. (1995). *Jewish Thought and Scientific Discovery in Early Modern Europe*. Detroit: Wayne State University Press.

Runia, D. (1986). *Philo in Early Christian Literature*. Minneapolis: Fortress Press.

Russell, G. (1992). ' "The Owl and the Pussy Cat": The Process of Cultural Transmission in Anatomical Illustration'. In Ekmeleddin Ihsanoglu, editor (1992), pp. 180-212. *Transfer of Modern Science and Technology to the Muslim World*. Istanbul: Research Center for Islamic History, Art & Culture.

Sabra, A. I. (1994). 'Science and Philosophy in Medieval Theology: The Evidence of the Fourteenth Century'. *Zeitschrift für Geschichte der Arabisch-Islamischen Wissenschaften* **9**, pp. 1-42.

Shatzmiller, J. (1994). *Jews, Medicine and Medieval Society*. Berkeley: University of California Press.

Silver, D. (1965). *Maimonidean Criticism and the Maimonidean Controversy 1180-1240*. Leiden: E. J. Brill.

Sterling, G. E. (1995). 'Jewish Self-Identify in Alexandria'. *The Studia Philonica Annual* **7**, pp. 1-18.

Stiefel, T. (1976). 'Science, Reason and Faith in the Twelfth Century: The Cosmologists' Attack on Tradition'. *Journal of European Studies* **6**, pp. 1-16.

Tarn, W. W. & Griffith, G. T. (1966). *Hellenistic Civilization*. 3rd edition. London: Edward Arnold & Publishers.

Tirosh-Rothschild, H. (1997). 'The Eve of Modernity'. In Frank & Leaman (1997), pp. 499-573.

Troeltsch, E. (1960). *The Social Teachings of the Christian Churches*. New York: Harper Torch Books.

Watt, W. M., editor & translator (1953). *The Faith and Practice of al-Ghazzâlî*. Lahore: Shaikh Muhammad Ashraf.

——— (1970). *Bell's Introduction to the Qur'an*. Revised & enlarged edition. Edinburgh: Edinburgh University Press.

——— (1974). *The Formative Period of Islam*. Edinburgh: Edinburgh University Press.

———, translator (1994). *Islamic Creeds: A Selection*. Edinburgh: Edinburgh University Press.

Wensinck, J. (1932). *The Muslim Creed*. Cambridge: Cambridge University Press.

White, L., Jr. (1962). *Medieval Technology and Social Change*. New York: Oxford University Press.

Winston, D. (1981). 'Introduction'. In *Philo of Alexandria*, pp. 1-37. New York: Paulist Press.

Wolfson, H. (1948). *Philo. Foundations of Religious Philosophy In Judaism, Christianity and Islam*. 2 volumes. Cambridge MA: Harvard University Press.

Wright, L. (2003). 'The Kingdom of Silence'. *The New Yorker*, 5 January 2003, pp. 48-73.

# 22

# Karl R. Poppers Aktualität für die Kritik an fundamentalistischen Weltanschauungen

## Kurt Salamun

Ich werde hier mehrere miteinander zusammenhängende Thesen vertreten, die man folgenderweise zusammenfassen könnte:

(1) Poppers Philosophie ist in ihren Grundannahmen zutiefst anti-fundamentalistisch.

(2) Der Totalitarismusbegriff, den Popper in seiner Sozialphilosophie verwendet, weist erhebliche Parallelen zu dem heute so aktuellen Begriff des Fundamentalismus auf.

(3) Die kritischen Argumente, die Popper in seinen sozialphilosophischen Hauptwerken gegen totalitäre Denkformen vorbringt, eignen sich ausgezeichnet auch zur Kritik an jenem Phänomen, das heute „Fundamentalismus" genannt wird.

(4) Poppers anti-fundamentalistische Philosophie gewinnt in der Gegenwart eine neue Aktualität im Zusammenhang mit der Kritik an fundamentalistischen Weltanschauungen, seien diese nun religiöser, politischer, szientistischer oder sonst irgendwelcher Natur.

## 1 Zu den Begriffen der Weltanschauung, des Fundamentalismus und des Totalitarismus

Unter einer „Weltanschauung" möchte ich hier ein „System von kognitiven und normativen Orientierungsmustern" verstehen, „mit dessen Hilfe die Wirklichkeit in ihrer Komplexität reduziert und für das Handeln interpretativ vorstrukturiert wird". Mit Wilhelm Dilthey gesprochen, könnte man auch sagen, dass eine Weltanschauung einen strukturellen Zusammenhang bildet, „in welchem auf der Grundlage eines Weltbildes die Fragen nach Bedeutung und Sinn der Welt entschieden und hieraus Ideal, höchstes Gut, oberste Grundsätze für die Lebensführung abgeleitet werden" (Dilthey 1931, p. 82). Diesem weiten Verständnis zufolge gelten dann auch Mythen, Religionen und politische Ideologien als spezifische Ausprägungen von Weltanschauungen.

Was den heute so oft verwendeten Begriff des Fundamentalismus betrifft,
ist man sich in der aktuellen Diskussion über die Extension dieses Begriffs
alles andere als einig. Wie bei so vielen wichtigen Begriffen mit denen wir versuchen, Ereignisse, Phänomene und Tendenzen in unserer gesellschaftlichen,
politischen und kulturellen Wirklichkeit zu beschreiben, gibt es dafür keine all-
gemein akzeptierte Definition. Der französischen Politikwissenschaftler Gilles
Kepel, der mit seinem 1991 erschienenen Buch *Die Rache Gottes. Radikale
Moslems, Christen und Juden auf dem Vormarsch* eine wichtige Studie zu
dem hier zur Diskussion stehenden Phänomen vorgelegt hat, warnt z. B.
ausdrücklich davor, die von ihm diagnostizierten radikalen religiösen Erneuerungsbestrebungen im Islam, im Christentum und im Judentum gemeinsam
unter das Etikett „Fundamentalismus" zu subsumieren (Kepel 1991, p. 16).
Er meint, damit würden wesentliche Unterschiede zwischen diesen
Bestrebungen verwischt. Andere Autoren sehen zwischen den radikalis-
tischen Erneuerungsbestrebungen in den verschiedenen Religionen so
viele Gemeinsamkeiten, dass sie es als berechtigt erachten, von einem
protestantischen, einem katholischen, einem islamischen und einem
jüdischen Fundamentalismus zu sprechen. Nicht wenige Autoren fassen
das Wort „Fundamentalismus" so weit auf, dass auch von einem „Hindu-
Fundamentalismus", einem „marxistischen Fundamentalismus" oder einem
„ökologischen Fundamentalismus" die Rede ist. (Voll 1989; Heimann 1989).
Eine derartige Verwendung ist nur dann möglich, wenn man unter
„Fundamentalismus" gewisse strukturelle Eigenheiten von Weltanschauungen
versteht, die unabhängig von den oft so verschiedenen Inhalten weltan-
schaulicher Gedankengebilde nachweisbar sind. In diese Richtung gehen
etwa Auffassungen, die unter „Fundamentalismus" etwas Ähnliches wie
„Dogmatismus" verstehen. Die folgende Bestimmung des Politikwissenschaft-
lers Thomas Meyer, dessen Buch *Fundamentalismus. Aufstand gegen die Moderne* im deutschen Sprachraum sehr verbreitet ist, weist in diese Richtung
wenn er feststellt (Meyer 1989b, p. 161).

> Der Fundamentalismus setzt an die Stelle des Zweifels und der generellen Un-
> gewissheit ein absolutes Wissen, das allem vernünftigen Zweifel enthoben wird.
> An die Stelle des prinzipiell unabschließbaren und für alle Argumente offenen
> Diskurses, der die Wissensform der Moderne ist, tritt ein zum festen Fundament
> allen weiteren Fragens und Handelns dogmatisiertes absolutes Wissen, das der
> wissenschaftlichen Prüfung und der relativierenden öffentlichen Debatte entzo-
> gen wird.

Ich möchte nicht weitere Definitionen aus der Fundamentalismus-Debatte
anführen, sondern auf meine eingangs genannten Thesen zurückkommen. Was
den Begriff des Totalitarismus bei Popper betrifft, so verwendet er die Wörter
„totalitär" und „Totalitarismus" in einer zweifachen Grundbedeutung. Wir
finden den Totalitarismusbegriff in der *Offenen Gesellschaft* (Popper 1957-
1958) zunächst auf politische Bewegungen und Herrschaftssysteme bezogen.
In dieser Verwendung entspricht er dem Totalitarismusverständnis, wie man

es bei den Vertretern der so genannten Totalitarismustheorie vorfindet, etwa bei Carl J. Friedrich, Zbigniew Brzezinski, Leonard Shapiro, im deutschen Sprachraum bei Hans Buchheim und Karl Dietrich Bracher. Dort dienen die Wörter „totalitär" und „Totalitarismus" zur Bezeichnung eines bestimmten Typus von Herrschaftssystem und den Methoden der Herrschaftsausübung in diesem System. Der Totalitarismusbegriff ist in diesem Zusammenhang ein institutioneller Begriff. Er bezieht sich primär auf Institutionen und Herrschaftspraktiken in einem politischen System. Als totalitäre politische Systeme in diesem Sinne wurden von den Vertretern dieser Theorie (Friedrich 1956; Brzezinski; Shapiro; Buchheim 1962; Bracher 1969, p. 381) das nationalsozialistische Herrschaftssystem in Deutschland, das stalinistische Herrschaftssystem in der Sowjetunion und ihren Satellitenstaaten, sowie mit gewissen Einschränkungen das faschistische Herrschaftssystem im Italien Mussolinis bezeichnet. Als strukturelle Hauptcharakteristika dieses Typs von Herrschaft gelten: ein Führer, ein Terrorsystem, ein technologisch ermöglichtes Monopol in der Massenkommunikation, die zentrale Überwachung und Lenkung der gesamten Wirtschaft, die Unterwerfung des Rechts unter die Willkür des Führers, das Geltendmachen der Herrschaftsgewalt bis in den Privatbereich, ein Aktivitätssyndrom, ein spezifischer Herrschaftsapparat neben dem Staat, sowie eine dieses Herrschaftssystem legitimierende Ideologie. Von einer „totalitären Ideologie" ist in diesem Kontext dann die Rede, wenn sie Bestandteil des totalitären Herrschaftssystems ist und dieses rechtfertigt.

In einer zweiten Grundbedeutung, die sich bei Popper ebenfalls findet und die in unserem Zusammenhang relevant ist, bezieht sich der Totalitarismusbegriff auf bestimmte Weltanschauungen, Weltbilder, Denksysteme, Ideologien und Philosophien. Von Popper werden bekanntlich auch die Moraltheorie Platons und die Staatstheorie Hegels als „totalitär" bezeichnet. In dieser Verwendung zielt dieser Begriff auf spezifische strukturelle Komponenten von Weltanschauungen ab, u. zw. unabhängig davon welche Inhalte diese Weltanschauungen haben. Die spezifischen strukturellen Komponenten von Weltanschauungen, die Popper als totalitär bezeichnet, — und das ist wieder eine meiner Eingangsthesen — sind auch Kennzeichen von solchen Weltanschauungen, mit denen man heute das Attribut „fundamentalistisch" verbindet.

## 2  Strukturelemente fundamentalistischer Weltanschauungen

Welches sind nun wesentliche Strukturelemente von fundamentalistischen Weltanschauungen und worin besteht deren unversöhnlicher Gegensatz zu den Basisannahmen von Poppers Kritischem Rationalismus, wie ich dies eingangs betont habe als ich Poppers Philosophie als zutiefst anti-fundamentalistisch bezeichnet habe? Dies sei im Folgenden durch vier Gegensatzpaare verdeutlicht.

## 2.1 Hypothetischer Wahrheitsanspruch versus absoluten, ausschließlichen Wahrheitsanspruch

In diesem Zusammenhang geht es um die Frage nach der Wahrheit und der Möglichkeit der Begründung von Wahrheitsansprüchen. Aus fundamentalistischer Sicht gibt es die absolute Wahrheit, sie geht auf eine unhinterfragbare metaphysische Instanz zurück. In religiös-fundamentalistischen Weltanschauungen ist diese Instanz eine Gottheit oder ein gottgesandter Prophet, der die Wahrheit den Menschen in einem einmaligen Offenbarungsakt kundgetan hat, so dass diese fortan Anteil an dieser Wahrheit haben können. Die Wahrheit ist ein für allemal in bestimmten heiligen Texten niedergelegt und diese Texte sind in ihren zentralen Aussagegehalten sakrosankt und auf ewige Zeiten unrevidierbar. Versuche einer vernunftmäßigen Prüfung oder Begründung des absoluten Wahrheitsanspruchs erscheinen aus fundamentalistischer Sicht als modernistisch-rationalistisches Sakrileg, denn jedes vernünftige Begründenwollen absoluter Glaubenswahrheiten mindert nur die Glaubensgewissheit. Diese Gewissheit ist eine Gnade, die Gott dem Rechtgläubigen in einer Zeit gewährt, in der Unsicherheit und Ungewissheit herrschen und alles in Frage gestellt wird. In unmittelbarem Zusammenhang mit dem absoluten Wahrheitsanspruch steht in fundamentalistischen Weltanschauungen stets auch ein Ausschließlichkeitsanspruch. Dieser äußert sich in einer zweifachen Überzeugung, u. zw. (a) in der Gewissheit, dass die Manifestation der absoluten Wahrheit ausschließlich in der eigenen Weltanschauung gegeben sei, und (b) in der unerschütterlichen Ansicht, dass nur die eigene Gesinnungsgemeinschaft im Besitz dieser Wahrheit sei und keine andere.

Dem fundamentalistischen Wahrheitsverständnis steht in Poppers Kritischem Rationalismus die These von der prinzipiellen Fehlbarkeit und Irrtumsanfälligkeit der Vernunft entgegen. Mit dieser These werden absolute Wahrheitsbehauptungen entschieden abgelehnt. Für Popper ist die absolute Wahrheit bloß eine regulative Idee oder ein Annäherungsideal. Allerdings argumentiert er nicht so, wie dies in populistischen Popper-Deutungen fälschlich nahe gelegt wird, dass es prinzipiell keine absolute Wahrheitserkenntnis geben könne. Popper vertritt vielmehr die Ansicht, dass der Mensch als irrtumsanfälliges und fehlbares Wesen niemals mit Sicherheit wissen kann, ob eine Erkenntnis oder ein Wissen im absoluten Sinne wahr sind, d.h. ein für allemal gültig und in alle Zukunft unwiderlegbar. Aus diesem Grund empfiehlt es sich von vornherein, jegliches Wissen als bloß hypothetisch und vorläufig zu betrachten. Poppers Wahrheitsverständnis ist ein relatives, hypothetisches oder plurales. Es ist nicht relativistisch in dem Sinne dass allen Wahrheitsansprüchen der gleiche Wahrheitswert zugesprochen wird. Wenn es *relativ* genannt wird, so bedeutet dies, dass bei allen Wahrheitsansprüchen die Möglichkeit des Irrtums und der Revision nicht von vornherein ausgeschlossen wird, wie dies bei absoluten Wahrheitsansprüchen der Fall ist. Ich kann hier nicht auf weitere erkenntnistheoretische Argumente eingehen, die Popper in seiner subtilen Kritik an der Idee einer absoluten Wahrheitsgarantie vorbringt. Er hat diese Idee, soweit sie eine Letzbegründung von Erkenntnissen und absolute Gewissheit vorgaukelt, in fast allen seinen Werken kritisiert. Für ihn ist die absolute Wahrheit stets nur eine regulative Idee bzw. ein den Erkenntnisprozess stimulierendes Annäherungsideal, (Popper 1930-1933, Einleitung 1978; Popper 1989, Kap. X, Abschnitt 84; Popper 1957-1958; Popper 1984, Kap. II, Abschnitt 6; Popper 1994, Einleitung, Abschnitt III; Popper 1990, Teil I, Kap. 3).

Sicherlich kommt die Idee einer absoluten Wahrheitsgarantie Gewissheits- und Sicherheitsbedürfnissen entgegen, die das Resultat von negativen Emotionslagen sind, wie Gefühlen der Ungewissheit, Ungeborgenheit und Isolation, des Auf-sich-allein-gestelltseins in pluralistisch strukturierten Entscheidungssituationen, des Bedrücktseins aufgrund der Last persönlicher Verantwortlichkeit usw. Diese negativen Emotionen sind der Preis, den der Mensch aus der Sicht von Popper für die Emanzipation von der archaischen Lebensform in geschlossenen Stammesgesellschaften zu bezahlen hat. Für diese negativen Stimmungslagen, die Popper unter Hinweis auf Sigmund Freuds Analysen in der Schrift *Das Unbehagen in der Kultur* die „Last der Zivilisation" nennt (Popper 1957-1958, Bd. I, Kap. 10, Abschnitt II, Bd. II, Kap. 14, Abschnitt III; 1992, Kap. 10, Abschnitt II, Kap. 24, Abschnitt III), würde die Idee einer möglichen absoluten Wahrheitsgarantie und unbezweifelbaren Gewissheit in vielen Situationen zweifellos eine ausgezeichnete Kompensationsmöglichkeit bieten. Dieser Überzeugung sind viele Vertreter von religiösen Glaubenspositionen wenn sie absolute Glaubenswahrheiten pragmatisch zu rechtfertigen versuchen, indem sie auf deren Trostfunktion bzw. deren psychische Entlastungs- und Stabilisierungsfunktion verweisen. Dass Popper von seiner kritisch-rationalistischen Position aus absolute Wahrheitsgarantien als Kompensationsmöglichkeit für die genannten negativen Emotionen ablehnen muss, hängt nicht nur mit dem Vernunftverständnis und dem Aufklärungsethos seiner Philosophie zusammen. Dies folgt auch aus der philosophisch-anthropologischen Rahmenvorstellung, die seinem gesamten Philosophieren zugrunde liegt. Ich meine damit die Vorstellung von einem sinnvollen Leben, bei dem der Mensch als ein höchst aktives Wesen gesehen wird, das sich ständig auf der Suche nach neuen Problemlösungen und nach Verbesserung von Hypothesen, Institutionen und Lebenseinstellungen befindet. Der Mensch ist ein Lebewesen, das stets von neuem ins Unbekannte, Ungewisse und Unsichere vorstoßen und permanent um Verwirklichung von mehr Freiheit, Offenheit, Pluralität und von größerer Humanität im Sinne der Leidminimierung ringen muss. Die Idee der absoluten Wahrheitsgarantie spiegelt Gewissheit, Sicherheit und Geborgenheit vor, was eher einem statisch-kontemplativen Menschenbild entspricht, als jenem dynamisch-kreativen Menschenbild, das Popper als Idealbild vom Menschsein vor Augen hat und das er in der Schlusspassage des l. Bandes der *Offenen Gesellschaft* deutlich ausgesprochen hat, wenn es dort heißt (Popper 1957-1958, Kap. 10, Abschnitt VIII):

> Aber wenn wir Menschen bleiben wollen, dann gibt es nur einen Weg, den Weg in die offene Gesellschaft. Wir müssen ins Unbekannte, ins Ungewisse, ins Unsichere

weiter schreiten und die Vernunft, die uns gegeben ist, verwenden, um, so gut
wie wir dies eben können, für beides zu planen: nicht nur für Sicherheit, sondern
zugleich auch für Freiheit.

## 2.2 Demokratisches Erkenntnisideal versus elitär-autoritäres Erkenntnisideal

Das zweite Gegensatzpaar mit dem ich den grundlegenden Gegensatz zwischen
Poppers Philosophie und fundamentalistischen Weltanschauungen verdeutlichen möchte, betrifft ebenfalls die Erkenntnis- und Wissensauffassung, u. zw.
die Frage nach dem Zugang zu jenem Wissen, das politisch und gesellschaftlich
relevant ist. Fundamentalistische Positionen basieren auf einem elitär-autori-
tären Erkenntnis- und Wissensideal. Sie räumen Einzelpersonen oder elitären
Gruppen, von Gott auserwählten Führerpersönlichkeiten oder Priestereliten,
von vornherein einen privilegierten Zugang zu einem Wissensbestand ein,
der als besonders bedeutsam hingestellt wird. Nicht selten wird dieses Wissen sogar zu einem Heils- und Überlebenswissen für eine ganze Gruppe,
eine Gesinnungsgemeinschaft, ein Volk oder gar für die gesamte Menschheit
hochstilisiert. Von metaphysischen Instanzen (Gott, der Geschichte, dem
Schicksal usw.) angeblich auserwählte Glaubensautoritäten und charismatische Führerpersönlichkeiten erhalten ein Interpretationsprivileg oder Erkennt-
nismonopol auf das höhere Wissen zugesprochen, das allen anderen Menschen prinzipiell nicht zugänglich und in keiner Weise überprüf- und kon-
trollierbar ist. Mit diesem Erkenntnisprivileg wird stets auch die alleinige
Kompetenz verbunden, darüber entscheiden zu können, welche Personen zu
den rechtgläubigen Anhängern der betreffenden fundamentalistischen Weltanschauung zu zählen sind und welche zu den Abtrünnigen und Verrätern. Das
Denkmotiv eines nicht kontrollierbaren höheren Wissens und eines privilegierten Zugangs zu diesem Wissen, das in vielen autoritären oder totalitären
politischen Ideologien anzutreffen ist, ist ein uraltes Denkmotiv, es findet
sich u. a. bereits in der Staatslehre Platons. Popper hat die Vorstellung von
den „königlichen Philosophen" in Platons Staatslehre und die Grundhaltung
eines „autoritären Intellektualismus" nachhaltig kritisiert. Er warnt mit Recht
vor der mystischen Aura der Auserwähltheit, die um politische, religiöse und
intellektuelle Führer entsteht, sobald ihnen mittels einer „mystischen Theorie
intuitiven Verstehens" gewisse nicht überprüfbare intuitive Einsichten zuge-
billigt oder prophetische Fähigkeiten eingeräumt werden, (Popper 1957-1958/
1992, Kap. 7). Das elitär-autoritäre Denkmotiv in Platons Staatsphilosophie
hat neben Popper übrigens auch der Rechtsphilosoph Hans Kelsen scharf kritisiert (Kelsen 1964, pp. 229f.), der in den Zwanzigerjahren an der Wiener
Universität, an der Popper studierte, gelehrt hat.
    In Poppers Kritischem Rationalismus wird dem elitär-autoritären Erkennt-
nisideal, ein demokratisches Erkenntnis- und Wissensideal entgegengesetzt.
Es ist durch die Auffassung charakterisiert, dass jedes Wissen zumindest
im Prinzip für jedermann einsehbar sein muss und keine Gruppe oder
Person von vornherein davon ausgeschlossen werden darf. Jeder Erkennt-

nisanspruch muss intersubjektiv prüfbar und in Aussagen formuliert sein, die möglichst klar und informationshaltig sind. Diese Aussagen müssen immer wieder im Rahmen einer kritischen Öffentlichkeit diskutiert werden, damit das in ihnen artikulierte Wissen kontrolliert, modifiziert und verbessert werden kann. An diesem Diskussionsprozess können sich im Prinzip alle zurechnungsfähigen Menschen aufgrund ihrer Vernunftbegabtheit beteiligen, falls sie sich der Mühe unterziehen, sich die notwendigen Fachkompetenzen anzueignen. Die kritisch-rationale Diskussion von Problemlösungsvorschlägen in der Öffentlichkeit durch möglichst viele vernünftige Individuen und nicht die autoritäre Entscheidung einzelner oder weniger Menschen aufgrund eines unkontrollierbaren Geheimwissens, macht einen Kernbestandteil des demokratischen Wissens- und auch Politikverständnisses aus. Wie stark bereits Poppers frühes Wissenschaftsverständnis und seine Auffassung vom wissenschaftlichen Erkenntnisfortschritt mit der Idee einer kommunikativ-kritischen Öffentlichkeit verbunden ist, hat Ian Jarvie in seinem Buch *The Republic of Science. The Emergence of Popper's Social View of Science 1935-1945* anschaulich herausgearbeitet (Jarvie 2001, pp. 35f., pp. 212f.). Das Objektivitätskriterium von Erkenntnissen ist bei Popper notwendig an das Prinzip der Offenheit für Kritik, der öffentlichen Prüfung und der Konfrontation mit konkurrierenden und alternativen Erkenntnisansprüchen gebunden. Nicht das Dogmatisieren eines Erkenntnisanspruchs sondern der Theorienpluralismus, die Konkurrenz mehrerer Theorien um die bestmögliche Problemlösung ist ein Kerngedanke von Poppers Wissenschaftsauffassung.

*2.3 Betonung von Individualität, Pluralität und Offenheit versus Fixierung auf Einheit, Ganzheit und Geschlossenheit*

Das dritte Gegensatzpaar, das ich hervorheben möchte, betrifft die Grundeinstellung zum Verhältnis von Individualität, Vielfalt (Pluralität) und Offenheit einerseits und Einheit, Ganzheit, Geschlossenheit andererseits. In fundamentalistischen Weltanschauungen wird eine Einheit, Ganzheit, Totalität, oft auch eine einheitliche Geschlossenheit beschworen (Eisenstadt 1968, pp. 77f.), sei es in Bezug auf den Glauben, das Wissen, die Gesinnungsgemeinschaft, den Zusammenhalt in der eigenen Gruppe, die Gesellschaft, den Staat, usw. Alles Individuelle, Singuläre, Unvollständige, Differenzierte, Vielfältige, Deviante wird als bloß vorläufig, vordergründig und unzulänglich hingestellt. Unterscheidung, Abweichung, Pluralität und Individualität erscheinen im Vergleich zur beschworenen Einheit und Ganzheit als minderwertig, ja oft sogar als subversiv in Bezug auf die Verwirklichung der erstrebten Einheit und Ganzheit. Fundamentalistische Weltanschauungen kommen mit Einheits- und Ganzheitsmythen latenten Bedürfnissen und Sehnsüchten entgegen, wie Sehnsüchten nach Unkompliziertheit der Lebensverhältnisse, nach Eindeutigkeit, nach einem Zustand, in dem man sich als Teil eines Ganzen geborgen fühlen kann, eine Einheit mit diesem Ganzen bildet und von diesem Ganzen her in seinen individuellen Lebensentwürfen gestützt wird. Einheits - und Ganzheitsideale sind im Rahmen fundamentalistischer Weltanschauungen wichtige Hilfsmittel, um für einzelne Menschen die „Last der Zivilisation" zu mildern, der der Mensch seit dem Verlassen der geschlossenen Stammesgesellschaften ausgesetzt ist. Diese Ideen können individuelle Leiderfahrungen beträchtlich abschwächen wenn diese in den Kontext eines Sinnganzen, etwa eines heilsgeschichtlichen Endziels, gerückt sind und man sich einzureden vermag, das persönliche Leid müsse im Kontext des Ganzen schon irgendeinen Sinn haben, für irgendetwas gut sein. Im äußersten Fall ist man sogar dazu bereit, im Dienste des übergeordneten Sinnganzen sein Leben zu opfern, um damit das verheißene endgültige Heilsziel herbeiführen zu helfen. Auch Entscheidungsängste können reduziert werden, wenn man der festen Überzeugung ist, nur als Teil eines Ganzen im Sinne dieses Ganzen zu handeln; die Last der Verantwortung für getroffene Entscheidungen und getätigte Handlungen lässt sich auf die ganzheitliche Wesenheit abschieben, in deren Interesse oder gar in deren Auftrag man gehandelt zu haben meint.

In Poppers Philosophie wird im Gegensatz zu Einheit, Ganzheit und Geschlossenheit der Wert von Vielfalt, Pluralität, Individualität und Offenheit besonders akzentuiert. Popper hat Ganzheitsideen, sofern sie ein wesentliches Ganzes im Gegensatz zum Einzelnen und Individuellen als eigentliches Sein hochstilisieren, nachdrücklich kritisiert, u. zw. in seiner Auseinandersetzung mit „essentialistischen" und „holistischen" Denkformen. (Popper 1965, Abschnitte 7, 10, und 23). Solche Denkformen degradieren den Einzelnen zu einem willkürlich manipulierbaren Mittel im Dienste einer übergeordneten Ganzheit, für die er seine Entscheidungs- und Meinungsfreiheit preisgeben muss. Sie stehen in krassem Widerspruch zu den Werten und Prinzipien, die Popper aus seiner liberalen Weltsicht als bestimmend für ein lebenswertes Dasein ansieht. Solche Werte und Prinzipien sind: das Bemühen um Herstellung und Bewahrung der größtmöglichen individuellen Freiheit, soweit dadurch die Freiheit anderer nicht beeinträchtigt wird und die notwendigen Einschränkungen, die durch das soziale Zusammenleben unvermeidlich werden, möglichst gleichmäßig verteilt sind; die Anerkennung der Würde und Autonomie der menschlichen Person im Sinne der Kantischen Ethik; das Respektieren der freien und persönlichen Meinungsbildung; das Toleranzprinzip, aus dem sich die Respektierung des Verschiedenartigen, Fremden, Nichtkonformen und vom einheitlichen Ganzen Abweichenden ergibt; das Verantwortungsprinzip, das die individuell zurechenbare Verantwortung und nicht die anonymisierte Verantwortlichkeit eines Kollektivsubjekts betont; das ethische Prinzip des negativen Utilitarismus, das nicht die Verwirklichung des Glücks für ein Kollektivsubjekt, wie eine politische oder religiöse Gesinnungsgemeinschaft, ein Volk, eine Nation oder gar die Menschheit verlangt oder gar verspricht, sondern vielmehr konsequent darum bemüht ist, das Leid von Individuen zu verkleinern.

*2.4 Gradualismus versus Alternativ-Radikalismus*

Das vierte und letzte Gegensatzpaar das ich hier als wesentliches Unterscheidungsmerkmal zwischen Poppers Philosophie und fundamentalistischen Weltanschauungen hervorheben möchte, ist der Gegensatz zwischen einer gradualistischen und einer alternativ-radikalistischen Denkweise. (Albert 1991, p. 210). Fundamentalistische Weltanschauungen sind von Denkformen geprägt, die radikale Alternativen nahe legen, keine graduellen Abstufungen und Differenzierungen zulassen, sowie Kompromisse grundsätzlich ablehnen. Auf der Sprachebene manifestieren sich solche Denkformen in emotional aufgeladenen Polarisierungskategorien und Schwarz-Zeichnungen des politischen, gesellschaftlichen und kulturellen Geschehens. Es werden komplexe Sachverhalte und Beziehungen immer wieder auf ein Entweder-Oder, ein Für-mich oder Gegen-mich, ein Freund-Feind-Schema reduziert. In der Regel enthalten fundamentalistische Konzeptionen auch manichäische, eschatologische und messianische Ideen, die den Alternativ-Radikalismus mit bedingen. Solche Ideen äußern sich in der Überzeugung, das Übel in der Welt, das Böse, die Sünde, der Abfall vom wahren Glauben, das soziale Elend der Glaubensbrüder, die menschliche Entwürdigung der eigenen Gruppe, müsse zuerst einen Höhepunkt erreichen, um dann in einer radikalen Umkehr, das ist einer möglichst radikalen Revolution oder radikalen Tat, ein für allemal aus der Welt geschafft zu werden. Die radikale Erlösungstat einer Einzelperson oder der auserwählten Gruppe der Rechtgläubigen werde die Rückkehr in die Heilsentwicklung und die Verwirklichung des ersehnten Heilszustands für alle bringen. Solche Ideen legen im politisch-gesellschaftlichen Bereich die gefährliche Illusion nahe, man müsse durch eine besonders radikale, gewaltsame Revolution möglichst alles von einer bestehenden Gesellschaft zerstören, um dann in das entstehende gesellschaftliche Vakuum hinein eine ganz andere, von allen Übeln der alten Gesellschaft gereinigte, neue Gesellschaft bauen zu können.

Im Gegensatz zu solchen alternativ-radikalistischen Denkweisen in fundamentalistischen Weltanschauungen sind in Poppers Philosophie gradualistische Denkschemata dominant. Ein Zustand darf nie undifferenziert als total schlecht oder total gut angesehen werden, sondern es gilt differenzierende Überlegungen sowohl über Vorteile als auch über Nachteile anzustellen. Auch weitergehende Veränderungen in einer Gesellschaft zum Zwecke der Vergrößerung individueller Freiheitsspielräume, der Ausweitung demokratischer Institutionen zur effektiveren Machtkontrolle, der Veränderung von Zuständen im Sinne der Leidminimierung, werden nicht in Form der Notwendigkeit einer einmaligen radikalen Heilstat vor Augen gestellt, sondern vielmehr als ein kontinuierliches graduelles Bemühen, bei dem mögliche negative Folgen eines Eingriffs in eine Gesellschaftsordnung verantwortungsbewusst mitbedacht werden müssen. Ein Musterbeispiel für diese gradualistische Denkweise ist das Konzept des piecemeal-social engineering, das Popper in *Das Elend des Historizismus* (Popper 1965, Abschnitt 21) einmal folgendermaßen umschrieben hat: Der Gesellschaftsveränderer und Sozialreformer

... mag zwar einige Vorstellungen von der idealen Gesellschaft „als Ganzem" haben, ... aber er ist nicht dafür, daß die Gesellschaft als Ganzes neu geplant wird. Was immer seine Ziele sein mögen, er sucht sie schrittweise durch kleine Eingriffe zu erreichen, die sich dauernd verbessern lassen. ... Daher wird er nur Schritt für Schritt vorgehen und die erwarteten Resultate stets sorgfältig mit den tatsächlich erreichten vergleichen, immer auf der Hut vor den bei jeder Reform unweigerlich auftretenden unerwünschten Nebenwirkungen. Er wird sich auch davor hüten, Reformen von solcher Komplexität und Tragweite zu unternehmen, daß es ihm unmöglich wird, Ursachen und Wirkungen zu entwirren und zu wissen, was er eigentlich tut.

Ich habe hier vier Gegensatzpaare hervorgehoben, die prinzipielle Gegensätze zwischen Poppers Philosophie und fundamentalistischen Weltanschauungen verdeutlichen sollten. Ich hoffe damit zugleich auch das fundamentalismus- und ideologiekritische Potential von Poppers Philosophie vor Augen geführt zu haben. Man könnte dieses Potential, das für eine politische Bildung im liberal-demokratischen Sinne fruchtbar gemacht werden sollte, abschließend in vier Fragenbündel formulieren, von denen man aus jede Weltanschauung beurteilen sollte:

(1) Finden sich im strukturellen Kontext einer Weltanschauung dogmatische Behauptungen über absolut wahre Einsichten und Grundprinzipien? Wird für die behaupteten absoluten Wahrheiten ein Ausschließlichkeitsanspruch erhoben? Wieweit werden die als absolut wahr behaupteten Einsichten und Prinzipien gegen Kritik immunisiert? Wie sind die Strategien beschaffen durch die diese Immunisierung erfolgt?

(2) Finden sich im gesellschaftlichen Unterbau einer Weltanschauung elitäre Gruppen oder autoritäre Einzelpersonen und charismatische Führerpersönlichkeiten, die ein Interpretationsprivileg auf die Deutung bestimmter Fundamentalbereiche einer Weltanschauung beanspruchen? Wieweit wird damit eine inappellable Kompetenz in Bezug auf die Entscheidung behauptet, wer ein rechtgläubiger Anhänger bzw. rechtgläubige Anhängerin der betreffenden Weltanschauung ist und wer ein Abweichler, Verräter der wahren Lehre, Häretiker, Revisionist usw?

(3) Wieweit ist in einer Weltanschauung die Tendenz zum monistischen Totalitätsstreben oder zu einem „essentialistischen Totalismus" ausgeprägt? Werden ganzheitliche essentialistische Entitäten, wie der Staat, die Volksgemeinschaft, die Religionsgemeinschaft, die Klasse, die Nation, die Partei usw. zu perfektionistischen Absoluta hochstilisiert? Wieweit wird in einem damit alles Partikulare, Individuelle, Deviante, Unabgeschlossene, Unfertige von vornherein diskriminiert? Wird aus der monistischen Totalitätstendenz der Dualismus zwischen Erkenntnis und Wertung preisgegeben, so dass Wertauffassungen getarnt als Tatsachenerkenntnisse auftreten und damit für erstere der gleiche Geltungs- und Wahrheitswert suggeriert wird wie für gut bewährte oder bestätigte Tatsachenbehauptungen?

(4) Wieweit sind in einer Weltanschauung Tendenzen zum Alternativ-Radikalismus ausgeprägt, die sich in dogmatisierten Schwarz-Weiß-Kategorisierungen, Freund-Feind-Schemata, Entweder-Oder-Perspektiven, Verschwörungstheorien usw. äußern? Ist im Zusammenhang mit holistisch-essentialistischen Denkmustern, welche utopische Harmonieideale vor Augen stellen, die Illusion verbunden, diese Ideale ließen sich unmittelbar (etwa durch einen radikalen revolutionären Sprung) in die Wirklichkeit umsetzen? Oder sind diese Ideale bloß als Annäherungsziele formuliert, an denen sich politisches Handeln langfristig orientieren soll? Welche Realisierbarkeitsüberlegungen finden sich im Kontext solcher Ideale oder sind gradualistische Realisierbarkeitsüberlegungen gänzlich ausgeblendet?

# Literatur

Albert, H. (1991). *Traktat über kritische Vernunft*. 5. verbesserte und erweiterte Auflage. Tübingen: J. C. B. Mohr (Paul Siebeck).

Bracher, K. D. (1969). *Die deutsche Diktatur*. Köln: Kiepenheuer & Witsch.

Buchheim, H. (1962). *Totalitäre Herrschaft*. München: Kösel.

Dilthey, W. (1931). *Weltanschauungslehre*. In *Wilhelm Diltheys Gesammelte Schriften*, Band VIII. Leipzig & Berlin: Teubner.

Eisenstadt, S. (1998). *Die Antinomien der Moderne. Die jakobinischen Grundzüge der Moderne und des Fundamentalismus*. Übersetzt und mit einem Nachwort von Georg Staudt. Frankfurt/Main: Suhrkamp.

Friedrich, C. J. (1956). *Totalitäre Diktatur*. Stuttgart: Kohlhammer.

Heimann, H. (1989). „Marxismus als Fundamentalismus?" In Meyer (1989a), pp. 213-230.

Jarvie, I. C. (2001). *The Republic of Science: The Emergence of Popper's Social View of Science 1935-1945*. Amsterdam & Atlanta: Editions Rodopi B.V.

Kelsen, H. (1964). *Aufsätze zur Ideologiekritik*. Hrsg. von Ernst Topitsch. Neuwied: Luchterhand.

Kepel, G. (1991). *Die Rache Gottes. Radikale Moslems, Christen und Juden auf dem Vormarsch*. München: Piper.

Meyer, T., Hrsg. (1989a). *Fundamentalismus in der modernen Welt. Die Internationale der Unvernunft*. Frankfurt/Main: Suhrkamp.

——— (1989b). *Fundamentalismus. Aufstand gegen die Moderne*. Reinbek: Rowohlt.

Popper, K. R. (1930-1933). *Die beiden Grundprobleme der Erkenntnistheorie*. 1. Auflage 1979. Tübingen: J. C. B. Mohr. (Paul Siebeck).

——— (1957-1958). *Die offene Gesellschaft und ihre Feinde*. Band I und II. Bern: Francke Verlag. English edition 1945. *The Open Society and Its Enemies*. London: George Routledge & Sons. 5th edition 1966. London: Routledge.

——— (1965). *Das Elend des Historizismus*. Tübingen: J. C. B. Mohr (Paul Siebeck). English edition 1957. *The Poverty of Historicism*. London: Routledge & Kegan Paul.

——— (1984). *Objektive Erkenntnis. Ein evolutionärer Entwurf*. 4. Auflage. Hamburg: Hofmann u. Campe. English edition 1972. *Objective Knowledge*. Oxford: Clarendon Press. 2nd edition 1979.

——— (1989). *Logik der Forschung*. 9. Auflage. Tübingen: J. C. B. Mohr (Paul Siebeck). English edition 1959. *The Logic of Scientific Discovery*. London: Hutchinson.

——— (1990). *Auf der Suche nach einer besseren Welt. Vorträge und Aufsätze aus dreißig Jahren*. 4. Auflage. München: Piper. English edition 1992. *In Search of a Better World*. London: Routledge.

——— (1992). *Die offene Gesellschaft und ihre Feinde*. Band I und II, 7. verbesserte Auflage. Tübingen: J. C. B. Mohr (Paul Siebeck).

——— (1994). *Vermutungen und Widerlegungen*. Teilband I. Tübingen: J. C. B. Mohr (Paul Siebeck). English edition 1963. *Conjectures and Refutations*. London: Routledge & Kegan Paul. 5th edition 1989. London: Routledge.

Voll, K. (1989). „Fundamentalistische Tendenzen unter Hindus und Moslems in Indien". In Meyer (1989a), pp. 155-192.

# 23

# World 3: A Critical Defence

Ilkka Niiniluoto

## 1 Introduction

Ever since Karl Popper introduced his new ontological doctrine of three worlds in 1967 (see Popper 1972, Chapters 3 and 4), his views have been praised by allies (Magee 1974), attacked by critics (Feyerabend 1981; Cohen 1985), and in the worst case ignored by philosophers working with similar problems (Searle 1995).

The hypothesis of World 3 is difficult to assess, since — besides being an ontological doctrine — it is an essential ingredient of Popper's epistemology, philosophy of mathematics, philosophy of biology, philosophy of mind, philosophy of art, philosophy of culture, hermeneutics, philosophy of history, and philosophy of the social sciences. In a single paper, it is not possible to do justice to all interesting and important aspects of Popper's approach (see also Niiniluoto 1984b, 1984c, 1992, 1994, 1999a, 1999b).

With some justification, Popper's expositions of his theory of World 3 can be accused of being sketchy and incoherent. In this paper, I attempt to give a critical defence of what I take to be the rational core of Popper's argument: the thesis of the existence of World 3 entities is an ontological hypothesis that gives the most plausible account of culture in terms of emergent materialism. This interpretation is the opposite of Mario Bunge's (1981, p. 138) claim that in 1967 Popper had a sudden 'conversion ... to objective idealism'.

Already our natural language involves ontological commitments to cultural and social entities such as artefacts, works of art, languages, norms, social institutions, and numbers. More generally, human mind, culture, and society are complex products of evolution, created and reproduced by men, but also capable of influencing the growth and development of new human individuals in their culture-producing activities. For these reasons, the traditional dichotomy of materialism and idealism is clearly perplexing in the case of culture. As culture is, *per definitionem*, something 'cultivated' by human beings, it is mind-dependent or mind-involving. But to say that culture is only 'in our heads', and to reduce it to our subjective experiences, is not at all convincing. The attempts of some materialist philosophers to reduce cultural entities to merely physical objects or practical activities are equally artificial. The ontological theory of World 3 should avoid the problematic features of reductionist materialism, but at the same time help us to understand the peculiar 'super-individual' character of cultural formations and social institutions without platonist, idealist, or supernaturalist assumptions. On the other hand, the analysis of the concept of emergence should make it clear how real World 3 entities differ from unreal fictions. The Popperian approach also has to reject what might be called the imperialist view of World 3, that makes even the material World 1 a part of man-made reality.

## 2  Sir Karl's three worlds

According to Popper (1972, p. 106), there is, in addition to the world of physical objects or physical states (World 1) and the world of consciousness or mental states (World 2), the 'third world': 'the world of *objective contents of thought*'. Its inhabitants include, among other things, theories, problems, problem situations, critical arguments, states of critical discussion, contents of journals, books and libraries, numbers, and works of art. The third world is a natural product of man, in many cases a non-intended by-product of our acts, but, simultaneously, it is relatively 'autonomous' and 'independently existing' because of its 'feed-back effect' upon us. Objective knowledge grows in a Darwinian way through the interaction between ourselves and the third world. (See also Popper & Eccles 1977; Popper 1974a, 1980, 1987.)

Popper's description of the physical World 1 represents a dynamic *process ontology* that is compatible with common sense and science. In his account of World 2, Popper grants that consciousness is a genuinely novel feature, which has appeared in material organisms as a result of emergent evolution. The mental states that belong to World 2 are 'real', since they are capable of causal interaction with objects of World 1 (Popper & Eccles 1977, p. 36). But unlike his interlocutor John Eccles, who supported interactionist dualism with an independently existing spiritual self, Popper declared himself to be an agnostic with respect to questions concerning religion and immortality of the soul. Popper thus accepted the basic ideas of *emergent materialism* (see Beckermann et al. 1992).

In his autobiography Popper mentioned Bernard Bolzano's 'sentences in themselves' (*Sätze an sich*) and Gottlob Frege's 'thoughts' (*Gedanke*) as points of departure for his theory of World 3 (Popper 1974a, pp. 144-146). Popper did not try to use World 3 as a solution to the problem of universals, the problem of the existence of universal concepts. I myself would be ready to accept among World 3 entities — in addition to propositions expressed by sentences — properties expressed by terms (such as the colour blue), that the human mind has abstracted from individual qualities related to World 1 objects (such as the blueness of the shirt I am wearing, the blueness of my eyes). (See the discussion on 'tropic realism' in Niiniluoto 1999a.)

While some philosophers think that the postulation of World 3 is 'a serious ontological extravagance' (Haack 1979, p. 325), some others have suggested that Popper's three worlds are not enough, but at least four worlds are needed. E. D. Klemke (1979) argues that 'the proper third world', consisting of the cognitive contents of sentences, is not man-created. This means that Klemke is advocating a return to platonism. However, the most important difference between platonism and Popper is the fact that World 3 is *created by human beings* — comparable to birds' nests and spiders' webs. The entities of World 3 are not located outside time, but have their own history like all artefacts. They emerge as products of human social action, and they can also be destroyed or rediscovered (*pace* Bunge 1981, p. 144). In this sense, Popper's theory about World 3 is a kind of 'poor man's platonism': as no higher being has created the World 3 objects, man must himself make them (cp. Niiniluoto 1992). This idea is compatible with antireductionist, emergent materialism: World 3 is produced and develops through cultural evolution, which continues the biological evolution. Therefore, World 3 would not exist without Worlds 1 and 2, and World 2 would not exist without World 1.

## 3 Carnap on the construction of the world

In addition to Plato, Hegel, Bolzano, and Frege, there seems to be one interesting historical predecessor of Popper's ontology of three worlds that Popper himself does not mention: Rudolf Carnap's *Der logische Aufbau der Welt* (1928/1967).[1]

In his *Aufbau* Carnap distinguished three types of objects. Firstly, *physical objects*, which always have spatial location, temporal location, form, size, position, and some property (such as colour, weight, or temperature). Secondly, *psychological objects* (acts of consciousness connected with some subject, such as perceptions, representations, emotions, thoughts, and volitions, including unconscious acts), which have a temporal location, no spatial location, and no perceptible sensational qualities. Thirdly, *cultural objects*, historical and sociological phenomena studied by the cultural sciences, such as customs that are tied to a group whose members possibly change. Cultural objects are temporarily located, but they need not be actualized at every moment.

In his 'pre-systematic' consideration Carnap said that cultural objects 'are not composed of' physical or psychological objects. Thus, Carnap's thesis about three kinds of objects seems to be essentially the same as Popper's 40 years later in the distinction between Worlds 1, 2, and 3.

As a logical positivist of the 1920s, Carnap, however, did not let himself use an ontological or 'material' mode of speaking, but formulated the distinction physical object – psychological object – cultural object as a 'formal' thesis concerning linguistic terms. In his *phenomenalist* constitution theory he then tried to show that the whole world can be 'logically constructed' starting from subjective experiences and proceeding from the autopsychological to the physical, then to the heteropsychological, and eventually to culture.

---

[1] I have discussed the relation of Carnap's *Aufbau* and Popper's three worlds ontology in a book published in Finnish in 1990. The only other mention of this connection, known to me, is in Herbert Keuth (2000/2004), § 15.31.

According to this programme, cultural objects are built from their psychological manifestations.

Thus, in Carnap's system, cultural objects do not after all form any relatively independent ontological level, like Popper's World 3. However, Carnap
can be said to have bravely — but, according to our present view, unsuccessfully — attempted to reduce World 3 to World 2 (and, in the end, the whole
World 1 to the part of World 2 that consists of the stream of experiences of
one single subject).

## 4  The inhabitants of World 3

Popper distinguished 'embodied' and 'unembodied' World 3 objects (see
Popper & Eccles 1977, p. 41). The former include, firstly, *material artefacts*
— such as books, furniture, clothes, utility articles, money, sculptures, and
paintings — which are, simultaneously, members of both World 1 and World
3. For example, a book as a material body and a coin as a piece of metal
belong to World 1: they have perceptible and measurable physical properties,
such as weight, form, spatio-temporal location, colour, odour, taste, and so on.
On the other hand, depending on the ambient human practice (author, users,
language, economic system), they have also relations to Worlds 2 and 3, that
is, non-physical relational properties (such as content, meaning, value, price,
purpose of use), through which they become cultural entities of World 3.

Popper's thoughts can be elaborated by noting that the distinction between a cultural object and its physical 'core' object is parallel to the usual
distinction between a human *act* and mere *behaviour*. Behaviour (for example,
the moving of a pen on a piece of paper) is an event of World 1 that consists
of bodily movements. Acting, however, is behaviour that is related to intentions in World 2 and to social institutions in World 3 (for example, writing
the name of a society, signing a bank cheque). If artefacts are *cultural objects*
of World 3 (cp. Margolis 1984), then acts and sequences of acts — from the
raising of one's hat and shaking hands, to sports competitions, congresses,
and wars — are, in a corresponding sense, *cultural events*. John Searle (1995)
includes artefacts (for example, screwdrivers, money) and cultural events (for
example, weddings, elections) among *institutional facts* that are created by
social acts involving 'collective intentionality'.

Secondly, *social institutions* are examples of elements of World 3: they do
not have as their constituents any specific physical objects (as most artefacts
do); still, they require continuous 'support' from Worlds 1 and 2. For example,
the Philosophical Society of Finland, founded by Professor Thiodolf Rein in
1873, is a historical entity, whose operation is regulated by, among other
things, the law of associations and statutes written down and accepted by the
register of associations. At every moment of time the Society has members and
officials chosen to represent and to maintain it. However, the attempt to define
an organization as a system of all of its members — past, present, future, and

perhaps even possible — would be ontologically artificial and problematic. These organizations as 'legal persons' are also typical agents of social action.

Thirdly, some in themselves *abstract* elements of World 3 can be copied, recorded, and reproduced through 'embodiments' that belong to Worlds 1 and 2. For example, a poem can be written on a paper (World 1) or recorded in people's memories (World 2); a symphony may be 'realized' as the composer's idea or as a listener's experience (World 2), as acoustic waves, as a record and a recording tape, or as notes on a score (World 1); a number can be written on a paper as a numeral, or it can exist in a mathematician's mind as a 'mental construction'. It would be completely arbitrary to identify this kind of an abstract entity with one of its embodiments and thereby to try to reduce it to World 1 or World 2.

It is important to add that World 3 should not be thought to include *all* real entities. The minimum assumption of ontological realism, as opposed to subjective and objective idealism, is that there is a mind-independent reality (see Niiniluoto 1999a); that is, the physical World 1 is both temporally and ontologically a precondition of World 3. This means that one should reject such 'imperialist' views of World 3 (for example, internal realism, social constructivism) that claim that all physical objects and facts are relative to human beings, their languages, practices, and social activities.

## 5 Getting rid of platonism

In his answer to Eccles, Popper (1974b) called by the name *World 3.1* that part of World 3 that has been in a way or another 'materialized' and 'stored up' in libraries or people's memories. Correspondingly, *World 3.2* is the part of World 3 which 'has been grasped or understood by some people'. According to Popper's thesis, Worlds 3.1 and 3.2 do not exhaust World 3: there are unembodied abstract objects that lie outside of the realms 3.1 and 3.2 and that no one has so far discovered. The natural numbers are a paradigmatic example: man has created an infinite set of natural numbers in World 3, though actually we can write on a paper or construe in our minds only a finitely many of these numbers.

O'Hear (1980) argues against Popper by noting that natural numbers become autonomous World 3 entities only if we separate them from the calculation practices originally related to them. Rather than finding objects of a new ontological realm created by ourselves, we should be satisfied with studying our own rules and practices. In the case of natural numbers, the issue is actually about what we can deduce from the definitions and postulates we have presented (see also Currie 1978). This counterargument is, however, not very convincing. Gödel's incompleteness theorem demonstrates that there are truths that cannot be logically deduced from the axiom systems of arithmetic, but yet are true of the set of natural numbers created by the mathematician.

Bunge (1981) presents a 'materialist' theory of culture, attempting to get along without World 3 and without falling into vulgar materialism. For him, culture is a material *system* consisting of 'cultural activities' performed by living individuals. Without doubt, Bunge is right in holding that at every moment the material basis of culture and society consists of individuals, their activities, and the material substance, instruments, and results of these activities. This individualistic-practical view provides, however, only a theory of culture as *activity*; it tells nothing about the actual *results* of this activity.

The talk about social facts and institutions produced, maintained, and reproduced by human practices is not unnecessary or unauthorized *reification* — or a result of *alienation*, as O'Hear (1980, p. 198), referring to Lukács, says. Social facts or constructions (for example, a party meeting, the present legal order, language as a system of norms, scientific knowledge) have super-individual and institutional features that cannot be distributed to Worlds 1 and 2 without remainder. World 3 entities are more than their *actual* instances in human behaviour; the Wittgensteinian slogan that 'meaning is use' (cp. Bloor 1974) should include the *potential* uses of linguistic expressions (see Niiniluoto 1999b). Concerning social entities, the theory of World 3 supports a Durkheimian holism instead of an ontological version of 'methodological individualism' frequently related to the Popperian tradition (cp. Niiniluoto 1984c; Currie & Musgrave 1985; Watkins 1957).

Popper insisted that there are 'autonomous' logical relations (such as entailment) between propositions in World 3. In this sense the products of the human spirit begin to 'live their own lives'. Constructions may transcend their creators' intentions, so that we do not have complete 'maker's knowledge' about our own productions (see Niiniluoto 1984c). From this it does not, however, follow that objective knowledge in the realm of World 3 would, for Popper, be an autonomous process entirely independent of us, as, for example, Bunge (1981, p. 155) interprets Popper (see also Haack 1979). Knowledge grows precisely through the interaction in which we as inhabitants of Worlds 1 and 2 put forward hypotheses as solutions to scientific problems and test them.

Popper's thesis that World 3 helps to analyse 'knowledge without a knowing subject' has led many critics to think of World 3 as a huge theory or a network of theories. As Popper allowed true and false propositions, and even inconsistent theories in World 3, is World 3 itself inconsistent? As contradictions logically entail 'anything whatever', World 3 appears to be 'over-full' (Cohen 1985; Gilroy 1985). In my view, this is not the right way to look at the construction of the third world. Suppose that $L$ is a well-defined formal language, with a fixed vocabulary and rules of formation. (This condition is not satisfied by natural languages.) Then the class $S(L)$ of all sentences of $L$ is an entity in World 3. If we now introduce a theory $T$ in $L$, and $T$ is inconsistent, then the class $Cn(T)$ of logical consequences of $T$ in $L$ is simply the set of all sentences of $L$. But this set $S(L)$ was already in World 3, and nothing new is added in World 3.

Another point is that a set like $S(L)$ is inconsistent in the sense that it contains for each sentence also its negation. But this is 'innocent' in the sense that such propositions as World 3 entities are not *asserted*: not everything included in World 3 belongs to human 'knowledge'.

In some respects Popper's description of the unembodied part of World 3 is, however, too platonistically coloured. In emphasizing the nature of World 3 as a 'by-product' of the creation of language, he seemed to locate in World 3 all propositions, theories, and arguments that *could* be formulated in a language and *could* be grasped by someone, even though no one ever produced and understood them (see Popper 1972, p. 116). This idea is analogous to the view that in the framework of musical scales created by man there 'exist' a lot of possible compositions that no one ever will compose. In this sense, the creation of a new symphony means that the composer discovers one of these previously unrealized possibilities.

Possible symphonies are 'man-made' only in the very weak sense that man has created the scales necessary for formulating them. However, maybe the different scales were already existent as possibilities waiting for their discoverer? If we think in this way, we will end up with pure platonism, in which everything that can be thought is accepted as real or 'existent'. However, there is a significant ontological difference between composed and possible symphonies — as well as between proposed and possible theories, painted and possible paintings, founded and possible associations, or already construed and possible mathematical objects. Only the former members of these pairs actually belong to the culture created by man.

To avoid platonism, some limitation is needed in defining World 3. One way of doing this is to admit in World 3 entities that are man-made and maintained by man or otherwise are included in such entities. This does not refute Popper's thesis, according to which some abstract objects in World 3 are not, at a given moment, embodied in Worlds 1 or 2. Here we are talking about man-made, well-defined totalities (for example, the set of natural numbers, theories as sets of sentences closed under deduction, the legal order prescribed by law) whose all elements or parts have not been studied yet. The set of possible symphonies is not in this sense well-defined, since the allowed principles for the construction of compositions are not specified as exactly as, for example, the rules of 'constructing' natural numbers.

## 6 The reality of World 3

Bunge (1981, p. 146) mistakenly claims that Popper does not tell us what the 'reality' of World 3 objects means. Popper, however, made it completely clear that, in his sense, an object is 'real' if, and only if, it is either a physical object of ordinary size or capable of causally influencing such objects (Popper & Eccles 1977, p. 9; Popper 1974a, p. 147). The formations of Worlds 2 and 3 that have emerged through evolution from matter are thus real, because they have the power of 'downward causation'.

According to Popper, Worlds 1 and 2 can interact, as well as Worlds 2 and 3. Between Worlds 1 and 3 there is, however, no direct contact. Their interaction takes place through the agency of World 2 (Popper 1974a, p. 147). This thesis is in many ways problematic. If the Louvre burns to ashes as a result of a lightning strike, this process belonging to World 1 results in the annihilation of a class of artworks in World 3, for example, da Vinci's *Mona Lisa*. Not all of Popper's examples of the effect of World 3 on World 1 are convincing either. They include unsolved mathematical problems causing scientists' activities in solving them, a sculptor's latest work stimulating other artists to imitate or modify it, the deduction of previously unknown consequences from scientific theories and then their application in technology to the manipulation of the environment. If the effect of World 3 objects is always transmitted through World 2, could these causal chains not be analysed as relations between Worlds 2 and 1, in which the postulation of World 3 would be unnecessary? (See Currie 1978; O'Hear 1980, p. 183. Cp. Watkins 1996.)

In my opinion, the following examples illuminate the causal powers connected with World 3 objects. (a) In a train somebody hands me a piece of paper on which there is written the English sentence 'The bridge has been blown up'. As I grasp the content of the message, I stop the train by pulling the emergency brake. Here it is essential that the message has information content that I can understand; a note written in Chinese would not have causal power over me. (b) The Communion wine enjoyed by a religious person — and the force of the religious tradition swallowed along with it — helps him or her to keep on the strait and narrow. (c) In a shop I pay for chocolate with a coin of one euro. (d) I sign a piece of paper and the bank takes care of a money transfer to a foreign account. (e) Ville commits a tax fraud against his better judgement, and thereby, according to the Finnish judicial system, he becomes a violator of the law. The fraud is discovered, and Ville is sentenced to prison. (f) I do not walk against a red light, because I know that the existing road traffic ordinance imposes an on-the-spot fine for it.

Most of these examples involve institutional facts in Searle's (1995) sense. But the sociologist Emile Durkheim offered already in 1894 excellent examples of the 'coercive influence' of social facts (such as super-individual institutions, established customs, fashion, social trends) on individual consciousness and behaviour (see Durkheim 1894). Thus, according to Durkheim's holism, social facts are World 3 entities: they are 'of our own making'; however, a 'coercive influence to the individual consciousness' is characteristic of them.

Capability of causal influence is, without doubt, a sufficient condition of reality. It is not clear, however, that it should also be a necessary condition — as, among others, Popper and Bunge suppose. Why should it be the case that the entire realm of reality constitutes a causally closed unity? According to the traditional definition formulated by Charles S. Peirce things 'whose characters are independent of what anybody may think them to be' are *real* (Peirce 1931-1935, § 5.405; cp. Niiniluoto 1984b, p. 212). According to this definition, the physical objects of World 1 and the mental states of World 2 are real, as well as the cultural entities, social facts, and institutions that belong to World 3. In addition, many abstract but public objects — even though it is not appropriate to ascribe causal powers to them — are, in this sense, real. Concepts, propositions, symphonies, and natural numbers are good examples. Any natural number that has not been previously studied is, in an objective sense, either a prime number or a composite number — entirely independently of the opinions of me, you, or the discoverer of the number in question. On the other hand, merely possible abstract objects that no one so far has even indirectly construed and thereby brought into public consideration are not real in Peirce's sense.

*Fictional objects*, such as Santa Claus or Anna Karenina, are not real, either, according to Peirce's definition. If I believe in Santa Claus, my belief itself is a real mental state in World 2, but Santa Claus is merely a product of my imagination. The status of fictional beings in World 3 is, however, a problematic question. Popper said that 'myths and fictions should not be excluded from World 3', because scientific theories emerge through the criticism of myths. However, saying that *The Kalevala* and the novel *Anna Karenina* belong to the man-made World 3 is different from claiming that Väinämöinen and Anna Karenina belong to it. Similarly, saying that a scientific theory (for example, the theory of phlogiston) belongs to World 3 is different from maintaining that entities postulated by such a theory (for example, phlogiston) belong to it.

Would it nonetheless be possible that some collective fantasies of human society might become public enough, so that objects related to them could be considered as cultural objects of World 3? What about earth spirits, drying barn brownies, angels, gods, and devils? At least according to the causality criterion these entities are not real: a belief in brownies may have causal effects, but brownies themselves have none. According to Peirce's criterion these entities do not have the same kind of a real status as for example the numbers construed by a mathematician have, either: by what kind of objective methods could, for example, the properties of angels be studied? Therefore, it is reasonable to conclude that the reification of these entities as members of World 3 is unauthorized.

## 7  Conclusion

In this paper, I have defended World 3 as a theory of human culture. On the whole, cultural objects are things that are as necessary in our ontology as are physical objects, theoretical entities, and human persons. Simply, we 'want to talk about them', as Hilary Putnam once remarked about the theoretical entities studied by science. World 3 entities do not, it is true, exist 'in themselves' (*an sich*), but are created and in many ways reproduced and maintained by human beings. From this it does not follow that World 3 is not a part of reality.

# Bibliography

Beckermann, A., Flohr, H., & Kim, J., editors (1992). *Emergence or Reduction? Essays on the Prospects of Nonreductive Physicalism*. Berlin: de Gruyter.

Bloor, D. (1974). 'Popper's Mystification of Objective Knowledge'. *Science Studies* **4**, pp. 65-76.

Bunge, M. (1981). *Scientific Materialism*. Dordrecht: D. Reidel.

Carnap, R. (1928). *Der logische Aufbau der Welt*. Berlin-Sprachtensee: Weltkreis-Verlag. English translation, 1967. *The Logical Structure of the World*. Berkeley and Los Angeles: University of California Press.

Cohen, L. J. (1985). 'Third World Epistemology'. In Currie & Musgrave (1985), pp. 1-12.

Currie, G. (1978). 'Popper's Evolutionary Epistemology: A Critique'. *Synthese* **37**, pp. 413-431.

Currie, G. & Musgrave, A. E. editors (1985). *Popper and the Human Sciences* Dordrecht: Martinus Nijhoff.

Durkheim, E. (1894). 'Les règles de la méthode sociologique'. *Revue philosophique* **37**, pp. 465-498, 577-607; **38**, pp. 14-39, 168-182. Book version 1895. Paris: Alcan. English translation 1938. *The Rules of Sociological Method*. Chicago: University of Chicago Press.

Feyerabend, P. K. (1981). Review of Popper's *Objective Knowledge*. In *Philosophical Papers 2*. Cambridge: Cambridge University Press.

Gilroy, J. D. (1985). 'A Critique of Popper's World 3 Theory'. *Modern Schoolman* **62**, pp. 185-200.

Haack, S. W. (1979). 'Epistemology *with* a Knowing Subject'. *Review of Metaphysics* **33**, pp. 309-335.

Keuth, H. (2000). *Die Philosophie Karl Poppers*. Tübingen: Mohr Siebeck. English translation, 2004. *The Philosophy of Karl Popper*. Cambridge: Cambridge University Press.

Klemke, E. D. (1979). 'Karl Popper, Objective Knowledge, and the Third World'. *Philosophia* **9**, pp. 45-62.

Magee, B. (1974). *Popper*. London: The Woburn Press.

Margolis, J. (1984). *Culture and Cultural Entities*. Dordrecht: D. Reidel.

Niiniluoto, I. (1984a). *Is Science Progressive?* Dordrecht: D. Reidel Publishing Company.

——— (1984b). 'The Evolution of Knowledge'. In Niiniluoto (1984a), pp. 61-74.

——— (1984c). 'Realism, Worldmaking, and the Social Sciences'. In Niiniluoto (1984a), pp. 211-225.

——— (1992). 'Reality, Truth, and Confirmation in Mathematics — Reflections on the Quasi-Empiricist Programme'. In J. Echeverria, A. Ibarra, & T. Mormann, editors (1992), pp. 60-78. *The Space of Mathematics*. Berlin: de Gruyter.

——— (1994). 'Scientific Realism and the Problem of Consciousness'. In A. Revonsuo & M. Kamppinen, editors (1994), pp. 33-54. *Consciousness in Philosophy and Cognitive Neuroscience*. Hillsdale NJ: Lawrence Erlbaum Associates.

——— (1999a). *Critical Scientific Realism*. Oxford: Oxford University Press.

——— (1999b). 'Rule-following, Finitism, and the Law'. *Associations* **3**, pp. 83-90.

O'Hear, A. (1980). *Karl Popper*. London: Routledge & Kegan Paul.

Peirce, C. S. (1931-1935). *Collected Papers*, volumes 1-6. Cambridge MA: Harvard University Press.

Popper, K. R. (1972). *Objective Knowledge*. Oxford: Clarendon Press. 2nd edition 1979.

——— (1974a). 'Intellectual Autobiography'. In Schilpp (1974), pp. 1-181. Reprinted as *Unended Quest* (1976). London & Glasgow: Fontana/Collins.

——— (1974b). 'Replies to My Critics'. In Schilpp (1974), pp. 961-1197.

——— (1980). 'Three Worlds'. In S. M. McMurrin, editor (1980), pp. 141-167. *The Tanner Lectures on Human Values 1980*, volume I. Salt Lake City UT: University of Utah Press, and Cambridge: Cambridge University Press.

——— (1987). 'Natural Selection and the Emergence of Mind'. In G. Radnitzky and W. W. Bartley, III, editors (1987), pp. 139-155. *Evolutionary Epistemology, Theory of Rationality, and the Sociology of Knowledge*. LaSalle IL: Open Court.

Popper, K. R. & Eccles, J. C. (1977). *The Self and Its Brain*. Berlin: Springer International.

Schilpp, P. A., editor (1974). *The Philosophy of Karl Popper*. La Salle IL: Open Court.

Searle, J. (1995). *The Construction of Social Reality*. New York: The Free Press.

Watkins, J. W. N. (1957). 'Historical Explanation in the Social Sciences'. *The British Journal for the Philosophy of Science* **8**, pp. 104-117.

——— (1996). 'World 1, World 2 and the Theory of Evolution'. In S. Amsterdamski, editor (1996), pp. 9-24. *The Significance of Popper's Thought*. Amsterdam & Atlanta: Editions Rodopi B.V.

# PART 3
# Metaphysics and Epistemology

## B: Our Knowledge of the World

# 24

# The Nature of Philosophical Problems
## Popper versus Wittgenstein

### Herman Philipse

## Introduction

One of the most heated, and most unsatisfactory, philosophical debates of
the twentieth century took place on the evening of Friday, 25 October 1946,
during a meeting of the Moral Sciences Club in Cambridge. The two main
protagonists, guest speaker Dr Karl Popper and the chairman of the Club,
Professor Wittgenstein, clashed over the question: Are There Philosophical
Problems? Popper's account of the evening in his intellectual autobiography,
*Unended Quest* (1974/1976) has been the subject of trenchant criticisms, and
recently two BBC journalists, David Edmonds and John Eidinow, have tried
to reconstruct the debate and its background in their excellent popular book
*Wittgenstein's Poker* (Edmonds & Eidinow 2001).

The issue that I shall raise in this paper is the very question with which Edmonds and Eidinow conclude their book: Who won on 25 October 1946? Or
rather: whose conception of philosophical problems is more fruitful, Popper's
or Wittgenstein's? Before we can answer this question, however, we have
to settle two preliminary issues. First, it is possible that there *could* be no
interesting debate on the nature of philosophical problems between Popper
and Wittgenstein, because Popper misunderstood Wittgenstein completely.
This is suggested by a note Wittgenstein sent to Rush Rhees shortly after the
Moral Sciences Club meeting, in which he speaks of 'a lousy meeting ... at
which an ass, Dr Popper, from London, talked more mushy rubbish than I've
heard for a long time' (Edmonds & Eidinow 2001, p. 227). A similar view has
been defended by E. D. Klemke in a paper of 1981. Klemke concludes by saying that Popper's critical remarks on Wittgenstein's *Tractatus* 'are worthless
and can lead only to more confusions and misunderstanding' (Klemke 1981,
p. 260). In my first section I shall argue that, even if Popper misunderstood
Wittgenstein, this does not exclude a real and interesting disagreement on
the nature of philosophical problems and on the issue of demarcation.

Popper's criticisms of Wittgenstein are all concerned with the *Tractatus
Logico-Philosophicus*. But after 1929 Wittgenstein rejected many of the views
central to the *Tractatus*, sometimes for reasons similar to Popper's. The second preliminary issue is, then, whether there could be a substantial debate

on the nature of philosophical problems between Popper and Wittgenstein in 1946. For in 1946, Popper was confronted by the 'later' Wittgenstein and not by the Wittgenstein of the *Tractatus*. This I shall discuss in my second section. In the third section I argue that it may be fruitful for the historian of philosophy to consider the competing conceptions of philosophical problems of Popper and of Wittgenstein as rival diagnostic hypotheses to be tested by the historical material. Depending upon the issue under consideration, Wittgenstein's or Popper's conception of philosophical problems will turn out to be more fruitful. And this result holds generally for all philosophical problems.

## 1 Did Popper misunderstand Wittgenstein's *Tractatus*?

One cannot expect Popper to have been an accomplished Wittgenstein scholar. Rather, Popper read Wittgenstein's *Tractatus* as an attempt to solve a problem he himself was interested in, the problem of demarcation, and he saw the book very much as the main source of inspiration for Logical Positivism. Although I agree with Klemke that Popper initially misunderstood the *Tractatus* to some extent and failed to reformulate his criticisms in the light of later Wittgenstein scholarship, I cannot accept the dismissive verdict with which Klemke concludes his analysis of Popper's critique. After having praised Popper as 'one of the greatest philosophers of our time', Klemke writes (1981, p. 260):

> But I do wish that he [Popper] would stick to the areas in which he is competent and in which he so often offers brilliant insights. In those areas, he has much to say that is of profound value. But as a critic of Wittgenstein, his remarks are worthless and can lead only to more confusions and misunderstanding. Hence, if I may paraphrase a famous statement in the *Tractatus*, I offer this advice: Whereof one does not have the competence or knowledge to speak one ought to remain silent.

There are three reasons why this verdict is grossly unfair. First, it is perfectly legitimate to read the *Tractatus* as a contribution to the problem of demarcation, that is, as an attempt to distinguish scientific or empirical statements and theories from metaphysics, even though this was not its central problem. Second, Wittgenstein's *Tractatus* is not a book written by an author who did his best to communicate his thoughts to the reader. Hence it was not necessarily Popper's fault if he misunderstood the *Tractatus*. Finally, and most importantly, we shall see that Popper's misunderstandings with regard to the *Tractatus* can be easily corrected without destroying the disagreement between Wittgenstein and him concerning demarcation and the nature of philosophical problems. In order to show this, I shall first summarize Popper's interpretation and critique of the *Tractatus*, to the extent that it is concerned with these two topics. Then I discuss some of Klemke's objections to Popper's critique and argue that they do not eliminate a real disagreement between Popper and Wittgenstein.

In the Preface to the *Tractatus*, Wittgenstein wrote: 'The book deals with the problems of philosophy, and shows, I believe, that the reason why these problems are posed is that the logic of our language is misunderstood.' He claimed that he had found, 'on all essential points, the final solution to these problems', and that he solved the problems by drawing a limit to the expression of thoughts in language, adding that 'what lies on the other side of the limit will simply be nonsense' (*einfach Unsinn*; 1921, p. 3). Popper linked the Preface of the *Tractatus* to aphorism § 6.53 in which Wittgenstein describes what he calls 'the correct method in philosophy':

> The correct method in philosophy would really be the following: to say nothing except what can be said, i.e. propositions of natural science — i.e. something that has nothing to do with philosophy — and then, whenever someone else wanted to say something metaphysical, to demonstrate to him that he had failed to give a meaning (*Bedeutung*) to certain signs in his propositions. Although it would not be satisfying to the other person — he would not have the feeling that we were teaching him philosophy — *this* method would be the only strictly correct one.

Popper interpreted these remarks as saying that, according to Wittgenstein, there are neither genuine philosophical problems nor genuine metaphysical or philosophical propositions. Philosophical problems would be mere symptoms of misunderstandings concerning the logic of our language, and any attempt to formulate philosophical or metaphysical propositions would fail, either because it would violate 'the logic of our language' or because 'no meaning was given to certain signs'. Consequently, philosophy cannot put forward propositions; it can consist only in an activity, the activity of 'logical clarification of thoughts' as Wittgenstein says in aphorism § 4.112. It follows that philosophy is strictly demarcated from the sciences, since Wittgenstein claimed that 'The totality of true propositions is the whole of natural science' (1921, § 4.11).

Popper raised many objections to the demarcation between metaphysics and science that he attributed to Wittgenstein. Let me mention the three most important ones:

(1) Popper accused Wittgenstein of blurring the problem of demarcation by supposing that there is something 'essentially' scientific and something 'essentially' metaphysical, and that the scientific coincides with what is meaningful or has sense, whereas metaphysics is senseless. According to Popper, a criterion of demarcation should be a practical proposal that serves the aim of maximizing the growth of knowledge. Wittgenstein's distinction between what has sense and what is senseless is practically useless as a criterion of demarcation for two reasons. First, since Wittgenstein holds that every meaningful proposition must be logically reducible to elementary propositions that are pictures of reality, his criterion of demarcation, if consistently applied, would reject 'as meaningless those natural laws the search for which, as Einstein

says, is the "supreme task of the physicist" ' (Popper 1959, § 4), because laws of nature are not logically reducible to elementary propositions. Second, the terms 'senseless' and 'meaningless' have the drawback of being emotionally coloured, so that 'these terms are better fitted for giving vent to one's personal indignation about metaphysicians . . . than for a technical characterization of a line of demarcation' (Popper 1945, Chapter 11, note 51).[1]

(2) Wittgenstein identifies the totality of true propositions with the whole of natural science. According to Popper, this implies that Wittgenstein 'excludes all those hypotheses from "the sphere of natural science" which are not true.' But 'since we can never know of a hypothesis whether . . . it is true, we can never know whether or not it belongs to the sphere of natural science' (ibidem). This is yet another reason why Wittgenstein's criterion of demarcation is practically useless. As Popper acknowledges, Wittgenstein in 1931 endorsed the view that scientific theories do not really consist of propositions, so that they would not have sense at all. Popper concludes: 'Theories, hypotheses, that is to say, the most important of all scientific utterances, are thus thrown out of the temple of natural science, and therefore put on a level with metaphysics' (ibidem).

(3) According to Popper, Wittgenstein's demarcation between science and metaphysics implies a doctrine of 'deeply significant nonsense', which Popper rejects. In the Preface to the *Tractatus*, Wittgenstein writes: '. . . the *truth* of the thoughts that are here communicated seems to me unassailable and definitive' (1961, p. 5). In aphorism § 6.54, he says, however, that the propositions of the *Tractatus* are elucidating on condition that the reader recognizes them as nonsensical (*unsinnig*). Popper combines these quotes and concludes: 'now we have a new kind of nonsense at our disposal, nonsense that communicates thoughts whose truth is unassailable and definitive; in other words, *deeply significant nonsense*.' He continues ironically as follows: 'I do not deny that Wittgenstein's thoughts are unassailable and definitive. For how could one assail them? Obviously, whatever one says against them must be philosophical and therefore nonsense. And it can be dismissed as such. We are thus faced with that kind of position which I have described . . . as a *reinforced dogmatism*' (1945, Chapter 11, note 51).

---

[1] In 1959, Popper assumes that Wittgenstein's elementary propositions are statements of experience, and that the problem of logical reduction is the same problem as the problem of induction. As an interpretation of the *Tractatus*, the first assumption is debatable. But one might confront the *Tractatus* with the dilemma that either the postulated elementary propositions are propositions of experience, or Wittgenstein will be unable to say what they are. The second assumption is mistaken, because in the *Tractatus* Wittgenstein was not interested in epistemology but in the logical structure of language. His question was not: how can we know that scientific laws are true, but rather: how can general statements have sense? Even so, Popper is right that the theoretical laws of physics cannot be logically reduced to elementary propositions of experience, because they are not truth-functional combinations of such propositions.

In his article of 1981, Klemke admits that Popper's second criticism may be correct (Klemke 1981, p. 254). But with regard to the other criticisms, he argues that they are mistaken. Popper projected on to the *Tractatus* a simplistic distinction between on the one hand meaningful statements that express propositions or thoughts and on the other hand pseudo-propositions or meaningless statements, whereas in fact Wittgenstein distinguished three categories with regard to statements: having a sense (*sinnvol*), having no sense (*sinnlos*), and nonsense (*unsinnig*). Klemke argues that these categories have a technical use in the *Tractatus*. Propositions have 'sense' because they are a picture of a possible state of affairs. Consequently neither tautologies nor contradictions have a sense (they are *sinnlos*), because they do not picture possible states of affairs (1921, § 4.461). Yet tautologies and contradictions are not nonsensical (*nicht unsinnig*), Wittgenstein says, because they are part of the symbolism as correctly used (ibidem, § 4.4611). Klemke concludes that Wittgenstein's distinction between statements having a sense and utterances without a sense coincides neither with his distinction between statements that have sense and nonsensical utterances, nor with his distinction between science and metaphysics, as Popper thought (Klemke 1981, pp. 243-249). And in this, Klemke is right.

But is Klemke also correct in thinking that wherever Wittgenstein calls philosophical and metaphysical statements 'nonsensical' (*unsinnig*), this 'does not entitle us to jump to saying that they are nonsensical in the ordinary sense of the word' (Klemke 1981, p. 246)? According to Klemke, Wittgenstein uses 'unsinnig' in a technical sense as well: 'to say that a proposition (*Satz*) is nonsensical is merely to say that it neither has sense nor lacks sense .... It simply falls into a third category' (ibidem, p. 244). Klemke develops this point as follows (ibidem):

> Now it is perhaps unfortunate that Wittgenstein chose words like 'nonsensical' and 'without sense', for we tend to think of them as pejorative. But it is clear that Wittgenstein does not intend them to be used in a pejorative sense at all. Once one understands their meanings, they become very neutral, technical terms and could be replaced with arbitrary and even newly invented labels.

Thus, when Wittgenstein qualifies as *unsinnig* metaphysical and philosophical statements, including his own philosophical statements, this cannot have a pejorative connotation. Klemke offers two further arguments for this interpretation. First, the *Tractatus* presents 'an astonishingly rich and incredibly beautiful ontology'. How can one think, then, with Popper, that Wittgenstein was an anti-metaphysician (Klemke 1981, p. 250)? Second, Wittgenstein said that philosophical statements have the function of elucidations. So how can they be nonsensical in the ordinary, pejorative sense of the term (Klemke 1981, p. 247)?

The problem for Klemke is, however, that Wittgenstein *did* use the word '*unsinnig*' in a pejorative sense. He calls statements nonsensical whenever there is something *wrong* with them. The reason Wittgenstein calls '[m]ost of the propositions and questions to be found in philosophical works' nonsensical is that they 'arise from our failure to understand the logic of our language' (1921, § 4.003). Nonsensical pseudo-statements arise, for instance, if one uses a formal concept such as 'object' as if it were a proper concept-word (ibidem, § 4.1272), or if one interprets identity as holding between two objects (ibidem, § 5.53ff.). According to Wittgenstein's view of the formal essence of language, there is also something wrong with the metaphysical statements in the *Tractatus* which Klemke finds 'incredibly beautiful': these statements purport to *say* something of which Wittgenstein holds that it can only be *shown*, to wit, the logical structure of language and the world.

Correcting Klemke, we might summarize Wittgenstein's views on the senseless (*sinnlos*) and the nonsensical (*unsinnig*) as follows. All utterances that do not form a picture of a possible state of affairs are senseless (*sinnlos*) in Wittgenstein's technical sense. There are two categories of senseless utterances. One of them consists of tautologies and contradictions, which are part of the symbolism as correctly used. A second category consists of all nonsensical utterances, in which the symbolism is not correctly used. As against Klemke, I defend the view that nonsensical utterances constitute a subclass of senseless utterances; they are not 'a third category' apart from what has sense and what is senseless. Among the nonsensical utterances, we may distinguish at least four kinds. First, trivial and apparent nonsense, such as '2 + 2 at 3 o'clock equals 4' (ibidem, § 4.1272). Second, the latent and therefore misleading nonsense of which most of traditional metaphysics consists, that is, utterances in which either no reference is given to terms (ibidem, § 6.53) or which arise from our failure to understand the logic of our language (ibidem, § 4.003). Third, ethical, aesthetic, and religious utterances, which cannot express propositions or thoughts either (ibidem, §§ 6.42, 6.421, 6.432). Finally, there is the illuminating philosophical nonsense of Wittgenstein's *Tractatus*. The function of this latter type of nonsense is to elucidate what cannot be said but what is shown by all (well formed) propositions.

I conclude that Wittgenstein's essentialist view of language in the *Tractatus* implies a rigid demarcation between science (everything empirical) and philosophy in terms of 'sense' or 'meaning' (*Sinn*). No philosophical statement can be 'meaningful' in the sense of having a factual content. Philosophical problems are typically bound up with language, both in traditional philosophy, because they spring from our failure to understand the logic of our language, and in Wittgenstein's *Tractatus*, because ultimately they are concerned with the question of how language relates to the world. In all these things, Popper was basically right about the *Tractatus*.

Popper did not overlook the fact that Wittgenstein defined 'having a sense or meaning (*Sinn*)' in a peculiar and technical manner. Rather, this was the very move Popper objected to. In § 10 of *The Logic of Scientific Discovery* (1959) he wrote: 'nothing is easier than to unmask a problem as "meaningless" or "pseudo". All you have to do is to fix upon a conveniently narrow meaning for "meaning", and you will soon be bound to say of any inconvenient question that you are unable to detect any meaning in it' (see also 1945, Chapter 11, note 51). This is precisely what Wittgenstein did in the *Tractatus*, by arguing that only sentences that are pictures of possible states of affairs have *Sinn*. The result was that all moral and political discussions, for example, and issues of normative scientific methodology, which for Popper were among the most important ones a philosopher could be concerned with, did not have a 'sense' and could not form legitimate discursive philosophical concerns.

It follows that, even if one corrects Popper's many simplifications of the *Tractatus*, there remains a real disagreement between Wittgenstein and Popper on the nature of philosophical problems and their demarcation from scientific problems: should we formulate demarcation in terms of sense (*Sinn*) or meaning (Wittgenstein and the logical positivists) or in terms of degrees of testability (Popper)? And are all philosophical problems ultimately problems of logical grammar (Wittgenstein), or are there also substantial philosophical problems, the solution of which may contribute to our knowledge of the world and to ethics and politics (Popper)?

## 2   Was the dispute merely verbal?

That Popper really disagreed with the *Tractatus* on the nature of philosophical problems becomes even clearer when one reads the paper 'The Nature of Philosophical Problems and their Roots in Science' of 1952, in which Popper sketches his own view of philosophy and philosophical problems (1963, Chapter 2).

Popper begins this paper by saying that a discussion of questions like 'What is philosophy?' is both insignificant and futile. It is insignificant because 'the function of a scientist or of a philosopher is to solve scientific or philosophical problems, rather than to talk about what he or other philosophers are doing or might do'. And it is futile because such a discussion presupposes 'the naïve belief that there is an entity such as "philosophy", or perhaps "philosophical activity", and that it has a certain character or essence or "nature" ' (ibidem, § I). But if one wants to discuss the question at all, one should put it in a slightly better form, that is: 'What is the character of philosophical problems?' The reason is that *disciplines* such as philosophy or physics are distinguished on quite accidental grounds: 'partly for historical reasons and reasons of administrative convenience . . . , and partly because the theories which we construct to solve our problems have a tendency to grow into unified systems' (ibidem, § I).

Genuine philosophical *problems*, Popper then argues, are 'always rooted in urgent problems outside philosophy', so that they typically 'cut right across the borders of any subject matter or discipline' (ibidem, § III; ibidem, § I). The reason we may nevertheless call these problems 'philosophical' is that we find that, although they originally arose in connection with extra-philosophical concerns and theories, they are 'more closely connected with the problems and theories which have been discussed by philosophers than with theories nowadays treated' in these extra-philosophical disciplines (ibidem, § III). Popper further claims that a philosophical problem may well contain factual, mathematical, and logical elements. 'To say that since it deals with factual issues it must belong to science rather than to philosophy is not only pedantic but clearly the result of an epistemological, and thus of a philosophical, dogma' (ibidem, § III).

There is no doubt, then, that Popper's anti-essentialist view of philosophical problems is very different from the conception Wittgenstein defended in the *Tractatus*.[2] One may wonder, however, whether there could have been a real debate on the nature of philosophical problems between Popper and Wittgenstein in 1946, for Popper was now confronted with the later Wittgenstein. In a footnote to the 1952 paper, Popper says that during the Moral Sciences Club meeting he found Wittgenstein's views unchanged on 'the most fundamental and influential part of his teaching', the 'doctrine of the non-existence of philosophical problems' (ibidem, note 8). If Popper refers to the view that 'the problems of philosophy ... are posed' because 'the logic of our language is misunderstood' (Wittgenstein 1921, Preface), his assessment is confirmed by the sections on philosophical problems in Wittgenstein's *Philosophical Investigations* (1953, I, §§ 109-133). Wittgenstein wrote, for example(§§ 109, 111, 132):

> ... philosophical problems ... are, of course, not empirical problems; they are solved, rather, by looking into the workings of our language ... Philosophy is a battle against the bewitchment of our intelligence by means of language ... The problems arising through a misinterpretation of our forms of language have the character of *depth*. They are deep disquietudes; their roots are as deep in us as the forms of our language .... The confusions which occupy us arise when language is like an engine idling, not when it is doing work.

Yet the later Wittgenstein rejected many doctrines of the *Tractatus*, and sometimes he did so for the reasons that Popper also adduced. For example, in § 65 and § 92 of Part I of *Philosophical Investigations* (1953), Wittgenstein repudiates the essentialism inherent in the *Tractatus*. The Tractatarian idea that there is one hidden logical essence of all possible languages, an essence that is the same as the essence of the world, is now replaced by the notion of a family resemblance of language games. Furthermore, the idea that formal logic as developed by Frege and Russell constitutes the deep structure of language is also abandoned. Formal calculi are useful in representing ordinary language for specific aims, but one should not 'predicate of the thing what lies in the method of representing it' (1953, I, § 104).

---

[2]In the 1952 paper, Popper partly justifies the Tractatarian conception of philosophical problems by arguing — somewhat maliciously — that it is an adequate diagnosis of degenerate forms of philosophy, produced either by the inbreeding of philosophical schools, or by a *prima facie* method of teaching philosophy: the method of reading the great philosophers without exploring the extra-philosophical background of their problems.

On these points, then, Popper and Wittgenstein agreed in 1946. For Popper not only accused the *Tractatus* of essentialism (1945, Chapter 11, §II). He also blamed the early Wittgenstein for not distinguishing between ordinary language and the artificial calculi of logic (1963, Chapter 2, end of §II):

> I believe that even Wittgenstein's original adaptation of Russell's theory rests upon a logical mistake. From the point of view of modern logic there no longer appears to be any justification for speaking of pseudo-statements or type mistakes or category-mistakes within ordinary, naturally grown languages (as opposed to artificial calculi) so long as the conventional rules of custom and grammar are observed.

Given this agreement, one might wonder whether in 1946 there still was room for a real dispute on the nature of philosophical problems between Wittgenstein and Popper. For surely, we should apply Wittgenstein's anti-essentialism and his notion of a family resemblance also to the very ideas of philosophy and of philosophical problems, even though, surprisingly, Wittgenstein did not do so himself. In 1946, Wittgenstein could have accepted Popper's anti-essentialist view of intellectual disciplines. And he could also have accepted the idea that the set of philosophical problems is constituted by a family resemblance.

If so, we should re-interpret Wittgenstein's statements on philosophical problems in *Philosophische Untersuchungen* in a non-dogmatic and anti-essentialist way. Wherever Wittgenstein speaks of 'philosophy' and 'philosophical problems', we should not take him as dogmatically asserting things about *all* philosophical problems, for that would violate the idea that the notion of philosophy is based upon a family resemblance. Rather, we should read these statements as claims about a number of paradigmatic problems in which Wittgenstein was interested. Given the fact that in the *Tractatus* Wittgenstein was primarily concerned with the limits of what can be expressed in language, and that he developed his later philosophy mainly as a criticism of this earlier work, it is no wonder that these paradigmatic problems are concerned with language and with what can be meaningfully expressed in it as well.

If we apply a similar anti-essentialist interpretation to what Popper says about the nature of philosophical problems, the very possibility of a substantial dispute between Popper and Wittgenstein seems to evaporate. Admittedly, the pronouncements of Popper and Wittgenstein on the nature of philosophical problems and on philosophical method seem to contradict each other. For Wittgenstein, philosophical considerations cannot be scientific (1953, I, § 109), whereas for Popper, they may cut through many disciplines, including scientific ones. According to Wittgenstein, the philosopher should not put forward theories, explanations, or hypotheses (1953, I, § 109), whereas Popper holds that '[o]ur main task as philosophers is ... to enrich our picture of the world by helping to produce imaginative and at the same time argumentative and critical theories'.[3] For Wittgenstein, there are typical methods of philosophy,

---

[3] Quoted from 'On the Theory of the Objective Mind'; Popper (1972), Chapter 4, proem.

which are like therapies. Their aim is to give a perspicuous survey of the rules
of our language in which we have become entangled, and the result of applying them should be 'that the philosophical problems ... *completely* disappear'
(1953, I, §§ 125, 133). Popper holds, on the contrary, that there is no specific
philosophical method: '*any* method is legitimate if it leads to results capable
of being rationally discussed' (1963, Chapter 2, § III). The philosopher should
not make philosophical problems disappear, but attempt to solve them. And
if there are no substantial problems to be solved, Popper 'would give up philosophy' (1963, Chapter 2, § I).

But in fact, there is no disagreement on the nature of philosophical problems, if Popper and Wittgenstein were talking about different sets of paradigmatic problems. What Wittgenstein says is true of the problems he is interested in. What Popper says is true of very different problems, the problems
that fascinated Popper. On this assumption, the only thing we can say is that
Popper and Wittgenstein were interested in different types of problems, but
that both types may be called 'philosophical'. It would follow that the dispute
in 1946 between Popper and Wittgenstein was merely verbal. Nobody could
win, for there was no real disagreement.

## 3   Or does the dispute end in a draw?

This diagnosis of the 1946 debate on the nature of philosophical problems
as a merely verbal dispute is confirmed by Popper's autobiography. In § 26
of *Unended Quest*, Popper mentions a list of philosophical problems he had
prepared beforehand and which he handed to Wittgenstein during the debate.
According to Popper, Wittgenstein dismissed all Popper's problems as non-
philosophical. For instance, the problem of induction was disqualified because
it is merely a logical problem, and the problem of whether there is potential
or actual infinity was put aside as mathematical.[4] So it seems that Popper
and Wittgenstein merely had an uninteresting verbal dispute about which
problems should properly be called 'philosophical'.[5]

The same diagnosis applies to one of the two examples that Popper discusses in his paper of 1952 in order to substantiate his view that philosophical
problems are always rooted in urgent problems outside philosophy. This example is the theory Plato defends in *Timaeus* 53E-55C on the geometrical
construction of the elements out of triangles. Popper argues that the theory
should be seen as a solution to the problem caused for Greek atomism and for
the Pythagorean school by the discovery of irrationals in mathematics. This

---

[4]One may wonder to what extent Popper's account is accurate on this point, or whether
Wittgenstein was inconsistent. For Wittgenstein discussed induction both in the *Tractatus*
(§ 6.31 and § 6.363) and in *Philosophische Untersuchungen* (1953, I, § 325).

[5]This was also Popper's view of the matter. Cp. 1963, Chapter 2, § IX: 'But I shall not
pursue the question of the proper application of the label "philosophy" any further; for this
problem, which is Wittgenstein's problem, clearly turns out to be one of linguistic usage;
it is indeed a pseudo-problem, and one which by now must be rapidly degenerating into a
bore to my audience.'

discovery, Popper claims, was a fatal blow both to atomism and to Pythagore-anism, because both theories 'were based on the doctrine that all measurement is, ultimately, counting of natural units, so that every measurement must be reducible to pure numbers' (1963, Chapter 2, § VII). By advocating a geo-metrical theory of nature instead of a numerical one, and by incorporating irrationals into the ultimate elements of which the world is built, Plato sought to overcome the crisis in atomism and Pythagoreanism. At least this is what Popper argues, diving deeply into the history of Greek mathematics. Prob-ably, Wittgenstein would have dismissed this problem as non-philosophical. How we are to conceive of elementary particles may have been a 'philosoph-ical' problem in Plato's time. Today, the problem belongs to physics and not to philosophy.

Such a reaction is less plausible with regard to Popper's second example, the Kantian problem of how necessarily true knowledge of nature is possible. For the Kantian question is not only a paradigmatic philosophical question for Popper; it is also for Wittgenstein. Here we have a case, then, in which Wittgenstein and Popper point to one and the same problem in order to sub-stantiate very different views of philosophical problems. With regard to Kant's problem there seems to be a real difference of diagnosis between Popper and Wittgenstein. Whose analysis of the Kantian problematic is more instructive, that of Wittgenstein or that of Popper?

Wittgenstein would have diagnosed Kant's view that the principle of caus-ality and geometrical or arithmetical propositions are synthetic a priori, that is, necessarily true of reality, as a typical philosophical illusion, produced by the attempt to predicate of reality what in fact are features of our method of representing it (cp. 1953, I, § 104). Within the framework of Newtonian phys-ics, the principle of causality prescribes that whenever we notice deviations from inertial movements, we seek for an external cause. Similarly, the propos-itions of geometry do not a priori describe actual absolute space, as Newton and (early) Kant thought, but constitute a system of rules for describing spa-tial objects and relations. Kant's problem of the synthetic a priori may be seen as a typical example of 'problems arising through a misinterpretation of our forms of language' (1953, I, § 111).

Popper's diagnosis of Kant's problem is very different. Kant's problem was triggered by the eighteenth-century conviction that Newtonian mechan-ics realized the ancient ideal of demonstrable knowledge of nature. But Hume had shown that universal demonstrable knowledge is impossible on an em-pirical basis. In order to resolve this conflict between Hume's results and the contemporary view of Newton, Kant argued that Newtonian physics should be deducible, at least in part, from substantial non-empirical principles, the synthetic a priori propositions, and he wondered how such propositions are possible. Popper concludes that the Kantian problem was not a linguistic puzzle. Yet it was insoluble, because its assumption that Newtonian mechan-ics realizes the ancient ideal of demonstrable knowledge of nature, is false. Newton's theory, says Popper, 'is no more than a marvellous *conjecture*, an astonishingly good approximation; unique indeed, but not as divine truth, only as a unique invention of a human genius; not *epistēmē*, but belonging to the realm of *doxa*' (1963, § x).

With regard to the Kantian question of the synthetic a priori, we may consider the conceptions of the nature of philosophical problems defended by Wittgenstein and by Popper, respectively, as rival diagnostic hypotheses, to be tested by the historical materials. In this particular case, both hypotheses contain valuable insights. Concerning the role of Newtonian physics and the ideal of demonstrative science in Kant's problematic, Popper's view is correct, and Wittgenstein is of no help whatsoever. But with regard to Newton's and Kant's interpretation of geometry as a system of truths about actual space, Wittgenstein's diagnosis is more insightful.

Popper's strength lies in his attempt to reconstruct the 'situational logic' of a philosophical problem that arose at a particular point in intellectual history, and to reveal the philosophical and extra-philosophical assumptions that informed the problem.[6] But Popper completely lacked Wittgenstein's *esprit de finesse* for diagnosing transgressions of the bounds of sense. Indeed, his own speculations on the nature of the human mind or on the 'third world' as a reservoir of objective thought contents that can be grasped by us humans would have profited greatly from a Wittgensteinian critique, which would have cleansed the valid core of Popper's views of the many misleading expressions of it.

We may conclude that the dispute between Popper and Wittgenstein on the nature of philosophical problems was merely verbal only in part. For there is a substantial overlap between the sets of philosophical problems considered as paradigmatic by Wittgenstein and by Popper, respectively, whereas each of them advocated a radically different approach of the problems they had in common. Unfortunately, neither of these Viennese prima donnas was prepared to learn something from the philosophical compatriot whom he met only once, on the evening of Friday, 25 October 1946. But we are well advised to learn from both of them, because our philosophical toolbox should contain not only the instrument of Popper's situational analysis, the use of which will prevent us from concluding prematurely that what philosophers say or said does not make sense, but also the techniques of linguistic therapy à la Wittgenstein, which will preclude us from advocating bold philosophical conjectures the meaningfulness of which is dubious.

---

[6]Cp. (1972), Chapter 4, § 9, and (1957), §§ 31f.

# Bibliography

Edmonds, D. & Eidinow, J. (2001). *Wittgenstein's Poker. The Story of a Ten-Minute Argument Between Two Great Philosophers*. London: Faber & Faber.

Klemke, E. D. (1981). 'Popper's Criticisms of Wittgenstein's *Tractatus*'. *Midwest Studies in Philosophy* **6**, pp. 239-261.

Plato. *Timaeus*.

Popper, K. R. (1945). *The Open Society and its Enemies*. London: George Routledge & Sons. 5th edition 1966. London: Routledge & Kegan Paul.

———— (1957). *The Poverty of Historicism*. London: Routledge & Kegan Paul.

———— (1959). *The Logic of Scientific Discovery*. London: Hutchinson.

———— (1963). *Conjectures and Refutations. The Growth of Scientific Knowledge*. 5th edition 1989. London: Routledge.

———— (1972). *Objective Knowledge*. Oxford: Clarendon Press. 2nd edition 1979.

———— (1974). 'Intellectual Autobiography'. In P. A. Schilpp, editor (1974), pp. 1-181. *The Philosophy of Karl Popper*. La Salle IL: Open Court. Reprinted as *Unended Quest* (1976). London & Glasgow: Fontana/Collins.

Wittgenstein, L. J. J. (1921). *Tractatus Logico-Philosophicus*. London: Routledge & Kegan Paul. German text with a new English translation by D. F. Pears & B. F. McGuinness, 1961. London: Routledge & Kegan Paul.

———— (1953). *Philosophical Investigations*. Oxford: Blackwell. German text with an English translation by G. E. M. Anscombe. 3rd edition 1967.

# 25

# Gödel, Kuhn, Popper, and Feyerabend*

## Jonathan P. Seldin

## 1  The dispute between Kuhn and Popper

Thomas Kuhn (Kuhn 1962/1970a) has presented a view of the history of science that differs from the previously commonly held view of science as a gradual accumulation of knowledge. He presents the history of science as a succession of periods of 'normal science', each of which is determined by a 'paradigm'. When for some reason the paradigm is no longer adequate for normal science to proceed in the usual way, there is a 'scientific revolution', and normal science resumes only when a new paradigm is accepted by the scientific community involved. Usually, this is a group of specialists, but sometimes it may be a larger group than that.

One of the most controversial aspects of Kuhn's ideas is his view that successive paradigms are not completely compatible. He says, for example, 'Like the choice between competing political institutions, that between competing paradigms proves to be a choice between incompatible modes of community life.' (1962/1970a; all citations from Kuhn 1962, will be from the 1970 edition.)  Later (ibidem, p. 111), he says, 'In so far as their only recourse to that world is through what they see and do, we may want to say that after a revolution scientists are responding to a different world.'

As readers of this volume will be aware, Karl Popper is known for the view that science consists of the bold formation of theories as hypotheses, which are then subjected to attempts to falsify them. This seems in many ways close to the ideas that Kuhn proposed. However, Popper objected to Kuhn's views on the grounds that they represented relativism. Popper writes (1970, p. 56):

> ... Kuhn suggests that the rationality of science presupposes the acceptance of a common framework. He suggests that rationality *depends* upon something like a common language and a common set of assumptions. He suggests that rational discussion, and rational criticism, is only possible if we have agreed on the fundamentals.

*This work was supported in part by a grant from the Natural Sciences and Engineering Research Council of Canada. A preliminary version of this paper was presented at a forum of Sigma Xi held at McGill University in Montreal on 18 April 1997. A later preliminary version was presented at a colloquium of the Department of Philosophy at the University of Lethbridge in January 1999. I should like to thank the anonymous referees for their helpful suggestions.

> This is a widely accepted and indeed a fashionable thesis: the thesis of *relat-ivism*. And it is a *logical* thesis.
>
> I regard this thesis as mistaken.

(The emphasis in the original.) And he goes on to say later on the same page (author's footnote omitted):

> I should like just to indicate briefly why I am not a relativist: I do believe in 'absolute' or 'objective' truth, in Tarski's sense (although I am, of course, not an 'absolutist' in the sense of thinking that I, or anybody else, has the truth in his pocket.) I do not doubt that this is one of the points on which we are most deeply divided; and it is a logical point.

And again later on the same page:

> The central point is that a critical discussion and a comparison of the various frameworks is always possible. It is just a dogma — a dangerous dogma — that the different frameworks are like mutually untranslatable languages.

Popper was not the only one who thought that Kuhn was relativist: 'There is nobody else than Thomas Kuhn who contributed more to the widespread acceptance of cognitive relativism in the recent years' (Watanabe 1991, p. 25).

Popper did eventually accept that he had misinterpreted Kuhn's views. He says of the view that comparison of different scientific theories requires an agreement on the general framework, a view with which he disagrees (Popper 1994, Chapter 2, footnote 19):

> ... I originally had in mind Thomas Kuhn .... However, as Kuhn points out, this interpretation was based on a misunderstanding of his views [see Kuhn 1970b, and his 'Postscript 1969' to Kuhn 1970a], and I am very ready to accept his correction. Nevertheless, I regard the view here discussed as influential.

There seem to be other disagreements between Kuhn and Popper. Kuhn concludes that it may not be possible to say that as science progresses it is bringing scientists close to the truth (Kuhn 1970a, p. 170):

> ... scientific progress is not quite what we had taken it to be. ... In the sciences there need not be progress of another sort. We may, to be more precise, have to relinquish the notion, explicit or implicit, that changes of paradigm carry scientists and those who learn from them closer and close to the truth.

On the other hand, Popper says about scientific theories: 'The aim is to find theories which, in the light of critical discussion, get nearer to the truth.' (Popper 1970, p. 57) An indication of what Popper means by this is as follows (Popper 1963, Chapter 10, § X; author's footnote omitted):

> I shall give here a somewhat unsystematic list of six types of case in which we should be inclined to say of a theory $t_1$ that it is superseded by $t_2$ in the sense that $t_2$ seems — as far as we know — to correspond better to the facts than $t_1$, in some sense or other.

(1) $t_2$ makes more precise assertions than $t_1$, and these more precise assertions stand up to more precise tests.

(2) $t_2$ takes account of, and explains, more facts than $t_1$ (which will include, for example the above case that, other things being equal, $t_2$'s assertions are more precise).

(3) $t_2$ describes, or explains, the facts in more detail than $t_1$.

(4) $t_2$ has passed tests which $t_1$ has failed to pass.

(5) $t_2$ has suggested new experimental tests, not considered before $t_2$ was designed (and not suggested by $t_1$, and perhaps not even applicable to $t_1$); and $t_2$ has passed these tests.

(6) $t_2$ has unified or connected various hitherto unrelated problems.

If we reflect upon this list, then we can see that the *contents* of the theories $t_1$ and $t_2$ play an important role in it. (It will be remembered that the *logical content* of a statement or theory $a$ is the class of all statements which follow logically from $a$, while I have defined the *empirical content* of $a$ as the class of all basic statements which contradict $a$.) For in our list of six cases, the empirical content of theory $t_2$ exceeds that of theory $t_1$.

This suggests that Popper is aiming to give a set of deductive rules to express the idea that one theory is nearer to the truth than another. The idea presupposes the kind of relationship between theories that Kuhn claims does not always exist between paradigms, but is rather excluded by their incommensurability. Some of Popper's remarks seem to indicate that he thought that Kuhn's notion of incommensurability implied the impossibility of comparison between paradigms. However, Kuhn (1983, pp. 670f.) explicitly denied this, claiming that his idea of incommensurability was really *local incommensurability*:

> Applied to the conceptual vocabulary deployed in and around a scientific theory, the term 'incommensurability' functions metaphorically. The phrase 'no common measure' becomes 'no common language'. The claim that two theories are incommensurable is then the claim that there is no language, neutral or otherwise, into which both theories, conceived as sets of sentences, can be translated without residue or loss. No more in its metaphorical than its literal form does incommensurability imply incomparability, and for much the same reason. Most of the terms common to the two theories function the same way in both; their meanings, whatever those may be, are preserved; their translation is simply homophonic. Only for a small subgroup of (usually interdefined) terms and for sentences containing them do problems of translatability arise. The claim that two theories are incommensurable is more modest than many of its critics have supposed.
>
> I shall call this modest version of incommensurability 'local incommensurability'. Insofar as incommensurability was a claim about language, about meaning change, its local form is my original version.

I believe that if Popper had taken more account of Gödel's incompleteness theorem, he would have found his position much closer to that of Kuhn than he realized. (Popper was certainly aware of Gödel's incompleteness theorem; he refers to it, for example, in 1963, Chapter 11, § 4, and at the end of Chapter 14. But he seems to have missed this particular application of it.)

## 2  Gödel's incompleteness theorem and the Kuhn-Popper dispute

Gödel's incompleteness theorem says that any consistent formal system that includes the elementary theory of natural numbers is necessarily incomplete. It is proved by mapping the formal objects of the formal system to the natural numbers using a one-to-one mapping so that some sentences about natural numbers become, via this mapping, sentences about the formal system itself and then constructing a sentence of the formal system that, via this mapping, asserts its own unprovability. The condition that the formal system includes the elementary theory of natural numbers is often expressed by saying that the system is 'strong enough to be interesting'.

Gödel's incompleteness theorem applies directly only to formal systems, that is, to deductive theories that are so strictly formalized that it is possible to determine mechanically whether or not a sequence of sentences constitutes a valid proof. But indirectly it applies to theories that are capable of this complete formalization, even if they are not presented in this fully formalized form. If one considers the process by which large parts of mathematics were formalized in the late nineteenth and early twentieth centuries, one can see that the process that led to these formal systems was a matter of bringing hidden assumptions into the open, a process that required the analysis of some concepts that had not been previously analysed. It would thus appear that most deductive theories could be formalized if somebody were willing to do the necessary work.

Furthermore, there are a number of results related to Gödel's incompleteness theorem. As an example, there is the undecidability of the halting problem, which says that for an idealized computer with unlimited memory and time, there is no program that will take as input another program and input data and return the answer to whether or not the computer running the second program with the given input data will stop after a finite amount of time or continue forever in an infinite loop. There are a number of other such examples. A consideration of all of these related results suggests strongly that even where Gödel's incompleteness theorem itself does not apply directly, it would be a mistake to assume completeness.

To see how these results might apply to the dispute between Popper and Kuhn, suppose that $t_1$ and $t_2$ are two scientific theories to be compared. For example, $t_2$ might be a theory that has replaced $t_1$ in what Kuhn calls a scientific revolution. Any comparison would have to be carried out in some theory, $t'$ (which might be one of $t_1$ or $t_2$). The theory $t'$ will have to be strong enough to include references to $t_1$ and $t_2$ and to draw conclusions from those references. Assuming that $t_1$ and $t_2$ are 'strong enough to be interesting', $t'$ will also have to be 'strong enough to be interesting'. This means that assuming completeness would be a mistake. (Even if we are thinking in terms of semantics [model theory], where the basic definitions do seem to imply completeness, the comparison is likely to involve deductions, and the definitions used in model theory are insufficient to allow a determination of the validity of all possible deductions.) It follows that there cannot be a guarantee that it will be possible in $t'$ to obtain a complete comparison of all aspects of $t_1$ and $t_2$. This is why I claim that Kuhn's notion of incommensurability, especially in the version of local incommensurability of (Kuhn 1983) should be considered an expected consequence of Gödel's incompleteness theorem.

(It should be noted that Kuhn's claims for [local] incommensurability were based on historical considerations.)

A similar argument will, I believe, show why we cannot talk about science progressing to theories that come ever close to the truth about the world. To say that one theory, say $t_1$, is close to the truth than another, say $t_2$, requires a theory, $t'$, in which to carry out this reasoning. Since we are dealing with scientific theories, it is reasonable to suppose that $t'$ would also be 'strong enough to be interesting', and so it would be a mistake to assume completeness for it. This would imply that it would be a mistake to assume that there is a complete definition of truth, and therefore that it is not always possible to say that newer theories are close to the truth than older ones. Thus, we should consider it a consequence of Gödel's incompleteness theorem that we cannot always talk about scientific progress getting close to the truth.

It thus appears that Popper was originally more mistaken about Kuhn's views being relativist and subjective than he later realized. This seems especially likely since Kuhn implies in (1970a) that every paradigm will eventually be found inadequate: surely this implies that there is some sort of objective reality against which these paradigms are being tested. The implication of the incommensurability of paradigms is that our ability to *know* and *talk about* this objective reality is limited, not that this objective reality does not exist. In fact, Kuhn himself points out (1970b) that except for this one difference, (that is, Popper's claim that the incomparability of paradigms implies relativity) his views are very similar to Popper's, and when he and Popper are analysing the same historical episode in science their analyses are usually very much alike. Perhaps we can say that, roughly,

$$\text{Popper} + \text{Gödel} = \text{Kuhn}.$$

## 3   Gödel's incompleteness theorem and Paul Feyerabend

Gödel's incompleteness theorem also has something to tell us about the views expressed by Paul Feyerabend in (1975). Feyerabend thinks that he is arguing that there is no such thing as a scientific method. But when his arguments are stripped of rhetoric, what is left is a catalogue of instances in which various descriptions of scientific methodology fail to correspond with the way science has actually progressed. Feyerabend argues correctly that this shows that the descriptions of scientific methodology of which he is speaking do not fit science as it has actually occurred, and he goes on to suggest that no complete and consistent description of scientific methodology is possible.

Feyerabend then argues that the absence of a sound and complete description of the scientific method means that there is no such method. But, again, this argument is based on the same kind of claim of completeness as Popper's. In fact, Gödel's incompleteness theorem and related results should lead us to *expect* that no description of scientific method can be both sound and complete. Feyerabend may have produced some evidence that we can never soundly and completely *describe* the scientific method, but he has no evidence whatever that there is no such method. (If there can be no sound and complete description of a scientific method, perhaps 'method' is the wrong word: perhaps we should be speaking of a scientific approach.) The evidence Feyerabend presents in his (1975) simply does not support his thesis that 'anything goes' in science.

(This argument applies only to what Feyerabend says in his 1975, and perhaps not to any of his other works.)

## 4  The objective truth of science

At this point some readers may wonder what we can say to those who really deny the value or truth of science. I think there is an answer to them, but it is not the same kind of answer that Popper seems to have been seeking. The answer I have in mind does not try to prove the truth of *every* assertion of the accepted scientific paradigms. Instead, it concentrates on those questions that are of interest to legislative bodies and courts involving matters of public policy or the value of scientific testimony. Legislative bodies and courts are interested in *evidence* for their conclusions on these issues. And I think that the refereeing procedure that is standard in the best scientific journals is the procedure that generates the best evidence for or against the assertions involved. Ayala & Black (1993) argue from the position of Popper that the courts should pay attention to refereed scientific journals. This idea gives us a basis for saying that there is an objective basis for these assertions. Of course, at a later time, the evidence may change with regard to any particular question, but *at the time the question is being considered*, a consensus of the literature by specialists on the matter in question in refereed scientific journals, if such a consensus exists, is the best evidence available on that question. It is possible that at a given time there is no consensus of the literature by specialists on the matter in refereed scientific journals; in this case, the legislatures and courts would have to conclude that there is insufficient scientific evidence to settle the matter at hand scientifically. This is a way we can refer to science as embodying objective truth.

This idea seems to have something in common with the Popper's discussion of the establishment of basic statements in (Popper, 1959, Chapter V), especially the last two pages on jury verdicts. What is common is the idea that the determination of truth involved is not absolute and unchanging, but depends on the (scientific or legal) context. However, unlike Popper, I am not assuming any characterization of the logical forms of questions which come before legislatures and juries, as Popper seems to do.

There is one important qualification we must make here: it is important that this refereeing process be conducted in a way consistent with the practices of the scientific specialty in question and is free from external influences, such as economic interests. I think most of us know from our own personal experience that if we have a reason to want something to be the case, it is easy to convince ourselves that it is the case even if the evidence does not support that conclusion. This means that each of us must constantly be on guard against making this kind of mistake in our own individual work. Economic interest can cause a very powerful desire for something to be the case even if it is not. This suggests that in areas of science in which there are important economic interests that are affected by the results of scientific research, special efforts are needed to protect the process of scientific research and refereeing from the effects of those economic interests. For a troubling example showing how medical research financed by a pharmaceutical company may be affected by economic interests, see Canadian Association of University Teachers (2001).

Of course, there are questions that arise in science that are never considered by courts or legislative bodies: an example is the question that arose in the early days of the special theory of relativity, when there was an alternative theory due to H. A. Lorentz based on classical physics, which made exactly the same predictions as Einstein's theory. Einstein's arguments for his approach did not constitute the same kind of evidence from the point of view of courts and legislative bodies as, say, the scientific evidence that AIDS is caused by the HIV virus. But then these arguments of Einstein were on a subject unlikely to get before a court or legislative body. It is at the point at which science touches public policy or trials through courts and legislative bodies that we are best able to talk about the objective reality of science. (I am thus dividing science in something like the way Hilbert divided mathematics into its real and ideal parts.)

# Bibliography

Ayala, F. J. & Black, B. (1993). 'Science and the Courts'. *American Scientist* **81**, pp. 230-239.

Canadian Association of University Teachers (2001). *Report of the Committee of Inquiry on the Case Involving Dr. Nancy Olivieri, the Hospital for Sick Children, the University of Toronto, and Apotex Inc.* www.caut.ca/en/issues/academicfreedom/OlivieriInquiryReport.pdf/.

Feyerabend, P. K. (1975). *Against Method: Outline of an Anarchistic Theory of Knowledge*. London and Atlantic Highlands: New Left Books and Humanities Press.

Kuhn, T. S. (1962). *The Structure of Scientific Revolutions*. Chicago: University of Chicago Press. All references are to the 2nd edition, Kuhn (1970a).

———— (1970a). *The Structure of Scientific Revolutions*. 2nd edition. Chicago: University of Chicago Press.

———— (1970b). 'Reflections on My Critics'. In Lakatos & Musgrave (1970), pp. 231-278.

———— (1983). 'Commensurability, Comparability, Communicability'. In P. D. Asquith & T. Nickles, editors (1983), pp. 669-688. *PSA 1982: Proceedings of the 1982 Biennial Meeting of the Philosophy of Science Association*, Volume 2. East Lansing MI: Philosophy of Science Association.

Lakatos, I. & Musgrave, A. E., editors (1970). *Criticism and the Growth of Knowledge*. Cambridge: Cambridge University Press.

Popper, K. R. (1934). *Logik der Forschung*. Vienna: Julius Springer Verlag. English translation, Popper (1959).

———— (1959). *The Logic of Scientific Discovery*. London: Hutchinson.

———— (1963). *Conjectures and Refutations. The Growth of Scientific Knowledge*. London: Routledge & Kegan Paul. 5th edition 1989. London: Routledge.

———— (1970). 'Normal Science and Its Dangers'. In Lakatos & Musgrave (1970), pp. 51-58.

———— (1994). *The Myth of the Framework. In Defence of Science and Rationality*. London: Routledge.

Watanabe, S. (1991). 'The Foundations of Cognitive Relativity'. *Annals of the Japan Association for the Philosophy of Science* **8**, pp. 23-48.

26

# Science Wars
## Remarks from a
## Critical Rationalist's Point of View<sup>*</sup>

Karsten Weber

## 1  The beginning of Science Wars

Actually, the Science Wars did not start with Sokal's hoax. The term was coined by Andrew Ross, editor of the journal *Social Text*, in reaction to Paul R. Gross's and Norman Levitt's book *Higher Superstition*. In that text, Gross & Levitt attacked postmodernism:[1]

> Once a postmodern critic has at hand a license to read every proposition as its opposite when it suits his convenience, analytic skills of the more traditional sort are expendable and logic is effaced in the swirling tide of rhetoric. Once it has been decided that determinate meaning is chimerical and not worthy of slightest deference from the well-honed poststructuralist postmodernist, the entire edifice of hard-won truth becomes a house of cards. Once it has been affirmed that one discursive community is as good as another, that the narrative of science holds no privileges over the narratives of superstition, the newly minted cultural critic can actually revel in his ignorance of deep scientific ideas.

In some sense, Gross's & Levitt's attack just repeats what C. P. Snow already wrote in 1959 about the 'two cultures'. Snow had a pessimistic view on the divide or gap between science on the one hand and literature, humanities, and those academic disciplines which today are called 'cultural studies' on the other hand:[2]

> The non-scientists have a rooted impression that the scientists are shallowly optimistic, unaware of man's condition. On the other hand, the scientists believe that the literary intellectuals are totally lacking in foresight, peculiarly unconcerned with their brother men, in a deep sense anti-intellectual, anxious to restrict both art and thought to the existential moment.

---

[*]The numerous and detailed comments and criticisms of two anonymous referees helped me to improve the text significantly. I should like to thank them very much for their assistance.

[1]Gross & Levitt (1994), p. 85.

[2]Snow (1959), p. 5.

So, one can say that already in 1959 the skirmishes of the Science Wars began. However, until 1996 there was only minor public awareness of what was going on. This situation changed tremendously when Alan Sokal's text *Transgressing the Boundaries. Toward a Transformative Hermeneutics of Quantum Gravity* was published in the American postmodernist journal *Social Text*[3]. Even newspapers reported Sokal's hoax after it was revealed. Sokal had written a strange mélange of mathematics, physics, postmodernist jargon, and a vast number of citations of postmodernist and poststructuralist authors. In fact, the text is complete nonsense. Actually, it was written so as to appear to be really intelligent, really sound, really progressive, really political correct. But still, it remains complete nonsense.

It was an experiment by Sokal to test whether the editors of *Social Text* were able to recognize the nonsense within the text. Sokal thought that intelligent people should be able to see that the mathematics and physics in his paper were improper and that it is impossible to prove anything with them within the realm of social sciences. And he thought that in case the editors were not able to decide whether the text was gibberish or not, they would be intelligent enough to take the advice of mathematicians or physicists. But the fact that the editors of *Social Text* published Sokal's article without any question and obviously without any kind of peer reviewing showed clearly that those editors were able to do neither the first nor the second.

To Sokal the behaviour of the editors of *Social Text* showed clearly the complete absence of scientific standards within the realm of postmodernist and poststructuralist social science. To him this is a scientific as well as a political problem. The scientific part of the problem is quite obvious; the political part has to be explained.

Mainstream social sciences or, better to say, mainstream social scientists are politically moderate leftists or liberals — so says Sokal.[4] If they are, in any sense, politically active, they stand up for women's liberation, emancipation, anti-racism, anti-colonialism, civil rights, economic justice, and so on. And Sokal goes along with all those political objectives. For instance, he went to Nicaragua during the Sandinista regime to be a lecturer in physics and mathematics at a local university — the Universidad Nacional Autónoma de Nicaragua — to support the socialist revolution. He speaks about himself as an old leftist political activist. And from his point of view science and scientific knowledge are not merely discourses relative to social, political, cultural, historical, or economical conditions. To him scientific knowledge is not only a kind of sophisticated story without any priority to any other story. To Sokal, the postmodernist and poststructuralist approach to science and scientific knowledge is totally wrong and misguided. From his point of view, science

---

[3]Sokal (1996a). The four papers by Sokal mentioned in this and succeeding footnotes are available at http://www.physics.nyu.edu/faculty/sokal/.

[4]It is questionable whether this is true or not. As one of the anonymous referees stressed, one obviously will find other than leftist or liberal political positions and convictions among, for instance, economists.

and scientific knowledge are important, maybe the most important, weapons against ignorance, injustice, and political and economic inequality.

After his essay was published in *Social Text* Sokal tried to start a discussion within the social sciences about scientific standards. He wrote a second paper to uncover his hoax and again he sent it to *Social Text*. However, this time, the editors refused to publish the essay, because they had the opinion that the text did not fit in with their scientific and intellectual standards. But it is more than obvious that this was not the real reason for the rejection. The editors would have made themselves ridiculous had they revealed that they had published complete nonsense in their journal. Sokal revealed his hoax then in a paper called 'A Physicist Experiments With Cultural Studies' that was published in *Lingua Franca*[5] three weeks after publishing the hoax. Then in autumn 1996 the paper 'Transgressing the Boundaries: An Afterword' appeared in *Dissent*[6] and, slightly amended, in *Philosophy and Literature*.[7]

After the publication of Sokal's articles about his hoax a really polemical debate started. On the one side of the battle line of the now intensely fought Science Wars we can find some of those authors who felt that they were attacked unjustifiedly by Sokal — for instance Stanley Aronowitz, cofounder of *Social Text*, and Andrew Ross, editor of the same journal.[8] On the other side of the line authors such as Paul R. Gross, Norman Levitt & Martin W. Lewis,[9] Noretta Koertge,[10] and Mario Bunge[11] defended Sokal's critique of postmodernism and poststructuralism in the social sciences as justified and necessary. To understand why those debates were very aggressive and polemical it is necessary and helpful to take a short look at Sokal's central arguments against postmodernist thinkers. Surprisingly, at least for critical rationalists, one will see that Sokal added them to the legions of postmodernist supporters. And more surprisingly, almost none of them responded to Sokal and his attack. On Sokal's web site[12] one can find a vast amount of texts, reviews, criticisms, replies to criticisms, and so on. But as far as I can see almost no critical rationalist can be found among the authors of all those texts.[13] Why is this?

## 2  A brief description of Sokal's hoax

In the debates that followed the uncovering of his hoax Sokal explained his critique of postmodernist and poststructuralist social sciences in more detail. Together with Jean Bricmont he summarized his arguments in 1997 in the

---

[5] Sokal (1996b).

[6] Sokal (1996c).

[7] Sokal (1996d).

[8] For more scholars who fought on that side see, for instance, Ross (1996) and Ashman & Baringer (2001).

[9] Gross, Levitt, & Lewis (1996).

[10] Koertge (1998).

[11] Bunge (1999).

[12] http://www.physics.nyu.edu/faculty/sokal/.

[13] Sokal lists the book of Noretta Koertge (1998), but one cannot find, for instance, Miller (1999), Miller (2000), and Niemann (1999).

book *Impostures Intellectuelles*, which in 1998 was published in the UK as *Intellectual Impostures* and in the USA as *Fashionable Nonsense*. In German the book is entitled *Eleganter Unsinn* and was published in 1999.

In their book Sokal & Bricmont analysed postmodernist and poststructuralist authors, their texts and ideas. With a broad discussion of examples of some writings of those authors, they showed in detail that within those texts one can find absolutely wrong uses of concepts of mathematics and physics, misunderstanding of those concepts, metaphorical uses of scientific technical language without any meaning, and so on. The authors Sokal & Bricmont criticized included Jacques Lacan, Julias Kristeva, Luce Irigaray, Jean Baudrillard, and Bruno Latour. Those writers used mathematics and physics to prove their own ideas and theories about literature, history, feminism, or gender studies. Sokal & Bricmont tried to show that the scientific concepts used made no sense within the context of the discussed problems. According to Sokal & Bricmont this is due to one major reason: almost none of the cited authors understands the theories and concepts which they use, or they understand them only rudimentarily and fragmentarily. Sokal & Bricmont made it obvious that the use of concepts of mathematics and physics by postmodernist authors is arbitrary and without understanding. But sometimes the impression seems reasonable that the misuse or even the abuse of concepts of science is consciously wrought by many postmodernist and poststructuralist authors.

Although Sokal stressed that '[f]rom the mere fact of publication of my parody, I think that not much can be deduced',[14] one should not underestimate the case. Of course he is right in writing that '[i]t doesn't prove that the whole field of cultural studies, or the cultural studies of science — much less the sociology of science — is nonsense. Nor does it prove that the intellectual standards in these fields are generally lax.'[15] Perhaps from the point of view of an American scholar the situation seems to be more or less unproblematic because mainstream social sciences seem to be, or even are, more than postmodernist and poststructuralist cultural studies. But in other countries, for instance in Germany, one can often find a large divide within the social sciences themselves. Economics and sociology, and this is only one possible example, are often separated with respect to personnel, institutions, and — as a consequence — research. Or to put it another way: Economists and sociologists who use, for instance, a kind of Rational Choice Theory are separated from the rest of social scientists because the first insist on concepts of science, truth, and reality, which are closer to those of the (natural) sciences than to those of the latter. Broadly speaking, in such cases it seems that the gap between Snow's 'two cultures' is still deepening.

---

[14] Sokal (1998).
[15] Ibidem.

Anyway, there is no reason to be surprised about the described misuse of scientific concepts. Postmodernist[16] scholars do not make any secret of what they think about science. To most of them, science is nothing but a complex and sophisticated story told by scientists — Lyotard's *La condition postmoderne* as well as Baudrillard's *Simulacra et simulation* are good examples of that opinion. The scientific story is one among many others like myths, sagas, religion, literature, and so on. All those stories are equal and indifferent. No one of them has any superiority on the others. One cannot speak about them in terms of false and true. For postmodernist scholars stories like myths and science make sense only in the context of a language game or the context of a certain culture. Myths and science are both 'true' or 'false' only within a certain cultural, social, political, or historical context. Their 'truth' or 'falsity' is relative to those contexts. Most postmodernist and poststructuralist authors not only deny the possibility of knowledge of reality and truth; they also deny the very existence of a mind-independent reality. They stress that any 'reality' is man-made; it is constructed by means of social interactions of people within the shared context of culture, religion, language, and so on. Outside this context, for postmodernist thinkers it is senseless to speak about anything called 'reality'.[17]

From the point of view of this postmodernist and relativistic epistemology the production of scientific knowledge is not guided by the regulatory idea of truth; it is not a quest for truth and knowledge. To postmodernist authors science is guided by the interests of scientists and their customers. Those interests are in the end political and economic: power and wealth. The aim of postmodernist and poststructuralist thinkers is to uncover this fact. They want to show that science isn't practised for the sake of truth, but that it serves or even seeks power. They deny that the question which theory temporarily should be accepted or used is answered by experiments, observations, and so on. Postmodernist scholars stress that such decisions are made by means of scientific influence, reputation, or bare power. To them, the acceptance of scientific theories is dependent on sex, race, religion, and political and economic power. From their point of view the so called *context of justification* is a mere *context of authority*. It is not the results of experiments or observations that decide whether a scientific theory can be accepted temporarily or has to be abandoned because of it has been falsified. Instead, those who have power decide what is 'true' and what is 'false'.

Sokal & Bricmont, however, didn't attack only postmodernist authors; they also attacked critical rationalism. Popper's rejection of inductive science and his denial of the possibility of verification are, as they pointed out, the

---

[16] Although postmodernism and poststructuralism are dissimilar in many ways, there are some common aspects, especially epistemological and moral relativism, anti-realism, and constructivist views on science and society. See Bricmont & Sokal (2001).

[17] A surely incomplete list of examples of this relativistic and constructivist view on science and reality is, for instance: Pickering (1984), Collins & Pinch (1996), Latour (1987), (1991), Knorr-Cetina (1999).

gateways to epistemological relativism and thus critical rationalism seems to
be a kind of a predecessor of postmodernism. The two authors argue that the
scepticism that lies within Popper's philosophy of science and the surrender
of a criterion of truth cannot be accepted within the realm of science. Like
Popper they admit that theories cannot be confirmed once and for all, but
they stress that there are some theories that are supported by such strong
evidence that there is no space for any reasonable doubt. To them, such
theories are proved or verified: they are true. In reaction to the critique of
Sokal & Bricmont, David Miller tried to clarify the case. He argues that the
authors mix up relativism and scepticism:[18]

> But *Intellectual Impostures* contains also a chapter ... that grapples with a more
> serious concern: the doctrine, now so common, that there is no absolute truth,
> that truth is never more than a matter of opinion, or of consensus, or of (per-
> haps unconscious) social construction. Sokal & Bricmont rightly object to this
> pernicious doctrine of radical relativism, according to which western science is
> just one item on a menu of competing but not really comparable ideologies or
> superstitions. Unfortunately they mistakenly identify radical relativism with a
> doctrine that is decisively different from it: the doctrine of radical scepticism,
> according to which nothing that we call knowledge, science included, is known
> with any authority, that we cannot know anything in the traditional sense of the
> word (very crudely: knowledge = justified true belief).

Much of Miller's text is focused on this point. But one can disagree with
Miller's argumentation. Sokal & Bricmont differentiate between relativism and
scepticism or, at least, they do not mix up those epistemological positions.
All they do is to say that we should not overestimate Hume's scepticism and
that we should trust in common sense:[19]

> The universality of Humean scepticism is also its weakness. Of course, it is
> irrefutable. But since no one is systematically skeptical (when he or she is sincere)
> with respect to ordinary knowledge, one ought to ask *why* skepticism is rejected
> in that domain and *why* it would nevertheless be valid when applied elsewhere,
> for instance, to scientific knowledge. Now, the reason why we reject systematic
> skepticism in everyday life is more or less obvious and is similar to the reason
> we reject solipsism. The best way to account for the coherence of our experience
> is to suppose that the outside world corresponds, at least approximately, to the
> image of it provided by our senses.

Looking on Popper's own argumentation for his realist point of view one can
find a quite similar formulation in his book *Objective Knowledge*:[20]

> My thesis is that realism is neither demonstrable nor refutable. Realism like
> anything else outside logic and finite arithmetic is not demonstrable; but while
> empirical scientific theories are refutable, realism is not even refutable. (It shares

---

[18] Miller (2000), pp. 157f.; (2006), p. 134.
[19] Sokal & Bricmont (1998), p. 53; (1999), p. 55. Miller cites this passage too.
[20] Popper (1972), p. 38.

this irrefutability with many philosophical or 'metaphysical' theories, in particular also with idealism.) But it is arguable, and the weight of the arguments is
overwhelmingly in its favour.'

One page later, Popper again returns to this way of argumentation:[21]

> Thus idealism is irrefutable; and this means, of course, that realism is indemon-
> strable. But I am prepared to concede that realism is not only indemonstrable
> but, like idealism, irrefutable also; that no describable event, and no conceivable
> experience, can be taken as an effective refutation of realism. Thus there will be
> in the issue, as in so many, no conclusive argument. *But there are arguments in*
> *favour of realism*; or rather, *against idealism*.

Here Popper himself argues in a quite pragmatic way in favour of realism. In
fact, he decides to accept realism. Actually, this decision could be understood
to be irrational in the sense Popper uses the word 'irrational', because all his
arguments are somehow inductive. For instance, he stresses 'that realism is
an important part of common sense'[22] — obviously that argument can be
translated into the sentence 'all those common people cannot err'. Clearly,
to trust in common sense is an inductive attitude. So, presupposing that
Miller accepts Popper's view, we may ask why doesn't he accept Sokal's and
Bricmont's? To reject their critique of critical rationalism, it would be too
simple to accuse them of arguing from a standard positivist and justificationist
point of view.

Of course, to Sokal & Bricmont Popper isn't a relativist in the strong
sense of the word. But they stress that, in succession to Popper, authors
such as Thomas S. Kuhn and Paul Feyerabend promoted a strong relativistic
epistemology. Actually, Kuhn and Feyerabend were often cited by postmodernist authors. At least Feyerabend was once a critical rationalist and perhaps
Kuhn can be seen as one with respect to the broad discussion in *Criticism*
*and the Growth of Knowledge*.[23] And so, to those who did not know the
internal discussions of critical rationalists and their harsh critiques of Kuhn
and Feyerabend the impression can arise that all critical rationalists support a
relativistic epistemology. Actually, it seems to be obvious that Sokal & Bricmont didn't know the differences between Popper, Kuhn, and Feyerabend.
However, *cum grano salis*, Sokal & Bricmont made a point that has to be
taken into account. They argue that falsification is an ambiguous concept.
Miller, a little bit outraged, puts it that way: 'It is really rather shocking of
Sokal & Bricmont to suggest as they do that "ambiguities or inadequacies in
Popper's *The Logic of Scientific Discovery*" (p. 59) bear some responsibility
for the rising tide of irrationalism in the philosophy of science.'[24] Perhaps,
the argumentation of Sokal & Bricmont does not work very well, but it seems
to be possible to improve it slightly. If one examines Popper's *The Logic of*

---

[21] Ibidem, p. 39; italics in the original.
[22] Ibidem.
[23] See Lakatos (1970).
[24] Miller (2000), p. 171; (2006), p. 145.

*Scientific Discovery*, one can learn about several problems raised by the concept of falsification and, in general, by scientific methodology. For example, Popper wrote:[25]

> I regard conventionalism as a system which is self-contained and defensible. Attempts to detect inconsistencies in it are not likely to succeed. ... the conventionalist seeks in science 'a system of knowledge based upon ultimate grounds', to use a phrase of Dingler's. This goal is attainable; for it is possible to interpret any given scientific system as a system of implicit definitions.

While reading this passage, it is obvious that any postmodern poststructuralist will say 'Hurrah, this is all we need to know! Popper gave us approval. All that we need to do is to replace the term "implicit definitions" by "uncircumventable social constructions". That's all!' But the problem with conventionalism goes further. Popper wrote some pages later that '[e]xperiences can *motivate a decision*, and hence an acceptance or a rejection of a statement, but a basic statement cannot be *justified* by them — no more than by thumping the table'.[26] And in the next section, he stressed that '[b]asic statements are accepted as the result of a decision or agreement; and to that extent they are conventions.'[27] Nothing more and nothing less would, for instance, Karin Knorr-Cetina or Bruno Latour say to this topic: Facts, or better statements about facts, are accepted in a discursive process. And they will add that the decision to accept a statement about a fact heavily depends on factors like power, the social status and the interests of the involved scientists, their sex, and so on. So, the mere acceptance of basic statements that are used to corroborate or to falsify a hypothesis is in both conceptions of science, in Popper's as well as in a relativistic one, one of the most important principles.

Of course, reading Popper this way violates the principle of charity. And so do Sokal & Bricmont. But it is hard to deny that Popper can be understood that way because even some critical rationalists did so, for instance Imre Lakatos[28] and surely Kuhn — even if one really can deny with good arguments that Kuhn is a critical rationalist. There are several other problems with Popper's view on the logic of scientific discovery, for instance the inductive aspects of the principle of corroboration, which Sokal & Bricmont did not address. But this brief discussion shows that while their critique was written from a standard positivist and justificationist point of view and hence can be challenged with all the standard arguments against induction and justification, Popper's (crypto-)conventionalism opens the door to relativistic positions if one only wants to go through. Feyerabend did it, Kuhn did it too, and Lakatos was half way through.

---

[25]Popper (1959), § 19.
[26]Ibidem, § 29.
[27]Ibidem, § 30.
[28]See Lakatos (1970).

## 3   Under fire!

Critical rationalism has fallen between two stools. On the one side one finds Sokal & Bricmont who accuse critical rationalism of being relativistic or at least of leading to relativism. On the other side a large majority of scholars in the humanities and social sciences accuse critical rationalism of being positivistic and unaware of the impact of social, historical, cultural, political, and economical factors on science itself.

Critical rationalists took sides neither for Sokal & Bricmont nor for the postmodernist party. As far as I can see one can find almost no texts by Critical Rationalists in which the Science Wars were discussed.[29]  Of course it is a difficult situation, since arguing against Sokal & Bricmont could be understood as support of postmodernist ideas and arguing with Sokal & Bricmont would implicate acceptance of their critique. But these are not the only alternatives.

At first, critical rationalists should make clear that fallibilism as a methodological principle of science as well as of the social sciences does not imply endless scepticism at least in the field of daily research. Scientists, as Sokal & Bricmont wrote explicitly, know that in principle any theoretical assumption as well as any observation or any result of an experiment could be called in question. However, there is no dispute about this, since Popper wrote that '[e]very test of a theory, whether resulting in its corroboration or falsification, must stop at some basic statement or other which we *decide to accept*. If we do not come to any decision, and do not accept some basic statement or other, then the test will have led nowhere.'[30]  In principle, we can challenge any basic statement but in practice, we have to accept them at least for the moment — and this moment can last a very long time.[31]  In addition, most critical rationalists emphasize that theories should not be abandoned after the first empirical falsification. As Imre Lakatos pointed out, Popper and most critical rationalists are not naïve falsificationists. A sensible limitation on universal criticism and on relativism has already been elaborated.[32]

In addition, critical rationalists should also argue against postmodernist authors that they know well that, in the context of justification, non-scientific factors can always interfere in the results of research. But they should also stress that the critical rationalists' distinction of science and non-science and the requirement of empirical testability of theories and assumptions are proper means to avoid or control such factors as personal interests, political influence, and so on. The existence of non-scientific influence on science is not something that was discovered by postmodernist authors; for instance, it was

---

[29]For exceptions see footnote 13 above.

[30]Popper (1959), § 29.

[31]To put it rather polemically: anybody who denies this difference between principle and practice and keeps insisting on an endless scepticism in daily research, seems to have never worked empirically.

[32]See footnote 36 below.

already stressed by Max Weber[33] and Robert K. Merton.[34] And those authors already mentioned ways to reconcile individual partisanship, social contexts, and scientific objectivity. So critical rationalists can and did adopt this.[35]

## 4 Conclusion

If one looks back a few decades, the current discussion concerning the Science Wars could be understood as a sequel of the so called *Positivismusstreit* in German social sciences in the 1960s and 1970s. Scholars of the Frankfurt School argued at that time that critical rationalism is a kind of 'rationalism halved by positivism'. Theodor W. Adorno and especially Jürgen Habermas, among others, attacked critical rationalism for not being sufficiently critical against existing circumstances of society and not willing to change them actively. The core of the charges of the *Positivismusstreit* and the Science Wars is quite the same: (a) Critical Rationalists want to describe the world as it is. Critical Theorists and the postmodernist thinkers — to adapt Marx — want to change it. (b) Critical Rationalists assert that there is a mind-independent and society-independent world and knowledge about the world; Critical Theorists and postmodernist thinkers assert that they know better.

But this contrast is totally wrong. Actually, Popper and other scholars tried to adopt the principles of critical rationalism to support social change, for instance in Popper's *The Open Society and its Enemies* or *The Poverty of Historicism*. The difference is that critical rationalists, unlike the Frankfurt School, learnt that comprehensive rationalism is an illusion.[36] As a consequence, critical rationalists deny that a just society could be conceived by mere thinking and they deny that it should be implemented by a revolution. And unlike postmodernist and poststructuralist thinkers critical rationalists know that relativism and particularism cannot support democracy and human rights. In the 1940s and 1950s universal human rights and scientific insights were the weapons against colonialism and in the late 1980s against communist dictatorship. Now, in many countries the new bondage of people and society

---

[33] Max Weber (1904).

[34] Robert K. Merton (1942).

[35] For example Hans Albert (1968), pp. 74-81.

[36] One of the anonymous referees mentioned Bartley's Comprehensively Critical Rationalism (1962) as a possible alternative to a comprehensive rationalism. Actually, I do not have any good arguments for or against Bartley's kind of critical rationalism in which everything can be criticized, but I should like to mention the following moral intuition as a counterargument: there are some basic rights that belong to human beings and cannot be subject to criticism. To think that it is possible to discuss those rights is in the end to think that it is possible that they do not belong to human beings. Of course my position is in a way dogmatic, but my question is: do we really want to discuss the freedom to speak? Even Richard Rorty argues that there is no duty to argue with those who deny that we have a right to argue. From my point of view, there are some conditions that must be met before we can start the process of criticism. Those conditions cannot be criticized. So as a consequence, Comprehensively Critical Rationalism is practically impossible or even contradictory.

and sometimes even dictatorship are justified with relativistic and particularistic arguments. *This* is the important message of Sokal's hoax.

# Bibliography

Albert, H. (1968). *Traktat über kritische Vernunft*. Tübingen: J. C. B. Mohr (Paul Siebeck). 5th edition 1991.

Ashman, K. M. & Baringer, P. S., editors (2001). *After the Science Wars*. London & New York: Routledge.

Bartley, III, W. W. (1962). *The Retreat to Commitment*. New York: Alfred A. Knopf. 2nd edition 1984. La Salle and London: Open Court Publishing Company.

Bricmont, J. & Sokal, A. (2001). 'Science and Sociology of Science: Beyond War and Peace'. In J. A. Labinger & H. Collins, editors (2001), pp. 27-47. *The One Culture?* Chicago & London: The University of Chicago Press.

Bunge, M. (1999). *The Sociology-Philosophy Connection*. New Brunswick & London: Transaction Publishers.

Collins, H. & Pinch, T. (1996). *The Golem. What Everyone Should Know about Science*. Cambridge: Cambridge University Press.

Gross, P. R. & Levitt, N. (1994). *Higher Superstition. The Academic Left and its Quarrels with Science*. Baltimore MD: The John Hopkins University Press.

Gross, P. R., Levitt, N., & Lewis, M. W., editors (1996). *The Flight from Science and Reason*. New York: The New York Academy of Sciences.

Knorr-Cetina, K. (1999). *Epistemic Cultures*. Cambridge MA & London: Harvard University Press.

Koertge, N., editor (1998). *A House Built on Sand*. New York & Oxford: Oxford University Press.

Lakatos, I. (1970). 'Falsification and the Methodology of Scientific Research Programmes'. In I. Lakatos & A. E. Musgrave, editors (1970), pp. 91-195. *Criticism and the Growth of Knowledge*. Cambridge & elsewhere: Cambridge University Press.

Latour, B. (1987). *Science in Action*. Cambridge MA: Harvard University Press.

—— (1991). *Nous n'avons jamais été modernes. Essai d'anthropologie symétrique*. Paris: Éditions La Découverte.

Merton, R. K. (1942). 'Science and Technology in a Democratic Order. *Journal of Legal and Political Sociology* 1. pp. 115-126. Reprinted as 'The Normative Structure of Science' in R. K. Merton (1974), pp. 267-278. *The Sociology of Science*. Chicago: University of Chicago Press.

Miller, D. W. (1999). 'Being an Absolute Skeptic'. *Science* **284**, 4.vi.1999, pp. 1625f.

—— (2000). 'Sokal & Bricmont: Back to the Frying Pan'. *Pli – The Warwick Journal of Philosophy* **9**, pp. 156-173. Reprinted as Chapter 6 of D. W. Miller (2006). *Out of Error*. Aldershot: Ashgate.

Niemann, H.-J. (1999). 'Die "Krise in der Erkenntnistheorie" – Sokal, Bricmont und die wissenschaftlichen Standards in der Philosophie'. *Conceptus*, 80, pp. 1-35.

Pickering, A. (1984). *Constructing Quarks. A Sociological History of Particle Physics*. Chicago & London: The University of Chicago Press.

Popper, K. R. (1959). *The Logic of Scientific Discovery*. London: Hutchinson.

——— (1972). *Objective Knowledge*. Oxford: Clarendon Press. 2nd edition 1979.

Ross, A. (1996). *Science Wars*. Durham NC & London: Duke University Press.

Snow, C. P. (1959). *The Two Cultures*. Cambridge: Cambridge University Press.

Sokal, A. (1996a). 'Transgressing the Boundaries. Toward a Transformative Hermeneutics of Quantum Gravity'. *Social Text*, 46/47, pp. 217-252.

——— (1996b). 'A Physicist Experiments With Cultural Studies'. *Lingua Franca*, May/June 1996, pp. 62-64.

——— (1996c). 'Transgressing the Boundaries: An Afterword'. *Dissent*, 43/44, pp. 93-99.

——— (1996d). 'Transgressing the Boundaries: An Afterword'. *Philosophy and Literature* **20**, pp. 338-346. Revised version of Sokal (1996c).

——— (1998). 'What the Social Text Affair Does and Does Not Prove'. In Koertge (1998), pp. 9-22.

Sokal, A. & Bricmont, J. (1998). *Intellectual Impostures*. London: Profile Books. American edition 1999. *Fashionable Nonsense. Postmodern Intellectuals' Abuse of Science*. New York: Picador.

Weber, M. (1904). 'Die "Objektivtät" sozialwissenschaftslicher und sozialpolitischer Erkenntnis'. *Archiv für Sozialwissenschaft und Sozialpolitik* **19**, pp. 22-87.

# 27

# On the Idea of Logical Presuppositions of Rational Criticism

## Jonas Nilsson

In this paper I shall discuss an idea that has been used by many philosophers, philosophers who otherwise have widely divergent philosophical standpoints. These philosophers claim that certain logical laws and inference rules must be regarded as immune to rational criticism and revision. The reason these laws and rules cannot be rationally criticized is supposed to be that they are presuppositions of rational criticism as such. The idea is that these laws and inference rules cannot be put into question in a rational way, because in putting them into question one would always have to make use of the same laws and rules and already regard them as valid. My aim is to criticize this idea of uncriticizable presuppositions of criticism.

Arguments that draw upon this idea have been put forward by Karl-Otto Apel, Jürgen Habermas, William Bartley, and Thomas Nagel, for example.

## 1 Shared assumptions and a point of disagreement

I assume that all parties to the discussion about the criticizability or un-criticizability of logic agree that not all laws and inference rules in classical logic must be treated as uncriticizable. It is usually acknowledged, for example, that the law of excluded middle be open to potential criticism. It is also agreed by all that every argument (and thus every piece of rational criticism) has some logical presuppositions. The issue is instead whether or not there is some core of logic that is uncriticizable. Must any general logical laws and inference rules, such as the law of noncontradiction, modus ponens, and other laws and rules of classical logic be viewed as uncriticizable presuppositions of criticism?

To be even more specific, my aim is to criticize a type of argument for the claim that certain inference rules and laws must be regarded as uncriticizable and unrevisable. The idea behind this kind of argument is that certain basic laws and inference rules cannot be put into question in a rational way, because in putting them into question one would always have to make use of the same laws and rules and already regard them as valid. In the following, I criticize this idea of logical presuppositions of rational criticism and the kind of argument for uncriticizability that draws upon it. I try to suggest how one can avoid presupposing the validity of the rules that, in a certain critical argument, are targeted for criticism. What I want to defend is the claim that *we do not have to be dogmatic* concerning logical laws and inference rules.

## 2  Some proponents of the idea

The idea of logical presuppositions that cannot themselves be criticized and revised is an important ingredient in the philosophies of Apel and Habermas. They claim that there are certain rules that are necessary presuppositions for the possibility of meaningful argumentation. Some of these rules are logical inference rules. It is not clear exactly which rules are supposed to have this status. Presumably, they do not think it applies to all logical rules, but rather that there is some core of basic rules that are immune to criticism. If one tries to criticize such rules, or denies their validity, so called 'performative contradictions' arise (Apel 1987; Habermas 1990).

A performative contradiction occurs when an asserted proposition contradicts the propositional content of some presupposition of the asserting speech act (Habermas 1990, p. 77). An example would be if I uttered the statement 'I do not exist'. It is contradicted by something that is presupposed in my speech act, to wit that I, the speaker, exist. Concerning basic logical rules, the idea is that performative contradictions would arise in the following way. Assume that I make the statement: 'the logical rule R is not valid'. According to Apel and Habermas, in performing that speech act I claim to be able to defend the statement by arguing for it. A performative contradiction would then arise if arguing for the statement were to depend upon using the very rule R that I purport to reject.

They also think that one can *show* that a certain rule is a necessary presupposition for argumentation, by showing that a performative contradiction arises if one tries to challenge it. This way of justifying logical (and other) rules, Apel calls 'transcendental-pragmatic reflection'. Apel even thinks that in this way one can give ultimate justifications of these rules, justifications which establish their validity with absolute certainty.

But this idea of logical rules that cannot be criticized because they are presuppositions of all rational criticism has also attracted philosophers who present themselves as fallibilists.

Even a critical rationalist like William Bartley has such a view of logic. Bartley's position is that rationality is exclusively a matter of (negative) criticism, and that everything can and ought to be held open to criticism. However, he qualifies his claim that everything can be held open to criticism, by saying that there is what he calls a 'minimal logic' which is an 'absolute presupposition of argument' (Bartley 1962/1984, p. 134). Critical argumentation as such is necessarily connected with this minimal logic. If we are to argue at all, some logical laws and inference rules must be regarded as uncriticizable presuppositions of argumentation. Such laws and rules — minimal logic — are conditions of the possibility of rational criticism, and there can be no critical argument that does not already presuppose that they are valid.[1]

Bartley does not say precisely *which* laws and inference rules are included in this minimal logic. The only law he explicitly mentions is the law of non-contradiction (Bartley 1962/1984, p. 251).

Thomas Nagel expresses a similar view of logic in *The Last Word* (1997). Nagel writes about 'a framework of methods and forms of thought that reappear whenever we call any specific propositions into question' (ibidem, p. 69). He writes also (p. 62): 'There just isn't room for skepticism about basic logic, because there is no place to stand where we can formulate or think it without immediately contradicting ourselves by relying on it.'

The logical examples Nagel refers to are thoughts about the validity of such general inference rules as modus tollens and modus ponens. Concerning the latter, he writes: 'Nothing would permit us to attribute to anyone a disbelief in modus ponens' (ibidem, p. 77).

## 3   Different kinds of criticism of logic

It is true that every critical argument has logical presuppositions. But is it really the case that general logical laws and inference rules such as the law of noncontradiction, modus tollens, and modus ponens are presupposed whenever we criticize something, and that therefore they cannot themselves be criticized? I would like to complicate this idea of the logical presuppositions of criticism.

To begin with, logical laws and inference rules may be criticized in different ways. First, one may try to show that a law is not true or that an inference rule is not valid. For example, one could argue that there is some true contradiction, in order to criticize the law of noncontradiction, or one could try to find a counterexample to an inference rule, in which the rule permits an inference from true premises to a false conclusion.[2]

Alternatively, one could argue that an inference rule, although valid, is not appropriate in some context or for some purpose.[3] Intuitionists, for example, think that certain rules of classical logic should not be used in mathematical proofs. The study of inconsistent theories might be another example. In classical logic, any statement whatsoever can be derived from a contradiction. Therefore, one might propose to use a weaker logical system, dispensing with some classical rules, in order to investigate an inconsistent theory.

Third, one might criticize logical inference rules from an epistemological point of view. A justificationist rationalist might for example worry about how to reply to a skeptic who argues that logical rules are not justifiable.[4]

---

[1] For a critical discussion of Bartley's views on logic, see Andersson (1998).

[2] Graham Priest argues that there are true contradictions, so that the law of noncontradiction is false. He also argues that certain rules of classical logic are invalid and should be rejected (see Priest 1989 and 1998).

[3] See Bartley (1980).

[4] This is the worry that, for example, Boghossian addresses (see Boghossian 2001).

What is then criticized is perhaps a claim to the effect that it is rational to make inferences in accordance with certain inference rules.

Fourth, one might argue more radically that the practice of logical argumentation (along with the value attached to the ideas of truth and validity) is in some way suspect. Perhaps one should avoid being constrained by logic, in order to achieve something that is more valuable than truth and valid argumentation.

My discussion is not concerned with the fourth alternative. I am dealing with the question of whether someone who is trying to inquire and reason *rationally* can and should treat logic as criticizable and revisable.

It seems that in each of the three first kinds of criticism of logic, some argumentation must take place if the criticism is to be rational, and that that criticism will presuppose some logic. If one argues that there is a counterexample to a logical inference rule, or that a certain rule should not be used in mathematical proofs, or that a certain rule is unjustified, one will have to argue in a way that presupposes some logic (otherwise there would, I suppose, be no distinction between good and bad arguments).

The idea of logical presuppositions of criticism which is supposed to show that certain rules cannot be rationally criticized, seems to be applicable primarily in the first and third kinds of cases. If the criticism is aimed at showing that an inference rule is invalid, then it is of course problematic if in the critical argument one presupposes the validity of the same rule. Similarly, if the argument is intended to show that an inference rule is unjustifiable and hence that reasoning in accordance with it is not rationally permitted, it is problematic if the critical argument is based on the presuppositions that the rule is valid and that reasoning in accordance with it is rational.

On the other hand, if the aim is instead to show that in some particular context it is preferable not to use a certain inference rule, the same rule may be used in the critical argument without this giving rise to a problem. The context in which the criticism occurs may be different from the context in which the rule is claimed to be inappropriate, and presupposing that it is valid in the critical context does not have to be incompatible with its being inappropriate in a different context (say, in mathematical proofs or in the investigation of inconsistent sets of statements).

## 4   Logical presuppositions in criticism of logic

In the rest of my discussion, I shall focus on the type of criticism that is directed against claims that inference rules are valid (or that logical laws are true). If an inference rule is valid, one cannot derive a false conclusion from true premises with its help. If one finds a case where a rule permits the derivation of something false from true premises, one has found a counterexample, which shows that the rule is invalid.

I take it that the inference rules of classical propositional and predicate logic are truth-preserving, and that therefore there can be no counterexamples to them. So there can be no effective criticism against them showing that they are not valid. Thus the project of criticizing them by means of counter-examples is in this sense impossible. However, I shall argue that the reason for this is *not* that any criticism against them would presuppose those very rules. One does not have to *presuppose* them. It is just that they are *valid*.

Let us say that I think I have found a counterexample to an inference rule R, a case where R permits me to derive a false conclusion from true premises. I use the example to argue that R is invalid. The proponents of the idea of logical presuppositions of rational criticism would claim that if R is one of the basic rules, then at least one step in my critical argument would be an instance of R, so in accepting that step as valid I have to presuppose that R is valid.

The basic idea in this kind of argument for uncriticizable inference rules is that if I accept as valid a particular argument that instantiates a certain general inference rule, then I must presuppose the validity of that general inference rule. It is this idea that I suspect is mistaken and shall criticize. For the purpose of constructing a particular critical argument, one can make do with rather weak logical presuppositions, and there are ways in which one can avoid presupposing any inference rule that has been targeted for criticism.

Let us assume, again, that we have found what we think is a counterex-ample to an inference rule R, and that we use it in order to argue that R is invalid.

It might well be the case that we *actually*, in our critical argument, make use of the rule R in question — or that at least we are implicitly presupposing precisely that rule. But when criticizing a rule like R, does one really *have to* use the very same rule that has been targeted for criticism? Does one really have to presuppose the rule one wants to criticize?

No, I do not think that one has to. There are ways of avoiding such logical presuppositions.

First of all, there will be other inference rules than R. It is reasonable to think that an argument presupposes a certain inference rule only if that rule is actually used in it. It may be possible to reconstruct one's critical argument in such a way that R is not used in any step.

Second, it should be noted that R is assumed to be a general rule. Inference rules are usually presented in the form of argument schemas. Take the elim-ination rule for material implication (modus ponens) as an example. It says that from $A$ and $A \rightarrow B$ one may derive $B$. The antecedent $A$ and the conse-quent $B$ stand for arbitrary statements, and as long as they are well formed and meaningful, the rule contains no restrictions on, for example, what logical structure the statements $A$ and $B$ may have.

If one finds a counterexample to an inference rule, it may be possible to identify some special characteristic of the statements that are used, some characteristic that makes the example differ from instances of the rule one regards as unproblematic. It may be, for example, that the premises in the counterexample have a complex logical structure. If the rule in question is

modus ponens, say, the counterexample might be such that the consequent
$B$ itself contains material implications.[5]

A possibility is then to propose a *more strict* version of R, a version that
contains a *restriction* that rules out all cases with the special characteristic of
the counterexample. If the rule criticized is modus ponens, and the proposed
counterexample is such that the consequent $B$ itself contains a material implication, the restriction might be one that rules out application of the rule
whenever the consequent ($B$) itself contains an implication. The counterexamples would not affect this, more strict, rule. Then one can try to use only
this strict rule when criticizing the general version of modus ponens.

If one does so, then one does have access to an inference rule that can be
used to criticize modus ponens, and in that criticism modus ponens would
not itself have to be used or presupposed.

It is important at this point to be clear about what it means to deny that
(or question whether) an inference rule or logical law is valid. If a rule is valid,
then every instance of it, every argument that instantiates it, is valid. When
one claims that a rule is invalid, one does *not* claim that every instance of it
is invalid. Instead, what one claims is that some instance of the rule is invalid,
that is, that not every instance of it is valid.

Similarly, when someone like Graham Priest denies the law of noncontradiction and claims that there are true contradictions, he is of course not
suggesting that all contradictions are true (see Priest 1989 and 1998).

Therefore, denying the validity of an inference rule does not have to amount
to claiming that all previous arguments that instantiated the rule are invalid.
It does not have to lead to the breakdown of our argumentative practices.
If, for example, it were to be the case that some rule of classical logic is
invalid, then it might still be the case that most instances of that rule are
also instances of some other rule that *is* valid — for example some more strict
version of the rule as I proposed earlier.

So far, I have assumed that when we criticize a logical inference rule,
our critical argument must appeal to some general inference rule, which our
argument instantiates. But is this really necessary? Is it not sufficient if each
particular step in the argument is valid and one can recognize it as valid —
without knowing which general rule such a step is an instance of? It seems
reasonable to accept that this could be rational, since in general people can
recognize the validity or invalidity of particular arguments without knowing
anything about the general inference rules the arguments instantiate.

---

[5] Cp. McGee (1985): 'A Counterexample to Modus Ponens'. The counterexamples McGee
presents have this structure: in each of them there is a premise that is a conditional whose
consequent itself contains a conditional. However, the rule McGee criticizes under the name
'modus ponens' is not modus ponens in formal logic (that is, the elimination rule for material implication). He refers to it as a rule governing indicative conditionals in the English
language, and says explicitly that these conditionals are not material implications. Thus
his discussion does not concern the validity of any rules in classical logic.

I accept that a particular inference is valid only if it is an instance of a valid general inference rule.[6] But from an epistemological point of view, it seems to be more difficult to decide if a general inference rule is valid than if a particular inference is. This, I think, speaks in favour of the idea that a particular critical argument could be rational, although one leaves open the question of which general rule it is that makes it a valid one.

## 5 Conclusions

In conclusion, I should like to say that the idea of uncriticizable logical presuppositions of rational criticism is not at all as uncomplicated and self-evident as many philosophers seem to think.

When criticizing a certain logical law or inference rule, one does not have to make very strong assumptions about what logical laws and rules are valid. Thus, the correct claim that all criticism has logical presuppositions, does not mean that such general logical laws and rules as the law of noncontradiction, modus ponens, or modus tollens must be presupposed in any attempt at rational criticism. If one wants to avoid presupposing the rule that is criticized at the time in question, there are ways of avoiding such a presupposition. One strategy is to try to reconstruct the argument, using other rules that are not criticized in that situation. One way of doing this is to introduce restrictions on the rules one uses in the criticism, restrictions that are such that they exclude the kinds of counterexamples one is working with. Another possibility is to judge the validity of every *particular* step in the argumentation, while refraining from making any assumptions about which *general* rules and laws are valid.

If nevertheless there *are* parts of logic that are necessary presuppositions of all rational criticism, then it seems to be difficult to specify exactly what these presuppositions are. At least the idea of logical presuppositions of rational criticism that I have discussed here does not support the view that such general laws and inference rules as the law of noncontradiction or modus ponens must be regarded as immune to rational criticism.

The argument of this paper is bad news for all those who have hoped that any interesting standards of rationality, such as classical inference rules, can be *justified* by showing that they are inescapable presuppositions of rational criticism. If I am right, the kinds of justificatory strategies proposed by philosophers like Apel and Habermas do not look promising.

Conversely, another consequence of the argument is that a rationalist does not have to be *dogmatic* about logic. If he thinks that the rules of classical logic are valid, then of course he thinks that there can be no counterexamples to those rules. But if challenged with a proposed counterexample against some rule, he can discuss it rationally without being forced to presuppose

---

[6] For an expression of the opposite view, see Searle, who writes that 'the rules of logic play no role whatever in the validity of inferences. The arguments, if valid, have to be valid as they stand' (Searle 2001, p. 20).

the rule in question. He can also rationally discuss whether using a certain rule is perhaps inappropriate in a certain context or whether a certain rule is rationally acceptable or justifiable or criticizable and so on.[7] This is good news for the rationalist who wants to avoid being dogmatic about his rationalism and his standards of rational reasoning.

---

[7]This means that, as far as logic is concerned, a rationalist need not be open to the kind of *tu quoque* argument discussed by Bartley (see Bartley 1962/1984, pp. 71-77). Indeed, contrary to Bartley's own claims, a rationalist can consider a challenge to purportedly basic logical laws and inference rules without being forced to view this as a challenge to the very practice of critical argumentation.

# Bibliography

Andersson, G. (1998). 'Die kritisierbarkeit der Logik'. In V. Gadenne, editor (1998), pp. 61-75. *Kritischer Rationalismus und Pragmatismus*. Amsterdam & Atlanta: Editions Rodopi B.V.

Apel, K.-O. (1987). 'The Problem of Philosophical Foundations in Light of a Transcendental Pragmatics of Language'. English translation in K. Baynes, J. Bohman, & T. McCarthy, editors (1987), pp. 250-290. *After Philosophy: End or Transformation?* Cambridge MA: MIT Press. Originally published 1975. *Man and World* **8**, pp. 239-275.

Bartley, III, W. W. (1962). *The Retreat to Commitment*. New York: Alfred A. Knopf. Page references are to the 2nd edition 1984. La Salle IL and London: Open Court Publishing Company.

———— (1980). 'On the Criticizability of Logic – A Reply to A. A. Derksen'. *Philosophy of the Social Sciences* **10**, pp. 67-77.

Boghossian, P. (2001). 'How Are Objective Epistemic Reasons Possible?' *Philosophical Studies* **106**, pp. 1-40.

Habermas, J. (1990). 'Discourse Ethics: Notes on a Programme of Philosophical Justification'. In S. Benhabib & F. Dallmayr, editors (1990), pp. 60-110. *The Communicative Ethics Controversy*. Cambridge MA: MIT Press. Excerpted from J. Habermas (1983). *Moralbewusstsein und kommunikatives Handeln*. Frankfurt/Main: Suhrkamp.

McGee, V. (1985). 'A Counterexample to Modus Ponens'. *Journal of Philosophy* **82**, pp. 462-471.

Nagel, T. (1997). *The Last Word*. Oxford: Oxford University Press.

Priest, G. (1989). 'Reductio ad Absurdum et Modus Tollendo Ponens'. In G. Priest, R. Routley, & J. Norman, editors, (1989), pp. 613-626. *Paraconsistent Logic: Essays on the Inconsistent*. Munich: Philosophia Verlag.

———— (1998). 'What Is So Bad About Contradictions?' *Journal of Philosophy* **95**, pp. 410-426.

Searle, J. R. (2001). *Rationality in Action*, Cambridge MA: MIT Press.

# 28

# Constructing a Comprehensively Anti-Justificationist Position

## Antoni Diller

## 1 Introduction

The central epistemological problem in a justificationist philosophy is that of justification. This is the problem of how we can justify our theories or beliefs. Virtually all philosophical systems in the Western tradition, from the time of Descartes until the twentieth century, have been justificationist ones. These philosophies can be distinguished by the different ways in which they solve the problem of justification. The revolutionary nature of Popper's thought is due to the fact that he removed the problem of justification from its central position in epistemology and replaced it with the problem of criticism, that is to say, the question of how theories can be criticized. By doing this he showed that the problem of justification is irrelevant to epistemology (Popper 1983, Part I, § 2(I)). Popper criticized many aspects of justificationism in his first published book (Popper 1935), but he was not fully aware of just how radical he was being. In that book Popper was particularly interested in the problems of induction and demarcation and he developed his solutions partly in the context of a debate with several logical positivists, especially Carnap, who were thoroughly justificationist in their thinking. It was Bartley, in the 1960s, who realized that Popper's originality was not restricted to solving particular problems, like that of induction and demarcation, but involved a thoroughgoing re-orientation of the problem situation in epistemology.

Bartley was interested in the problem of the limits of rationality and his discussion of this is largely conducted in the context of a debate with various liberal theologians who made much use of the *tu quoque* (you too) or boomerang argument. One version of this goes as follows: '(1) [For] certain logical reasons, rationality is so limited that *everyone* has to make a dogmatic irrational commitment; (2) therefore, the Christian has a right to make whatever commitment he pleases; and (3) therefore, no one has a right to criticize him for this' (Bartley 1962, p. 90). This argument is persuasive only if a justificationist conception of knowledge is presupposed. Bartley also thought that there were remnants of justificationism in Popper's critical rationalism, which led to what he saw as Popper's fideism. This emerges in Popper's discussion of rationality where, unable to justify his critical rationalism logically, he says that his minimal concession to irrationalism is to make a decision to believe in reason (Popper 1945b, Chapter 24, § II). In forging his comprehensively critical rationalism, later rechristened 'pancritical rationalism', Bartley sought to present a solution to the problem of rationality free from any taint of justificationism. It is not surprising, therefore, that the term 'anti-justificationism' was used to describe his views (Watkins 1969, p. 60).

Bartley's anti-justificationist ideas came to be accepted by many in the Popper camp, including Watkins, Agassi, and Lakatos (Bartley 1962, p. 157), though some later recanted. As Bartley's ideas spread, differences of emphasis began to emerge and various facets of anti-justificationism were stressed by different thinkers. Disputes arose between people who actually had a great deal in common. The purpose of this paper is to present a systematic account of anti-justificationism. I hope thereby to show that the debate between justificationism and anti-justificationism is far more important than arguments within anti-justificationism. I start by characterizing justificationism, mentioning some of the criticisms that have been brought against it, and then I characterize anti-justificationism. Having a clear characterization of anti-justificationism it is easier to see what distinguishes it from justificationist philosophies and this enables me to present a novel argument showing the superiority of anti-justificationism. (I do not wish to suggest that all conceivable epistemologies are either justificationist or anti-justificationist ones, but I do not have the space to consider other approaches here.)

## 2  Justificationism

I am not trying to answer the question, 'What is justificationism?' I agree with Popper that such questions are not helpful. Instead, I identify the main features of justificationism.

(1) In justificationism knowledge is defined to be justified true belief. This is known as the *standard analysis* and Bartley takes it to be the unique determining feature of justificationism (Bartley 1962, pp. 172f.). Not only do justificationists accept the standard analysis, they also think that this definition is important and many of them have been seriously troubled by examples that show that it is flawed (Gettier 1967). Recently, however, Wright has sought to draw the sting of Gettier's counterexamples by conceding that 'knowledge is not really the proper concern of epistemological-sceptical enquiry' (Wright 1991, p. 88). He explains, 'We can live with the concession that we do not, strictly *know* some of the things we believed ourselves to know, provided we can retain the thought that we are fully justified in accepting them.' Thus, Wright accepts the standard analysis and the validity of Gettier's counterexamples, but is not troubled by them. This is because he thinks that epistemologists should be concerned with justified true belief even if this is not knowledge! Wright's approach to epistemology shows that he regards the standard analysis as a real or, what Popper calls, an essentialist definition

(Popper 1945b, Chapter 11, § 11). When people ask what-is? questions, they are looking for real definitions. The standard analysis arises when philosophers take the pseudo-problem, 'What is knowledge?', seriously. Popper, and most anti-justificationists, do not accept the existence of real definitions.

(2) One consequence of the standard analysis is that knowledge is taken to be something subjective. Thus, the epistemological focus for justificationism is the knowledge that some individual or other possesses. There is, certainly, knowledge in this sense, but Popper has persuasively argued that it is not the primary concern of epistemology. Instead, he argues that the study of objective knowledge should be the primary focus of philosophy (Popper 1972, Chapters 3 and 4). Popper follows such thinkers as Frege and Bolzano in singing the praises of objective knowledge. Such knowledge has many advantages over the subjective variety. For example, objective knowledge can stand in logical relations to other objective knowledge, whereas subjective knowledge cannot. Objective knowledge can be grasped by many people, whereas an individual's subjective knowledge is unique to that individual. Objective knowledge has a permanence that fleeting subjective knowledge does not have.

(3) Another consequence of the standard analysis is that knowledge is understood as being certain. This has led many epistemologists to engage in what Popper, following Dewey, calls 'the quest for certainty' (Popper 1972, Chapter 2, § 13). Lakatos, in comments he made at the 1966 Denver Colloquium, describes how the quest for certainty, rigorously applied by a justificationist empiricist, continually diminishes the class of things that can be known for certain (Lakatos 1970, p. 221):

> [Justificationism] inexorably leads to a step by step reduction of the field of rational inquiry. The most important pattern of such reduction is this: First cast doubt on any source of indubitable knowledge about the world except for sense-experience and arrive at (realistic) empiricism; then cast doubt on whether sense-experience was a proof of the external world and slip into solipsism; then cast doubt on the coherence of your ego and replace solipsism by the mist of 'fleeting bundles of perception' — the infinite abyss of doubt leaves one with nothing spared.

Anti-justificationists can have a lot of fun with any philosopher who claims that a particular class of statements or some specific proposition is certain and, therefore, immune from criticism, because, with a little effort, luck, and creativity, it is possible to find a way of criticizing any given statement.

(4) In the standard analysis knowledge is defined to be justified true belief. A justification involves three components, namely the foundational statements that form the premises of the justification, the collection of acceptable logical procedures or rules of inference that allow the conclusion or statement being justified to be inferred from the foundational statements and a non-logical and non-linguistic rational authority that establishes the truth of the foundational statements. A specific justificationist philosophy is obtained by choosing a

particular rational authority that validates foundational statements and by choosing the collection of allowable logical procedures. The choice of rational authority then determines the class of foundational statements. The reason why justificationists need such a rational authority is in order to ensure that justifications contain only a finite number of steps. This is how they prevent the occurrence of an infinite regress of reasons. There are, however, other ways of dealing with the threat of such an infinite regress (Armstrong 1973, pp. 150-161; Bartley 1962, pp. 211-216), but I do not have the space to discuss them here. The currently most popular version of justificationism is empiricism. Here, the rational authority is sense experience or observation and the class of foundational statements consists of those that can be validated by sense experience or observation. Concerning the collection of acceptable inference rules, most empiricists in the 20th century have accepted the rules of classical, bivalent logic, though in recent years the work of Dummett and other anti-realists have made intuitionistic logic fashionable. Furthermore, justificationist empiricists accept some form of induction as a legitimate way of inferring conclusions from premises in justifications.

In recent years the idea of justification has become increasingly important in analytical philosophy. I shall only quote a few representative opinions on the matter (Williamson 1997, p. 717; Aspenson 1998, p. 28; Swinburne 2001, p. 1). It should be noted that, although Williamson acknowledges that the trend in analytical philosophy is for philosophers to occupy themselves increasingly with issues relating to justification, this is not a trend he favours.

> Tradition has it that the main problems of philosophy include the nature of knowledge. But, in recent decades, questions of knowledge seem to have been marginalized by questions of justification.

> Though epistemologists talk a good deal about knowledge, they talk much more about *justification*, that is, about the varieties of good reasons for believing something.

> 'Justification' is a central notion in contemporary epistemology in the analytic tradition. Epistemologists are concerned with the kind of justification that is indicative of truth.

Many more passages could be quoted to show just how much the idea of justification dominates the study of epistemology by analytical philosophers, but these should be sufficient.

Many introductory texts on informal logic are written from a justificationist perspective and as a consequence of this they give incorrect advice. In one such text we find the maxim (Gilbert 1979/1996, p. 32):

> *Always attack the reasons for a claim, not the claim itself.*

(Anti-justificationists, by contrast, would directly criticize any claims they objected to.) The author of the text himself, however, clearly states the limitations of his advice (ibidem, p. 34):

Someone who believes something without reason is being irrational. In terms of argument, being rational means providing reasons for belief. In the end all of us may be irrational, since sooner or later we reach a point of ultimate beliefs (for which it is impossible to provide reasons).

This admission comes from a person who is upholding and advocating rationalism! His honest comment reveals the tensions inherent in justificationism.

There are also other ways of criticizing the idea of a justification. For example, Popper criticized the validity of induction, which plays a large part in justificationist empiricism, and he criticized also the idea that sense experience or observation can confer certainty on foundational statements.

(5) In justificationism criticism is fused with justification. Bartley was the first to realize this (Bartley 1962/1984, p. 261, note 1). He distinguished two ways in which such criticism can operate. In the first a theory is rejected if it cannot be justified from the acceptable foundational statements and in the second a theory is rejected if it conflicts with justified statements (Bartley ibidem, pp. 142-144).

(6) Because a justification has to proceed from a collection of foundational statements that cannot themselves be justified logically, the collection of foundational statements has to be thought of as being immune from criticism. Justificationists, therefore, are forced to admit that some propositions cannot be criticized.

(7) Because of the way knowledge is defined in the standard analysis, it must be certain. This means that knowledge can grow only in a non-evolutionary and non-revolutionary manner. This is because, if something is granted the status of knowledge, then, as it is certainly true, there is no way that it could turn out to be false. Thus, once something is accepted as knowledge, it remains knowledge forever. If knowledge is seen to grow in an evolutionary or revolutionary manner, by contrast, successor theories contradict their predecessors and thus the predecessor theories could not have been correct. In fact, a safe assumption to make for anyone who accepts an evolutionary or revolutionary theory of the growth of knowledge is that all scientific theories are false. Justificationists, however, abide by the principle that all genuinely scientific theories must be true.

## 3   Anti-justificationism

It is important to stress that anti-justificationism is not obtained by negating justificationism. Anti-justificationism was created by certain philosophers providing better solutions to the genuine epistemological and methodological problems that justificationism attempts to solve. Anti-justificationism does not try to solve all the problems that justificationism does because some of these are pseudo-problems. These it exposes as not being real problems. Therefore, in order to characterize anti-justificationism, it is not possible to go through the features of justificationism listed above and simply state the corresponding aspect of anti-justificationism. Thus, I will label the main properties of anti-justificationism using the capital letters (A), (B), (C) and so on.

(A) Anti-justificationists do not try to define knowledge. This is because of their views about definition rather than any specific opinion about knowledge.

(B) Anti-justificationists are, following Popper, primarily interested in objective knowledge. Although not all anti-justificationists follow Popper in accepting the reality of World 3, they all think that the objective content of a theory is far more important than any particular individual's subjective understanding of that theory.

(C) Not only do anti-justificationists focus primarily on objective knowledge, they also agree with Popper that such knowledge is conjectural, fallible, and revisable. Knowledge is not thought of as being certain, but rather as being tentative and hypothetical.

(D) Because they deny that certain knowledge exists, anti-justificationists are not engaged in a quest for certainty. What they are primarily interested in are true theories and, thus, they replace the quest for certainty with a quest for truth. Rather than trying to justify their beliefs, they endeavour to devise better theories to solve the problems they are interested in.

(E) Anti-justificationism is anti-authoritarian. Recall the idea of a justification of some statement. This is a logical argument that has that statement as its conclusion and whose premises are either foundational statements, which are validated by some rational authority, such as sense experience, or statements that can be logically inferred from such foundational statements. As criticism is fused with justification, the collection of foundational statements cannot be subjected to criticism. Anti-justificationism is anti-authoritarian in the sense that everything can be criticized. There is no privileged class of propositions that are beyond criticism. There are no infallible authorities.

(F) Justificationists and anti-justificationists have very different ideas about criticism. The way in which a justificationist empiricist, for example, criticizes a theory is either by showing that it does not follow from observation statements or by showing that it does not conflict with observation statements. Anti-justificationists, by contrast, have a different conception of criticism and use various strategies in order to criticize theories. In justificationism emphasis is placed on proving the correctness of what you believe. Therefore, not a lot of thought has been expended by justificationists on the manifold ways in which theories can be criticized. One of the many strengths of anti-justificationism is that it employs a wide selection of methods of criticism. Because of this, I devote a considerable amount of space to discussing anti-justificationist methods of criticism:

(i) One way of criticizing a theory is to ask, 'Is this theory consistent?' If we discover that a theory is inconsistent, then the inconsistency needs to be removed. Although people sometimes work with inconsistent theories, this is just a stop-gap measure until the source of the inconsistency can be located and a more acceptable solution found.

(ii)     Another method of criticizing a theory is to ask, 'What problem is this theory intended to solve?' According to Popper, theories are put forward in order to solve problems and one way to criticize a theory is to show that it does not solve a genuine problem.

(iii)    A further method of criticizing a theory put forward to solve a real problem is to ask, 'Does this theory successfully solve the problem it was put forward to solve?' Even if a theory is put forward in order to solve a genuine problem, it may be that it does not solve it very well.

Item (i) corresponds to the check of logic (Bartley 1962, p. 158) and items (ii) and (iii) elaborate the check of the problem (ibidem, p. 159).

The methods of criticism mentioned so far can be applied to any type of theory, but there are differences between the way in which empirical, mathematical, and metaphysical theories are criticized. The following ways of criticism are some of those that can be used against empirical theories:

(iv)     One way of criticizing an empirical theory is to ask, 'Is this theory consistent with observed facts?' If a theory, together with some initial conditions, entails a prediction that is contradicted by an observation report, then that theory has been falsified, unless we have good reasons to think that either the initial conditions or the observation report are at fault.

(v)      Another way of criticizing an empirical theory is to ask, 'Is this theory better than its rivals?' Even if a group of two or more theories are all consistent, have all adequately solved the same problems and none of them has been falsified, it may still be possible to think that one of the theories is better than its rivals. We may decide, for example, to pick the simplest theory.

(vi)     A further way of criticizing an empirical theory is to ask, 'Is this theory in conflict with some other scientific theory that has survived a lot of criticism?' If there is a conflict of some sort, then either we have to give up or modify the proposed theory or else we have to give up the other theory. In order to decide what to do we would need to subject both theories to further criticism.

(vii)    Yet another way of criticizing an empirical theory is to ask, 'Is this theory in conflict with the methodology of its parent discipline?' If there is a conflict, then either the theory or the methodology has to go, but we would need to submit both to further criticism in order to decide which it is.

(viii)   A further method of criticizing an empirical theory is to ask, 'Is this theory in conflict with some elements of the dominant cultural world view?' This method of criticism is analogous to that in which there is a conflict between a newly introduced empirical theory and an old, established empirical theory. In fact, whether the older theory is empirical or metaphysical should not matter. What is important is how well the older theory has stood up to criticism. If the older theory happens to be non-empirical, but it has withstood rational criticism, then a conflict between it and a fledging theory is important. If there is such a conflict, then either the theory or the element of the world view involved has to give way. To decide which we would have to submit both to further criticism.

Item (iv) is the check of sense experience and (v) is the check of scientific theory (Bartley 1962, pp. 158f.). Items (vi), (vii), and (viii) are based on Laudan's analysis of conceptual problems (Laudan 1977, Chapter 2). Although he is not a Popperian, some of Laudan's views on the ways in which theories can be criticized can profitably be incorporated into anti-justificationism.

(G) Anti-justificationists agree with Popper that the origins of a theory are irrelevant to its truth (Popper 1994, Chapter 1, § XIII). The consequences of a theory are far more important in the task of assessing its value.

(H) Anti-justificationists agree with Popper that science begins with problems.

(I) Anti-justificationists see knowledge as growing in an evolutionary or revolutionary manner. I do not distinguish between these as the key feature of each of them is that new theories are propounded that contradict existing theories.

(J) Proliferation is encouraged in anti-justificationism. It is thought by many that Feyerabend is the originator of the idea that proliferation of theories is beneficial to the growth of science and knowledge in general. It is true that Feyerabend proposed a principle of proliferation around 1965, which Preston quotes as, 'Invent, and elaborate, theories which are inconsistent with the accepted point of view, even if the latter should happen to be highly confirmed and generally accepted' (Preston 1997, p. 138). Popper (1945a, § 32), however, was singing the praises of proliferation many years before Feyerabend.

> [We] must realise that with the best institutional organisation in the world, scientific progress may one day stop. There may, for example, be an epidemic of mysticism. This is certainly possible, for since some intellectuals *do* react to scientific progress by withdrawing into mysticism, everyone *might* react in this way. Such a possibility may perhaps be counteracted by devising a further set of social institutions, such as educational institutions, to discourage uniformity of outlook and encourage diversity.

Furthermore, in his later years Popper frequently wrote about his tetradic schema of problem solving. The benefits of proliferation are clear in those versions of this schema in which several theories are proposed as solutions to a single problem (Popper 1972, Chapter 6, § XVIII(8)).

## 4  Prospering in the scientific marketplace

Whereas many philosophers have written about the fact that scientists sometimes work with several competing theories, the fact that members of the scientific community accept several different methodologies is not discussed nearly so frequently. It is not the case that there is a single methodology that all scientists accept. Some scientists accept justificationism and some accept anti-justificationism. (There are probably others who accept non-justification- ist methodologies other than anti-justificationism. To simplify my argument I ignore this possibility.) Whereas this poses a real problem for justificationists, anti-justificationists can take it in their stride. The considerations that I am about to present constitute an *ad hominem* argument, that is to say, I draw out unacceptable consequences for justificationists on the assumption that their views about knowledge and methodology are correct. In connection with the other arguments that have been put forward against justificationism (some of which have been briefly mentioned or alluded to above) I think that this constitutes a refutation of justificationist empiricism.

Although individual scientists have their own goals and aims, the aim of science is the production of true explanatory and predictive theories. In doing their work scientists have to make use of information that was obtained from other people. On the whole justificationist empiricists see scientific knowledge as growing through a non-evolutionary process of accumulation. What is im- portant to them is that this knowledge was obtained using a fairly reliable method. I am not suggesting that all justificationists are reliabilists or that they all accept a reliability theory of knowledge. What I am saying is that they all accept some form of the inductive method and they think that know- ledge that is obtained by means of this method is generally reliable. For them the pedigree of a piece of information is of crucial importance.

Anti-justificationists sees things very differently. For them the way in which a theory is produced is irrelevant from an epistemological or methodological point of view, though it may be interesting from a psychological perspec- tive. What is important for them is how a theory is criticized using methods that do not involve the attempt to justify it. Anti-justificationists disregard what they know about the origins of a theory when they are involved in the task of assessing the value of that theory. If they come across a theory that is claimed by its author to have been produced using an inductive method, they disregard this information when they are criticizing that theory. They are prepared to entertain, and even accept, a theory allegedly obtained by using the inductive method just as much as one obtained in any other way. Hence, the existence of justificationists in the scientific community presents no epistemological problems. Their presence slows down scientific progress and acceptance of their methodology creates the illusion that scientific knowledge is especially reliable, but anti-justificationists can accommodate themselves to these things. They are willing to consider the theories propounded by justific- ationists on their merits irrespective of their origins. They consider the time justificationists spent arguing for their theories inductively as having been wasted. They would have taken the theory seriously, if it had intrinsic merit, even if there were no such argumentation present.

Justificationists, however, have real difficulties accommodating the existence of anti-justificationists in the scientific community. Anti-justificationists propound theories and then they try to falsify them. They spend much of their time criticizing theories rather than trying to establish them conclusively. They are not concerned with the origins of their theories nor do they claim they have a pure pedigree. Yet sometimes their theories are generally accepted and become, for a time at least, part of the fabric of knowledge. The way in which they work ensures that the knowledge they produce does not have a pure pedigree. Justificationists have to make use of knowledge produced by other people, but they cannot ascertain the pedigree of every piece of information that they use. Their goal of adding a few stones to the growing edifice of scientific knowledge is undermined by the fact that anti-justificationists build in the air. The presence of anti-justificationists spoils the pedigree, for justificationists, of a great deal of scientific knowledge and, from their point of view, they cannot always know which pieces of information have been infected. For justificationists, if they thought the matter through, this state of affairs would be intolerable. Thus, in a community of scientists using different methodologies, anti-justificationists have a definite advantage.

## 5  Conclusion

In this paper I have made a start on the task of providing a systematic characterization of anti-justificationism, which, amongst other things, rejects the idea that justification is central to philosophy. It is, thus, fundamentally opposed to the analytical tradition of philosophy. I argued above that justificationist scientists, if they thought the matter through, would find the presence of anti-justificationists in the scientific community intolerable. Most scientists, however, have not thought the matter through. Since justificationist philosophers are likely to have done so, this partly explains their hostility to anti-justificationists. Unable to answer their arguments they pretend they do not exist. I think it is a pity that anti-justificationists spend so much time criticizing each other on fairly minor points when there is so much that unites them. They have far more in common with each other than they have with analytical philosophers. By attempting to systematize anti-justificationism I hope to redraw some philosophical battle lines. Rather than these running through the anti-justificationist camp, they should lie between that camp and that of the justificationists. By trying to systematize anti-justificationism, I hope to make it easier for anti-justificationists to take on the analytical tradition. Analytical philosophy, the descendant of logical positivism, has done little to advance philosophy and it is, therefore, imperative, for the sake of philosophy, that it be attacked.

# Bibliography

Armstrong, D. M. (1973). *Belief, Truth and Knowledge*. Cambridge: Cambridge University Press.

Aspenson, S. S. (1998). *The Philosopher's Tool Kit*. London: M. E. Sharpe.

Bartley, III, W. W. (1962). *The Retreat to Commitment*. New York: Alfred A. Knopf. 2nd edition 1984. La Salle IL & London: Open Court Publishing Company.

Gettier, E. (1967). 'Is Justified True Belief Knowledge?' *Analysis* **23**, pp. 121-123.

Gilbert, M. A. (1979). *How to Win an Argument*. New York: McGraw Hill. Page references are to the 2nd edition 1996. New York: Wiley.

Lakatos, I. (1970). Discussion of 'Scepticism and the Study of History' by R. H. Popkin. In W. Yourgrau & A. D. Breck, editors (1970), pp. 220-223. *Physics, Logic, and History*. New York & London: Plenum Press.

Laudan, L. (1977). *Progress and its Problems*. London: Routledge & Kegan Paul.

Popper, K. R. (1935). *Logik der Forschung*. Vienna: Julius Springer Verlag.

———— (1945a). 'The Poverty of Historicism', Part III. *Economica* **XII**, pp. 69-89. Reprinted as Part IV of K. R. Popper (1957). *The Poverty of Historicism*. London: Routledge & Kegan Paul.

———— (1945b). *The Open Society and its Enemies*. London: George Routledge & Sons. 5th edition 1966. London: Routledge & Kegan Paul.

———— (1972). *Objective Knowledge*. Oxford: Clarendon Press. 2nd edition 1979.

———— (1983). *Realism and the Aim of Science*. London: Hutchinson.

———— (1994). *The Myth of the Framework* London: Routledge.

Preston, J. (1997). *Feyerabend: Philosophy, Science and Society*. Cambridge: Polity.

Swinburne, R. G. (2001). *Epistemic Justification*. Oxford: Clarendon Press.

Watkins, J. W. N. (1969). 'Comprehensively Critical Rationalism'. *Philosophy* **44**, pp. 57-62.

Williamson, T. (1997). 'Knowledge as Evidence'. *Mind* **106**, pp. 717-741.

Wright, C. (1991). 'Scepticism and Dreaming: Imploding the Demon'. *Mind* **100**, pp. 87-116.

# 29

# Rationality without Foundations

## Stefano Gattei

One man come he to justify
One man to overthrow
Paul Hewson[1]

Orthodoxy, especially in light of the enormous impact of Thomas Kuhn's ideas, presents us with a picture of a sharp and massive break, of a true revolution: Kuhn is viewed as a philosopher whose main achievement is to have undermined a whole philosophical tradition. I think this is wrong. From many and often fundamental points of view Kuhn did not manage to break entirely with the preceding philosophical tradition of Logical Positivism (or Logical Empiricism): his works are laden with principles belonging to that very empirical philosophy he was determined to reject. Furthermore, only a partial challenge of positivism and empiricism can actually account for the genesis of Kuhn's philosophical perspective — incommensurability, the notion of progress, the rejection of the concepts of truth and verisimilitude, and the very thesis of 'world change' (one of the theses deemed most radical and characteristic of Kuhn's philosophical stance) are all consequences of the empiricist elements that his philosophy retains. Appearances to the contrary notwithstanding, the implicit presuppositions and the stated principles of Kuhn's philosophy are not very different from those of the logical positivists or logical empiricists he saw himself to be distancing himself from.

Far from spelling the 'demise'[2] of Logical Positivism, then, Kuhn's philosophy is its natural continuation (which is, perhaps, the reason why Carnap welcomed his book so favourably[3]). Like Copernicus, who, while fetching the first fatal blow to the Aristotelian-Ptolemaic world view, was also irrevocably soaked in that very same way of thinking, so Kuhn can be regarded as the last exponent of the philosophical tradition he was determined to reject. In

---

[1] U2, 'Pride (In the Name of Love)', from the album *The Unforgettable Fire*, October 1984 (single released in September 1984).

[2] See Friedman (1991), p. 1; for a criticism, see Gattei (2000) and (2001), pp. 818-822.

[3] See Carnap's letters to Kuhn, published in Reisch (1991); for the relationship between Carnap and Kuhn, see also Irzik & Grünberg (1995), Friedman (1991), (1992), (1993) and (2001), pp. 18-19, 22, 41-43 and 56, Earman (1993), Axtell (1993), Irzik (2002) and Gattei (2004), Chapter 5. In a recent article, Michael Friedman explicitly outlines his project, namely, to rescue Logical Positivism through a reassessment of Kuhn's philosophy: see his (2003).

*The Copernican Revolution* Kuhn wrote that Copernicus is like the middle point of a bend in a road: from one point of view it is the last point of one stretch of the road; from the other, it is the beginning of the next. In this sense, Kuhn is the last of the neo-positivists and, at the same time, the first of their successors. In particular, Kuhn's later 'linguistic turn' marks a clear step back into inductivism and justificationism, completely disregarding Popper's philosophical revolution and turning Kuhn's followers into foundationalist philosophers.

## 1  Kuhn on truth and realism

Having dealt with the complex relationship between Kuhn and Logical Positivism more broadly elsewhere,[4] in the present paper I shall focus on what I take to be a central issue for understanding both this relationship and the Popper-Kuhn debate. It is the notion of truth.

In the first edition of *The Structure of Scientific Revolutions* (1962) Kuhn hardly refers to the concept of truth: he has no need of it, not even in order to characterize and explain progress.[5] In the 1969 'Postscript' to the second edition of the book he introduces two arguments against the notion of truth implicit in the traditional view of progress as increasing verisimilitude.[6] Later, he relates his rejection of truth to incommensurability.[7]

---

[4]In Gattei (2004).

[5]See Kuhn (1962), pp. 170-173. In fact, in the first edition of *The Structure of Scientific Revolutions* the term 'truth' appears only in a quotation from Francis Bacon (on p. 18). In the closing pages of the book, Kuhn writes: 'The developmental process described in this essay has been a process of evolution *from* primitive beginnings — a process whose successive stages are characterized by an increasingly detailed and refined understanding of nature. But nothing that has been or will be said makes it a process of evolution *toward* anything' (ibidem, pp. 170f.). He then urges us to give up the concept itself in order to get rid of some of the problems that have afflicted the history of Western thought (p. 171):

> We are all deeply accustomed to seeing science as the one enterprise that draws constantly nearer to some goal set by nature in advance. But need there be such goal? Can we not account for both science's existence and its success in terms of evolution from the community's state of knowledge at any given time? Does it really help to imagine that there is some one full, objective, true account of nature and that the proper measure of scientific achievement is the extent to which it brings us closer to that ultimate goal? If we can learn to substitute evolution-from-what-we-know for evolution-toward-what-we-wish-to-know, a number of vexing problems may vanish in the process. Somewhere in this maze, for example, must lie the problem of induction.

[6]See Kuhn (1970b), pp. 205-207. On p. 206 he writes:

> A scientific theory is usually felt to be better than its predecessors not only in the sense that it is a better instrument for discovering and solving puzzles but also because it is somehow a better representation of what nature is really like. One often hears that successive theories grow ever closer to, or approximate more and more closely to, the truth. Apparently generalizations like that refer not to the puzzle-solutions and the concrete predictions derived from a theory but rather to its ontology, to the match, that is, between the entities with which the theory populates nature and what is 'really there'. Perhaps there is some other way of salvaging the notion of 'truth' for application to whole theories, but this one will not do.

[7]See Kuhn (1989), (1991), (1992), and (1993).

Indeed, as a consequence of Kuhn's later characterization of incommensurability, which is attributed both an inevitable and a functional role for the
growth of scientific knowledge, there is no need for the notions of 'truth' and
'approximation to the truth'. Kuhn has always opposed the correspondence
theory of truth and criticized its applications to the relation between scientific
theories and reality: as history can show, he says, there is[8]

> no theory-independent way to reconstruct phrases like 'really there'; the notion
> of a match between the ontology of a theory and its 'real' counterpart in nature
> ...seems to me illusive in principle. Besides, as a historian, I am impressed
> with the implausibility of the view. I do not doubt, for example, that Newton's
> mechanics improves on Aristotle's and that Einstein's improves on Newton's
> as instruments for puzzle-solving. But I can see in their succession *no coherent
> direction of ontological development.*

In its stead, he argues, a weaker concept of truth can be retained: we can talk
about truth only within the context of a given lexicon.[9] Indeed, within such
a lexical structure a claim may be properly said to be true or false, but that
does not hold for the system of categories embedded in the lexicon, which is
not itself capable of being true or false.[10] Truth is internal to lexicon in the
sense that its use is restricted to assessing claims made within the context of
the lexicon: truth claims in one lexicon are not relevant for those made in
another, nor can truth be applied to a lexicon itself. In other words, Kuhn
rejects the idea that the structure which constitutes the theory might reflect
the way the world is, independently from theory. The lexicon has the status of
a linguistic convention which may be judged only on the basis of how well it
serves a particular purpose, rather than how well it reflects reality. As a result,
though Kuhn assumes the existence of an independent reality throughout his
work, his position involves idealistic leanings.[11]

'Lexicons are not ...the sorts of things that can be true or false', writes
Kuhn:[12] their logical status is that of general meanings, that of a convention

---

[8]Kuhn (1970b), p. 206; italics added. Such expressions as 'zeroing in on the truth', or
'getting closer and closer to the truth' are meaningless as a consequence of incommensurability: see also Kuhn (1993), p. 330.

[9]The notion of truth involved may be provided, Kuhn suggests, by 'something like a
redundancy theory of truth' (Kuhn 1991, p. 8).

[10]Reaffirming his opposition to the traditional, correspondence theory of truth, Kuhn
sketches his position about the nature of truth in the context of the idea of variant lexical
structures. Scientific theories are the source of alternative sets of taxonomic categories which
are imposed on the world by theories. Such categories do not reflect reality: it is impossible
for them to do so — they are, at most, ways of ordering experience (taxonomy). The sets
imposed on the world depend on theories and vary with them. In a Kantian way (but with
mobile categories), the taxonomic categories of the scheme provide a structure for possible
experience. Thus we can say, following Kuhn's own image, that as theories change, the
world changes with them. See Kuhn (1991) and Sankey (1997b).

[11]See Hoyningen-Huene (1989a/1993), pp. 267-271, and (1989b); see also Sankey (1993),
(1997b), and (1997c).

[12]Kuhn (1993), p. 330. See Wittgenstein (1969), § 205: 'If the true is what is grounded,
then the ground is not *true*, nor yet false'; and '...why should the language-game rest on

that we can justify only in a pragmatic way. A lexicon marks the distance between the reality as described by a theory and the theory that describes it in different ways: 'Experience and description are possible only with the described and describer separated, and the lexical structure which marks the separation can do so in different ways, each resulting in a different, though never wholly different, form of life. Some ways are better suited to some purposes, some to others. But none is to be accepted as true or rejected as false; none gives privileged access to a real, as against an invented, world. The ways of being-in-the-world which a lexicon provides are not candidate for true/false':[13] they are assessed on the basis of their ability to serve a particular function, not to reflect reality.

## 2   The background of Kuhn's position

Kuhn's position is rooted both in justificationism and in a particular way of posing problems that is typical of Wittgenstein and his followers.[14] Taken together, these two closely interwoven aspects work together and reinforce each other, enforcing the compartmentalization of knowledge and the limitation of rationality. One problem lies at the root of both of them: the problem of induction. Their entire development hinges on the assumption that the problem of induction cannot be solved. Once we understand that the problem of induction has been solved, and what the consequences of its solution to methodological issues and philosophy are, we shall see things from a radically different perspective.

From David Hume (1711-1776) onwards — but we might go as far back as Aristotle —, it has been asserted that there are two kinds of inference: deductive inference, which defines logic; and inductive inference, which defines the natural sciences.[15] The two apply, so to say, to different fields, and

---

some kind of knowledge?' (§ 477; see also § 559). According to Wittgenstein, a language game presents no gaps, since together with its possible moves it also defines the space which makes those very moves possible: just as the rules of the game define which moves belong to it, so the grammar of the language circumscribes what is meaningful. Nothing meaningful can therefore remain outside its boundaries and establish itself as a mark of the incompleteness of the language game (*incommensurability*). A game to which new rules are added is not a richer game, but simply a new game (*paradigm shift*). Therefore, a language game is autocriterial — like the sample standard metre preserved at the International Bureau of Weights and Measures of Sèvres, near Paris, it is not itself measurable, since it is not possible to measure what is to be the unit of measurement: its having a length cannot be ascertained, but it is a feature which displays itself in the way we use it when measuring (see Wittgenstein 1953, Part I, § 50 and § 241). 'If you tried to doubt everything you would not get as far as doubting anything. The game of doubting itself presupposes certainty' (Wittgenstein 1969, § 115; see also § 160, § 450, and § 625). Doubting the paradigm means, on the one hand, condemning oneself to silence; on the other, extending the practice of doubt beyond what it is reasonable (that is, meaningful) to doubt.

[13] Kuhn (1991), p. 12.

[14] Following Bartley's suggestion, we could call the latter the 'Wittgensteinian problematic': see Bartley (1990), Chapters 14f.

[15] 'Instead of being a faulty sort of deduction, induction is fundamental, defining science — just as deduction is fundamental, defining logic' (Bartley 1990, p. 219).

must not be confused: the problem of induction is simply dissolved once we learn not to apply the standards of deductive logic to judge inductive inference. Once we realize that the two principles cannot be unified, the task of the philosopher is simply that of describing and clarifying the standards of deductive and of inductive reasoning. Most positivists, while maintaining the unity of the sciences, accepted this 'methodological' division. Wittgenstein extended this approach: each discipline, or field, or 'language game', or 'form of life' is alleged to have its own standards, or principles, or 'logic', which need not conform to or be reducible to any other standards and which, again, is the special task of the philosopher to *describe* and *clarify* — but not at all to judge, defend or criticize.[16] There is no arguing or judging among disciplines: criticism, evaluation, and explanation are no longer proper philosophical aims. *Knowledge is essentially divided, and description is all that remains to the philosopher.* All he can do is to describe the logics, grammars, or first principles of the various kinds of discourse, and the many sorts of language games and forms of life in which they are embedded. *Philosophical critique is no longer of content, but of the application of criteria*: as Paul Feyerabend put it, all that is left are 'consolations for the specialist'.[17]

Regardless of Kuhn's own intentions, his philosophy drastically impoverishes the reasons, aim, and scope of philosophical critique. Confrontation is often banned, criticism discouraged. Philosophical and scientific values of truth and rationality are replaced with commitment to the dominant tradition and consensus within a community of experts.[18]

---

[16]See Wittgenstein (1953), part I, §66: 'don't think, but look!'; '...we may not advance any kind of theory. There must not be anything hypothetical in our considerations. We must do away with all *explanation*, and description alone must take its place' (§109); see also §89, and his (1969), §189. It is no accident that Wittgenstein had already used the term 'paradigm' to refer to the ruling principles of an activity very similar to Kuhnian 'normal science': see his (1953), Part I, §50 and §54.

[17]See Feyerabend (1970). 'Consolations for the Specialist' is the title of Feyerabend's critical remarks on Kuhn's paper delivered at the 1965 Bedford College Colloquium in London (see Kuhn 1970c; a revised and expanded version of Feyerabend's paper is his 1978). The affinities between Kuhn's position and Wittgenstein's are substantial: see, in particular, Wittgenstein (1921), §4.112; (1953), Part I, §109; and (1969), §189. To Wittgenstein, philosophy has no cognitive function — rather, it has a 'therapeutic' function (see his 1953, Part I, §§109, 133, and 255). The descriptive task that characterizes philosophy concerns the rules governing the use of our language, that is, the grammar of the terms that constitute it: 'description' refers to the description of language games, and it aims at showing the rules of those games and hence the structures that characterize them. Concerning rules, and not facts, description has an exemplary value. There is a close parallelism between the role of Kuhn's 'exemplars' ('or exemplary problem solutions') and Wittgenstein's 'examples': see Kuhn (1970b) and (1974) (both written in 1969, a crucial year for Kuhn's philosophical development), and Wittgenstein (1953), Part I, §§71 and 133.

[18]Despite Kuhn's talk of revolutions and acknowledgement of the existence and necessity of revolutionary periods in the growth of scientific knowledge, the notions of paradigm (or lexicon) and normal science dominate Kuhn's picture: they are required if we want to progress, they constitute the very essence of scientific enterprise. Just as for Kant's 'light dove' — that in her free flight feels the resistance of air and might think that she could fly much more easily in an empty space (see Kant 1781, p. 47) — air is not an annoying friction: it is what renders her very flight possible. So, for Kuhn, normal science is not an

By contrast, as Mark Notturno rightly notices,[19] Popper's solution to the problem of induction offers an account of how scientific knowledge can be objective and rational without being certain and without grounding itself upon expert opinion, consensus, and the solidarity of belief. By regarding criticism, not description, as the alternative to justification, it offers an account in which truth, and not power, is the key element.

The core difference between Popper and Kuhn is not about the possibility of falsification, incommensurability, or the existence of normal science. It is about the role of truth, the value of criticism, and the nature of the bond that unites scientists into a community. Popper and Kuhn agree that there is no objective criterion for truth, but Kuhn takes this to mean that truth plays no role at all in theory appraisal and theory choice, while Popper maintains that truth plays the role of a regulative idea. As a consequence, Kuhn characterizes the bond uniting scientists in terms of shared beliefs: since it is not possible to prove the truth of such beliefs, scientists cannot but commit themselves to them uncritically.[20] Popper, on the other hand, characterizes this bond in terms of the search for truth, believing that only truth and the critical attitude enable a scientific community to be an open society.

## 3  Faith in reason

According to Popper, all proposed sources of knowledge are fallible and epistemologically insufficient — but all are welcome, given that they can be criticized. Nothing is or needs to be justified: everything is criticized. Contrasted with Kuhn's, the perspective is opposite: 'Instead of positing infallible intellectual authorities to justify and guarantee positions, one may build a philosophical program for counteracting intellectual error. One may create an ecological niche for rationality.'[21]

In *The Logic of Scientific Discovery* Popper sharply separates the concepts of justification and criticism, thus eliminating the notion of justification from that of criticism.[22] But the attitude of rational argument cannot be grounded

---

annoying period but renders progress itself possible: 'What the tradition sees as eliminable imperfections in its rules of choice I take to be in part responses to the essential nature of science' (Kuhn 1977, p. 330).

[19] See Notturno (2000), Chapter 10, especially pp. 238f.

[20] In hindsight, the radical challenge of *The Structure of Scientific Revolutions* was not to rationality, but to realism: Kuhn's thrust was actually directed not so much against the rationality of theory appraisal and theory choice, as against the epistemic, or truthlike, character of the theories so chosen, since it is not possible to say that they are better approximations to the truth, that is reality.

[21] Bartley (1962/1984), pp. 112f. For a discussion of Bartley's criticism of Popper's views of rationality see my (2002a).

[22] Popper's original proposal (as developed in his 1935), was that a theory is scientific if and only if it can be overthrown with the help of experience, and that we gain theoretical knowledge from experience when and only when such revolutions occur. There is nothing explicit about corroboration, namely about the failure to refute hypotheses. However, in his later works (especially his 1963, Chapter 10) Popper claimed that corroboration *is* important, and not only enlightening as discovery and increasing of explanatory power

on rational argument. Critical rationalism ultimately relies upon an 'irrational faith in reason', a consequence of a moral decision in favour of rationalism: 'whoever adopts the rationalist attitude does so because he has adopted, consciously or unconsciously, some proposal, or decision, or belief, or behaviour; an adoption which may be called "irrational". . . . we may describe it as an irrational *faith in reason*'.[23]

For Popper, rationalism requires a complementary notion of reasonableness, that is 'an attitude of readiness to listen to critical arguments and to learn from experience'.[24] It is the moral core of Popper's fallibilism: having realized how little we know, not only must we be fully prepared to correct our mistakes, but we are also required to have doubts about our knowledge. The process of doubting must be a conscious *attitude* of openness to criticism, which has an individual and a social aspect. On the one hand, each participant in the game of critical discussion is required to be prepared to listen to criticism, to be able to accept criticism, to practice self-criticism, and to engage in mutual criticism with others. On the other, once a subjective attitude or moral stance has been adopted by the individuals, reasoning must be conceived as a social process of intersubjective confrontation.

---

of a hypothesis. Corroboration thus became even *essential* to science, since it constitutes an encouragement to our research: not only should a good theory be capable of being refuted, but also it should not be refuted too soon. We want positive evidence before we get negative evidence, so as to be assured that knowledge grows. With that, Popper changed his view of science from a theory of conjectures and refutations to a theory of conjectures, corroborations, and refutations. As Joseph Agassi correctly remarked, 'either Popper assigns no value to positive evidence *qua* positive evidence, or he is in the same boat as the inductive philosophers who cannot bring positive evidence to support their theories of positive evidence' (Agassi 1968, p. 27). If our aim is to learn from experience, Popper's second thoughts are redundant: we learn from experience by repeatedly positing explanatory hypotheses and refuting them experimentally, thus approximating the truth by stages. Corroborations are entirely irrelevant, they have no epistemological significance. On this, see Miller (1994), p. 120. On the contrary, testing matters and bears methodological significance. For a more detailed discussion, see Gattei (2002b).

[23] Popper 1945/1966, Chapter 24, § II. See also Popper (1935/1959), Chapter I, § 4: 'Thus I freely admit that in arriving at my proposals I have been guided, in the last analysis, by value judgments and predilections. But I hope that my proposals may be acceptable to those who value not only logical rigour but also freedom from dogmatism; who seek practical applicability, but are even more attracted by the adventure of science, and by discoveries which again and again confront us with new and unexpected questions, challenging us to try out new and hitherto undreamed-of answers"; and Chapter V, especially § § 29f., where he discusses the acceptance of basic statements in terms of decisions; and Popper (1930-1933), Zweiter Teil, Frag. VII (p. 395): 'We thus share the conventionalist standpoint that the ultimate foundation of all knowledge ought to be sought in an act of free determination, that is, in the setting of a goal that cannot, in its turn, be further rationally grounded. And this is, though in a different form, Kant's idea of the primacy of practical reason' (my translation).

[24] Popper (1945/1966), Chapter 24, § I. The very realization of this would have saved much time for those who become prisoners of unending discussions about naïve, sophisticated, or methodological falsificationism, whose overdetailed writings 'may or may not give an image similar to Sterne's detailed and chaotic but rather charming picture of inept provincial life' (Agassi 1971, p. 323). Moreover, if we ignore the ethical character of Popper's reasoning, we risk reducing a remarkable system of ideas to a soulless body of unsolved problems.

Reasoning is engaging in communication with others; it requires non-epistemic values of social conduct. Central among these is the moral imperative to take others and their arguments seriously, that is, to respect them, to be ready not only to allow differences to exist, but to try to learn from them. Popper chooses reason primarily because of its beneficial consequences: rationalism comprises a set of principles that are both epistemological and ethical, and set the social and political rules for the human cooperation necessary for the acquisition of knowledge.

When we argue in favour or against something, we have already adopted or accepted a rational attitude, no matter how tentatively. Rationality is just a word to describe the correct way of finding out what is going on by using unlimited criticism. It has nothing to do with discovering thoughts or assuming stances; it does not allow us to follow a procedure that would be 'right' and would lead us to the desired results. *Reason is the negative faculty of relentless criticism.* Do we wish to become more rational or less rational? Once we accept it this way, we are already rational to some degree. After asking, we can go one way or the other, but the very ability to ask it tells us that we are.

## 4 Rationality without foundations

The appropriate standards of criticism are not those that appeal to justification, but those that appeal to truth.[25] As soon as we give up the idea that we can justify our theories, the epistemic problem becomes the problem not of what to believe, but of how to criticize our beliefs. While traditional philosophy regards the justification of beliefs as the goal, and the critical method a way of reaching it,[26] for Popper the goal is truth, and it is the method of investigation itself that is rational. Rationality, in other words, is not a property of knowledge, but a task for researchers: being rational means nothing but being willing to appeal to reason and arguments, as opposed to violence and force, to resolve our disputes. It requires no foundation, no grounding upon expert opinion or consensus. It needs only critical dialogue.

The history of Western philosophy is marked by attempts to provide our knowledge with a bedrock foundation. The twentieth century opened with profound crisis in both mathematics and physics: the foundations of these disciplines were shaken and so was the entire edifice of science. More than ever, perhaps, philosophers witnessed the crisis of foundationalism and tried to respond to it. Some of them have concluded that scientific knowledge is unjustified and hence irrational after all; some others — indeed, the majority — have opted for retaining the idea that scientific knowledge is justified, but for weakening either the idea of truth as correspondence with reality or the idea of justification. Neither of these responses frees itself from the ghost of foundationalism. Popper offers an alternative.

---

[25]See Notturno (2000), especially Chapter 5.
[26]That is why, for example, errors are often regarded as something to be avoided and not as something we can learn from.

The crisis of foundationalism has no implication for truth. It does not show that truth does not exist, and it does not show that it is solidarity and consensus. It shows that — as Socrates beautifully said — we are living in the twilight zone between knowledge and ignorance, where the views that we hold may be true, but where we are unable to know that they are. The failure of foundationalism is not the failure of epistemology: however difficult to reach, Socrates' twilight zone between knowledge and ignorance is an ideal well worth holding on to.

Popper's proposal is that of a *rationality without foundations*. Like the foundationalists and the irrationalists he believed that we must, in science, ultimately make some sort of unjustified decision. Indeed, he saw the rational attitude as a moral obligation and as a clear option against violence, deeming both dogmatism and voluntarist irrationalism to be irresponsible.[27] It is an attitude of dialogue, accepted with the full awareness of the difficulty of such a task.[28] Those who accept it do so because, consciously or unconsciously, they have adopted a proposal, or decision, like an 'irrational faith in reason': a minimal concession to irrationalism that cannot be determined by argument, even though we can argue in its favour — by explaining its consequences, for instance. It may be assisted by arguments, and we can assess the potential consequences of the decision. It is not, however, 'determined' by such consequences, and remains the responsibility of the individual.[29]

The problem of rationality is perhaps the most important of philosophical problems and, in a sense, the core of philosophy itself. It concerns the choice of one's principles and values, says Popper; it concerns the choice of one's lifestyle, says Agassi.[30] Rationality is a part of our way of life, and that goes alike for the rationalist and the irrationalist. What we can decide is whether we like it or not, whether we wish to drive it to its limit and expand it, or take it as it comes and be content, or even try to avoid and repress it and then succeed to some measure.

The solution to the problem of rationality is the very starting point of every philosophical approach, the very choice of one's lifestyle. Popper's approach to philosophy is his solution to the problem of rationality: his whole life is

---

[27]See Artigas (1999) and Agassi (2003), Chapter 1.3.

[28]Believing in reason is not sufficient; we must put it into action and practise it — particularly with people whose views and styles are different from, and therefore more of a challenge to, our own. That is the first way we have to respect others (and not merely tolerate them), that is, to allow them to make a difference to us, to affect our views and to have an impact on our own lives.

[29]'The choice before us is not simply an intellectual affair, or a matter of taste. It is a moral decision .... For the question whether we adopt some more or less radical form of irrationalism, or whether we adopt that minimum concession to irrationalism which I have termed "critical rationalism", will deeply affect our whole attitude towards other men, and towards the problems of social life' (Popper 1945/1966, Chapter 24, § III).

[30]See, for example, Agassi (1982), (1988a), and (1990). But see also the Introduction to Popper (1994). Important choices in life, such as philosophical viewpoints and ethical standards, are not usually the result of argument or logical reflection any more than scientific theories are the result of sense observation.

the very embodiment of his understanding of rationality and his solution to its fundamental problem.[31]

Traditional epistemology sets itself the task of finding what it calls the foundations of our knowledge, that is, a (restricted) body of knowledge that is absolutely certain and from which we can obtain the rest in a simple and straightforward fashion. On the contrary, 'any decision against methods creating certainty will be at the same time a decision against the acceptance of foundations of knowledge ... ; *it will be a decision in favour of a form of knowledge that possesses no foundation.* And it will therefore also be a decision to leave the traditional path of epistemology and to build up knowledge in an entirely new fashion'.[32] Popper showed that there are at least two possible forms of life, which are connected with two forms of knowledge. The choice between them involves one's personal responsibility, and must therefore be made individually.

We are confronted with a decision that will affect our whole approach to philosophy and life in general. And since the situation cannot be resolved by any proof but only on the basis of our demands and preferences, we have to give up the desire of certainty, the wish to escape our responsibilities. 'Reason also is choice', wrote John Milton:[33] the very act of reasoning implies that of a choice. We are called upon to decide what we like better. Our choice in favour of reason does not guarantee that we will be successful in our search for the truth, nor in the discovery of our errors. It does not even necessarily lead to the avoidance of violence.[34] Why be rational, then? Maybe just because we do not want to give up, or voluntarily limit, the use of our intellect. We are free to make the best use of our freedom. It is up to us to leave us the freedom to arrange our lives in the manner we find most congenial. Our choice has therefore an inescapable ethical nature: 'epistemology, or the structure of the knowledge we accept, is grounded upon an ethical decision'.[35]

---

[31]Indeed, we may read Popper's theory of rationality and freedom as an attempt to maintain a coherence between the political and the epistemological: see the story of his struggle with problems, studded with failures and successes, as told in Hacohen (2000).

[32]Feyerabend (1961), pp. 55f.

[33]Milton (1667/1674), Book III, 108. Of course, not deciding is already a decision, but of the worst kind.

[34]Of course, it may lead to these things — but it also may not, and faith in reason may become important precisely when it does not.

[35]Feyerabend (1961), p. 56.

# Bibliography

Agassi, J. (1968). 'Science in Flux: Footnotes to Popper'. In R. S. Cohen & M. W. Wartofsky, editors (1968), pp. 293-323. *Proceedings of the Boston Colloquium for the Philosophy of Science, 1964-1966. In Memory of Norwood Russell Hanson*. Dordrecht: D. Reidel Publishing Company. Reprinted in Agassi, J. (1975). *Science in Flux*, pp. 9-39. Dordrecht & Boston MA: D. Reidel Publishing Company.

———— (1971). 'Tristram Shandy, Pierre Menard, and All That: Comments on *Criticism and the Growth of Knowledge*. *Inquiry* **14**, pp. 152-164. Reprinted as 'Kuhn and His Critics: Rational Reconstruction of the Ant Heap'. In J. Agassi (1988a), pp. 315-328.

———— (1982). 'In Search of Rationality — A Personal Report'. In P. Levinson, editor (1982) pp. 237-248. *In Pursuit of Truth. Essays on the Philosophy of Karl Popper on the Occasion of His 80th Birthday*. Atlantic Heights NJ: Humanities.

———— (1988a). *The Gentle Art of Philosophical Polemics: Selected Reviews and Comments*. La Salle IL: Open Court.

———— (1990). *The Siblinghood of Humanity. An Introduction to Philosophy*. Delmar NY: Caravan Books. 2nd edition 1991.

———— (2003). *Science and Culture*. Dordrecht, Boston MA, & London: Kluwer Academic Publishers.

Artigas, M. (1999). *The Ethical Nature of Karl Popper's Theory of Knowledge*. Berne: Peter Lang AG.

Axtell, G. S. (1993). 'In the Tracks of the Historicist Movement. Re-assessing the Carnap-Kuhn Connection'. *Studies in History and Philosophy of Science* **24**, pp. 119-146.

Bartley, III, W. W. (1962). *The Retreat to Commitment*. New York: Alfred A. Knopf. 2nd edition 1984. La Salle IL: Open Court.

———— (1990). *Unfathomed Knowledge, Unmeasured Wealth: On Universities and the Wealth of Nations*. La Salle IL: Open Court.

Earman, J. (1993). 'Carnap, Kuhn, and the Philosophy of Scientific Methodology'. In Horwich (1993), pp. 9-36.

Feyerabend, P. K. (1961). *Knowledge without Foundations*. Two Lectures Delivered on the Nellie Heldt Lecture Fund. Oberlin OH: Oberlin College.

———— (1970). 'Consolations for the Specialist'. In Lakatos & Musgrave (1970), pp. 197-230.

———— (1978). 'Kuhns Struktur wissenschaftlicher Revolutionen. Ein Trostbüchlein für Spezialisten?' In P. K. Feyerabend (1978), pp. 153-204. *Der Wissenschaftstheoretische Realismus und die Autorität der Wissenschaften: Ausgewählte Schriften*. Braunschweig: Friedrich Vieweg & Sohn.

Friedman, M. (1991). 'The Re-evaluation of Logical Positivism'. *Journal of Philosophy* **88**, pp. 505-523. Reprinted as 'Introduction' in Friedman (1999), pp. 1-14.

—— (1992). 'Philosophy and the Exact Sciences: Logical Positivism as a Case Study'. In J. Earman, editor (1992), pp. 84-98. *Inference, Explanation, and Other Frustrations. Essays in the Philosophy of Science*, Los Angeles: University of California Press.

—— (1993). 'Remarks on the History of Science and the History of Philosophy'. In Horwich (1993), pp. 37-54.

—— (1999). *Reconsidering Logical Positivism*. Cambridge & elsewhere: Cambridge University Press.

—— (2001). *Dynamics of Reason*. Stanford: CSLI Publications.

—— (2003). 'Kuhn and Logical Empiricism'. In T. Nickles, editor (2003), pp. 19-44. *Thomas Kuhn*, Cambridge & elsewhere: Cambridge University Press.

Gattei, S. (2000). Review of Friedman (1999). *Newsletter of The History of Philosophy of Science (HOPOS) Working Group* **5**, pp. 18f.

—— (2001). Review of Hacohen (2000). *The British Journal for the Philosophy of Science* **52**, pp. 815-825.

—— (2002a). 'The Ethical Nature of Karl Popper's Solution to the Problem of Rationality'. *Philosophy of the Social Sciences* **32**, pp. 240-266.

—— (2002b). 'The Positive Power of Negative Thinking'. *Cladistics* **18**, pp. 446-452.

—— (2004). *Incommensurability, Rationality and the Search for Truth: A Critical Assessment of Thomas Kuhn's Philosophy in the Light of the Twentieth Century's Crisis of Foundationalism*. PhD dissertation, University of Bristol.

Hacohen, M. H. (2000). *Karl Popper – The Formative Years, 1902-1945. Politics and Philosophy in Interwar Vienna*. New York: Cambridge University Press.

Horwich, P., editor (1993). *World Changes. Thomas Kuhn and the Nature of Science*. Cambridge MA & London: MIT Press.

Hoyningen-Huene, P. (1989a). *Die Wissenschaftsphilosophie Thomas S. Kuhns: Rekonstruktion und Grundlagenprobleme*. Braunschweig: Friedrich Vieweg & Sohn. English translation, 1993. *Reconstructing Scientific Revolutions: Thomas S. Kuhn's Philosophy of Science*. Chicago & London: University of Chicago Press.

—— (1989b). 'Idealist Elements in Thomas Kuhn's Philosophy of Science'. *History of Philosophy Quarterly* **6**, pp. 393-401.

Irzik, G. (2002). 'Carnap and Kuhn: A Belated Encounter'. In P. Gärdenfors, J. Wolenski, & K. Kijana-Placek, editors (2002), pp. 603-620. *In the Scope of Logic, Methodology and Philosophy of Science*. Dordrecht, Boston MA, & London: Kluwer Academic Publishers.

Irzik, G. & Grünberg, T. (1995). 'Carnap and Kuhn: Arch Enemies or Close Allies?' *The British Journal for the Philosophy of Science* **46**, pp. 285-307.

Kant, I. (1781). *Kritik der reinen Vernunft*. Riga: Verlag Johann Friedrich Hartknoch. 2nd edition 1787. English translation by N. Kemp Smith 1929. *Immanuel Kant's Critique of Pure Reason*. London & elsewhere: Macmillan. New edition, with an introduction by H. Caygill, 2003. New York: Palgrave Macmillan.

Kuhn, T. S. (1962). *The Structure of Scientific Revolutions*. Chicago & London: University of Chicago Press. 2nd edition 1970.

——— (1970a). *The Structure of Scientific Revolutions*. 2nd edition. Chicago & London: University of Chicago Press.

——— (1970b). 'Postscript–1969'. In Kuhn (1970a), pp. 174-210.

——— (1970c). 'Logic of Discovery or Psychology of Research?' In Lakatos & Musgrave (1970), pp. 1-23.

——— (1974). 'Second Thoughts on Paradigms'. In F. Suppé, editor (1974), pp. 459-482. *The Structure of Scientific Theories*. Urbana, Chicago, & London: University of Illinois Press. 2nd edition 1977.

——— (1977). *The Essential Tension. Selected Studies in Scientific Tradition and Change*. Chicago & London: University of Chicago Press.

——— (1989). 'Possible Worlds in History of Science'. In S. Allén, editor (1989), pp. 9-32. *Possible Worlds in Humanities, Arts and Sciences. Proceedings of Nobel Symposium 65*. Berlin: Walter de Gruyter & Co.

——— (1991). 'The Road Since Structure'. In A. Fine, M. Forbes, & L. Wessels, editors (1991), pp. 3-13. *PSA 1990: Proceedings of the 1990 Biennial Meeting of the Philosophy of Science Association*, Volume 2. East Lansing MI: Philosophy of Science Association.

——— (1992). *The Trouble with the Historical Philosophy of Science*. An Occasional Publication of the Department of the History of Science, Harvard University. Cambridge MA: Harvard University.

——— (1993). 'Afterwords'. In Horwich (1993), pp. 311-341.

Lakatos, I. & Musgrave, A. E., editors (1974). *Criticism and the Growth of Knowledge*. Cambridge: Cambridge University Press.

Miller, D. W. (1994). *Critical Rationalism. A Restatement and Defence*. Chicago & La Salle. Open Court Publishing Company.

Milton, J. (1667). *Paradise Lost. A Poem Written in Ten Books*. London: Peter Parker, Robert Boulter, & Matthias Walker. 2nd edition 1674. *Paradise Lost. A Poem, in Twelve Books*. London: S. Simmons.

Notturno, M. A. (2000). *Science and the Open Society. The Future of Karl Popper's Philosophy*. Budapest: Central European University Press.

Popper, K. R. (1930-1933). *Die beiden Grundprobleme der Erkenntnistheorie*. First published 1979. Edited by T. E. Hansen. Tübingen: J. C. B. Mohr (Paul Siebeck). 2nd edition 1994.

——— (1935). *Logik der Forschung*. Wien: Julius Springer Verlag. English translation, 1959. *The Logic of Scientific Discovery*. London: Hutchinson.

——— (1945). *The Open Society and Its Enemies*. London: George Routledge & Sons. 5th edition 1966. London: Routledge & Kegan Paul.

——— (1963). *Conjectures and Refutations. The Growth of Scientific Knowledge*. London: Routledge & Kegan Paul. 5th edition 1989. London: Routledge.

——— (1994). *The Myth of the Framework. In Defence of Science and Rationality*. London & New York: Routledge.

Reisch, G. A. (1991). 'Did Kuhn Kill Logical Empiricism?' *Philosophy of Science* **58**, pp. 264-277.

Sankey, H. (1993). 'Kuhn's Changing Concept of Incommensurability'. *The British Journal for the Philosophy of Science* **44**, pp. 759-774. Reprinted in Sankey (1997a), pp. 21-34.

——— (1997a). *Rationality, Relativism and Incommensurability*. Aldershot: Ashgate.

——— (1997b). 'Kuhn's Ontological Relativism'. In Sankey (1997a), pp. 42-65.

——— (1997c). 'Taxonomic Incommensurability' In Sankey (1997a), pp. 66-80.

Wittgenstein, L. J. J. (1921). 'Logisch-philosophische Abhandlung'. *Annalen der Naturphilosophie* **14**, 1921, pp. 185-262. English translation by D. F. Pears & B. F. McGuinness, 1961. *Tractatus Logico-Philosophicus*. London: Routledge & Kegan Paul.

——— (1953). *Philosophical Investigations*. Oxford: Basil Blackwell.

——— (1969). *On Certainty*. Oxford: Basil Blackwell.

# 30

# Is Popper's Philosophy Anti-Foundationalist?

## Hubert Cambier

## 1 Introduction

Karl Popper presented his philosophy as a choice and a commitment in favour
of reason, and claimed that this choice and this commitment were themselves
rational. From a philosophical point of view, such a claim is highly problematic, however. It is not enough to say that such a choice is the only way to
regulate the relations between individuals who, too often, have the tendency
to settle their quarrels by violence, nor that it is the most efficient way to
make progress in scientific research. The choice in favour of reason must itself
be rationally founded. At least, this is what Karl-Otto Apel has emphasized
since the beginning of the 1970s, reminding us that any choice which was not
rationally founded would be arbitrary, or, to put it even more bluntly, an
irrational one (1973, T.2; 1980, pp. 262ff.). He was thus directly arguing with
Hans Albert who, a few years before, had denounced such an approach, and
emphasized that the originality of Popper lay precisely in his rejection of the
foundation which has led most of the great philosophies into deadlock (1968,
Chapter 1, § 2). For Albert, foundationalism cannot escape the challenge of
what he calls the 'Münchhausen trilemma': it must choose between either an
infinite regress — the necessity to go further and further back in the search
for foundations —, or a logical circle in the deduction — statements are used
in the process that are themselves in need of foundation —, or a dogmatic
breaking-off of the process at a particular point — which involves an arbitrary
suspension of the principle of sufficient reason. None of these possibilities offers even the beginnings of a solution. It has simply to be accepted, explains
Albert, that a rationalist philosophy cannot itself establish its own foundation (1968, Chapter 1). The value of the falsificationist/fallibilist conception
is to oblige us to accept this, without however falling into scepticism. The
Popperian methodology shows us how scientific progress can be achieved —
and is indeed achieved; the same methodology gives us guidelines with which
to organize our societies so as to ensure that freedom and all our rational
values can become reality.

It is not my intention in this paper to go deeper into this dispute. I referred
to it simply in order to stress that both Apel and Albert, the first criticizing

Popper and the other defending him, take as their starting point the assumption that his philosophy is 'anti-foundationalist'. And this is, in fact, the way his philosophy is generally understood. To take another example: Malachi Hacohen in his book: *Karl Popper – The Formative Years* (2000), pp. 224-235, supports exactly the same point of view. Indeed we can say that there is a general consensus that a rejection of foundationalism is a basic feature of Popper's philosophy. Popper is read as an anti-foundationalist philosopher, as Ludwig Wittgenstein — correctly in the latter case — is seen to have been. The advantage, of course, is that this allows a bringing together of the philosophies of these two authors. Mistakenly, I should say, because — and this is the thesis that I shall defend here — Popper's philosophy is not anti-foundationalist. It is anti-justificationist, but it is not anti-foundationalist, and anti-justificationism should not be confused with anti-foundationalism.

What does this mean? Justification refers to a 'logic of justification', as opposed to a 'logic of investigation'. In this conception, presented initially by Hans Reichenbach (1938), pp. 6f., the epistemologist has to make a clear distinction between the way scientists carry out their investigations, and arrive at a discovery, and the way they present their results in a logically articulated form. The process of investigation is a very pragmatic one, a very contingent one also. It relies on the experience of the scientists, on the circumstances, on their psychologies; and sometimes simply on luck. Science, however, is more than that. A discovery has to be formulated as a proposition, or as a theory, and has to take place within the general architecture that characterizes the science at a given time. It is only at this moment that the epistemologist or the logician enters the stage. How is a theory organized? How are universal propositions ('laws') related to empirical ones ('experience')? How can we say that analytic propositions are true? How are synthetic propositions ('new knowledge') possible? Under which conditions can we say that these synthetic propositions are true, or false? All these questions, and many others, are at the core of most of the theories of knowledge — at least all those that, in one way or another, belong within the Kantian tradition. They are questions that refer to the way a proposition can or cannot be justified; they presume the existence of a logic of justification that imposes its rules and its standards on any discovery that claims to be acknowledged as a scientific contribution.

Justification, from this perspective, is a relation between propositions. Any kind of theoretical proposition, whether new or not, needs to be justified, based on well-identified rules of deduction or derivation. I do not wish to enter here the long-standing debate about the validity of rules of induction: the Vienna Circle members, in line with the whole empirical tradition, considered that these rules exist, and that they can be elaborated under the form of a logic of induction; Popper opposed them, and did not believe that such a logic would ever make sense. But this does not really affect the core of the present issue. The Vienna Circle considered that all empirical propositions should, ultimately, find their justification in initial, singular propositions — what they called 'protocol statements'. Popper criticized this approach, not so much because he refused their protocol statements — the basic statements he proposed in their stead were protocol statements formulated in a non-subjective way —, but because he opposed the doctrine that all propositions require justification — a doctrine that eventually leads to basic or ultimate propositions. Justificationism, in this sense, is the conception that all our knowledge, all our propositions, need to be justified by logical derivation from other propositions, which could be protocol statements, initial empirical propositions — this was the Vienna Circle doctrine — or self-evident propositions, axioms established a priori as true. Justificationism can be associated with an empirical conception of knowledge, such as that of the Vienna Circle; but this is not necessary. Justificationism is primarily linked with a logicist conception of knowledge.

Foundation refers to a different tradition. Founding a philosophy requires identifying a first principle on which that philosophy can hang. In that sense, most of the philosophies of the past can be said to have been foundationalist. Empirical, scientific knowledge has been considered as in need of some foundation, a task that falls within the specific remit of philosophers. Natural philosophies and political or moral philosophies have been formulated in order to meet this supposed need. The problem, however, is that these philosophies do not contain their own principles. They need to be founded in their turn, which could be done only by referring to another discipline, usually called metaphysics, or the knowledge of first principles. Would the knowledge of first principles suffice to found all knowledge? Many philosophers felt it necessary to go one step further, and to guarantee the value of this knowledge through some extra-philosophical reality, by some God, which could be only a non-deceiving God. Ultimately, it is this supra-reality that provides the foundation not only for all our knowledge but also for the world, for all the reality that we know. Of course, this supra-reality can take different forms, it does not necessarily have to be a God. But it has to be a reality that is more real than the day-to-day reality in which we live, if this supra-reality is to provide the foundation for our worldly reality.

For centuries, metaphysics has been the main instrument for addressing the question of the foundation of our knowledge or our values. Since Kant, it is no longer the only approach. For Kant, there was indeed a need to deepen our philosophical reflection, and to search for its foundations, but he did so by refusing to look for it in another reality, in a reality that our human faculties do not have the capacity to know, at least in the usual meaning that we give to the word 'know'. Keeping the exercise of our reason within the limits of what our reason can achieve does not mean, however, that we should accept Humean scepticism, and that we should give up trying to establish the foundations of our knowledge. We can use our powers of reason to identify the transcendental conditions — the conditions existing in all human beings, considered as finite beings — of our knowledge. Ultimately, these conditions refer to a transcendental 'I', which alone can provide the foundations, that is, the necessary conditions of the categories of our understanding, and of the relation between our understanding and the phenomenal world that we perceive. This is the second way foundationalism can be understood. In this sense, the foundations do not refer to another world, another reality, beyond the present one, but to a philosophical and internal interrogation on the powers, the limitations, and the conditions of our reason.

Foundationalism can be associated with justificationism, but this is not necessary and is not always the case. Foundationalism, to use one of Schopenhauer's expressions, is a relation '*in re*', established 'in reality' or 'in things'. The search for first principles reflects the need to provide an ultimate explanation not only for this or that theory, but for all our knowledge, in the first place for the fact that we can know, and that our knowledge, at least sometimes, is true. Justificationism is a relation between propositions, it is an interrogation about what is said, '*de dicto*'. Foundationalism leads either to a metaphysical investigation, or, on the path opened by Kant, to transcendental search; justificationism is a question of logic or language analysis. *In fine*, justificationism could lead to the question of the choice of a logic, or of a language, and, when this logic is defined as reflecting the structure of the world, or the laws of thought, it could lead to foundationalist research. But it does not necessarily have to go as far as that. The Vienna Circle members were justificationist without being foundationalist; Popper was opposed to justificationism, but inclined — mildly at the beginning, more and more openly later — towards foundationalism. That is what I should like to show in this paper. But that will require proceeding step by step.

## 2   Anti-justificationism

It was W. W. Bartley, III — in his book *The Retreat to Commitment* (1962) — who first defended the point of view that one of the important features of the philosophy of Karl Popper is its 'non-justificational approach'. And it is the linking of this non-justificationist approach with an anti-authoritarian project that represents the main innovation of this philosophy. There are plenty of examples of philosophies, he explained, that define themselves as critical, or want to escape dogmatism. But all philosophies come up against the problem of what he terms an 'ultimate commitment'. All our propositions should be justified, which can be done only by using further propositions, which in their turn, also need to be justified. The truth of our propositions is therefore dependent on other propositions, whose truth cannot be justified without some first, fundamental propositions, whose truth can only be accepted, or asserted. This problem is unsolvable. The importance of Popper's philosophy, says Bartley, is that it shows that we do not have to solve it, simply because it is a false dilemma. We do not need to look for first, initial, true propositions. For Popper, all our propositions are hypotheses; they are hypotheses with which we should confront reality. In some cases, this confrontation will falsify the hypothesis we have just elaborated, and we shall need to propose a new one; in other cases, we shall accept it provisionally. We do not need first, true, hypotheses. The endless process can be stopped without hesitation. The real process of knowledge is a process of conjectures and refutations. And it does not make sense to look for the justification of a conjecture: either it passes the test or it does not pass it. There is nothing to be looked for beyond this.

Popper readily endorsed this interpretation of his philosophy. All of us remember the pages he devoted to this issue in *Realism and the Aim of Science* (1983, Part I, § 2). The critical approach, he maintains, endorses the claims of both scepticism and rationalism. With the sceptics, Popper acknowledges that we 'cannot give any positive justification or any positive reason for our theories and our beliefs ... we cannot give any positive reasons for holding our theories to be *true*' (Part I, § 2). And he adds: 'the belief that we can give such reasons, and should seek for them is itself neither a rational nor a true belief, but one that can be shown to be without merit' (ibidem). Does that mean that Popper's philosophy can be defined as a variant of scepticism? No. Popper himself rejects this interpretation by stressing that, whilst his philosophy does not consider that it is possible to find any justification, this does not imply that all propositions and all beliefs can be regarded as equally valid. Some of our propositions, he says, can be considered closer to the truth than others, and it is the role of the theory of knowledge to provide us with a methodology that enables us to discriminate between them. The theory of falsification provides this; it does not give any criteria to establish the truth of a proposition; but at least it tells us when a proposition is false. And if we can say that some propositions are false, then at least we have a basis on which we can build and develop our knowledge. This knowledge will always have to be reviewed, corrected, some of the propositions we thought well-corroborated will show themselves to be false, at a later stage, but this is the practical process of science. What is important is that, by showing the possibility of identifying what is false, we can refute the sceptical point of view, which maintains that whether true or false, all our propositions are of equal worth.

In this sense, the Popperian theory of knowledge is anti-justificationist. All our propositions are problematic; it is pointless to look for any initial or basic propositions, whose truth can be established, and on whose truth all the truths of the others depend. Following here the position of Otto Neurath, Popper states explicitly that none of our propositions is privileged or can declare itself immune from any kind of falsification. What applies to universal laws applies equally to basic statements.

This leads, however, to some difficulties. If all our propositions must always be submitted to criticism, if all our propositions are at best provisionally corroborated, how can we be sure that we know something? By expanding the fallibilism of our reason, Popper runs the risk of falling into scepticism and relativism. He therefore felt — as is apparent already in *Logik der Forschung* (1935) — obliged to temper the harsh logical line of his theory of knowledge with softer pragmatic considerations. *De jure*, there are no privileges accorded to the basic statements; in practice, some basic statements are considered as good as true — building on what, at a given time, the scientific community agrees to regard as true. His most classic examples show that clearly: the validity of the universal law 'all swans are white', can never be established; but it is enough to find one black swan to falsify it. For Popper, one empirical fact falsifies any universal law, however corroborated that law may be. This means that, in practice, it is not so difficult to identify facts, and to accept that the basic statements which express them are true. From the epistemological point of view, this truth is provisional, and could always be challenged and submitted to further questioning; in practice, these basic statements operate as true propositions, since they correspond to the facts they express. To avoid scepticism and relativism, Popper has recourse to pragmatism, but, it must be said, at the expense of the consistency of his theory of knowledge.

## 3 Anti-foundationalism

If we agree that the Popperian theory of knowledge aspires to be anti-justificationist, should we also recognize that his philosophy is anti-foundationalist? At first sight, it seems that this could very well be the case, at least as long as we look at the first works of Popper — the ones he wrote in the 1930s. In *Die beiden Grundprobleme der Erkenntnistheorie* (1930-1933, published in 1979) as well as in *Logik der Forschung* (1935), he presents his theory of knowledge by clearly demarcating himself from other approaches such as:

the one defended by Descartes: we have to start from some first truths, that are clear and self-evident;

the one defended by Kant: all our knowledge relies on some main categories, produced by reason, and dependent on the subject;

the one defended by Hume and by many members of the Vienna Circle: all our knowledge relies on ideas that refer directly to experience.

We could therefore be tempted to say that, by criticizing these three philosophies, Popper is defending an anti-foundationalist point of view. He would, according to this interpretation, consider it to be wrong to look for any foundation on which we can strongly establish our knowledge — as well as our theory of knowledge — be it in first and self-evident truths, in the subject, or in experience. We should accept the facts that our knowledge and our theory of knowledge are both problematic; our knowledge is perhaps a priori, in its form, but being a priori in this way does not imply that it is a priori valid.

Such an interpretation raises problems as soon as we confront it with the later works of Popper. At the beginning of the 1960s indeed (1961, see also Popper 1972), and initially much to the surprise of his friends, colleagues, and students, Popper undertook to expand the scope of his philosophy by applying the principles of his theory of knowledge to evolutionary theory. This is not the right place to discuss the question of Popper's Darwinism — his approach is in fact closer to neo-Lamarckism than to neo-Darwinism. What is important here is that, in establishing a direct link between the cognitive processes of all living beings — beginning with the amoeba and culminating with Einstein — and the logical theory of knowledge he presented initially in his *Logik der Forschung*, Popper pursues a thought that goes far beyond the question of the logical justification of the Darwinian laws. In fact, he engages his philosophy in what can only be considered as an attempt to establish the foundations of his theory of knowledge. This new thought is openly presented as metaphysical; it makes use of biological observations and considerations, but clearly the biology here establishes only the background. A metaphysical theory means, for Popper, the setting up of a research programme for the sciences; but by presenting such a theory, he contributes also to the establishment of the foundations of these sciences. What was until then presented as *falsificationism*, or since *The Open Society and Its Enemies* (1945) as the theory of *conjectures and refutations*, became more and more the *methodology of trial and error*. The term *trial and error* appears at the beginning of 'What Is Dialectic? (1940), but rarely elsewhere before the 1960s; — Popper found it, indeed, in the Introduction to Bernard Shaw's *Back to Methuselah* (1921), which deals precisely with the evolutionist issue, in a neo-Lamarckian spirit. But what is important here is not the introduction of a new expression to characterize his theory of knowledge, but the fact that this expression designates both the activity of living beings — the way they organize themselves to survive and to adapt to a selective environment — and the process of the growth of knowledge, which we can see, in its most sophisticated form, in the sciences. From the beginning of the 1960s, science will be presented as a continuation, critically aware of its methods, of a process that is fundamentally the process of life. 'All knowledge is problem solving', he will say later ; as indeed life itself is also problem solving: *Alles Leben ist Problemlösen* (1994). This means that life — or problem solving — in fact provides the general principle for understanding the methodology and development of science; and it provides also, in the metaphysics Popper is working hard to formulate at this time, the foundation for this methodology, or for his theory of knowledge. The sciences, the methodology of science, and the theory of knowledge, are part of the life process — a process they lead to its most developed form. Sciences, the methodology of science, and the theory of knowledge, are founded on this process; and it is in this process that they find their ultimate foundation. If this is indeed the position that Popper defends in the 1960s and after, then we have no choice but to recognize that the previous interpretation — which considered Popper's philosophy as anti-foundationalist — does not correspond to his texts. And from the fact that it is wrong to say that Popper, in the 1960s, was anti-foundationalist, we can conclude that he was not anti-foundationalist in the 1930s either. To think differently would require the identification in the Popper's intellectual life of two different and even, on such a key issue as foundationalism, antagonistic philosophies, which would be a very costly hypothesis. Before coming to that, it would be better to reconsider our previous analysis, and consider whether our conclusions might have been premature.

## 4  Back to the 1930s

We need to go back to the texts of the 1930s. The interpretation I should like to defend is that Popper did indeed criticize the approaches of Descartes, Hume, and Kant, but he did so not because he was anti-foundationalist — he was not — but for different reasons, which I can only briefly indicate here.

(1) The reason why Popper criticized Descartes is relatively easy to understand. Descartes defended the principle of building on some first ideas, which should be clear, simple and self-evident. But these ideas were, for him, guaranteed by God, who can be only a God of truth. Popper could certainly not follow Descartes on this path, which for him could be only a mixture of an appeal to an external authority and an uncritical way of considering knowledge. Anti-justificationism and anti-authoritarian approaches adequately explain the opposition of Popper to Descartes and we do not need to see here any kind of anti-foundationalism.

(2) Why Popper criticized Hume and the Vienna Circle is also fairly obvious. For Popper, knowledge is not the product of experience alone; it does not proceed from experience, and its value cannot be reduced to what experience tells us. In fact, experience does have a function, and an important one, in his theory of knowledge. It is experience that falsifies, refutes a proposition. Experience is, as we could put it, the 'touchstone' of our propositions or hypotheses. But it was the same for Kant. The Popperian theory of knowledge is a rationalist one; it is a theory that keeps a place for experience, but in a subordinate way; it is a theory that opposes empiricism, because empiricism destroys all necessity, all true universality. This could sound at odds with many declarations expressed by Popper himself in the 1930s, as well as during the rest of his life. But it would not be too difficult to demonstrate that it is indeed the case. The difficulty lies here in the sometimes idiosyncratic use by Popper of some philosophical concepts, and also — but in that he is not alone — in the cross-over widespread in the Vienna Circle, of the notions of empiricism and positivism. Popper repeatedly criticized the positivists; but if we look more closely at these criticisms, we realize that, most of the time, the real target was empiricism and not positivism. I cannot develop this point further here. But what I think we can agree on is that, if Popper was an empiricist, it was in the way Kant was. In other words, he was not. This explains why he underlined his differences with Hume. Popper opposed the foundation of his theory of knowledge on experience, not because he was anti-foundationalist, but because he refused to be an empiricist, at least in the Humean way.

(3) Popper criticized Kant also. Why? Simply because when he read Kant, he approached him from the point of view of Jakob Friedrich Fries, and the interpretation Fries gave of the Kantian philosophy. Fries indeed questioned the foundations of the Kantian theory of knowledge, and emphasized the need to establish the categories on solid foundations. And these, as he saw them, could be found only in the psychology of human beings. This interpretation is shared by others. Hermann von Helmholtz also saw the Kantian categories as

features of human nature, and declared that it is the task of science to invest-igate them. It is this Kant, this 'psychologized' Kant, that Popper criticized. Or, in other words, what Popper refused in the Kantian philosophy is that it sends the truth of all our propositions back to the human subject — a human subject that Popper does not see as transcendental but as psychological. For Popper, this is subjectivism; which means, in a way, that it is also empiricism. A theory of knowledge, for him, cannot be established on empirical facts, or on empirical human nature. It needs to be objective and logical. What we could, at first sight, take as an anti-foundationalist approach is an anti-subjectivist one. This is a philosophical concern Popper has expressed repeatedly through-out his life. There is therefore no reason to reduce this anti-subjectivism to an anti-foundationalism that he has hardly ever presented as such.

We can therefore answer our question. Popper, in the 1930s, was not anti-foundationalist. He was indeed anti-Cartesian, rationalist opposed to empiri-cist, objectivist opposed to subjectivist. All these positions are important dimensions of his own philosophy, and he was to work on them, formulate them in a more systematic way in the 1950s — in the *Postscript to the Logic of Scientific Discovery* (Popper 1982a, 1982b, 1983) — and after. None of these positions implies that he was anti-foundationalist. He was indeed anti-justificationist, but this, as I tried to make clear at the beginning of this paper, is quite different. In the 1930s as well as later on, Popper, regularly, emphasized that we can never arrive at any first 'true' propositions, that the propositions that we know are always problematic. But in the 1930s as well as in the 1960s, for Popper, our knowledge itself, the very fact that we can know, is not itself problematic. The possibility of knowledge can be founded — and is already founded in *Die beiden Grundprobleme* — in biological reality. We can know, and our knowledge can meet reality, not, as Kant says, because we impose our categories of thinking on reality, but because we are a product of evolution, and it is due to evolution that we are cognitive organisms adapted to the reality we need to know or to act upon. In this, the position Popper defended in the 1930s, and in the 1960s or the 1970s, is fundamentally the same.

## 5  From the 1930s to the 1960s

There is a change however between the texts of the 1930s and the texts of the 1960s. In the 1930s, Popper was not anti-foundationalist, but did not feel the necessity to establish the foundations of his theory of knowledge. We find a few occurrences of his evolutionist conception in *Die beiden Grundprobleme* and in *Logik der Forschung*, but they are scarce and not systematic. After 1960, he seemed to consider that some foundation was necessary, and he worked hard to build his evolutionist theory of knowledge into a *Weltanschauung*, which begins with a definition of knowledge as a process of problem solving, but soon continues as a comprehensive theory of World 1 — the world of matter — leading to World 2 — the world of psychological processes — and then to World 3 — the world of objective theories and problems. There is a change there, not in the general orientation, but at least in the attention Popper devoted to the issue, which after 1960, clearly, becomes one of his central concerns.

The main problem Popper was confronted with was scepticism. In a way, he always opposed scepticism. In the 1930s, he thought that he could do it by proposing his theory of falsification. He argued that we cannot know when a proposition is true; but it is possible, at least from a logical point of view, to say that a proposition is false. In order to do so, the methodology requires submitting the hypotheses to the test of experience. At this time, Popper was fighting on two fronts, against scepticism but also against dogmatism. And to combat dogmatism, he relied, at least in a provisional way, on conventionalism and pragmatism. How do we know that we have a false proposition, and that on this basis — a negative one, but better than no basis at all — we can build authentic knowledge? In fact, we never know, because the falsification process rests on singular propositions that, themselves, can be questioned, and submitted to a falsification process that, in principle, can be endless. As we have seen above, the way devised by Popper to get out of this difficulty was to resort to pragmatism. The scientific community agrees, *hic et nunc*, to consider such and such a basic statement as valid. But this solution not only damages the logical consistency of his theory of knowledge, it is also a very fragile one.

This became apparent when Popper developed his thinking on moral issues. How can we know that what we consider to be our basic values are indeed values and that we should behave according to them? We cannot. All what we can do is to observe what are the consequences of our behaviour for social and human reality. But why should a particular value be preferred to others? Popper, at this time, tried once again to appeal to pragmatism. We should alleviate social sufferings, reduce the most obvious pains. Aiming at producing happiness, as the utilitarians say, is vain, and could be dangerous. The only utilitarianism that, for Popper, makes sense is a negative one. But the problem is the same: even if negative, utilitarianism must be founded on something. If not, we run the risk, once again, of falling into scepticism: a closed society would then be as good, or as bad, as an open one; promoting one's interest at the expense of the suffering of one's neighbours would be as good, or as bad, as trying to alleviate his pain. Reducing the most blatant evils, alleviating the most obvious suffering . . . all these expressions summarize the negative utilitarianism defended by Popper. They all, implicitly, refer to a human nature, to its biological — universally recognized — reality. This is the way in which he opposes scepticism. But it is also a temporary solution. To respond fully to scepticism, to respond to it both in the field of the theory of knowledge and in the field of ethics, Popper needs stronger arguments, philosophical ones. This requires a philosophical refinement of his philosophy. This is, in my opinion, the main reason why he decided to enter into metaphysics, a kind of thinking he had always, in the 1930s and the 1940s, strongly condemned. And it is also the reason why, having begun with an implicit, but not developed, foundationalist philosophy, he felt the need to develop explicitly the foundations on which his philosophy could be firmly established. In this, he followed Arthur Schopenhauer, a philosopher he always deeply respected. Both the theory of knowledge and morality need foundations. Schopenhauer provided these by calling in the biological-metaphysical reality of the Will. For Popper, such a theory is permeated with psychologism and subjectivism. For him, the fundamental reality is the natural — and objective — process of life. It is this biological and metaphysical reality that allows him to unify and to establish his philosophy, in all its dimensions, because it is life that gives the best refutation to scepticism, both in science and in practical actions. In this sense, there is indeed a change — some would say a turn — between the works of the 1930s and the works of the 1960s. It was started at the end of the 1940s — or the beginning of the 1950s. It was a metaphysical turn, an effort to provide foundations — biological-metaphysical ones, as Popper formulated them — to the theory of knowledge and to the philosophy of ethics elaborated earlier. And this was caused by the difficulties that Popper met in writing *The Open Society*, when he tried to establish the objectivity of values and of rationality — their transcendence *vis-à-vis* the subjective choices and decisions of individuals.

## 6  Back to the Introduction

If the philosophy of Popper is not the anti-foundationalist one it was thought to be, then the confrontation with the philosophy of Apel can be organized on a new basis. Both philosophers indeed place practical reason at the basis of theoretical reason; both of them have worked to provide foundations for the rational choice of reason. But the strategies used to establish these foundations are different. While Apel decided to follow the Kantian way, looking for the transcendental conditions of his *ethics of discussion*, Popper chose to take a more classical approach — the metaphysical one. How do these authors, each one with his own method, succeed in achieving their objectives — solving their problems? That is perhaps the best basis for a future — and more fruitful — dialogue.

# Bibliography

Albert, H. (1968). *Traktat über kritische Vernunft*. Tübingen: J. C .B. Mohr (Paul Siebeck). English edition, 1985. *Treatise on Critical Reason*. Princeton, Princeton University Press.

Apel, K.-O. (1973). *Transformation der Philosophie*. T.1: *Sprachanalytik, Semiotik, Hermeneutik*. T.2: *Das Apriori der Kommunikationsgemeinschaft*. Frankfurt/Main: Suhrkamp. References are to K.-O. Apel (1980). *Towards a Transformation of Philosophy*. London: Routledge & Kegan Paul.

Bartley, III, W. W. (1962). *The Retreat to Commitment*. New York: Alfred A. Knopf. 2nd edition 1984. La Salle and London: Open Court Publishing Company.

Hacohen, M. H. (2000). *Karl Popper – The Formative Years 1902-1945. Politics and Philosophy in Interwar Vienna*. Cambridge & elsewhere: Cambridge University Press.

Popper, K. R. (1930-1933). *Die beiden Grundprobleme der Erkenntnistheorie*. First published 1979. Edited by T. E. Hansen. Tübingen: J. C. B. Mohr (Paul Siebeck). 2nd edition 1994.

——— (1935). *Logik der Forschung*. Vienna.: Julius Springer Verlag. 10th edition 1994. Tübingen: J. C. B. Mohr (Paul Siebeck). English edition, 1959. *The Logic of Scientific Discovery*. London: Hutchinson.

——— (1940). 'What Is Dialectic?' *Mind* **49**, pp. 403-426. Paper read to a seminar at Canterbury University College, Christchurch, New Zealand, in 1937. Reprinted as Chapter 15 of Popper (1963).

——— (1945). *The Open Society and Its Enemies*. London: George Routledge & Sons. 5th edition 1966. London: Routledge & Kegan Paul.

——— (1961). 'Evolution and the Tree of Knowledge'. Herbert Spencer Lecture, University of Oxford. Reprinted as Chapter 7 of Popper (1972).

——— (1963). *Conjectures and Refutations. The Growth of Scientific Knowledge*. London: Routledge & Kegan Paul. 5th Edition 1989. London: Routledge.

——— (1972). *Objective Knowledge*. Oxford: Clarendon Press. 2nd edition 1979.

——— (1982a). *The Open Universe*. London: Hutchinson & Co.

——— (1982b). *Quantum Theory and the Schism in Physics*. London: Hutchinson & Co.

——— (1983). *Realism and the Aim of Science*. London: Hutchinson & Co.

——— (1994). *Alles Leben ist Problemlösen. Über Erkenntnis, Geschichte und Politik*. Munich & Zurich: R. Piper Verlag. English edition, 1999. *All Life Is Problem Solving*. London: Routledge.

Reichenbach, H. (1938). *Experience and Prediction. An Analysis of the Foundations and Structure of Knowledge*. Chicago: University of Chicago Press.

# 31

# Conceptual and Non-Conceptual Content and the Empirical Basis of Science

Robert Nola

## 1 Exposition of Popper's problem of the empirical basis of science

*1.1 The problem of an observational basis*

The topic of this paper concerns what Popper calls, in *The Logic of Scientific Discovery* (*LSD*), 'The Problem of the Empirical Basis' (this being the title of Chapter V). The empirical basis is to be found in observation statements; Popper calls these 'basic statements'. For our purposes we can treat these as the same. They commonly have the form of singular statements about 'observable' items, or they are restricted existential statements about 'observables'. What counts as an 'observable' need not concern us. As examples we can cite: 'the litmus paper turned red (at $t$)', or 'there is an $x$ in space-time region R, such that $x$ is a swan and $x$ is not-white'. These have a significant role in science; they are needed to show that a hypothesis, or theory, $H$, actually, or potentially, passes, or fails, some test. The concern of this paper is: on what grounds do we accept (believe, adopt) such basic statements?

If we use the hypothetico-deductive (H-D) method of test for $H$, then we compare the deductive consequences drawn from $H$ conjoined with auxiliary statements $A$, which will often include some basic statements, with yet other basic statements obtained independently by observation or experiment. However basic statements cannot, in turn, be tested in H-D fashion for two reasons: on this model we must conjoin them with some other auxiliary assumptions which may include further basic statements; and we must compare their deductive consequences with yet other basic statements that show that the deductive consequences pass or fail their test. Thus either some basic statements used in testing must be assumed to be true, or a regress of testing of basic statements threatens. To overcome these problems some assume that the observational basis of science is infallible. Like Popper we reject this; basic statements are contingent, empirically knowable, synthetic, and fallible.

*1.2 The regress*

The problem of a basis for knowledge in observation or experience has been
well known since Ancient Greek philosophy, particularly Sextus Empiricus'
*Outlines of Scepticism* with its account of the Five Modes of Agrippa. We
can extract from Agrippa the following trilemma, which faces any attempt
to justify our (observational) beliefs: either (i) the beliefs are unsupported,
or (ii) circularity arises in providing support, or (iii) a regress of reasons of
support arises. Popper mentions neither Sextus nor Agrippa but does cite the
1820s writings of Jakob Fries in posing what he calls 'Fries's trilemma', which
can be expressed as follows.

(A) Either we accept the statements of science dogmatically (cp. (i)), or we
justify them.

(B) A logical point: justification is a logical relation between statements, and
only statements.

(C) If one statement is to be justified by another, then a regress threatens (cp.
(iii)).

(D) Psychologism, which Popper describes as 'the doctrine that statements
can be justified not only by other statements but also by perceptual experience' (1959, § 25), has the regress stopping in non-propositional (immediate)
experience.

(E) Conclusion: a trilemma of dogmatism versus infinite regress versus psychologism.

Popper makes an additional point worth noting: 'the decision to accept
a basic statement, and to be satisfied with it, is causally connected with our
experiences — especially with our perceptual experiences' (ibidem, § 29). So
we may add:

(F) Our perceptual experience is a cause of our *decision to accept a basic
(observational) statement*.

Expressed counterfactually, this says: if we had not had a given perceptual
experience (for example, of red), then we would not have accepted some particular basic statement ('this is red').

This is an indication of Popper's adoption of some causal theory of perception linking perceptual experience with perceptual belief.

Psychologism is given a particular gloss when Popper tells us: 'In sense
experience we have "immediate knowledge": by this immediate knowledge,
we may justify our "mediate knowledge" ... [a]nd this mediate knowledge includes, of course, the statements of science.' (ibidem, § 24). Here psychologism
is linked to a theory of immediate knowledge and an associated 'veil of perception' doctrine. Popper spends several sections of Chapter V of *LSD* criticizing
this doctrine, or its linguistic counterpart; it was adopted by many positivists
and discussed in terms of whether or not there were protocol sentences. In

rejecting the 'veil' theory as Popper does, we can reject this understanding of psychologism as a solution to the trilemma.

The problematic notion in (D) is that of 'perceptual experience', an innocent enough phrase. But it leads to the unacceptable 'veil' doctrine. Is there a way of talking about perceptual experience that does not beg the questionable 'veil' doctrine? There is. Much of the paper will spell out a notion of the *non-conceptual content of experience*, which does not reify talk of sense data, impressions, veils of perception, mediate and immediate objects of perception, and the like. And it does allow, contrary to the trilemma, that there is some rational, non-inferential relation that can hold between the contents of experience (say of red) and the concepts that are contained in our beliefs about that experience (such as the concept *red* as contained in the belief about, say, a litmus strip, *that it is red*).

This raises a question about (B), namely, that reasons of justification must always be logical relations holding between statements, and cannot hold between a statement and something that is non-statement-like such as an experiential content. In accepting (B), some have built into the idea of experience a quasi-propositional content; somehow the world comes already conceptually prepared for us. Such hubris, or human chauvinism, we ought to resist. We shall depart from Popper and talk about rational, but non-inferential, transitions from the non-conceptual content of experience to the propositional content of a perceptual belief. Of course there will be irrational or unreasonable transitions as well. As we refine (D) and expand on (B), the force of the trilemma is dissipated, thereby bypassing Popper's 'solution'.

## 1.3 Popper's response to the trilemma

Popper's solution is to accept (C) and ride along with the infinite regress. At any stage we can make a decision to stop and accept the beliefs characteristic of that stage. In making such a decision an element of dogmatism threatens. In one sense this can be unproblematic. There is no reason why scientists cannot test hypotheses such as 'all swans are white' and simply accept that some item $n$ is a swan, or is black, without further testing these claims. But this is merely a practical point, and not the resolution of an epistemological problem. Popper's response can be deemed inadequate as an overall epistemological theory. It is important to realize that Popper is not adopting a convention about how we are to use words in a given circumstance. Rather, Popper's solution presupposes meaning conventions and involves a quite different kind of decision to accept some statement for the purposes of testing other statements.

Popper's solution is 'decisionist' when he says: 'if the test is to lead us anywhere, nothing remains but to stop at some point or other and say that we are satisfied, for the time being' (1959, § 29). Who are the 'we'? The individual scientist does not decide this but a community, 'the various investigators [who] are likely to reach agreement' (ibidem) 'And if there is no agreement then there would be a 'new "Babel of Tongues" ... [and i]n this new Babel the soaring edifice of science would soon lie in ruins' (ibidem). The acceptance or rejection of scientific theories turns on a sociological investigation into the formation of agreements in scientific communities, that is, that such-and-such a stopping point yields an acceptable basic statement for the community. Here the acceptance is based neither in meaning conventions, nor truth nor further evidence; rather it is mere overall acceptance for the purposes of testing.

Many have found Popper's decisionist epistemology unsatisfactory (for example, Habermas 1976). They look for hard, decisive criticisms of our theories using Popper's rules of method. But, alas, Popper's own methodological rules also have a decisionist flavour. As Popper says of his own conception of science: 'My criterion of demarcation will accordingly have to be regarded as *a proposal for an agreement or a convention.*' And '[t]he choice of that purpose must, of course, be ultimately a matter of decision, going beyond rational argument' (1959, §4). For many, Popper's philosophy of science, rather than being the deeply rationalistic theory it is often proclaimed to be, is really riddled with decisions that make the edifice of science rather arbitrary and liable to collapse like the tower of Babel.

Here I shall not be concerned with the decisionist character of his methodological principles. The focus will be on whether there is an account of observational/basic statements that overcomes Popper's decisionism due to his adoption of (C) as a 'resolution' of the trilemma. The resolution proposed here involves a modification of (C) and a reinterpretation of (D). The theory cannot be fully developed here (see Crane 1990; Peacocke 2001, and the papers collected in Gunther 2003). Rather a number of theses will be somewhat dogmatically proclaimed; they need much fuller development, but they do point in the direction of the proposed resolution.

## 2  Some theses concerning a solution of the problem of the empirical basis of science

### 2.1 The reliabilist epistemological background

The background epistemological theory assumed here is reliabilism, the view that we are, on the whole, and perhaps owing to our biological inheritance, reliable detectors of certain features of the world. In general we are reliable detectors of large objects such as elephants or trees or cars. But they have to be reasonably close up and not viewed at a great distance, or in a mist, or through haze, or when we are sleepy, drugged, or intoxicated. The basic point here can be summed up in two claims.

(i)     For a person $X$ and some object $b$ that is $F$, then if, as input to $X$ in 'normal' circumstances of perception $C$, it perceptually appears to $X$ that $b$ is $F$, then, as output for $X$, $X$ believes that $b$ is $F$;

(ii)    There is a high ratio of truths believed for given input, with few or no falsehoods; that is, $X$, in $C$, has a strong disposition, on the basis of the way $b$'s being $F$ appears to $X$, to form the correct belief that $b$ is $F$.

Importantly reliabilism accommodates the causal claim that Popper makes in (F) above.

Consider now the relata of the reliability relation, and the relation itself. One of the relata is (a) how a situation appears or looks to someone; more will be said about the non-conceptual character of this. Second, the other relatum is (b) a belief, the conceptual side of the relation. Finally, the relation between them is one of reliability, which for Popper, is the reliability of a causal connection. But more needs to be said if a case is to be made for a rational connection between (a) the non-conceptual content to our perceptions and (b) the conceptual content of our perceptual beliefs. Moreover, there are good reasons for (b) based in (a); the perceptual belief we acquire has to be 'appropriate' to, or 'right' for, the non-conceptual content of the perception.

## 2.2 Having a concept and having a belief

We shall simply assert the following thesis: A person $X$ has the concept $F$ (say, cat, mat, being on) if & only if $X$ has beliefs (such as *that the cat is on the mat*) in which the concept $F$ occurs (and make the right inferential connection between the beliefs). It follows from this that having beliefs involves having concepts; conversely, applying concepts will result in beliefs.

## 2.3 The informational content of a state of affairs

The states of affairs of the world contain informational content. This will not be defined and so is taken as primitive; but it can be illustrated. One example commonly cited in the literature is that of a tree that has 70 tree rings. Then this state of a bit of the world contains the informational content *that the tree is 70 years old*. Further, this state of the world represents another state of the world, namely *that the tree is 70 years old*. How the second informational content is to be extracted from the first need not concern us. All that is required is that informational content can be contained in states of the world, and can, under certain circumstances, be extracted. Analogously we can say that our perceptual systems, through the perceptual experiences we have (of, say, tree rings), are able to extract informational content (such as the tree's having tree-rings, the tree's having 70 tree rings, and so on). Of course there may much information contained in states of the world that our perceptual systems do not detect. But that is simply the way we have evolved to be perceptual detectors of the world.

Granted this notion of informational content, note that nothing has been said about *conceptual* content. Clearly there is no need to mention it. States of the world, such as a tree having 70 rings, or being 70 years old, contain no concepts at all. The are simply states of affairs that obtain, or not, as the case may be. The tree has no concept of itself as a thing with tree-rings, or 70 rings or of being 70 years old. But of course we can and do apply concepts to the world, and to our experience of it. A mark of our being able to do so is that we form beliefs about the world.

## 2.4 Non-conceptual content

The following definition is proposed:

> for any subject $X$ and state S of $X$, S has *non-conceptual content P*, if & only if subject $X$, being in S, does not entail that $X$ possesses the concepts that normally characterize $P$, or if $X$ possesses them $X$ does not apply them to S.

Some examples might help. Consider some subject, a tree $X$; it is in a certain state S, that of having 70 tree rings. But obviously the tree $X$ in state S does not have the concepts of 70, or tree rings, or even being a tree, even though it is in the state of having 70 tree rings. So the state, the tree has 70 tree rings, is a state that has non-conceptual content.

Turn now to the example of sentient being $X$, and $X$ sees the cat on the mat. Now $X$ might be a newly born infant, or an animal such as a dog, or a person who had never encountered cats or mats before. $X$ is in a certain visual state, S, the state that is described by saying: $X$ sees the cat on the mat. This is distinct from saying: $X$ sees *that* the cat is on the mat. This is a conceptual achievement quite different from $X$'s being in a state that has non-conceptual content, that is, seeing the cat on the mat. If $X$ is a newly born infant, or an animal, or a person unacquainted with cats and mats, then there are characteristic concepts, cat, mat, and so on, that pertain to S, but $X$ does not possess these characteristic concepts. So the state of $X$, seeing the cat on the mat, has content $P$, but it is non-conceptual content, since the possessor of the state has not, or cannot apply, the appropriate concepts. It is this idea of non-conceptual content of perception that will replace the idea of immediate experience that is so problematic in Popper's account of Fries's trilemma (but not there alone).

We normal people do possess the concepts that standardly characterize the state of the cat's being on the mat, and do apply them when we come across cats on mats. This is simply part of our normal cognitive repertoire. But there is a contingency to be noted here. It is not necessary that we do apply them, or even apply them correctly; and there are circumstances in which we may not apply the concepts, because we lack them. So even those who are cognitively competent may be in perceptual states S with a given non-conceptual content; but it is not the case that S also has a correct belief about that content.

## 2.5 Conceptual content

The definition to be proposed arises from the one just given:

> For any subject $X$ and state S of $X$, S has *conceptual content P*, if & only if a subject $X$ being in S entails that $X$ possesses the concepts that normally characterize $P$, and applies them to S.

As an illustration, if $X$ is a person who not merely sees the 70 tree rings, but sees *that* there are 70 tree-rings (not an easy achievement!), then this is a state S of $X$ that does have conceptual content that $P = that\ the\ tree\ has\ 70\ rings.$

## 2.6 The idea of a visual presentation

This adds to the distinction between conceptual and non-conceptual content in perception, such as in seeing. Consider a case of conceptual seeing, such as a person $X$'s seeing *that p* (= that the cat is on the mat). Now there is a world of difference between that and $X$'s *hoping that p, wondering whether p, dreading that p, believing p*, and so on for other intentional terms. Now the latter differ from *seeing that p* in that $X$ must have a *visual presentation* of the cat being on the mat. But all the examples share something, for they have the same conceptual content, *that p*. The different ingredient possessed only in the case of seeing *that p*, is the visual presentation. The same applies to a case of, say, hearing that $q$ (= *that the oboe is sounding middle C*). Here there is an auditory presentation absent in the cases of hoping, wondering, dreading, and so on, that $q$.

Now it can be agreed that the following entailment holds: $X$ sees *that* the cat is on the mat entails that $X$ believes *that* the cat is on the mat. Conceptual seeing that $p$ essentially involves belief, that is, the application of concepts. This is to be distinguished from non-conceptual seeing in which (a) this entailment does not hold, but (b) there is still a visual presentation.

An important thesis now emerges, namely that visual presentations are states of a person that do *not* have conceptual content, but they do have non-conceptual content. That is, there are perceptual states of people, such as seeings, hearings, touchings, and so on. Moreover these are not to be reified into a sense datum or an immediate experience of the sort that would permit the 'veil' doctrine to arise. Let us focus on visual states, $S_V$, or auditory states, $S_A$ (which provide more striking examples). These do have content that is non-conceptual. These states can arise in sentient subjects that also have well-developed conceptual capacities, or in subjects that do not have the appropriately developed concepts (the ignorant, or children), or subjects without concepts (neonates, animals).

## 2.7 The richness of non-conceptual content over conceptual content

This is the commonly made point in the literature that in a visual presentation there is a richness of non-conceptual content that surpasses that of conceptual content. For example, any visual presentation contains much that we do not even properly articulate in conceptual terms. Consider the cat and its mat. There are various shades and textures that are part of the visual presentation (assuming our eyes are in good working order) about which we might say nothing, or about which we cannot say anything. And even if we could, as when we say of the visual scene that the cat is on the mat, we leave out much that we could say on the basis of our visual presentation, such as the orientation of cat and mat, the position of the cat (sitting, standing, sleeping), and so on. The case of hearing, say, a symphony orchestra, is more striking. Only with much training in music can one, from one's auditory presentation and its non-conceptual content, say what instrument is playing, at what register, with what dynamics, what the chords are, how they are evolving, what the tempo is, and so on.

## 2.8 Non-conceptual seeing

Here we shall simply adopt the theory of non-conceptual seeing developed by Dretske. A central thesis is: $X$ non-conceptually sees object $b$, that is $F$, does not entail that there is some belief $p$ such that $X$ believes that $p$. The occurrence of '$b$' in the first clause is purely extensional and is open to existential quantification and substitution of equivalents. (For arguments for this thesis see Dretske 1969, Chapter II, and Dretske 2000, Part II, especially Chapter 6.)

But in non-conceptual seeing there is something that one does have, namely, a *visual presentation*. The world is visually presented to one, simply because one's eyes are open, in good working order and pointed in the right direction. One does not have to pay attention to any of it in order to see it; one just sees it, and cannot help but do so, unless one averts one's head or shuts one's eyes. Of course one can pay attention to it, and form beliefs about what one sees. As indicated, visual presentations contain some information, in a broad sense of 'information'. The visually presented scene is usually variegated with respect to objects, colours, shapes, movement, and the like. And the information content can be high as in a scene with much detail, or very meagre, as when one looks at a white wall close up.

This leads to a positive condition for non-conceptual seeing which can be expressed as follows:

> $X$ non-conceptually sees $b$ = (i) $b$ is an object at the terminus of the cone of $X$'s field of vision; and (ii) amongst $b$'s properties are visual properties that make it a distinct object with respect to its background within $X$'s field of vision (assuming the conditions of $X$'s seeing are normal).

Dretske expresses this condition as follows (Dretske 1969, p. 20): $b$ is a visually differentiated from its immediate environment by $X$. But this makes it appear that $X$ is more activist in seeing than Dretske intends, and that $X$ is busy doing some differentiation. But $X$ need not be busy in this way at all. $X$ does no special attending to $X$'s field of vision. Nor need $X$ be aware of anything in $X$'s field of vision. In particular, $X$ need not aware *that* $b$ is different from its surrounds. In the case of non-conceptual seeing the following need to be distinguished. (a) $X$ sees the difference between $b$ and its surrounds. (b) $X$ sees *that* there is a difference between $b$ and its surrounds. The latter entails awareness but not the former. One can non-conceptually see differences without seeing *that* they are differences; ignorance of the difference does not impair (non-conceptual) seeing the difference.

## 2.9 Conceptual seeing

Here I shall merely state some conditions that can plausibly be taken to apply to conceptual seeing. Again I shall adopt the proposal of Dretske (1969, Chapter III), but applied only to the case where object $b$ is an item in one's field of vision.

> $X$ (conceptually) sees that $b$ is an $F$ $=_{\text{Defn}}$
> (1)   $X$ sees $b$, which is $F$ (non-conceptual seeing);
> (2)   $b$ is $F$ (truth condition);
> (3)   the conditions under which $X$ sees $b$ are such that $b$ would not look to $X$ the way it does unless it were $F$ (the 'looks' condition, that is, $X$'s visual presentation);
> (4)   on the basis of (3), $X$ believes that $b$ is $F$ (the belief condition).

This is a proposal that has merit but will not be discussed here. But it shows how non-conceptual seeing, the having of a visual presentation, is necessary to conceptual seeing *that* $b$ is $F$, and thus believing that $b$ is $F$. Central to our concern is the passage from (1) and (3) to (4). Not only must $X$ have a visual presentation of $X$ (as in (1)), but $X$ must also pay attention to the visual presentation, or be aware of it. $X$ may not be able to identify everything in it because, as indicated in § 2.7, there is a richness of the non-conceptual content of $X$'s visual presentation such that either $X$ may not attend to all of that content, or $X$ lacks the requisite concepts to apply to aspects of that content. Condition (4) expresses the idea behind conceptual seeing. So what the above proposes is the following transitions:

(i)   a visual presentation in the sense of non-conceptual seeing;

(ii)   $X$ having a belief that $b$ is $F$ by conceptually seeing that $b$ is $F$;

(iii)   and (ii) is *via* the look to $X$ possessed by the items $X$ non-conceptually sees.

Contrary to Popper, the transition here from (i) to (ii) *via* (iii) is nothing like a decision. What Popper says will not help us at this point.

## 2.10 The transition from the visual presentation of non-conceptual content to conceptual content

This transition is the crux of the matter. In some cases there is no transition for those, such as neonates, aliens, or animals, who lack the requisite concepts. But even for us ordinary folk there can also be problems. We can be given some non-conceptual content, yet we make no transition to a belief with conceptual content. For example a musician plays a note on a clarinet, say, middle C. A person might hear a noise, and even identify it as a noise. But there is more content than this in the auditory presentation. A skilled musician might not only tell that it is a clarinet, and not (say) an oboe, but also tell what note it is. Thus there is a transition from an auditory state of a person, the state of hearing a clarinet sound middle C, and this state has non-conceptual content, to a state that does have conceptual content, that is, the person hears *that*, and so believes *that*, it is a clarinet playing middle C. So here, two stories need to be told about the skill we have in applying concepts, and how we get the appropriate concepts in the first place. But this is not the main issue to be focused upon here.

This issue is whether there is a rational transition here, in the sense that it can be justified. The first point, evident in the clarinet example, is that the connection is not obviously causal. But we can at least say, along with (F) of § 1.2, that if our auditory presentation did not have the non-conceptual content that it did, then we might not have had the belief that we did, the counterfactual expressing the causal relation holding between these items. What this indicates is that our ability to apply concepts to our perceptual presentations must be sensitive to those situations and not insensitive as when, in the case of the clarinet, we thinly characterize it as 'that sound now'. This is sufficient to identify it but not adequate to capture conceptually much of its rich non-conceptual content.

Now it has been abundantly argued that a person having the perceptual presentation of a clarinet, a cat, or red, need not also have the concept of that something, a clarinet, a cat, or red. So, what needs to be given is an account of what it is for person $X$ to have a concept of, say, clarinet playing middle C, and then, on the basis of $X$'s auditory presentations, for it to be sufficient for $X$ to say at least that it is a clarinet sound, or more fully that it is a clarinet sounding middle C. The connection is not causal. Rather it is a matter of the correct application, by $X$, of an observational concept to items that are perceptually presented in some way to $X$. And what kind of a connection is this? Clearly it is a connection that does have conditions of rightness, or correctness, or appropriateness, when, on the basis of what we perceive, we apply concepts. And it leaves room for fallibility in that a person can misclassify as when $X$ says 'it is an oboe (playing D above middle C)'.

In such a case there might be quite general demonstrative concepts that can be successfully used to refer, such as 'that sound now'; but one might not be able to classify further. Though correct, the richness of the auditory presentation goes beyond the thin concepts that are applied in this case. But such reference will not succeed in individuating the sound of a single instrument when there is a full orchestra playing. To individuate, finer concepts need to be applied to such a rich auditory presentation. And of course in all these cases there is fallible concept application.

Here there is a role for reason in the correctness or rightness relation that holds between some aspect of the non-conceptual content of, say, an auditory presentation of which we can be aware, and a concept, say, of a clarinet playing middle C. This is not the same as the logical relation of justification that holds between propositions, which was such an important feature of Popper's trilemma. Popper restricted such relations of reason only to those that can hold between propositions. But relations of reason can be much more varied than this. There are also the quite different relations of (a) whether an object falls under a concept, and (b) whether the possessor of a concept has correctly, or incorrectly, applied a concept to an item. Popper pays little attention to such matters. In fact his decisionist position helps him bypass it. But that is an error that leaves his rational scrutiny of our basic observational statements rather up in the air.

Given the above, a modification needs to be made to §2.2. Even though having a belief and applying concepts are closely related, it does not follow that both are to be justified in the same way. We can still claim that certain kinds of relation of justification hold only between propositions. However what has been argued for is a different, but nonetheless rational, relation that holds between (aspects of) a perceptual presentation and the application of concepts to it. This is not an inferential relation between propositions but a quite different non-inferential relation holding between two different items, non-conceptual contents and (perceptual) concepts. Reasonableness lies not in logical relations between propositions but in the conditions of correct application of concepts. And this makes possible incorrect application, and thus an element of fallibility.

So, what is it to apply concepts correctly to the objects that fall under them? There is a vast literature on this subject in philosophy that cannot be gone into here (but see §§IIIf. of Peacocke 2001). My thesis is that a way out of Fries's trilemma can be found through exploring this non-inferential relation. It rejects (B) of the trilemma, and does not involve (D), psychologism, since it concerns itself not with the properties of the 'veil' of immediate experience but rather with the rational and objective relation that concepts have to their objects that are non-conceptually presented to perceivers.

# Bibliography

Crane, T. (1990). 'The Nonconceptual Content of Experience'. In T. Crane, editor (1990), pp. 136-157. *The Contents of Experience: Essays on Perception*. New York: Cambridge University Press.

Dretske, F. (1969). *Seeing and Knowing*. London: Routledge & Kegan Paul.

———— (2000). *Perception, Knowledge and Belief*. Cambridge: Cambridge University Press.

Gunther, Y. (2003). *Essays on Nonconceptual Content*, Cambridge MA: MIT Press.

Habermas, J. (1976). 'The Analytical Theory of Science and Dialectics'. In Adorno, T. W., Albert, H., Dahrendorf, R., Habermas, J. & Popper, K. R. (1976). *The Positivist Dispute in German Sociology*. London: Heinemann.

Peacocke, C. (2001). 'Does Perception have Nonconceptual Content?'. *The Journal of Philosophy* **98**, pp. 239-264.

Popper, K. R. (1959). *The Logic of Scientific Discovery*. London: Hutchinson.

# 32

# Sprachliche und empirische Aspekte des Basisproblems[*]

## Herbert Keuth

Folgt man Carnap, so bildet die *Überprüfung von Beobachtungssätzen an der Wirklichkeit* „das *Kernproblem der Wissenschaftslogik*" (Carnap 1932b, p. 215; 1987, p. 457), und die „Erörterung der *Basisprobleme* gehört zu den wichtigsten Teilen" von Poppers *Logik der Forschung* (Carnap 1935, p. 290, H.i.O.). Zwar bezeichnet Popper selbst die Probleme der *Induktion* und der *Abgrenzung* als *die beiden Grundprobleme der Erkenntnistheorie*, aber jedes dieser drei Probleme hängt mit jedem anderen zusammen.

Was trägt Popper denn zur Lösung der Basisprobleme bei? Carnap diagnostiziert im „logistischen Positivismus [des Wiener] Kreises ... die verfeinerte Form eines *Absolutismus der Ursätze*" (Carnap 1932b, p. 228, m.H.; 1987, p. 469). Zu dessen Überwindung macht Popper einen Vorschlag, nach dem es „*keine absoluten Anfangssätze* für den Aufbau der Wissenschaft" gibt (Carnap 1932b, p. 224, H.i.O.; 1987, p. 466), ja, gar „*keine letzten Sätze*; [Poppers] *System stellt daher die radikalste Überwindung jenes Absolutismus dar*" (Carnap, 1932b, p. 228, m.H.; 1987, p. 469).

Doch zum einen ist der „Absolutismus der Ursätze" ein Rückfall hinter jenen Stand der Erkenntnistheorie, den Hermann Helmholtz schon 1867 erreicht hatte. Zum anderen wiederholt Popper auf sprachlicher Ebene — oder in „*,formaler'* Redeweise" — ein Argument, das Helmholtz in „*,inhaltlicher'* Redeweise" geführt hatte. Und weil Poppers Vorschlag *konventionalistisch* ist, wirft er das Problem *rationaler Entscheidungen* auf und ist — wegen der stillschweigenden Unterstellung freier Willensentscheidungen — letztlich antinomisch.

(1) Der Rückfall des Neopositivismus hinter Helmholtz hat verschiedene Ursachen. Dazu zählen vor allem (1.1) der Versuch, die metaphysische Annahme der *Existenz einer Außenwelt* zu vermeiden, und (1.2) das Streben nach *Sicherheit*.

(1.1) Folgt man Schlick, so scheint es zur „Frage nach der *Realität der*

---

[*]A sketch in English of the present argument may be found in Herbert Keuth, *The Philosophy of Karl Popper*, Cambridge University Press 2005, Chapters 4.1 and 4.2.

*Außenwelt* ... zwei Parteien zu geben: die des ,*Realismus*‘, welche an die Realität der Außenwelt glaubt, und die des ,*Positivismus*‘, welche nicht daran
glaubt“ (Schlick, 1932-1933, p. 4, m.H.). Einerseits „sprechen manche Natur-
forscher von der Notwendigkeit, die Existenz einer Außenwelt als eine *metaphysische* Hypothese an[zu]nehmen“ (Schlick, 1932-1933, p. 24, H.i.O.). Wenn
andererseits „die Ablehnung der Metaphysik durch den Positivismus so viel
bedeutet wie Leugnung der transzendenten Wirklichkeit, so scheint ... [der]
*Hauptgrundsatz des Positivisten* ... zu lauten: ,*Nur das Gegebene ist wirk-
lich*‘“ (Schlick 1932-1933, p. 4, m.H.).
    Aber weshalb leugnet der Positivismus eine transzendente Wirklichkeit?
Schlick erklärt: „es wäre ein *Selbstwiderspruch*, wenn man etwas *Unerkenn-
bares* [wie die Außenwelt] *hypothetisch annehmen* wollte“ (Schlick 1932-1933,
p. 25, m.H.). Denn er urteilt nach dem „Prinzip, daß die *Wahrheit* und Falsch-
heit aller Aussagen, ..., allein im ,Gegebenen‘ *geprüft* werden kann und daß
*daher* (H.i.O.) der *Sinn* aller Aussagen auch nur mit Hilfe des Gegebenen
formuliert und *verstanden* werden kann“ (Schlick 1932-1933, p. 26, m.H.).

(1.2)   Das Streben der logischen Positivisten nach *Sicherheit der empirischen
Basis* gab Anlaß zur *Protokollsatzdebatte*. So schreibt Carnap: „[G]ewisse
konkrete Sätze der Systemsprache [werden] als *Protokollsätze* genommen, d.h.
als Basis der Nachprüfung, als Sätze, hinter die man bei der Nachprüfung
der Systemsätze ... nicht mehr zurückgreift“ (Carnap 1932b, p. 223, H.i.O.;
1987, p. 464), und „bei den Protokollsätzen *kann nach einer Bestätigung
nicht gefragt werden*“ (Carnap 1932b, p. 221, m.H.). Zwar gibt er diese Position bald auf, aber Schlick behauptet weiterhin „Die *Konstatierungen* sind
*endgültig*“ (Schlick 1933-1934, p. 94, m.H.; 1959, p. 223), „es sind die einzi-
gen synthetischen Sätze, *die keine Hypothesen sind*“ (Schlick 1933-1934, p. 98,
H.i.O.; 1959, p. 227).

(2)   Wie überwindet Popper diesen „*Absolutismus der Ursätze*“? Er ver-
wirft Fries’ Idee, man könne Beobachtungssätze „auf Wahrnehmungserlebnisse
gründen“ (Popper 1935, Abschnitt 25; 1966, Abschnitt 25, p. 60). Denn
wir „können keinen wissenschaftlichen Satz aussprechen, der nicht über
das, was wir ,auf Grund unmittelbarer Erlebnisse‘ sicher wissen können,
weit hinausgeht“. Popper nennt das die „,*Transzendenz der Darstellung*‘“ und illustriert es mit dem Satz „,Hier steht ein Glas Wasser‘“.
Dieser Satz kann schon deshalb „durch keine Erlebnisse verifiziert werden“,
weil die „*Wort*[e] ,Glas‘“ und „,Wasser‘“ physikalische Substanzen von
„,*gesetzmäßigem* Verhalten‘“ bezeichnen (Popper 1935, Abschnitt 25; 1966,
Abschnitt 25, p. 61, m.H.). Hans Albert wies später auf eine „,*Transzendenz
der Wahrnehmung*‘“ hin, die den gleichen Effekt hat (Albert 1987, p. 56,
m.H.).
    Poppers *sprachliches* Argument ist das Gegenstück zu einem *natura-
listischen* Argument von Helmholtz (1867), nach dem alle *Eigenschaften*, die
wir *Objekten der Außenwelt* zuschreiben, „nur *Wirkungen* bezeichnen, welche

sie entweder auf unsere Sinne oder auf andere Naturobjekte ausüben. ... Da
... [wir immer] die eigentümliche Art der Wechselwirkung eintreten sehen, so
schreiben wir den Objekten eine dauernde und stets zur Wirksamkeit bereite
*Fähigkeit zu solchen Wirkungen* [m.H.] zu. Diese dauernde Fähigkeit nennen
wir *Eigenschaft*" (Helmholtz 1867, p. 444; 1910, pp. 19f., H.i.O.; 1962, p. 21).

Eigenschaften sind demnach *Dispositionen* zu regelhaftem Verhalten. Deshalb müssen Prädikate, die Objekten solche Eigenschaften zuschreiben, *Dis-
positionsprädikate* sein. Schon weil wir nicht die Dispositionen selbst wahr-
nehmen, sondern nur das, was wir mit ihrer Wirkung erklären, *transzendieren*
Aussagen, die Objekten Eigenschaften zuschreiben, jede Erfahrung. Das
erklärt die *Fehlbarkeit* aller Beobachtungssätze.

(3) Aber warum nimmt Poppers Argument zur Lösung des Basispro-
blems eine *konventionalistische* Wendung?    In der *Logik* schreibt er:
„Die Basissätze werden durch Beschluß, durch Konvention anerkannt, sie
sind *Festsetzungen*" (Popper 1935 Abschnitt 30; 1966, Abschnitt 30, p. 71,
H.i.O.), und er betont, „daß die Entscheidungen über die Basissätze
nicht durch unsere Erlebnisse ‚begründet' werden, sondern, logisch betrachtet, *willkürliche Festsetzungen* sind (psychologisch betrachtet, zweckmäßige
Reaktionen)" (Popper 1935, Abschnitt 30; 1966, Abschnitt 30, p. 74, H.i.O.).
Dennoch hat die Willkür solcher Festsetzungen ihre Grenzen, denn „Es
besteht ... eine entscheidende Asymmetrie zwischen Maßstäben und Tatsachen: Mit der Entscheidung, einen Vorschlag ... zu akzeptieren, schaffen
wir den dazugehörigen Maßstab ...; durch die Entscheidung, eine Aussage zu
akzeptieren, schaffen wir hingegen *nicht* die dazugehörige Tatsache" (Popper
1992, Volume II, Addendum I, Abschnitt 13, p. 478, H.i.O.).

Auch Carnap schreibt: „Die Sätze des wissenschaftlichen Systems werden
[durch empirische Prüfungen] *nicht* im strengen Sinne ‚verifiziert'. Die Auf-
stellung des Systems der Wissenschaft enthält *somit* stets ein *konventionelles*
Moment" (Carnap 1932a, p. 440; 1995, m.H.). — Ist „konventionell" also nur
ein anderes Wort für „nicht streng verifiziert"? — Er fährt fort: „*d.h.* die
Form des Systems ist *niemals vollständig durch die Erfahrung festgelegt*, sondern *stets auch durch Festsetzungen mitbestimmt*" (m.H.). Sind auch Poppers
Basissätze nur insofern „Festsetzungen", als ihre Annahme nicht hinreichend
begründet werden kann? Prüfen wir zunächst, welchen Beitrag die *Festsetzungen* und welchen die *Erfahrungen* zur Annahme wissenschaftlicher Sätze
leisten.

(3.1) Zweckmäßigerweise beginnen wir mit *verifizierbaren* Sätzen. Der Wahrheitswert des Satzes $p \lor \neg p$ ist nicht „durch die Erfahrung festgelegt", sondern
hängt allein von seiner Form ab. Seine Auswertung mit der Wahrheitstafel *be-
weist*, dass er eine Tautologie ist. Doch seine Annahme als wahr folgt nicht
*logisch* aus der Führung dieses Arguments. Erst die *Annahme des Resultats
eines Arguments als Beweis* impliziert die *Annahme des bewiesenen Satzes*

*als wahr.* Aber was *heißt* es, das Resultat eines Arguments werde als Beweis *akzeptiert*?

Ist seine Akzeptierung insofern eine „*willkürliche Festsetzung*", als unser Urteil über das Resultat von der Beschaffenheit des Arguments *im statistischen Sinne unabhängig* ist, oder *verursacht* ein korrektes Argument die Annahme seines Resultats als Beweis? Herbert Feigl erwägt immerhin, ein guter Logiker könne durch die Führung eines leicht überschaubaren Beweises *determiniert* sein, dessen Resultat zu akzeptieren.

Wir verwerfen diese beiden Extreme, stellen aber *probabilistische Abhängigkeiten* fest. Bei einfachen Beweisen ist die Wahrscheinlichkeit, dass Sachkundige ihr Resultat akzeptieren, sehr hoch. Doch von welcher Art ist diese Abhängigkeit? *Motiviert* uns die Führung eines Arguments, sein Resultat als Beweis zu akzeptieren, oder ist sie ein „*guter Grund*" dazu, oder ist die Annahme des Resultats eine *zweckmäßige Reaktion* auf das Argument? Die Verschiedenheit dieser Erklärungsversuche zeigt, dass wir über die Art des Zusammenhangs noch wenig wissen.

Ist aber wegen des erforderlichen Beschlusses der *Satz p ∨ ¬p* selbst eine *Festsetzung? Dass er eine Tautologie ist, resultiert aus Festsetzungen*, etwa aus der Definition seiner logischen Verknüpfungszeichen durch Wahrheitstafeln. Wenn wir nun sagen, eine Zeichenfolge, deren Annahme *ausschließlich von Festsetzungen abhängt*, habe selbst den Charakter einer Festsetzung, dann ist der Satz *p ∨ ¬p* in diesem Sinne eine Festsetzung.

(3.2) Dagegen hängt der Wahrheitswert eines *empirischen Satzes* von der Beschaffenheit der Welt ab; und deshalb hängt seine Annahme als wahr einerseits von „der *Erfahrung*" ab. Für solche Sätze kennt man nicht nur keinen Beweis, sondern man kann auch zeigen, warum für sie *kein Beweis* möglich ist. Bei *generellen* Hypothesen scheitert er am logischen *Induktionsproblem*, bei den singulären Beobachtungssätzen an der *Transzendenz der Darstellung* und der *Transzendenz der Wahrnehmung*, die auch den Komplex der *Sinnestäuschungen* umfasst.

(3.2.1.) Andererseits hängt die Annahme eines empirischen Satzes von *Konventionen* ab. *Welchen Sachverhalt er behauptet*, bestimmt sich nach *sprachlichen Regeln*, die wir als Konventionen betrachten. Und wollen wir festellen, *ob der behauptete Sachverhalt vorliegt*, so orientieren wir uns dabei an *methodologischen Regeln*. Auch sie gelten als Festsetzungen.

Neben *mathematischen Verfahren*, die — wie die statistischen Verfahren der Datenreduktion — dazu dienen, aus empirischen Sätzen andere empirische Sätze zu gewinnen, gibt es Regeln, denen — neben Sätzen der Logik und Mathematik — *empirische Hypothesen zugrunde liegen*. Da sind zunächst die *Festsetzungen von Maßeinheiten*, etwa nach dem internationalen Einheitensystem SI. Will man das Meter als den zehnmillionsten Teil des Erdquadranten definieren, so benötigt man *empirische Annahmen* über dessen Länge. Doch insofern man das Meter als einen *anderen* — etwa den tausendsten — Teil des Erdquadranten definieren könnte, liegt seiner Festsetzung auch eine

*Zweckmäßigkeitserwägung* zugrunde, die sich ihrerseits u.a. auf *Annahmen* über die Größe der zu messenden Objekte stützt. Andere *methodologische Regeln* entsprechen *hypothetischen Imperativen*, denen empirische Hypothesen zugrunde liegen. Zwar sind alle empirischen Hypothesen fehlbar, doch insoweit wir methodologische Regeln auf sie stützen, nehmen wir sie *durch Beschluss* einstweilen von der Kritik aus. Da die Annahme eines *empirischen Satzes* nicht allein von solchen Festsetzungen abhängt, macht diese Abhängigkeit ihn *nicht selbst* zu einer *Festsetzung*.

(3.2.2.) *Wie* hängt denn die *Annahme eines Beobachtungssatzes* von *Sinneseindrücken* ab? Helmholtz betrachtet die *Wahrnehmung* „als eine *Wirkung*, welche das wahrgenommene Objekt auf unsere Sinnlichkeit hat, welche Wirkung in ihren näheren Bestimmungen *ebensogut abhängt von dem Wirkenden wie von der Natur dessen, auf welches gewirkt wird*" (Helmholtz 1867, p. 456; 1910, p. 32, m.H.; 1962, pp. 35f.). Demnach resultiert die Wahrnehmung aus Einwirkungen der Außenwelt auf unseren Wahrnehmungsapparat und aus dessen Reaktionen. Schon wegen der Wirkungsweise der Nervenzellen kann die *Wahrnehmung* nur ein *probabilistischer Effekt* dieser *Einwirkungen* sein. Dennoch kann eine bestimmte Wahrnehmung insofern *zuverlässig* sein, als sie mit hoher Wahrscheinlichkeit bei bestimmten Stimuli und nur dort auftritt.

Wenn wir weiter fragen, *wie* die *Wahrnehmung* ihrerseits das *Urteil über Beobachtungssätze* beeinflusst, dann hängt die Antwort zunächst davon ab, welche Interpretationsleistungen man zur *Wahrnehmung* zählt und welche zur *Bildung des Urteils* über einen Beobachtungssatz. Helmholtz entwirft eine *Schlusstheorie der Wahrnehmung*, die besagt (Helmholtz 1867, p. 430; 1910, pp. 5f. m.H.; 1962, p. 4):

> Die psychischen Tätigkeiten, durch welche wir zu dem Urteile kommen, daß ein bestimmtes Objekt von bestimmter Beschaffenheit an einem bestimmten Orte außer uns vorhanden sei, sind … in ihrem Resultate einem [unbewußten] *Schlusse* (H.i.O.) gleich, insofern wir aus der *beobachteten Wirkung* auf unsere Sinne die *Vorstellung von einer Ursache* dieser Wirkung gewinnen, während wir in der Tat direkt doch immer nur die Nervenerregungen, also die Wirkungen wahrnehmen können, niemals die äusseren Objekte.

Demnach entwickeln wir zur *Erklärung* der Sinneseindrücke die Vorstellung von *Ursachen*. *Materialisten* vermuten als Ursachen Vorgänge in einer physischen *Außenwelt*, *Idealisten* die Aktivitäten von Göttern oder *Geistern*.

Aber wie weit *stimmen* angesichts dieser Schlusstheorie „unsere *Vorstellungen* überhaupt *mit ihren Objekten überein*" (Helmholtz 1867, p. 442; 1910, p. 17, m.H.; 1962, p. 19)? Es gibt keine Übereinstimmung in dem Sinne, dass Dinge, wie sie uns erscheinen, *Bilder* von Dingen an sich wären. Vielmehr betont Helmholtz: „Insofern die Qualität unserer Empfindung uns von der Eigentümlichkeit der äußeren Einwirkung, durch welche sie erregt ist, eine Nachricht gibt, kann sie als ein *Zeichen* derselben gelten, aber nicht als ein *Abbild*. … Ein Zeichen aber braucht gar keine Art der Ähnlichkeit mit dem zu haben, dessen Zeichen es ist" (Helmholtz 1878, p. 153, H.i.O.). Damit scheidet zwar eine *Abbildtheorie der Wahrheit* aus, aber nicht die *Idee der Wahrheit* selbst, denn „die Vorstellung von einem Dinge ist *richtig* für denjenigen, welcher danach richtig vorauszubestimmen weiß, welche sinnlichen Eindrücke er von dem Dinge erhalten wird, wenn er sich in bestimmte äußere Beziehungen zu ihm setzt" (Helmholtz 1867, p. 446; 1910, p. 22, m.H.; 1962, p. 23).

Nehmen wir einmal an, wir müssten es nicht mehr bei dem Vergleich mit einem unbewussten Schluss belassen, sondern verfügten über *bewährte* Hypothesen, die Geflechte *probabilistischer Zusammenhänge* nicht nur zwischen Stimuli und Wahrnehmungen, sondern auch zwischen *Wahrnehmungen* und *Urteilen über Beobachtungssätze* beschrieben. Auch dann *sicherten* die Wahrnehmungen zusammen mit solchen Hypothesen keineswegs die zutreffende Beurteilung der Sätze, denn die Hypothesen wären ja nicht nur *probabilistisch*, sondern auch *fehlbar*. Das gilt entsprechend für jene Hypothesen, nach denen wir unter bestimmten äußeren Umständen bestimmte Wahrnehmungen machen.

Um auszudrücken, dass Beobachtungen weder einen Beobachtungssatz *beweisen* noch seine Annahme *determinieren*, könnten wir, wie Popper, die *Urteile über Beobachtungssätze* durchaus „*Festsetzungen*" nennen, doch angesichts des soeben unterstellten *empirischen* „Wissens" um die Wirkungsweise unserer Wahrnehmungen wäre dieser Sprachgebrauch zumindest ungewöhnlich. Noch ungewöhnlicher wäre es, die akzeptierten *Beobachtungssätze* selbst „*Festsetzungen*" zu nennen.

Poppers späteres, vehementes Plädoyer für die Willensfreiheit lässt zudem vermuten, dass er sich die *Festsetzung eines Basissatzes* als rationale, *freie Willensentscheidung* denkt. Zwar hängt die Möglichkeit, Festsetzungen aller Art zu treffen, nicht von der Willensfreiheit ab. So könnte man bestimmte Sätze für empirisch und andere zu *Konventionen* erklären, selbst wenn man dazu determiniert wäre. Aber die Thesen, man sei *frei* bzw. man sei *determiniert*, wären bloß *metaphysisch*, wenn sie nicht *logisch fehlerhaft* wären, und zwar der *Determinismus* wegen des Problems der ersten Ursache, die Idee der *Willensfreiheit* wegen des Problems der erforderlichen stochastischen Unabhängigkeit „freier" Entscheidungen von *allen* anderen Ereignissen.

Sollten gehaltvolle empirische Hypothesen über *Assoziationen zwischen Vorgängen in der Welt und unseren Wahrnehmungen* sowie *zwischen Wahrnehmungen und Urteilen über Beobachtungssätze* sich bewähren, so erklärten sie auch, was heute als „*Motiv*" oder „*guter Grund*" gilt, einen Beobachtungssatz anzunehmen. Um die Möglichkeit solcher Erklärungen auszuschließen, müsste man auf einer *nicht-naturalistischen Erkenntnistheorie* bestehen. Aber die macht langfristig nur Sinn, wenn man annimmt, dass unsere kognitiven Aktivitäten nicht im *Gehirn*, sondern in einem davon zumindest partiell unabhängigen *Geist* stattfinden. Schließlich relativiert Helmholtzens naturalistische Wissenschaftslehre auch den *Prioritätenstreit* unter den Teilnehmern der Protokollsatzdebatte.

# Literatur

Albert, H. (1987). *Kritik der reinen Erkenntnislehre. Das Erkenntnisproblem in realistischer Perspektive*. Tübingen: J. C. B. Mohr (Paul Siebeck).

Ayer, A. J. (1959). *Logical Positivism*. New York: Free Press.

Carnap, R. (1932a). „Die physikalische Sprache als Universalsprache der Wissenschaft". *Erkenntnis* **2**, pp. 432-465. English translation with an introduction by Max Black, 1934. *The Unity of Science*. London: Kegan Paul, Trench, Trubner & Co. Reprinted 1995. Bristol: Thoemmes.

—— (1932b). „Über Protokollsätze". *Erkenntnis* **3**, pp. 215-228. English translation, 1987. „On Protocol Sentences". In *Noûs* **XXI**, pp. 457-470.

—— (1935). „Popper, Karl: Logik der Forschung. Zur Erkenntnistheorie der Naturwissenschaft" (Besprechung). *Erkenntnis* **5**, pp. 290-294.

Cohen, R. S. & Elkana, Y., editors (1977). *Epistemological Writings: the Paul Hertz/Moritz Schlick centenary edition of 1921 with notes and commentary by the editors*. Dordrecht & Boston MA: D. Reidel Publishing Company.

Helmholtz, H. v. (1867). *Handbuch der physiologischen Optik*, Bd. 3. Leipzig: Leopold Voss. English translation from the 3rd German edition 1910. J. P. C. Southall, editor (1924). *Helmholtz's Treatise on Physiological Optics*. Rochester NY: The Optical Society of America. Volume III reprinted 1962, pp. 1-37. New York: Dover.

—— (1878). „Die Tatsachen in der Wahrnehmung". Rektoratsrede 1878. In Helmholtz (1921), pp. 147-175. English translation in Cohen & Elkana (1977), pp. 115-146.

—— (1921). *Schriften zur Erkenntnistheorie. Kommentiert von Moritz Schlick und Paul Hertz*. Bonk, E., Hrsg. (1998). Vienna & New York: Springer. English translation Cohen & Elkana (1977).

Neurath, O. (1932). „Protokollsätze". *Erkenntnis* **3**, pp. 204-214. English translation: „Protocol Sentences". In Ayer (1959), pp. 199-208.

Popper, K. R. (1935). *Logik der Forschung*. Zur Erkenntnistheorie der Naturwissenschaft. Wien: Julius Springer Verlag. Zitiert nach der 2. Auflage 1966. Tübingen: J. C. B. Mohr (Paul Siebeck). English edition, 1959. *The Logic of Scientific Discovery*. New York: Basic Books.

—— (1945). *The Open Society and Its Enemies*. London: George Routledge & Sons. 5th edition 1966. London: Routledge & Kegan Paul.

—— (1992). *Die offene Gesellschaft und ihre Feinde*. 7. Auflage mit weitgehenden Verbesserungen und Anhängen der deutschen Übersetzung von Popper (1945). Tübingen: J. C. B. Mohr (Paul Siebeck).

Schlick, F. A. M. (1932-1933). „Positivismus und Realismus". *Erkenntnis* **3**, pp. 1-31.

—— (1933-1934). „Über das Fundament der Erkenntnis". *Erkenntnis* **4**, pp. 79-99. English translation: „The Foundation of Knowledge". In Ayer (1959), pp. 209-227.

# 33

# Test Statements and Experience

Gunnar Andersson

In order to test universal hypotheses scientists use singular test statements. For example, a singular test statement about an observed position of a planet can be used in order to test a universal hypothesis about the movements of the planets. By using such singular test statements scientists can corroborate or falsify universal hypotheses.

What is the relation between test statements and experience? Experience cannot prove a test statement to be true, since a statement can be proved only by other statements. In order to describe particular individual events, we must use universals such as 'planet', transcending the immediately given. Experience is therefore not an infallible criterion for the truth of test statements, but test statements are fallible, like universal hypotheses.

Which fallible test statements can be used in the critical discussion of scientific hypotheses and theories? According to Popper (1959), § 30, test statements are accepted by conventional decisions. Experience can motivate such decisions, but cannot justify them. Popper's answer to the question of how test statements are selected has the advantage that it does not support the vain hope of finding an infallible empirical basis for science. Nevertheless, Popper's conventionalism concerning test statements is unsatisfactory.

A typical convention in science is the decision to use a specific coordinate system in order to determine the positions of the stars in the sky. We can decide to accept a coordinate system using the local horizon. Such a system is useful for the amateur astronomer and the occasional observer. When I tell you that this evening in Vienna you can observe the planet Venus at ten o'clock in the evening almost in the West and a little more than $9°$ above the horizon, my choice of coordinate system is conventional and useful for those of you wanting to observe Venus this evening.[1] The professional astronomer wanting to test a hypothesis about the movement of Venus around the sun would probably choose another coordinate system, more useful for his purpose. The choice of

---

[1] More exactly, in Vienna on the fourth of July 2002 at 10.00 p.m. local mean daylight saving time the position of Venus is azimuth $282°30'$ and altitude $+9°32'$ using altazimuth coordinates. Its equatorial coordinates at the same time are right ascension (RA) $9h44.2m$ and declination $+15°24'$; its ecliptic coordinates are longitude $143°03'$ and latitude $+1°42'$. In these coordinate systems the local horizon, the celestial equator, and the ecliptic are used as basic lines of reference. The values of the coordinates have been calculated with the help of the computer programme Voyager II.

a specific coordinate system is conventional and may be useful or convenient, but the system itself is not true or false. Once a coordinate system has been chosen, the statement about the position of Venus is no longer conventional, but a true or false description of the world. My rather vague description of the position in Vienna of Venus this evening is a test statement that also is true or false. It should not be accepted or claimed to be true by conventional or 'free decisions' (Popper 1959, § 30), but only after empirical test, only after comparison with experience (cp. Andersson 1998, p. 161).

Although Popper says that test statements are accepted by conventional decisions, he nevertheless requires that they should describe observable events, that they must be testable, intersubjectively, by 'observation' (Popper 1959, § 28). For example, the test statement about the position of Venus is testable by observation. Before we claim that this test statement is true, we must first observe Venus. If we are empiricists, not only must we require that test statements should be testable by observation, but we must also require that they should actually have been tested by observation before they are claimed to be true. Otherwise empiricism is unwittingly thrown overboard.

It is obvious that Popper does not want to throw empiricism overboard. Why, then, does he call the decision to accept a test statement a conventional decision? When Popper wrote *The Logic of Scientific Discovery*, he was involved in discussions with members of the Vienna Circle. The problem of the relation between statements and the external world is a fundamental philosophical problem. When members of the Vienna Circle were confronted with such problems, they tried to show that they were metaphysical and meaningless, or they tried to solve them by introducing mere 'decisions' and 'conventions'. In retrospect, this attitude seems to us 'cavalier almost to the point of irresponsibility' (Davidson 1986, p. 327). When Popper wrote the *Logic of Scientific Discovery*, he avoided the use of the concept of truth as far as possible (Popper 1959, § 84). Not long after the publication of the book Popper got acquainted with Alfred Tarski's theory of truth and his hesitation to use the concepts of 'truth' and 'falsity' disappeared (Popper 1959, § 84, note *1). Had Popper known a satisfactory theory of truth earlier, his discussion of test statements would probably have been free of any conventionalism. Test statements are true or false descriptions of the external world. Their truth values can be tested with the help of experience. In this way a critical and empirical theory of test statements can be developed without any conventionalist fig leaves.

Philosophers in the Vienna Circle and later Davidson have doubted that we can compare statements with reality. They maintain that when we experiment and observe, we do not compare statements with reality in any but a metaphorical sense (Davidson 1986, p. 331). Let us consider our earlier discussed test statement about the position of the planet Venus west in the sky this evening. This test statement can be compared with observations of the sky this evening. Is this a comparison only in a metaphorical sense? Of course this comparison does not verify the truth of the test statement, does not provide an infallible criterion for the truth of the test statement, does not guarantee that the test statement corresponds to reality. In spite of the fact that the result of the comparison is not conclusive, a comparison in the literal sense of the word has been achieved.

Test statements can be compared directly with our experiences. As realists we assume that there is a (causal) connection between the independently existing reality and our experiences. With the help of experience we can indirectly compare statements with reality. In a fallibilist theory of knowledge this is enough. There we do not have to assume that we can observe reality with God's eye so to speak. In contradistinction to naïve direct realism about perceptions, which claims that external objects are perceived directly or immediately and as they really are, we maintain a sophisticated indirect realism about perception and claim that external objects are perceived indirectly or 'mediately' and not necessarily as they really are (Musgrave 1993, pp. 274f.). According to indirect realism perception is no infallible criterion of truth: test statements remain fallible after comparison with experience.

Those who, like Davidson and some members of the Vienna Circle, are attracted by a coherence theory, cannot satisfactorily explain how our theories are rationally constrained by experience. Unintentionally they throw empiricism overboard (cp. Popper 1959, § 26).

According to the correspondence theory of truth a statement is true if and only if it corresponds to the facts. This correspondence does not depend on conventional decisions, but can be tested with the help of experience. In this way it is possible to establish a theory of test statements that is an expression of robust realism and is without any ingredients of conventionalism. Traditional epistemologies try to verify test statements with the help of our subjective experiences. The new and critical epistemology tries to replace the classical idea of experience with the idea of objective, critical test.[2]

According to the classical idea, experience is a sufficient reason for the truth of a test statement. According to the new idea experience can be used for objective tests. Of course such tests cannot establish the truth of test statements, as justificationism required. According to the critical view, test

---

[2] Popper (1935), § 30, *Zusatz (1968) (2):

Das Kapitel [V der *Logik der Forschung*] stellt einen *robusten Realismus* auf und zeigt, daß dieser mit einem neuen, undogmatischen und nicht-subjektiven Empirismus vereinbar ist. ... Ich versuche, die klassische Idee der Erfahrung (Beobachtung) durch die der objektiven kritischen Prüfung zu ersetzen und die der *Erfahrbarkeit (Beobachtbarkeit)* durch die einer objektiven *Prüfbarkeit.*

The chapter [V of *The Logic of Scientific Discovery*] establishes a *robust realism* and shows that this realism can be combined with a new, undogmatic and non-subjective empiricism. ... I try to replace the classical idea of experience (observation) with that of an objective critical test and the idea of *perceivability* (*observability*) with that of objective *testability.*

(My translation (GA). The italics are Popper's.) This passage is replaced to a single sentence in Addendum (1972) to Chapter V in the 6th and subsequent impressions of Popper (1959).

statements can be intersubjectively tested by experience and can describe reproducible effects. In this way they can be objectively tested.

In spite of Popper's references to conventional decisions on test statements, there are ideas in the *Logic of Scientific Discovery* leading to a new critical theory of experience. The critical testing and critical discussion of test statements with the help of experience can lead to a tentative evaluation and selection of test statements governed by the regulative idea of objective truth, as Popper later explained his intentions.[3] After critical testing with the help of experience, test statements can be evaluated. Those test statements are selected that are in agreement with experience, that have survived the tests. It is reasonable to claim that such test statements are true. After having tested statements, we can rationally conjecture their truth value. The following principle is the heart of Critical Rationalism (cp. Albert 1968, § 5; Musgrave 1999, p. 324):

> It is rational (at time $t$) to claim that a statement $S$ is true if and only if $S$ has withstood serious criticism (at time $t$).

There is no reason to have one special principle of rationality for universal hypotheses and another for singular test statements. Both types of statements are testable and are claimed to be true first after critical tests. General hypotheses can be compared with singular test statements. Singular test statements can be compared with other test statements, but they can also be compared with experience. The direct comparison of a test statement with experience is the most simple form of an empirical test.

Is there any asymmetry in the epistemic situation between universal hypotheses and singular test statements (cp. Musgrave 1999, p. 342)? If we accept the principle of rationality above, there is no such asymmetry, but the same principle can be used in order to evaluate both universal hypotheses and singular test statements. Especially, there is no asymmetry of the kind Popper suggested (1959, § 30) such that test statements are accepted by conventional decisions and universal hypotheses after critical tests.

Do we have to make any concession to the epistemic primacy of sense experience (Musgrave ibidem)? Yes, we have to concede that test statements can be tested in a way that universal hypotheses cannot: namely by direct comparison with experience. It is easier to test singular test statements than to test universal hypotheses. In order to test a universal hypothesis we must

---

[3]Cp. Popper (1935), § 30, *Zusatz (1980) (6):

Der '*Begründungszusammenhang*' ... besteht in einer *kritische-rationalen Diskussion von Sätzen*. Sie führt zu deren vorläufiger Bewertung und Selektion. ('Kritisch-rational' bedeutet: 'geleitet von der regulativen Idee der Objektiven Wahrheit' ....)

The '*context of justification*' ... consists in a ... critical and rational discussion of statements. This discussion leads to the preliminary evaluation and selection of the statements. ('Critical and rational' means: 'guided by the regulative idea of objective truth' ....)

(My translation (GA). Popper's italics.) This addendum is not included in any English impression of (1959).

derive singular test statements and then compare the singular test statements with experience. But most singular test statements can be compared directly with experience. A singular test statement about an observable event can be tested directly by comparison with experience at some specific place and point of time. Universal hypotheses can be tested (indirectly) by many test statements and at many places and points of time.

Direct comparison with experience does not verify test statements or give sufficient reasons for their truth. But it makes it rational to claim that test statements are true. To compare a test statement with experience is an attempt to criticize it empirically. If the test statement withstands such criticism, it is rational to claim that it is true, according to our principle of rationality above. Such claims might very well be mistaken, as is to be expected from the point of view of consistent fallibilism. It is possible that our sense experience is mistaken, that observations are erroneous. Such mistakes can often be discovered by repeating the observation. But even if observations can be repeated and observed effects are reproducible, this does not guarantee that test statements are true. Sensory illusions occur and might be reproducible. (For example, the observations of the size of the brighter stars with the naked eye are now regarded as mistaken, as sensory illusions due to irradiation.)

In most cases we trust our senses and claim that a test statement is true after sensory experience without making further tests. Such tests are always possible, but usually they are not deemed to be necessary, at least not in ordinary life. In science, however, we require that important test statements should describe reproducible effects, that important test statements should be testable by other test statements (Andersson 1994, pp. 73-78). Important discoveries, say of a new planet or a new species must be testable by reproducible observations or experiments. Similarly, falsifications must be reproducible (cp. Popper 1959, § 22, on falsifying hypotheses), so that anybody who has learnt the relevant technique can reproduce the falsifying observation or experiment. Thus test statements cannot be tested only by comparison with experience, but also by comparison with other test statements.

If somebody should doubt a test statement that we claim to be true, we do not have to persuade him that we have had the corresponding perception. Instead, we can urge him to reproduce our observations and in this way test our test statements. This is especially important for test statements falsifying a theory. If somebody doubts that the theory is falsified, we can urge him to reproduce the falsifying observation. In principle, anybody who doubts a test statement should be able to test its truth value by repeating the relevant observation or experiment (cp. Andersson 1994, § 6.1.4, § 6.1.5, and § 8.3.2).

Ultimately, test statements are compared with individual experience. Such empirical tests do not verify test statements, but nevertheless make it rational to claim that some test statements are true. Should somebody doubt that the proposed test statements are true, it is open to him to repeat the relevant observations and experiments and to claim that other test statements are true, which perhaps (with background knowledge) falsify the earlier test statements. In this way we do not arrive at any infallible empirical basis, but at fallible test statements that we can test empirically and discuss rationally. The epistemological discussion has in the past been mainly a conflict between justificationism and scepticism. The discussion of test statements has been dominated by the same conflict. The justificationists searched for an infallible basis for knowledge and thought that they could find it in simple test statements or in immediate experience. Later, the fallibility and theory-dependence of test statements were discovered. These discoveries often led to relativism and irrationalism, as the recent discussion of the problem of incommensurability shows. When Popper wrote *The Logic of Scientific Discovery,* he realized that science has no firm empirical basis, that test statements cannot be verified by experience. Therefore he maintained that we have to accept test statements by conventional decisions. However, this idea inspired by conventionalism is mistaken and should be replaced by a critical conception according to which test statements should be tested by sense experience. In this way we avoid the shortcomings of justificationism and relativism and sail safely between these extremes.

Does the critical theory of test statements contain concessions to justificationism? It maintains that some truth claims are rational and even that some beliefs are rational (Musgrave 1999, Chapter 16). Beliefs have for a long time been an anathema for critical rationalists. They distrust all attempts to introduce subjective beliefs into the epistemological discussion. In the critical theory of knowledge presented here, subjective belief is not used as a criterion of truth. Instead an attempt is made to evaluate truth claims (or beliefs) with the help of critical testing and discussion. In contradistinction to classical or traditional justificationism, statements are not justified as true, but truth claims are evaluated as reasonable. A theory of knowledge without such an evaluation is sceptical. It is most important to understand that we do not have to choose between justificationism and scepticism, that there is a third possibility, namely a critical theory of knowledge. With such a theory we can overcome the shortcomings of justificationism, conventionalism, and scepticism.

# Bibliography

Albert, H. (1968). *Traktat über kritische Vernunft*. 5th edition, 1991. Tübingen: J. C. B. Mohr (Paul Siebeck).

Andersson, G. (1994). *Criticism and the History of Science: Kuhn's, Lakatos's and Feyerabend's Criticisms of Critical Rationalism*. Leiden: E. J. Brill.

——— (1998). 'Basisprobleme'. In H. Keuth, editor (1998), pp. 145-164. *Karl Popper, Logik der Forschung*. Berlin: Akademie Verlag.

Davidson, D. H. (1986). 'Empirical Content'. In E. Lepore, editor (1986), pp. 320-332. *Truth and Interpretation: Perspectives on the Philosophy of Donald Davidson*. Oxford: Blackwell.

Musgrave, A. E. (1993). *Common Sense, Science and Scepticism: A Historical Introduction to the Theory of Knowledge*. Cambridge: Cambridge University Press.

——— (1999). *Essays on Realism and Rationalism*. Amsterdam & Atlanta: Editions Rodopi B.V.

Popper, K. R. (1935). *Logik der Forschung*. Vienna: Julius Springer Verlag. 7th edition 1982. Tübingen: J. C. B. Mohr (Paul Siebeck).

Popper, K. R. (1959). *The Logic of Scientific Discovery*. London: Hutchinson. English translation of Popper (1935). 6th impression 1972.

# 34

# Basic Statements versus Protocols

Artur Koterski

## 1 Introduction

Even a beginning student of Popper's *Logik der Forschung* (*LdF*) (1935) easily understands that this important book is a strong critique of logical empiricism. Reading his other books and papers they quickly find, and may be somewhat surprised, that it was rather unusual for Popper to say anything without criticizing logical empiricism at the same time. Astonishment will increase when our student finds Popper fighting against logical positivism even after he had himself already killed it. Thus, he must be fighting a plague of apparitions!

One may respond that it is not at all surprising that Popper criticized logical empiricism for as long as he did. Logical empiricism was one of the most important and influential trends in the philosophy of science. It is proper and natural that one of the other leading figures in this field, Karl Raimund Popper, discusses their ideas and refutes them if, even though they are unacceptable, they are still alive here and there. This would be quite a good explanation. Unfortunately, it is false. To see why, we have to remember how Popper viewed logical positivism and the Vienna Circle: a group that blindly followed Mach in the wrong direction, regardless of the inconsistencies to which they were led. How then, we may ask, could it happen that such flawed ideas took over the philosophical market and became 'one of the most important and influential trends in the philosophy of science'?

Well, perhaps this is not so strange. Things like this do happen! In the Soviet Union tragically dim-witted Marxism was the most important and most influential ideology for over seventy years. But they had guns, tanks, internment camps, and many other tools to maintain their paradigm. Should we then say that logical empiricists held chairs in the most important and influential universities and blocked other views? But then, how is it that the two milestones of the so-called anti-positivist turn, *Logik der Forschung* (1935) and Kuhn's *The Structure of Scientific Revolutions* (1962) were published in two series edited by Schlick, Frank, Neurath, Carnap, and Morris?

But, maybe, the picture that Popper drew is simply wrong. Maybe, logical empiricism is not so primitive. Or, maybe, not primitive at all. And Popper is exorcizing his own ghost rather than engaging with real flesh-and-blood opponents, just like Don Quixote. This is the view I shall support by showing that his critique of Neurath's protocols missed the point.

## 2  Neurath's protocol sentences

Popper wrote that '...it is not quite easy to see what part the protocol sentences are supposed to play in Neurath's scheme' (Popper 1959, § 26). Perhaps it is the only remark he made on Neurath's conceptions which does not miss the truth. However, it was the Popperian critique that came to be seen as progressive once the empirical basis problem was considered.[1]

Following Thomas Uebel[2] I shall try to show how Neurath's protocols were supposed to function, and, on the basis of this analysis, I shall point out that Popper's basic statements proposal did not bring anything new.

The expression below (let it be $P$) is an example of one of Neurath's protocol sentences:

> Otto's protocol at 3.17 o'clock: [Otto's speech-thinking at 3.16 o'clock: (at 3.15 o'clock there was a table in the room perceived by Otto)].

This sentence can be decomposed in the following way:

(A)  Otto's protocol at 3.17 o'clock: [Otto's speech-thinking at 3.16 o'clock: (at 3.15 o'clock there was a table in the room perceived by Otto)].

(B)  Otto's speech-thinking at 3.16 o'clock: (at 3.15 o'clock there was a table in the room perceived by Otto).

(C)  At 3:15 o'clock there was a table in the room perceived by Otto.

(D)  At 3.15 o'clock there was a table in the room.

The first part, A ('protocol'), says that some sentence was minuted. It states the name of the person who took the protocol ('Otto') and it gives the title to that protocol ('Otto's protocol at 3.17 o'clock'). Accepting (A), we assume that under such and such conditions Otto noted down $P$.

Accepting (B) ('verbalization'), we agree that the observing person (again Otto) properly conceptualized the state of affairs he perceived.

Accepting (C) ('stimulation'), we say that Otto was sensually stimulated just as he would be if a table was present.

If we additionally accept (D) ('fact'), we agree that the event that is spoken about in (D) took place, and then we accept the $P$ as a whole.[3]

---

[1]At the time, but not any more. It has been questioned by some leading Popperians. Cp. Agassi 1966/1975, pp. 110f.; Andersson 1994, pp. 69f.; Andersson 1998, p. 164; Watkins 1984, pp. 250ff; see also footnote 12 below.

[2]Cp. Uebel 1992, 1992a, 1993; Cartwright et al. 1996, pp. 160ff. These books and papers contain detailed analysis of Neurath's stance. I use their results here in a highly simplified way.

[3]In his paper delivered at the AXIOMATIZATION OF NEURATH'S ENCYCLOPEDISM conference, Uebel (2002) provided some new arguments in favour of his interpretation. In particular, he described the 'fact' (or condition (D)) that must be satisfied when accepting $P$) as 'the no-defeater condition': one accepts part (D) when there is no reason to reject it. (As it will be shown later (cp. below § 4.1), Popper's basic statements look very similar to part (D) of Neurathian protocols. Some Popperians also talk about a kind of no-defeater condition; Miller (1994), p. 29, writes that: 'If [anyone] is unable to ...refute it [a basic

The very specific feature of protocol sentences, the one to secure their (higher) stability, was their non-extensionality. According to Neurath, in some cases one may reject individual parts of $P$, and still hold $P$ itself. Let us look at an example.

'Fire-swords appeared in the sky.' Firstly, let us put it into a $P$-form: Peasant Pierre's protocol, taken near Paris on 14 August 1357 at 3.17 o'clock: [Pierre's speech-thinking at 3.16 was: (at 3.15 o'clock there were fire-swords in the sky and Pierre saw them)].

To analyse the above statement we have to accept the historical fact that someone made it, that it was minuted — we must accept (A). Rejecting (A) we reject $P$, because we would then deny the very existence of such a sentence. We may also accept (B) and admit that Pierre chose his wordings correctly and consciously formulated $P$. Rejecting (B) we would say that Pierre was lying — that stimulation of the speech centre was not accompanied by stimulation in the sensory centre. Still later, we may accept (C), and then — unless we accept (D) — $P$ may be *Halluzinationsformulierung*, a sentence about a hallucination. But if we accept all four parts, then $P$ will satisfy the *formal condition* for being a 'reality statement'.

We accept a protocol statement because it allows us to check some scientific theory $T$. Nevertheless, our reality statement $P$ cannot be a testing statement yet — until the *pragmatical condition* is satisfied: $P$ has to be a 'binding statement'. We call $P$ a binding statement when $P$ entails a statement equivalent to a prediction entailed by $T$ or to the negation of that prediction — that is, when $P$ 'confirms' or 'shakes' $T$.

A reality statement that describes some anomaly may be counted as not binding, even if it was previously accepted as a protocol. We have to stress that there is always the possibility of changing the status of any reality statement: we can cancel it even if it was thought of as a binding statement.

According to Neurath, we cannot provide logical rules here: the acceptance, change, and rejection of a statement is the subject of appropriate (at that specific moment) agreement. (It is possible, however, to have a general desideratum: a good scientific theory should agree with as many protocol sentences as possible.) So, protocol sentences are chosen under agreement, they are not final; in a case of conflict with $T$ it is possible to save $T$ and reject $P$. But this does not mean that acceptance or rejection of $P$ is completely arbitrary. Firstly, the protocol sentence schema shows that to count $P$ as a reality statement one has to agree that some event took place (that is, the 'fact' of (D)), and that this 'fact' had some influence on the observer (Neurath is an empiricist). Secondly, contrary to Popper's or Lakatos's opinions (cp. Popper 1959, pp. 96f.; Lakatos 1970, p. 29; see also Watkins 1984, p. 253; O'Hear 1980, p. 75), Neurath gave the principles for rejecting $P$: those sentences are to be rejected (*qua* test statements) that do not satisfy formal and pragmatical conditions.

---

statement] — then clearly he has given no reason why the test statement should not be retained ....'

Let us consider now Popper's conception and compare it with Neurath's theory.

## 3  Basic statements in Popper

Popper's basic statements are individual existential statements, that — contrary to Neurath's proposal — have no *strictly* specified form[4] An example of a basic statement is $Q$: 'The pointer is over 5' (or, generally: 'An event $x$ of kind $E$ takes place at $k$'). Anyway, we can still talk about a *formal condition*. Additionally, $Q$ must satisfy a *material condition*; an event that happens in place $k$ has to be observable — basic statements must be intersensually and intersubjectively testable. Is it that we can accept every statement that satisfies the formal and material conditions? Of course not. Test sentences are accepted only during the testing process and only those that may give an answer to some significant question. This requirement looks like a *pragmatical condition*.

The great superiority of Popper's approach was, apparently, that it was the only one to solve the Fries's trilemma. This trilemma is encountered when trying to resolve the question of acceptance of basic statements. Firstly, we can say that sentences are to be accepted on the basis of a decision. This approach has a serious drawback, because we would never be able to reject statements thus accepted. So, to use that approach is to agree to some kind of (undesired) dogmatism. Acceptance requires justification and this leads to two other possibilities. One may justify the acceptance of a sentence by appealing to one's own sensations: I accept the sentence 'This wall is white' *as true*, because *I can see* that it is white. But this approach is also seriously defective and, therefore, unacceptable. The justification of a sentence through sensations amounts for Popper to 'thumping the table'. No sensation can justify any sentence because sentences are justifiable only by other sentences. This grievous error was called by Popper 'psychologism'.

There is only one way left open, free of dogmatism and psychologism: justification solely through other sentences. But even here there is a pitfall: it turns out that justification has no natural end — because to stop the regress one has to accept what is unacceptable, that is, either dogmatism or psychologism. So, there is no justification at all. Which way to go, then?

The truth lies somewhere in the middle. Popper's solution consisted in limited use of each of those three possibilities.

Popper says that basic statements are accepted by convention. But he is not in danger of dogmatism,[5] as he adds that all statements, including basic ones, are accepted only tentatively. This means that, if necessary, we can subject to further tests what has been thus far accepted by convention.

Avoiding the error of psychologism, Popper says that the acceptance of basic statements depends somehow (though quite mysteriously) on our ex-

---

[4]Popper claims also that *any* concrete statement may perform the test function.
[5]At least he thought so — see Schurz & Dorn 1988.

perience: sensations usually support our decisions (but they do not prove them). Though sentences are accepted only on the basis of other sentences, Popper is not concerned by the possibility of an infinite regress because he has introduced the mechanism of tentative decision.

This is not a complete solution, however. While testing a theory one has to accept as basic only those statements that are related by their content to the theory being tested; and only those that promise to answer some important questions, as has been observed earlier.

## 4 Basic statements and protocols

### *4.1 Was Popperian theory redundant?*

In a letter to Carnap, Popper, who was commenting on an early version of 'Über Protokollsätze' (Carnap 1932-1933), proposed to insert some changes into Carnap's work (22 October 1932 [ASP (RC) 102-59-72]):[6]

> First of all, we owe the overcoming of absolutism to *Neurath*; independently and in a different way, in his unpublished studies Popper reached a similar (and in his own opinion even deeper) view ....

Let us see then what is the novelty of Popper's theory.

(1) Is it the requirement of intersubjectivity and intersensuality of control statements? No; in his 'Protokollsätze' (Neurath 1932-1933) Neurath explicitly wrote that Otto is able to check Kalon's protocols.

(2) Is it the language that basic statements are formulated in? No; it is exactly the same language that the Vienna Circle called physicalistic language. Popper says (Popper 1959, § 28)

> ...that every basic statement must either be itself a statement about relative positions of physical bodies, or that it must be equivalent to some basic statements of this 'mechanistic' or 'materialistic' kind.

(3) Is it, then, the form of control statements? No; 'An event $x$ of kind $E$ takes place at $k$' is just a protocol statement in abbreviated form — namely, it is part (D) of Neurath's protocol. Neurath from time to time also uses shorter formulae.

(4) Is it that the novelty is hidden in the material condition (the requirement of the observability of $x$)? The answer is, obviously, no. After all, Neurath's protocols are, first and foremost, intended as an observability requirement.

(5) Is it, perhaps, the pragmatical condition — that we do not accept all the basic statements but only the useful ones? Surely not, since, as we saw, the pragmatical condition is already present in Neurath's conception.

---

[6] All excerpts from the Carnap Collection in the Archives of Scientific Philosophy (ASP), University of Pittsburgh, are quoted by permission of the University of Pittsburgh. All rights reserved. Excerpts from Popper's unpublished writings are quoted by permission of The Estate of Karl Popper. All rights reserved. The translations are the author's.

(6) Let us ask, finally, if the solution Popper gave to Fries's trilemma is not trying to break down an open door. To see if it is, we should frame the 'Fries–Popper' criterion *FPC*: a theory of protocol sentences satisfies *FPC* when it tells how to accept protocol sentences (respectively, basic statements) without falling into any one of the three pitfalls: dogmatism, psychologism, and infinite regress. If there was a conception that satisfied *FPC* before *LdF*, then '[t]he great superiority of Popper's solution' would be doubtful.

Such a theory did exist and, what is more, Popper must have known it.

If we ask whether Neurath is forced to accept protocol sentences 'dogmatically', then the answer is negative. As Popper, who commented on Neurath's views already in 1934, wrote (Popper 1935, § 26):

> Die Auffassung, daß die Protokollsätze nicht unantastbar sind, scheint mir ein erheblicher ... zu sein ....

In the English version of this fragment he explicitly refers to Neurath (Popper 1959, § 26):

> Neurath's view that protocol statements are not inviolable represents, in my opinion, a notable advance.

The cornerstone of Neurath's approach to protocol statements is their corrigibility. In addition, protocols are accepted or rejected on the basis of decisions.

Is Neurath's theory burdened with the sin of psychologism? Popper, in a convoluted way, tried to prove that it was. But he was wrong, as in Neurath's case sensations do not prove the truth of protocols. So, in this context, one cannot even speak of psychologism.[7] Strange as it might seem, when considering 'observation' there is no essential difference between Popper's and Neurath's views. When Neurath says 'at 3.15 o'clock there was a table in the room perceived by Otto', he talks about some behavioral stimuli — that one physical object (a table) has an effect on another (Otto's body). And what is Popper's view? He says (1959, § 28):

> ... it will now seem as though in demanding observability, I have, after all, allowed psychologism to slip back quietly into my theory. Admittedly, it is possible to interpret the concept of an *observable event* in a psychologistic sense.

Popper is right, one does immediately think about *psychologismus*. However Popper rushes to aid the confused reader by claiming that instead of talking about an 'observable' event we can use a different circumlocution (1935, ibidem):

---

[7] Popper said Neurath had not given the rules for rejecting his protocol statements. On the other hand, he claimed that Neurath had committed psychologism and opted for an invalid way of accepting protocols. But what Popper claims is simply inconsistent, as the methods of accepting and rejecting protocols are one and the same method.

... wenn wir wollten, statt von einem 'beobachtbaren Vorgang' auch von einem 'Bewegungsvorgang an (makroskopischen) physischen Körpern' sprechen könnten
....

We can read this as: 'instead of an "observable event" we could speak about a "movement-event" in (macroscopic) physical bodies'.[8] But, then, isn't it the case that 'movement' signifies (or could signify) behavioristically excited senses and that '(macroscopic) physical bodies' signify observers?

Just for the record we may add that Neurath's theory is safe from infinite regress. Even though in Neurath's conception sentences are justified by other sentences, as observed before, one can always decide to stop.

Popper, I suppose, would be highly dissatisfied with such a comparison. In the previously quoted letter to Carnap he wrote (22 October 10 1932 [ASP (RC) 102-59-72]):[9]

> *You* think that we owe the overcoming of absolutism to Neurath. Naturally, I cannot say anything against it. On the other hand, after Neurath's Vienna lecture it seems to me almost absurd that I would be headed 'towards the same position' as Neurath. Besides, I think that already in Burgstein I argued against metaphysical absolutism (which consists in a faith in the logical and formal distinction of all elementary or protocol sentences) ....

He seemed to be convinced that his conception is essentially (a) different and (b) better. He vehemently protested against being placed on the same level as Neurath — as a predecessor or as an ally (ibidem):

> ... it looks currently as if I have only developed Neurath's intentions. Even though Neurath in his Vienna lecture roughly *proves* that he is far from accepting the absolutism of protocol sentences, my considerations on this topic are, in any case, deeper and further-reaching than Neurath's. At the very most, Neurath's anti-absolutism is a pious wish — in [my conception] it is a derived consequence of the system, of deductivism.

### 4.2 Is Neurath's theory better?

Up to this moment we may at least say that these two theories are fairly similar. However, coming back to Popper's remark about the strange complexity of Neurath's protocols, one may say that even if these two conceptions give the same outcome in the Fries case, that of Popper is still better, as it is much

---

[8]The standard English translation is different, however: '... I am using it [that is, the notion of observable event] in such a sense that it might just as well be replaced by "an event involving position and movement of macroscopic physical bodies"' (Popper 1959, § 28). If this is a proper reading of the German text quoted above, then, of course, I am wrong on this point. But, still, Popper does no better. As Deutscher rightly points out, the explication of 'observable' cannot appeal to *makroskopischen physischen Körpern*, because 'macroscopic' *means* 'visible with the naked eye' — thus 'observable' (cp. Deutscher 1968, p. 281).

[9]They met in Burgstein in August 1932. There Popper learnt about the protocol sentences debate and Neurath's proposal.

simpler: one does not have to operate with outlandish reports that seem to be far from the practice of the real scientists.[10] This, of course, would be a clear advantage, unless Neurath's proposal were to provide a solution where Popper seems to be helpless. My task, therefore, consists in showing at least one such problem.[11]

When Popper published his *LdF* many people argued that his theory of basic statements broke the link with experience or with reality, due to his use of convention. However, to be sure, Popper was one of those — along with Schlick, Juhos, and Russell — who accused Neurath of 'throwing empiricism overboard'. But they were all wrong; Neurath and empiricism stayed 'on board'. The first argument against Popper was, I suppose, raised by Ayer (1937). Ayer restated his stance in the Schilpp volume (Ayer 1974). It seems that his argumentation softened Popper's position to some degree. In his replies Popper wrote (Popper 1974, p. 1114):

> Our experiences are not only motives for accepting or rejecting an observational statement, but they may even be described as *inconclusive reasons*. They are reasons because of the generally reliable character of our observations; they are inconclusive because of our fallibility.

Popper's comments awoke a measure of doubt among his pupils. Thus, for example, Watkins and Zahar opted for a break with strict Popperian anti-psychologistic policy.

One of the conditions a basic statement has to satisfy is testability. What if we wish to test it? If we wish to test a basic statement $p$ we have to infer another basic statement $q$ from the conjunction of $p$ and some additional hypotheses from background knowledge. Will we not fall into an infinite regress? Popper says that we may stop at any sentence which is very easily testable. However, we may ask after Watkins, if it is so easy to test, why not test it? But what if we really wish to test it? Then we have to repeat the aforementioned procedure — and infer yet another basic statement from the conjunction of $q$ and some additional hypotheses. And still, we do not get a reason to accept this one rather than the other one, as a basic statement. The situation would change if we agreed that perceptions may justify the acceptance of a statement, even if they did not justify it completely (cp. Watkins 1984, p. 253).

This is not a problem in Neurathian theory. Though his protocols are not formulated in phenomenal language and they are far from Watkins's 0-level sentences, they still are about perceptions, though not exclusively. Instead of relating them to a subjective experience, Neurath treats his protocols as descriptions of 'facts' — that somebody's nervous system reacted as if some event, also described in the protocol, took place. So, how do we accept a protocol? We accept it if it is in good agreement with the body of the already accepted statements. But how do we go about obtaining a protocol to consider

---

[10]I skip here the obvious fact that Neurath's protocols were designed as a reconstruction only, and not for conversational aims.

[11]We may, however, consider this as a purely rhetorical task; Wartofsky (1968, pp. 140-142) contended that Popperian basic statements do not exist.

its agreement or disagreement with our system? The method might be roughly reconstructed in the following way:

(D)  Let us say that there is an object $x$ in Otto's visual field.

(C)  And Otto looks at this object.

(B)  He, perhaps unconsciously, runs through his memory, finds the appropriate theory and identifies the object as a table.

(A)  Then he (or somebody else) formulates a sentence about all these 'facts'.

As sensations do not justify the acceptance of the protocol, Neurath is free from psychologism. But he is still able to point out the reason for which the protocol was made (and not just accepted) and that reason lies in Otto's perception.

Ayer urged that we can retain a relative, corrigible empirical basis, while accepting the existence of a causal link between experience and basic statements. That was not acceptable for Popper, at least not in 1935. Then, as Watkins and Zahar show, Popper's criterion of demarcation fails, as the asymmetry between verification and falsification disappears (cp. Zahar 1989, pp. 325f.; 1998, pp. 109ff).

This was never a problem for Neurath, who thought that both verification and falsification are a kind of Laplacean dream; and according to Neurath the criterion of demarcation was simply harmful.

Zahar[12] when he questioned the validity of Popper's solution to the empirical basis problem, talked about Popper's 'Robinson Crusoe objection'. In *Die beiden Grundprobleme der Erkenntnistheorie* Popper says (Popper 1930-1933, p. 133;[13] cp. also Agassi 1964, pp. 190f.):

> One can imagine a person, *Robinson [Crusoe]*, who though completely isolated, would master a language and develop some physical theory .... One can imagine ... that his 'physics' *coincides*, so to speak literally, with our modern physics; furthermore that that Robinson, who built a physical laboratory, tested it [that is, his 'physics'] experimentally as well.

> What Robinson constructs under the name of physics is *not a science*; this is so not because we arbitrarily *define* science in such a way that only intersubjectively testable theories can be termed scientific, but because the Robinson-objection starts from the false premise that science is characterized by its *results* rather than by its *method*.

Putting it simply, if we accept that science and, in particular, basic statements have to be intersubjectively testable, then Robinson Crusoe is not able to pursue science before Friday; for then there would be no possibility for different persons to repeat the same tests and hence to reach any intersubjective agreements. This, according to Zahar, is wrong. Robinson does not have to invent super-sophisticated theories of modern physics. However, he

---

[12]Cp. Zahar 1998, p. 116. See also Zahar 1995, pp. 58f.; Zahar 1983, pp. 161f.

[13]I have followed, with slight modifications, the translation on p. 161 of Zahar ibidem.

might discover and describe some important regularities such as the law of thermal expansion. Thus, Zahar says, the requirement of intersubjective basic statements is too strong and we should add to the arsenal of science also some 'private' sentences.

Could we turn this argument against Neurath? Not really. To be sure, Neurath had his own *Robinsoneinwand*, but it was directed against private language. If Robinson produces sentences in the so-called 'private language' then Robinson of tomorrow will not be able to understand Robinson of today — he will not be able to read his own diary. But Robinson had a diary. Thus he had his own small input into human history and psychology. He was able to pursue science. He would be able to test his own protocols in exactly the same way he would test Friday's protocols.

# Bibliography

ASP. Archives of Scientific Philosophy, University of Pittsburgh.

Agassi, J. (1964). 'The Nature of Scientific Problems and Their Roots in Metaphysics'. In Bunge (1964), pp. 189-211. Reprinted as Chapter 9 of Agassi (1975).

——— (1966). 'Sensationalism'. *Mind* **75**, pp. 1-24. Reprinted as Chapter 5 of Agassi (1975).

——— (1975). *Science in Flux*. Dordrecht & Boston: D. Reidel Publishing Company.

Andersson, G. (1994). *Criticism and the History of Science: Kuhn's, Lakatos's and Feyerabend's Criticisms of Critical Rationalism*. Leiden: E. J. Brill.

——— (1998). 'Basisprobleme'. In Keuth (1998), pp. 143-164.

Ayer, A. J. (1937). 'Verification and Experience'. *Proceedings of the Aristotelian Society* **37**, pp. 137-156.

——— (1974). 'Truth, Verification and Verisimilitude'. In Schilpp (1974), pp. 684-692.

Bunge, M, editor (1964). *The Critical Approach to Science and Philosophy*. New York: The Free Press of Glencoe.

Carnap, R. (1932-1933). 'Über Protokollsätze', *Erkenntnis* **III**, pp. 215-228.

Cartwright, N., Cat, J., Fleck, L., & Uebel, T. (1996). *Otto Neurath: Philosophy Between Science and Politics*. Cambridge: Cambridge University Press.

Cohen, R. S. & Wartofsky, M. W., editors (1968). *Boston Studies in the Philosophy of Science*, Volume III, *In Memory of N. R. Hanson*. Dordrecht: D. Reidel Publishing Company, & New York: The Humanities Press.

Deutscher, M. (1968). 'Popper's Problem of an Empirical Basis'. *Australasian Journal of Philosophy* **46**, pp. 277-288.

D'Agostino, F. & Jarvie, I. C., editors (1989). *Freedom and Rationality. Essays in Honor of John Watkins. From His Colleagues and Friends*. Dordrecht: Kluwer Academic Publishers.

Keuth, H., editor (1998). *Karl Popper, Logik der Forschung*. Berlin: Akademie Verlag.

Kuhn, T. S. (1962). *The Structure of Scientific Revolutions*. Chicago & London: University of Chicago Press. 2nd edition 1970.

Lakatos, I. (1970). 'Falsification and the Methodology of Scientific Research Programmes'. In Lakatos (1978), pp. 8-101.

——— (1978). *The Methodology of Scientific Research Programmes. Philosophical Papers*, Volume I. Edited by J. Worrall & G. Currie. Cambridge: Cambridge University Press.

Miller, D. W. (1994). *Critical Rationalism: A Restatement and Defence*. Chicago & La Salle IL: Open Court Publishing Company.

Neurath, O. (1932-1933). 'Protokollsätze'. *Erkenntnis* **III**, pp. 204-214.

O'Hear, A. (1980). *Karl Popper*. London: Routledge.

———, editor (1995). *Karl Popper: Philosophy and Problems*. Cambridge: Cambridge University Press.

Popper, K. R. (1930-1933). *Die beiden Grundprobleme der Erkenntnistheorie*. Edited by T. E. Hansen. First published 1979. Tübingen: J. C. B. Mohr (Paul Siebeck). 2nd edition 1994. 3rd edition to appear in *Gesammelte Werke in deutscher Sprache*, Volume 2. Tübingen: Mohr Siebeck.

——— (1935). *Logik der Forschung*. Vienna. Julius Springer Verlag.

——— (1959). *The Logic of Scientific Discovery*. New York: Basic Books, Inc.

——— (1974). 'Replies to My Critics'. In Schilpp (1974), pp. 961-1200.

Schilpp, P. A., editor (1974). *The Philosophy of Karl Popper*. La Salle IL: Open Court Publishing Company.

Schurz, G. & Dorn, G. J. W. (1988). 'Why Popper's Basic Statements are not Falsifiable. Some Paradoxes in Popper's "Logic of Scientific Discovery"'. *Zeitschrift für allgemeine Wissenschaftstheorie* **19**, pp. 124-143.

Uebel, T. (1992). *Overcoming Logical Positivism from Within. The Emergence of Neurath's Naturalism in the Vienna Circle's Protocol Sentences Debate*. Amsterdam & Atlanta: Editions Rodopi B.V.

——— (1992a). 'Rational Reconstruction as Elucidation? Carnap in the Early Protocol Sentences Debate'. *Synthese* **93**, pp. 107-140.

——— (1993). 'Neurath's Protocol Statements: A Naturalistic Theory of Data and Pragmatic Theory of Theory Acceptance'. *Philosophy of Science* **60**, pp. 587-607.

——— (2002). 'Neurath's Protocols Revisited'. Unpublished talk given at the Axiomatization of Neurath's Encyclopedism conference, Cracow 2002. http://neurath.umcs.lublin.pl/.

Wartofsky, M. W. (1968). 'Metaphysics as Heuristic for Science'. In Cohen & Wartofsky (1968), pp. 123-172.

Watkins, J. W. N. (1984). *Science and Scepticism*. Princeton NJ: Princeton University Press.

Zahar, E. G. (1983). 'The Popper-Lakatos Controversy in the Light of "Die beiden Grundprobleme der Erkenntnistheorie"'. *The British Journal for the Philosophy of Science* **34**, pp. 149-171.

——— (1989). 'John Watkins on the Empirical Basis and the Corroboration of Scientific Theories'. In D'Agostino & Jarvie (1989), pp. 325-341.

——— (1995). 'The Problem of the Empirical Basis'. In O'Hear (1995), pp. 45-74.

——— (1998). 'Falsifiability'. In Keuth (1998), pp. 103-123.

# 35

# Karl Popper and the Empirical Basis

Jeremy Shearmur

## 1 Introduction

Popper's approach to the 'empirical basis' in *The Logic of Scientific Discovery* is suggestive and I believe correct. But it is also set out much too briefly. In this paper, I first explore Popper's view, and discuss how it is best understood. I argue that it is to be distinguished from and to be preferred to foundationalist empiricism as a theory of the empirical basis. Second, I discuss criticisms of Popper's view by John Watkins and Elie Zahar. Watkins raises an interesting problem, but his own response is defective. What is needed to resolve it is an elaboration of Popper's view. Zahar's criticism, by contrast, rests on the assumption of the correctness of ideas that Popper gave us good reason to reject, while his positive suggestions are unworkable. Finally, I suggest that we may avoid misunderstandings of Popper, and what seems to a strong temptation to re-read him as an empiricist foundationalist, if we recognize him as having offered a distinctive kind of coherence theory of knowledge. I further suggest that Paul Feyerabend was correct in his earlier writings to see parallels between Popper's work and *certain* of the ideas of the later Wittgenstein.

## 2 Popper on the empirical basis

The best way into Popper's approach is by way of his discussion of scientific objectivity in Chapter 8 of *The Logic of Scientific Discovery*. This, Popper indicates,[1] draws on what Kant says in the *Critique of Pure Reason* about communication:[2]

> The touchstone whereby we decide whether our holding a thing to be true is conviction or mere persuasion is ... the possibility of communicating it and of finding it to be valid for all human reason.

The 'empirical basis' is that against which our theories should be appraised. Popper takes objectivity (understood as a product of intersubjective scrutiny[3]) to be an important aim, and argues more specifically for the significance

---

[1] Popper (1959), § 8.
[2] Kant (1781), Transcendental Doctrine of Method, Chapter 2, § 3.
[3] Compare, here, Popper's discussion in (1945), Chapter 23.

of intersubjective testability. This relates in turn to his requirements of repeatability, and to his view that what should be tested are claims about observable states of affairs.

In § 29 of *The Logic of Scientific Discovery*, Popper writes: 'Every test of a theory ... must stop at some basic statement or other which we *decide to accept*.' And, at the end of this section:

> the decision to accept a basic statement, and to be satisfied with it, is causally connected with our experiences — especially with our *perceptual experiences*. But we do not attempt to *justify* basic statements by these experiences. Experiences can *motivate a decision*, and hence an acceptance or rejection of a statement, but a basic statement cannot be *justified* by them — no more than by thumping the table.

Popper is concerned here with testing against what are taken to be true statements about the world. Accordingly, the decision that is being made is as to the tentative acceptance of some statement as a (fallible) candidate for this; something that is then open to intersubjective scrutiny. For the most part, this is simply what we see; in other special cases, we may have to decide when our scrutiny or checking will stop. *Pace* Susan Haack, it makes no sense of his argument to treat the truth of a basic statement as something that is decided by convention.[4]

This theme in Popper's work is not an isolated one — an aberration that can easily be detached from his other ideas. Related themes are to be found in his discussion of the social character of scientific knowledge in his *Open Society*, his endorsement of Marx's critique of psychologism, and his 'On the Sources of Knowledge and of Ignorance'.[5] Other relevant material is discussed in Jarvie's *The Republic of Science*.[6]

Popper's position is simple, straightforward, and I believe correct. It is concerned with intersubjectively acceptable statements of a kind that we need in order to test scientific theories. The simplest way of interpreting it, I would suggest, is as follows.

Our phenomenological experience is of objects in the world — of chairs, computers, pieces of laboratory equipment, and so on.[7] Such experiences are, plausibly, a product of an interplay between causal influences upon our bodies, and processes of interpretation. These processes of interpretation may be understood as going all the way down to the constitution of our sense organs and our physiology. We thus see things as trees, leaves and so on,[8] and our perceptual judgements are fallible — not least because of the degree of

---

[4]Cp. Haack (1993), p. 100.
[5]Cp. Popper (1945), Chapters 23f.; Chapter 14 (see text to note 1; note also Popper's use of 'Robinsonade'); and Popper (1963), Chapter 1.
[6]Jarvie (2001).
[7]Here, Austin (1962) seems simply correct.
[8]What we see are, thus, representations of the world, but in a realist mode. We each see things that we typically take to be there, and also accessible to other people.

interpretation that is involved. What is needed, in the face of this fallibility, is not an attempt to trace things back to supposedly uninterpreted elements of experience (which there is no reason to believe even exist) but, instead, the submitting of our observations to testing. This is ideally done by way of intersubjective testing. But — especially once, as adults, we have got used to it — we may do a reasonable job ourselves,[9] by means of checking our observations across time, or by using different forms of cross-checking, and so on. This differs from the empiricist account because it takes issue with the view that there are 'given' elements in our psychological experience that are certain and constitute a firm upon which other claims are to be assessed. (It may be possible for us to try to focus not upon the intersubjectively accessible objects of our day-to-day lives, but upon our subjective experience of them. But this can be very difficult and, outside of a wish to test theories about human experience,[10] it is not clear what the point of it would be.)

## 3  Some problems of foundationalism

Now there is a line of argument, going back to Descartes, that seeks to provide a foundation for scientific knowledge in statements that we can know for certain. The empiricist concern with statements about what we can be sure that we are experiencing, is a version of this research programme. But it is problematic. Let me illustrate why by considering two different ways in which such an approach might be understood.[11]

Suppose that we are looking at a red book. We might wonder if we are mistaken about what we are seeing. One empiricist approach involves our reducing the content of what we claim is there to be seen — for example, to a red oblong patch. This approach, however, faces a couple of difficulties.

The first is one to which Popper alerted us; namely, that when we make claims about the properties of such things, we attribute to them dispositional properties.[12] To refer to something as red, is to attribute to it a disposition to be red in the future (unless it undergoes some physical change), rather than some other colour. We attribute to it also standard rather than Goodmanesque

---

[9] If we are isolated for long periods of time, our judgement may become idiosyncratic.

[10] Compare Popper's discussion of the Würzburg School in *The Self and Its Brain* (Popper & Eccles 1977), Chapter P4, § 30, pp. 106f.

[11] These are loosely inspired by Price (1932/1950), and Ayer (1956), but my concerns are very different from theirs.

[12] I thus reject the criticisms made by Robert Nola (1983), pp. 25-44, and endorsed by Alan Musgrave in his (1983), pp. 45-62. Nola is correct that Popper also says things at odds with this idea; but this shows simply that Popper did not fully emancipate himself from the empiricism of which he offered such interesting criticism. Nola is incorrect in thinking that this view would mean that much of science is a priori; rather, the empirical issue would be to discern what there is (for example, water as understood in a particular manner, or something that in some ways resembles it). Against Musgrave, I would argue that all seeing turns out to be seeing as — although what we see things as may involve attributing to them only low-level theoretical properties.

dispositions.[13] In addition, we attribute to it dispositions that are intersubjective in their character: if I claim that there is a visible red patch in front of me, it is assumed that it will be visible as a red patch to others, too, provided that they are in the appropriate situation, and have the appropriate capacities.

There are ways that carry still less content in which it would be possible to state what one is claiming to see. I might claim that what I am experiencing is whatever there is in common between a red surface and its Goodmanesque versions. I might claim also that what I am seeing appears *to me* as red, leaving open the possibility that it would appear differently to others. However, the more content that is emptied out of our basic statements, the less we can do with them by way of criticism or corroboration.

The second problem relates to a claim that was made by Saussure in his *Course of General Linguistics* (1983).[14] He argued that the meaning of a colour term such as 'red' is to be understood in terms of that with which it is contrasted. What shades are understood by an individual as 'red' will relate to what terms are available to them in which to differentiate between colours. Clearly, it would be open to them to propose some new term — for example, to introduce a way of discriminating between two shades of an existing colour. But what they communicate to others will be limited by the discriminations made within their classificatory schemata. Further, what they convey to someone else will be affected by the other person's classificatory system, too. This may mean that there are possibilities for misunderstanding — in both directions — between those who are using a relatively crude and a highly sophisticated classificatory system. A printer may work with a highly sophisticated classificatory system. Many of the colours to which he refers may mean nothing to me, while, on the other hand, the crude classificatory system that I use may subsume a broad range of shades within each of the terms that I use, but may convey a more specific and possibly misleading meaning to them (or may leave indeterminate just what I wish to convey to him).

This does not mean that such misunderstandings cannot be resolved given time, and negotiation. In addition, Putnam's point about meaning — that we typically understand ourselves as having to defer to meanings and discriminations in our language, of which we are not personally aware[15] — also applies here. But a consequence of all this is that our first strategy is flawed. By limiting what one claims, one may be able to shed controversial theoretical content. To pursue this path may lead the individual further and further away from an intersubjective understanding of what the terms mean that they are

---

[13]I am, here, working with an interpretation of Goodmanesque predicates that differs from Goodman's own in his (1954), in that I understand them as dispositional properties of things in the world.

[14]Saussure (1983), Part Two, Chapter IV, pp. 111-122.

[15]See Putnam's discussion of the linguistic division of labour, in his 'The Meaning of "Meaning" ', now Chapter 12 of his (1975); especially pp. 226-229.

using to describe their experience. Yet it is the products of such an exploration that are needed to convey our points to others, and to relate our experience to the theories that we want to assess.

By contrast with our first approach, rather than moving from a dubitable book to a less dubitable red patch, we could move to a seeming book. Such an approach is able to avoid the dispositional and Goodmanesque problems that I have discussed above. In addition, it would seem to offer us the possibility of certainty — small problems about the misidentification of our experience, aside.

However, such statements are useless for any purpose other than the description of what we are experiencing. *Our* concern is with statements against which theories can be criticized or corroborated. But it is not clear with what such statements are compatible or incompatible. If we claim that we have seen a book, then we would simply judge ourselves to have been wrong if, when we looked again, we found that we were seeing something radically different. The same goes for red patches. But — and this is the other side of their immunity to the dispositional and Goodmanesque problems — it is not clear how seeming books will behave in the future.

Another problem is this. We know, from the history of science, from the study of myth, and from anthropology, that people's theoretical ideas influence how they see things; and, indeed, what they see. The subjectivization of the objects involved in statements about what we observe would have the effect of preserving all the (incompatible) theories that influence our observations, but in a ghostly form. We would end up with statements about seeming classical deities, witches, dephlogisticated air, and anything else that anyone has ever appeared to see. Such statements would be just about certain. But it is not clear what we would be expected to do with them, or how any theory that got built into them could ever be eliminated.

The most obvious alternatives to Popper's approach would thus seem to range from the defective to the completely useless *qua* basic statements.

## 4 A Popperian approach

Let us briefly explore what a Popperian approach would involve. As Paul Feyerabend argued, we need a setting of contending theoretical perspectives. Given that, for Popper, our theories influence how we see the world, we risk becoming prisoners of our theories if we are not confronted with alternatives to them. Evidence is thus best seen in the context of a dialogue, and as what one can get one's interlocutors to go along with. We want to obtain their agreement to claims that are as strong as possible — yet (and this goes back to Popper's discussion in *The Logic of Scientific Discovery*) — we want to be dealing with claims that we can take to be (tentatively) decided by observations that we can make.[16]

---

[16]If we do not have critical interlocutors to hand, we might make use of Adam Smith's idea of what an impartial spectator would go along with. Some aspects of observation can,

In the face of disagreement, we may try stripping aspects of our theoretical interpretation from our initial descriptions of what is the case, until the point where our interlocutor will agree as to what is there. In some cases, the currency in terms of which this is done may become relatively standardized (for example, we may make use of pointer readings); but such standard procedures may be called into question, if they are thought to be problematic in the light of the theories under contention. At the same time, such contestation is not to be undertaken lightly — proposals for revision have, themselves, to be cashed out in terms which will be intersubjectively acceptable. All this means that 'the empirical basis' is a product of active interpretation and of dialogue. Rather than as a *datum*, we may see it as an *artifact* — something we have to *work* our way towards.

But what about our experience? First, our interest is in a certain kind of public performance, to be made in appropriate circumstances, not in what experiences someone may have had while they are making it. Second, exactly what people are experiencing may differ: the focus of attention, and the quality of experience, may differ from person to person. As Popper says, an experience may prompt people to make the statement. But the relationship between the experience and the statement is complex. It is also beside the point. Provided someone can say: 'there is a cow here' when they are in front of one, it does not matter what they are experiencing. What is more, the public content of the statement may differ from what each person may be experiencing psychologically, depending on how they experience the world, what happens to strike them, what cows are associated with, how much attention they were paying and to what, and so on. Third, those who stress the priority of individual experience have got things precisely the wrong way round. Consider the extent to which what we experience — that is, the characteristics of our experiences — are structured by categories drawn from the public realm; most obviously, when we describe them, but also, I would suggest, when we experience them. In addition, given the mountain of literature that has been generated by Wittgenstein's claims about private language, I would not have thought that the general issue here of the primacy of the public character of meaning needs to be laboured. In saying this, I am not wishing to claim that we do not have private experiences, or, indeed, that there may not be problems if the categories available to us in the public realm are out of kilter with them.

To sum all this up, Popper's approach to the empirical basis has the following advantages. First it provides the kind of statements that we need, to test claims made in the sciences. Second, it is objective in the sense of being intersubjectively testable (by way of our being provided with a kind of recipe for how the test is to be reproduced, and also tested). Third, it is fallible — something that we have good reasons to wish for not least because we are familiar with the need to correct basic statements: Not only may we make

of course, be mechanized. But the acceptability of such procedures rests on intersubjective acceptability, as does the interpretation of whatever they deliver.

mistakes, but we may argue that hitherto accepted basic statements have been infected by theoretical ideas that, in our judgement, are false.

## 5 Two critics

Let me now turn to Popper's two critics. My treatment here can be only brief. First, John Watkins. His treatment of Popper's account of the empirical basis in *Science and Scepticism*[17] has two features; on the one side, there is a criticism; on the other, an attempt to respond to that criticism.

The criticism was (p. 253) that (if as I think is correct) Popper is to be interpreted as suggesting that perceptual experiences play no epistemological (or better, I would suggest, no justificatory) role in testing, then Popper simply did not explain what it actually is to test a theory.

Not much is here required to respond to his point. We can take a test to involve the undertaking of a test procedure, the observing of what has taken place, and the issuing of a statement about the state of an appropriate, publicly observable object: for example. that the temperature gauge said 98° Celsius. In this context, psychological experiences may motivate the person to make the statement, but they do not serve to give epistemological warrant to the truth of the claim, and are, in a sense, beside the point. At best, we might say that the occurrence of whatever experience we are having needs to be compatible with what we take to be the truth concerning the situation that we are in, and the public occurrence upon which we report. But this will equally be true if our report is, in fact, false. While if we experience something highly unusual — that while we are observing our apparatus, we have a strong visual impression of a hippopotamus — we will typically conclude that there is something wrong with us, and call a colleague for assistance. However, what the person is *doing* may be very much to the point; for example, if he shuts his eyes at the crucial point, or makes his statement under duress, or lies, then this undermines the value of the test.

My comment that psychological experiences are beside the point may be understood in two different ways. The first relates Austin's argument in *Sense and Sensibilia*[18] that what we experience are things, rather than sense data from which we draw inferences to the existence of things. If I were asked what is in front of me at this moment, I would say: a laptop computer on a desk — and that this is what I am seeing. Someone might ask me: what exactly are you experiencing? I could — perhaps with some difficulty — describe this. But it would require a shift of my attention from what I take to be there, to my experience and its characteristics. These are typically somewhat inchoate, such that the very request that I describe what I am experiencing in itself is likely to lead me to have to give attention to and to render specific, things that do not normally have this form. But it is also difficult to describe — in the sense that the terms in which I do so will usually be derivative from those

---
[17] Watkins (1984), Chapter 7.
[18] Austin (1962).

we use to describe the objects that I am observing. Rather than objects being constructed from my experiences, my experiences are typically constituted in terms drawn from the intersubjective realm of objects.

There is, however, a second and even more radical sense in which my suggestion may be understood. For it does not much matter what my experiences actually amount to — provided that I can give the appropriate descriptions when I am standing in the right kind of relationship to the objects; namely, observing them.

Thus, I don't think that there was *much* of a problem there to solve relating to the question that Watkins raises. What Watkins himself says in response to the problem is that we have various perceptual experiences, and interpret them, typically unconsciously, in various ways. He then invents the persona, Johnny Wideawake, who has conscious knowledge of the various different interpretative theories that are unconscious to John Watkins. He then, takes the perceptual experiences as something requiring explanation — the hypotheses thus being what is offered to explain them (pp. 260f.).

The final suggestion here is worthy enough; at least in the sense that that we can appeal to our claims to knowledge at a public level to explain our experiences, and also because we would, indeed, doubtless like to know about the processes through which we are led to make sense of the world. But there are three problems about Watkins's re-introduction of a form of psychologistic foundationalism.

The first is that it is not clear that there will necessarily be anything that is *consciously* given, at all. Our interactions with the world may operate by way of causal physical mechanisms, which it is odd to assume *must* be present as features of our *psychological* experience. Watkins seems to be assuming a particular model of how we understand the world, in which there are various causal interactions that lead to certain psychological experiences. These are taken as what is 'given', and our task, in epistemology, is then envisaged as being somehow to build our knowledge of the external world from such experiences. By contrast, Popper offers us a picture in which we come to the world with biologically pre-formed expectations (which may or may not correspond to what things are like). In addition, there are interactions with the world, which on Popper's account we interpret actively — the active interpretation being taken right down to what are, in effect, hypotheses built into our very sense organs and physiology. All this has the result that we may react in various standard ways to situations in which we find ourselves — as, say, do small babies when faced for the first time with visual situations that simulate a sharp drop.[19] We also, as Andrew Lock has argued, come into the world with the expectation not only that there will be language there, but others to help us learn it.[20] We come to live in an intersubjectively shared world, within which critical feedback from others plays a key epistemological role — in interplay with what we *make* of the world by various means.

---

[19]Cp. on this, Gregory (1966), pp. 188 and 201-203.
[20]Cp. Lock (1980), passim.

All told, we interact with the world and learn about it. But it is not clear that *anything* is psychologically 'given'. For the interaction may be purely physical, while what we make of this — from assumptions built into our sense organs,[21] right up to conscious efforts of interpretation — may *all* be seen as initiated by us.

Second, if as Popper suggests — and Watkins seems not unhappy with such suggestions — it is as if various hypotheses are built into our physiology, then the model with which Watkins is working (the given and its interpretation) looks problematic. For the problem with which Watkins is concerned seems part of the very empiricist tradition the Popperian critique of which Watkins would in other circumstances accept.

Third, we should separate, quite clearly, two different enterprises; the first, the attempt to explain what is going on when we see things in the world, which I would take to be part of science; and the second, epistemological issues. The latter seem best handled in terms of intersubjective accountability of the kind that Popper has described. To separate these things is important. This is, in part, for the reasons that Popper has stressed almost to the point of overkill: that tales of origins are a bad way to approach the issue of validity. It is also because, if either my first or my second suggestion in this section is correct, it is mistaken to try to tell our causal story in terms of the primacy of something that is psychologically certain or even given. There *may* be certain physical processes that play a key role when we are led to make statements about perceived objects that are veridical.[22] The content of these, however, may not be something that is known consciously to us at all, and there is no special virtue in trying to invent a bogus quasi-psychological story for things that are purely physical, just because one is attached to poor ideas in epistemology.

This brings me to Zahar.

His 'The Problem of the Empirical Basis' starts with a variety of flat-footed statements of epistemological ideas that Popper has given us good reason to question:[23] Thus on p. 59 Zahar tells us:

> as its name indicates, physical science is founded on man's relation to physical nature which acts on him through his senses and his brain, thus finally reaching his consciousness. *Only at this level does man's contact with nature occur unmediated* [the — astonished — emphasis is mine], which is why most scientists subscribe to the phenomenological and not to the consensual view of observation.

Second, Zahar is after criticism or justification by way of statements that are certain. He proposes that we achieve these, by having us talk about how

---

[21] This can of course be understood after the fashion of evolutionary epistemology, rather than assuming actual intentions.

[22] The extent to which this is true, however, must be very limited. First, if one could describe the 'content' of such interaction, it would radically underdetermine the content of what we wish to assert. Second, any such relationship will only hold good at the most basic of levels. Consider how our scientific theories are clearly underdetermined by any causal process in which we are involved, in respect to their generation.

[23] See Zahar (1995).

things appear, and emptying the terms that occur in such statements of any content that attributes properties to them that goes beyond what is being experienced at the time in question.

This one can do. But Zahar wants also to provide lawlike statements that link such things to real-world occurrences of such things as red palm trees, under certain conditions.[24] This, however, seems futile:

(1) The Zahar-statements (if I may so call them) will themselves be true, whether the palm trees are there or not.

(2) As Zahar notes, under his procedure, 'there is no guarantee that other people, or I at a later date, should attach the same meaning to "redness" as I do now'.[25]

(3) This makes the statements very odd, as they seemed, prima facie, to be about red palm trees. Zahar-statements, however, are about whatever I am experiencing now, where it is not clear that I or anyone else would be able to identify the content of this (such as it might be) on some later occasion. Indeed, if we follow Zahar's procedure, statements about my seeming to see a red palm tree now and at a later date may well have a different content. (Zahar's proposal is, in effect, that for the sake of achieving certainty, we create a private language.)

(4) But this would mean that to be able to link Zahar-statements to anything in the external world, we would need theories for each specific individual case in which we utter such a true statement, telling us whether or not it in fact corresponds to the facts, external to us.

(5) There would seem to be no way in which we could develop such things, not least given that, at the time at which we are making the statements, we presumably don't have the knowledge in question. (If we did, we could and presumably would say: I am experiencing something that looks like but is not a red palm tree.) Further, the path to objectivity concerning any statement that is supposed to make these links, is surely by way of intersubjective criticism — which gets us back to Popper's agenda, rather than Zahar's.

To sum all this up, Zahar's approach seems completely futile. We can make statements that are certain — or as good as makes no difference — about what we appear to be observing. But certainty comes with the penalty of a lack of content; and this lack of content seems to disable such statements as something that can sensibly be linked in a lawlike way to occurrences in the outside world. While what is true — or false — about the outside world would seem, anyway, to have to be approached by the kinds of procedures that Popper suggested.

---

[24]See Zahar (1989), pp. 330f.
[25]Zahar (1989), p. 336.

## 6 Concluding remarks

Did Popper say it all? No. I shall conclude with three comments that elaborate on this point.

First, Popper did not say anything like enough. The discussion of these issues in *The Logic of Scientific Discovery* — which is very rich and over-compressed — needs working over carefully, and expanding into a full philosophical theory. One source for regret is that Popper didn't take the opportunity to work upon these issues in much more detail, later in his life. There is, though, I think enough there to construct an interesting theory, not least, in terms of its relation to Kantian themes, albeit not of the usual kind. (The Marxian link too, to which I have referred above, suggests that attempts made in the 1970s[26] to relate Popper to Althusser were not as wild as some people may now think.) It would be useful for those interested in Popper's work to try to provide a full account, not least because of the philosophical inhibitions that Popper was himself under, when writing *Logik der Forschung*, against doing this himself.[27]

If these ideas are correct, then it was Feyerabend, in his earlier and more Popperian writings, who was attempting the kind of understanding of experience and its role that those interested in Popper's work should be developing. Feyerabend not only engaged in useful cross-fertilization with other theories — including some of the ideas of the later Wittgenstein.[28] But he also stressed the key role that needed to be played by competitive theoretical pluralism within such an approach. Those interested in the development of what is distinctive about Popper's approach — as distinct from its re-interpretation such that it becomes indistinguishable from the mainstream of the empiricist tradition — can only regret that Feyerabend shifted from this to a defence of pluralism as an end in itself.

Popper's ideas, however, do stand in need of further interpretation. One suggestion that I would make here, is that one might look at his epistemological ideas in terms of their being an intersubjective and 'layered' coherence theory rather than a foundationalist theory (of knowledge, rather than of truth).[29] Such a view is distinctive, in the sense that it would be a coherence theory that aspires to true and realistic knowledge. Within such an approach, and if one takes seriously Popper's non-justificationism, we can seek for (scientific rather than justificationist) solutions to the problem that underlies Watkins's concerns; namely, under what conditions do we, in fact, learn successfully about the world. But such an account must, by its very nature, be a matter of conjectural scientifically inspired metaphysics, rather than something that can play a role as part of a justificatory epistemology. Similarly, we may add to Popper's account a metaphysical theory of what we think is going

---

[26]See, for example the first edition of Chalmers (1976), and Curthoys & Suchting (1977).
[27]Cp. Popper (1972), Chapter 2, §5, note 9.
[28]Cp. also David Bloor's discussion of certain parallels in his (1997), pp. 108f.
[29]See, for some further discussion, my (2004).

on when we give priority to a tentative consensus about basic statements over richer, general theories. This may serve both to render coherent what we are doing, and to open it to criticism.

# Bibliography

Austin, J. L. (1962). *Sense and Sensibilia*. Oxford: Oxford University Press.

Ayer, A. J. (1956). *The Problem of Knowledge*. Harmondsworth: Penguin.

Bloor, D. (1997). *Wittgenstein, Rules and Institutions*. London: Routledge.

Chalmers, A. (1976). *What is This Thing Called Science?* St Lucia QD: University of Queensland Press.

Curthoys, J. & Suchting, W. (1977). 'Feyerabend's Discourse Against Method: A Marxist Critique'. *Inquiry* **20**, pp. 243-371.

Goodman, N. (1954). *Fact, Fiction and Forecast*. London: Athlone Press.

Gregory, R. L. (1966). *Eye and Brain*. London: Weidenfeld & Nicolson.

Haack, S. W. (1993). *Evidence and Inquiry*. Oxford: Blackwell.

Jarvie, I. C. (2001). *The Republic of Science*. Amsterdam & Atlanta: Editions Rodopi B.V.

Kant, I. (1781). *Kritik der reinen Vernunft*. Riga: Verlag Johann Friedrich Hartknoch. 2nd edition 1787. English translation b N. Kemp Smith 1929. *Immanuel Kant's Critique of Pure Reason*. London & elsewhere: Macmillan.

Lock, A. (1980). *The Guided Reinvention of Language*. London: Academic Press.

Musgrave, A. E. (1983). 'Theory and Observation: Nola Versus Popper'. *Philosophica* (Belgium) **31**, pp. 45-62.

Nola, R. (1983). 'Interpretation of "The Facts" in the Light of Theory'. *Philosophica* (Belgium) **31**, pp. 25-44.

Popper, K. R. (1945). *The Open Society and Its Enemies*. London: George Routledge & Sons. 5th edition 1966. London: Routledge & Kegan Paul.

——— (1959). *The Logic of Scientific Discovery*. London: Hutchinson.

——— (1963). *Conjectures and Refutations*. London: Routledge & Kegan Paul. 5th edition 1989. London: Routledge.

——— (1972). *Objective Knowledge*. Oxford: Clarendon Press. 2nd edition 1979.

Popper, K. R. & Eccles, J. C. (1977). *The Self and Its Brain*. Berlin: Springer.

Price, H. H. (1932). *Perception*. London: Methuen. 2nd edition 1950.

Putnam, H. (1975). *Mind, Language and Reality: Philosophical Papers*. Volume 2. Cambridge: Cambridge University Press.

de Saussure, F. (1983). *Course in General Linguistics*. London: Fontana.

Shearmur, J. F. G. (2004). 'Popper versus Analytical Philosophy'. In P. Catton & G. Macdonald, editors (2004), pp. 99-113. *Karl Popper: Critical Appraisals*. London: Routledge.

Watkins, J. W. N. (1984). *Science and Scepticism*. Princeton NJ: Princeton University Press.

Zahar, E. G. (1989). 'John Watkins on the Empirical Basis and the Corroboration of Scientific Theories'. In F. D'Agostino & I. C. Jarvie, editors (1989), pp. 325-341. *Freedom and Rationality: Essays in Honor of John Watkins*. Dordrecht: Kluwer.

———— (1995). 'The Problem of the Empirical Basis'. In A. O'Hear, editor (1995), pp. 45-74. *Karl Popper: Philosophy and Problems*. Cambridge: Cambridge University Press.

# 36

# The Epistemological Foundation of Methodological Rules

## Volker Gadenne

## 1 Methodological rules as a central part of critical rationalism

In *The Logic of Scientific Discovery* (*Logic*) (1959), Popper formulated a set of methodological rules, which he extended in later works. They deal, among other things, with the falsifiability and falsification of theories, with conventionalist stratagems, and the acceptance of basic statements. One rule states, for example, that scientific hypotheses should be severely tested; another says that hypotheses should never be regarded as finally verified. Johansson (1975) listed (and criticized) more than twenty rules he found in Popper's works (most from *Logic*, some from *The Poverty of Historicism*). Jarvie (2001) extracted fifteen rules from *Logic*. The latter ones are governed by a *supreme rule*, saying, 'the other rules of scientific procedure must be designed in such a way that they do not protect any statement in science against falsification' (Popper 1959, § 11). This supreme rule (SR) expresses an idea similar to what Popper later called *openness to criticism* though the latter idea is broader and not restricted to empirical science. We can say that SR demands openness to criticism in the realm of science. SR is also closely related to the idea of *fallibilism* since the insight that there can be no certain knowledge is the main reason for SR.

Though these methodological rules constitute a central part of critical rationalism, their status and function are still somewhat unclear. For instance, do the rules of falsificationism lead us to truth, or to progress? Can such an assumption be critically assessed and justified? Many questions of this kind are still quite controversial, even among people who consider themselves as followers of Karl Popper. In this paper, I want to discuss some problems connected with methodological rules, especially, their relation to the aim of science.

## 2 The means-end view of methodological rules

Methodological rules can be stated in one of the following forms: 'Apply method $M$', 'Avoid procedure $P$'; for example, 'Test theories critically', 'Never regard them as finally verified', and so on. Such rules always refer to certain problem situations. Let $S$ be a special type of problem situation in empirical science, and $M$ a procedure or method for this type of situation. For example, an experiment is to be planned to test a theory $T$, or it is to be decided how to proceed when some experimental results contradict $T$. A methodological rule such as 'Apply $M$' can then more exactly be stated in the form, 'If you are in situation $S$, apply procedure $M$.'

Popper realized that methodological rules could not be adequately conceived of as analytical statements, and not as empirical statements either. He therefore declared them as *conventions* that define the game of science (1959, § 11). As Jarvie (2001, p. 41) points out, Popper moved from the pure logic of science into aspects of scientific method that are social rather than logical. Methodological rules are social rules. Science requires cooperation of researchers; it is a 'republic of sorts' with specialized institutions. According to Jarvie, *Logic* is actually an embryonic institutional approach, which Popper developed further in *The Open Society and Its Enemies* (1945). The social character of science has been emphasized also by Agassi (1972), Albert (1985), and Wettersten (1992).

Let us come back to the form of methodological rules. Should they be interpreted as categorical norms or imperatives? This would not make much sense. It would be quite arbitrary and unconvincing to demand categorically, 'Be critical'. *Why* should we be critical? Actually, criticism causes a lot of conflict and trouble. Most people, including critical rationalists, very much dislike being criticized; some regularly feel offended. So there must be some gain associated with criticism that justifies these costs. What is it good for to be open to criticism?

Conventions cannot be true or false. As Popper argues, however, they may prove more or less fruitful (1959, ibidem). So they can be evaluated on the basis of their fruitfulness. What kind of fruitfulness had he in mind? Did he refer to the progress of empirical science? It does not seem so. He claimed that his definition of empirical science conformed to scientists' 'intuitive idea of the goal of their endeavours' (ibidem). And he said his methodological rules would also prove useful for philosophers by enabling them to detect inconsistencies and inadequacies in older theories of knowledge. But is methodology only an explication of scientists' 'intuitive ideas'? And is it helpful only for the philosophy of science, not for science itself?

Provided science has a goal, it should also be possible to interpret methodological rules as hypothetical norms: If you want to achieve $A$ (or contribute to $A$) in situation $S$, apply procedure $M$. $A$ may be roughly described as truth; or, more exactly, science aims at true theories of high explanatory power. We want to have as many true theories of high explanatory power as possible. Correspondingly, Albert (1985, p. 53) regards methodology as a specific *technology* with respect to this aim. Methodological rules claim *means-end rationality*, or *purposive rationality*. Albert also argues that such rules should not be taken as rigorous prescriptions. Their function is similar to that of *heuristic principles*; they give useful recommendations and hints but never require exactly one special solution.

If we understand methodological rules this way, the proposal and acceptance of such rules obviously presupposes that certain assumptions are true. The recommendation, 'Test theories critically in order to achieve true ones', makes sense if we assume that, other things being equal, critical testing contributes to finding true theories. There may be additional aspects that influence how scientists proceed, for example, expenditure of time and money. From an epistemological viewpoint, however, the proposal and selection of methods are guided by assumptions about what method best serves a special purpose that is related to the overall aim of science. We recommend $M$ on the basis of the assumption that $M$ is conducive to $A$. When there are rival procedures $M_1$ and $M_2$, both designed to achieve the same aim $A$, we have to ask whether $M_1$ or $M_2$ is more effective. If we recommend $M_1$ instead of $M_2$, our proposal is based on the *methodological hypothesis* that $M_1$ is more effective than $M_2$ with respect to $A$. Let us call the whole set of procedures proposed by critical rationalism *the critical method*. Critical rationalism then assumes that the critical method is conducive to the goal of achieving true, powerful theories. Obviously, the means-end view of methodological rules is based on *methodological hypotheses.* These hypotheses could be false. For example, too much criticism might discourage scientists. Or, even worse, God might decide to strike with blindness people who put everything into question. This seems to be quite trivial. However, some philosophers do not agree.

## 3   Is the critical method truth-conducive?

The means-end view of methodology is connected with the idea that following certain rules is helpful or conducive to approach the aim of science, especially, truth. Some fallibilists vehemently object to this idea. Miller (1994, p. 46) rejects the view that if one follows Popper's methodological rules one has a better chance to get nearer to the truth than otherwise. According to Miller, such a view is not suggested by critical rationalism, not even conjecturally. He also says that Popper never claimed that, by following the principles of falsificationism, scientists would be led to theories of greater verisimilitude. Jarvie (2001, p, 71) also emphasizes that Popper never promised that following his methodological rules leads us to progress.

Obviously, no method *guarantees* that we achieve the truth, or probably achieve it. Rules that we consider as fruitful and truth-conducive, may actually be ineffective or impeding. Furthermore, it would be quite naïve to specify exact probabilities with which the critical method leads to true hypotheses, or helps to avoid false ones. If this is what Miller and Jarvie want to emphasize, they are quite right. But let us assume that $A$ is the goal of science and our task is to decide whether procedure $M$ should be recommended with respect to $A$ or not. In this case, a rational person will recommend $M$ if and only if he or she *believes that $M$ contributes to $A$*, or that $M$ *gives us a greater* *chance to achieve A*. And this belief is reasonable if there are good arguments in favour of the hypothesis that $M$ is the best we can do to achieve $A$.

Having 'good arguments' in favour of a method $M$ does not mean that we can give a guarantee, that we can be certain to arrive at $A$. Popper liked the formulation that, even if we use the rules of falsificationism, we may only *hope* to make progress. But 'hope' is not a methodological or epistemological category. We may hope something even if our rational prediction says it will not happen. 'Guarantee' is too strong for a methodology that is committed to fallibilism. On the other hand, hope is not enough. The idea that applying a method is reasonable with respect to some goal must be something less than guarantee but stronger than mere hope. Someone who denies this can hardly claim rationality, even if he or she stresses the critical method. A position that proposes the critical method, declares truth as the aim of science, but then rejects the assumption that the critical method gives us a greater chance to arrive at true theories could appropriately be called 'critical irrationalism'.

Let us discuss this with the help of an example. In order to test a theory empirically, Popper recommended deriving from this theory a test statement that cannot be derived from other, rival theories. If possible, our test statement should even *contradict* those rival theories. Let us call this *the method of critical testing*. 'Critical' means that by tests of this kind one refutes at least one theory, or, more carefully, one gets evidence against one theory at least, either against the new theory to be tested, or against a rival theory, perhaps an established one.

We now have a choice between the following two positions. The first is: We recommend the method of critical testing; but we do not accept any methodological assumption connecting critical testing and truth.

This seems to me quite unconvincing. For what reason should we recommend a method if we do not assume that it contributes to our goal? Why should critical testing then be called a reasonable or rational method? Why should we make the effort of analysing and comparing theories in order to find out test statements that discriminate between those theories? We could as well do empirical research inductively or we could recommend Feyerabend's 'anything goes'.

The second position is: We recommend the method of critical testing; and we accept the assumption that critical testing contributes to achieving true theories.

In this case, we formulate a *methodological hypothesis* (which may be false). We can argue for this hypothesis in the following way. We want to have true theories. Since the truth of universal statements cannot be inductively proved we try to refute false ones. We now have the subgoal of detecting false theories. If there are several rival theories, a false one can be detected effectively by using test statements that follow from one theory and contradict another. The result will falsify at least one theory. Compare this *method of critical testing* $(M_1)$ to some other strategies of empirical research:

($M_1$) *Critical testing* Derive from the theory under test statements that do not follow from rival theories, or, even better, that contradict them.

($M_2$) *Simple testing* Test a theory by using any observational statement that follows from it.

($M_3$) *Data gathering*: Try to gather a lot of empirical data; then develop a theory that fits these data.

I think that $M_1$ is a more effective method than either $M_2$ or $M_3$ (or any other method yet known). We are justified in assuming that critical testing is superior to these other methods with respect to our subgoal, that is, to identify false theories.

Similarly, some other rules of falsificationism can be justified. Such rules claim means-end rationality. Their claim can be assessed by discussing them critically and comparing them to alternative methods. Therefore, they are no mere conventions, if 'convention' means that something cannot be rationally assessed. We can argue for methodological rules, in the same way we argue for other philosophical assumptions.

The methodological rules so far discussed are rules of *how to proceed* in certain problem situations. Note however that a methodology also needs rules for the *evaluation of results*. Procedures such as the method of critical testing do not automatically give us means to evaluate the outcome of a test. Consider a test of some competing empirical hypotheses. The critical method is designed to bring about a situation in which such competing hypotheses differ in corroboration. In the ideal case, one hypothesis is highly corroborated while all others are falsified. But the critical method, or the rules that define this method, do not tell us how such a result is to be evaluated. We therefore need, in addition, *principles of preference* that state, for example, that a corroborated theory is to be preferred to a falsified one with respect to truth: If we want to have true theories, we should reasonably prefer a corroborated theory to a falsified one (see Musgrave 1993 and 1999, p. 324, for principles of acceptance or preference). Such rules of evaluation are, as well as procedural rules, based on methodological hypotheses.

## 4 Methodological rules and the problem of induction

Many critics have objected that critical rationalism cannot dispense with an inductive principle, or that critical rationalism introduces induction in a hidden way. Miller (1994) discussed some objections of this kind and rejected them. For example, it has been claimed that empirical science has to presuppose the (inductive) assumption of a stable order in the world. But this is false. A stable order in the world may be necessary for science to be successful. This does not imply, however, that science has to accept a corresponding metaphysical assumption.

Another objection says that science, in order to predict future events, needs the inductive assumption that universal statements continue to hold tomorrow. Miller rejects this, too. A universal statement already has consequences about the future, so it can be used to predict future events without the help of an additional metaphysical principle.

Many arguments against critical rationalism that refer to the problem of induction are based on false premises. However, isn't it induction, too, to assume *that method M contributes to the aim A*, or that *M gives us a greater chance to achieve A?* It has indeed been argued that this is a kind of induction critical rationalism cannot dispense with.

Now critical rationalists have always stressed that we should never quarrel with words. We can of course decide to call any rule 'inductive' that cannot be reduced to principles of deductive logic. As a consequence, any methodology of the empirical sciences will turn out inductive in this broad sense. After all, methodology cannot be mere deductive logic and its application to science. However, the crucial question is not whether certain rules should be *called* inductive; it is rather: Provided these rules are 'inductive' in some sense, is it a problem? Remember some claims or principles associated with the idea of induction: The future is like the past. — The future is probably like the past. — All laws of nature were discovered by induction. — The empirical confirmation of a theory can be defined and calculated as its inductive probability.

All these claims or principles were criticized and in the end rejected because of serious difficulties. The history of this criticism begins with Hume's famous analysis. Popper used Hume's arguments in *Logic* when he rejected the inductive views of the logical positivists.

Now it has to be emphasized that the methodological rules and hypotheses discussed above are *not* induction as understood by its critics from Hume to Popper. Those rules and hypotheses are neither evidence-transcending inferences nor calculi of inductive probability. They may still be called 'inductive'. It seems to me not helpful, however, to use this term in such a broad sense. The problems connected with inferences from observations to theories, with the discovery of theories, with calculi of inductive probability, and with methodological rules as those discussed here, are quite different. This is perhaps why debates over the global question whether critical rationalism needs induction or not have not been very fruitful.

# Bibliography

Agassi, J. (1972). 'Sociologism in Philosophy of Science'. *Metaphilosophy* **3**, pp. 103-122.

Albert, H. (1968). *Traktat über kritische Vernunft*. Tübingen: J. C. B. Mohr (Paul Siebeck).

——— (1985). *Treatise on Critical Reason*. Princeton NJ: Princeton University Press. English translation of Albert (1968).

Jarvie, I. C. (2001). *The Republic of Science*. Amsterdam & Atlanta: Editions Rodopi B.V.

Johansson, I. (1975). *A Critique of Karl Popper's Methodology*. Stockholm: Akademiförlaget.

Miller, D. W. (1994). *Critical Rationalism: A Restatement and Defence*. Chicago & La Salle IL: Open Court Publishing Company.

Musgrave, A. E. (1993). 'Popper on Induction'. *Philosophy of the Social Sciences* **23**, pp. 516-527.

——— (1999). *Essays on Realism and Rationalism*. Amsterdam & Atlanta: Editions Rodopi B.V.

Popper, K. R. (1935). *Logik der Forschung*. Vienna: Julius Springer Verlag.

——— (1945). *The Open Society and Its Enemies*. London: George Routledge & Sons. 5th edition 1966. London: Routledge and Kegan Paul.

——— (1957). *The Poverty of Historicism*. London: Routledge & Kegan Paul.

——— (1959). *The Logic of Scientific Discovery*. London: Hutchinson. English translation of Popper (1935).

Wettersten, J. R. (1992). *The Roots of Critical Rationalism*. Amsterdam & Atlanta: Editions Rodopi B.V.

# 37

# The Lure of Induction

Shereen Hassanein

The key to understanding Putnam's and Quine's criticisms of Popper is to look at two major assumptions that underlie their arguments. The first assumption is that there is a continuity between human cognitive capacities and scientific methodology. This is to say that induction has a psychological component (namely: it is the way in which we understand our world), and that inductive reasoning is sufficient for science as it is how we determine the facts. The second assumption is that the descriptive justifies the prescriptive. Both of these assumptions are at the very core of Putnam's and Quine's attacks on Popper, and their support of induction.

Concentrating on Putnam's 'The "Corroboration" of Theories' (1974/1993), Quine's 'Natural Kinds' (1969/1993), as well as his 'On Popper's Negative Methodology' (1974), I intend to show that these key assumptions are necessary for the support of their arguments, and, in identifying the flaws in these assumptions, their criticisms of Popper are undermined. Although the two philosophers present substantially different arguments, these assumptions form the foundation of their arguments, and thus will be the topic of my concern.

## 1 Induction: A discontinuity between accounts

In 'The "Corroboration" of Theories' Putnam's main defence of induction is its naturalness, while his attack on falsification is based on the assertion that it too is essentially induction. His complaint then is that Popper is both condemning induction and supporting it when he endorses falsification. Dealing particularly with the issue of induction as natural, Putnam connects human activity with this particular cognitive process: 'ideas are not *just* ideas; they are guides to action. Our notion of "knowledge", "probability", "certainty", etc., are all linked to and frequently used in contexts in which action is at issue' (Putnam 1974, § 2). Since induction plays such a key role in human activity in general, it would be impossible for it to be absent from science. Speaking to this point, Putnam says (ibidem): 'Even if scientists do not inductively anticipate the future (and, of course, they do), men who apply scientific laws and theories do so. And "don't make inductions" is hardly reasonable advice to give these men.' What Putnam is getting at is that human activity is naturally guided by induction and that this notion will obviously extend to our scientific practices as well. Moreover, he suggests that we, as humans, cannot help but think inductively regardless of how hard we may try to curb these tendencies. If this is the case, Popper's request that we refrain from using induction is simply impossible to satisfy.

Putnam takes issue also with what he considers to be the unattainablility of Popper's notion of induction, citing this flaw as the source of much criticism. According to Putnam (ibidem, § 1), Popper 'uses the term "induction" to refer to any method for verifying or showing to be true (or even probable) general laws on the basis of observational or experimental data', but a method of induction such as this could not exist as it would be either 'synthetic a *priori* (a possibility that Popper rejects) or justified by a higher-level principle' (ibidem). To escape the problem of an infinite regress or the acceptance of synthetic a priori truths, Popper rejects induction as being independent from science. In his assertion of a psychologistic account of induction, Putnam rejects not only Popper's criticism of induction, but his description of it as well. What Putnam finds to be so unusual about Popper's methods is that 'his position is that empirical science does not really rely upon a principle of induction' (ibidem). It is important to note that Popper does not exclude induction from empirical science entirely, only from methodology. Inspiration and the creation of new ideas may very well be caused by induction, but this is neither problematic nor inconsistent with Popper's project. Clearly Putnam's incredulity is linked to the very concept of a non-inductive empirical science, since he views the success of empirical science to be determined by past successes. For Putnam, the circularity of a psychologistic account of induction is neither a surprise nor a concern: '[w]e do have a propensity — an *a priori* propensity, if you like — to reason "inductively", and the past success of "induction" increases that propensity' (Putnam ibidem, § 13). The very fact that our inductive reasoning in the past has often served us well actually serves as a justification for our tendency to think inductively. This circularity, however, does not worry Putnam (ibidem): 'Induction has no deductive justification; induction is not deduction.' Inductive success is sufficient for justification; rather than propose a methodology that is logically supported, Putnam is content to support induction on the basis of past successes. For example, the survival of our species has often depended on inductive reasoning (for example, tigers are dangerous and clean water quenches thirst) and therefore our survival suggests that induction is a useful tool. This form of *good in nature* is expected to continue upwards into all rational thought, including science. Thus his defence of induction is that since we *do* use it, and it seems to work, it must be good (on all levels).

A more serious point to consider would be Putnam's defence of induction as scientifically useful. Still critical of the inductivist position, he concedes that 'there is some truth in the "inductivist" view: scientific theories are shown to be correct by their successes, just as all human ideas are shown to be correct, to the extent that they are, by their successes in practice' (Putnam ibidem, § 8). The circularity of Putnam's argument cannot be overlooked; yet more importantly, his indifference to this circularity must be addressed. He explains that '[t]he fact that a justification is circular only means that that justification has no power to serve as a *reason*, unless the person to whom it is given as a reason already has some propensity to accept the conclusion' (Putnam ibidem, § 13). Strangely enough, however, his support for the circularity of induction is itself circular. He is right in asserting that inductive logic is *not* deductive logic, but his defence of induction should not be supported by induction and therefore its circularity is a real concern.

## 2 Falsification and induction

Putnam's attack on Popper is not that he *should* be doing induction, but that he already is but won't admit it. His complaint is that Popper presents falsificationism as an alternative to induction, given that induction is untenable. For Putnam, falsificationism is merely induction with different wording. The standard inductivist account of scientific method states that 'theory implies prediction ...; if prediction is false, theory is falsified; if sufficiently many predictions are true, theory is confirmed' (Putnam ibidem, § 4), while Popper's schema states that 'theory implies prediction (basic sentence); if prediction is false; theory is falsified; if sufficiently many predictions are true, and certain further conditions are fulfilled, theory is highly corroborated' (ibidem). Putnam's descriptions of induction and falsificationism seem structurally very similar when worded thusly, although his point is not deeply explored. Refraining from further analysis of potential similarities between the two, Putnam seems satisfied with the linguistic comparison. Asserting that both projects are concerned predominantly with the theory–prediction link, Putnam claims that '[b]oth schemes say: *look at the predictions that a theory implies; see if these predictions are true*' (Putnam 1974, p. 124). To some extent, this is true: both induction and falsification are connected in some way or another with the truth of predictions. Where they are fundamentally different is with what they do with this information. Where induction takes true predictions to be proof of a theory, falsificationism only tentatively holds that theory until at some future date it does get falsified. In induction, the theory–prediction link is set up to justify the adoption of a theory. In falsificationism, the theory–prediction link is used as an indicator of the type of theories that could be considered scientific. If a theory is highly corroborated, it is *tentatively* held until it is falsified. The point of the theory–prediction link is not to determine which theories will be accepted, but to determine a theory's capacity to be scientific.

Putnam's assertion of the similarities between induction and falsification is further undermined by his description of the nature of basic statements for Popper. He states: '[t]he ideal case is one in which a theory which rules out a great many basic statements implies a prediction which is very improbable relative to background knowledge' (Putnam, ibidem § 12). His use of falsification in this instance is quite contrary to the process of induction. Since the justification of a theory–prediction link is connected with past cases of success, falsificationism (which apparently makes predictions quite improbable relative to background knowledge) seems to be doing something else entirely. Actually, falsificationism would be doing something quite in opposition to induction were this the case, and thus Putnam's account of it remains fairly unclear.

Given that induction is a method of verification based on successful theory–prediction links that are cognitively strengthened by their resemblance to similar past experiences, it is clear that falsification is not a masked version of induction. While it may be tempting to see them as similar processes due to the fact that they both rely on the theory–prediction link in one way or another, there are simply too many differences to consider them to be equivalent.

## 3  Scientific methodology and science

Putnam accuses Popper's methodology of being too alienated from the practice of science; he asserts that scientists simply do not do what Popper says they do. 'What Popper consistently fails to see is that *practice is primary*: ideas are not just an end in themselves (although they are *partly* an end in themselves), nor is the selection of ideas to "criticize" just an end in itself' (Putnam ibidem, § 13). Not only is falsification separate from science, Putnam suggests that it might even be destructive in nature (ibidem). 'This "demarcation" is pernicious, in my view; fundamentally, it corresponds to Popper's separation of theory from practice, and his related separation of the critical tendency in science from the explanatory tendency in science' (ibidem). While it may be the case that Popper does not describe what scientists are doing, this is hardly problematic since Popper's intentions are not descriptive, but prescriptive. In introducing a scientific methodology, Popper's intentions are normative, not descriptive.

Putnam's attack on Popper's methodology, seeing it as separate from scientific practice, is unwarranted. Popper is suggesting a methodology for science; he is not *doing science*. Methodology is supposed to be separate from practice; it is what guides action, it is not itself the activity. Even if Popper's methodology were completely unlike science, this would not be a problem since a recommended guide for action need not resemble the current activity. For Putnam, we allow induction to guide our actions because of its success. In a Humean sense, we cannot but expect the future to be like the past and thus we allow these beliefs to guide our actions. The reason why we continue to behave in this manner is because of its impressive success rate. Essentially, we are using induction to justify itself. As human beings, scientists and non-scientists, this would certainly describe how we go about our daily lives, yet everyday human activity is not what Popper wants to regulate. That we have managed to survive partly due to our inductive tendencies (however reasoned they may be) has very little to do with scientific methodology; it should be relegated to the realm of psychology. Popper admits that psychology plays a part in the conception of new ideas, but it is the testing of new ideas that he is concerned with: his recommendations are confined to the latter.

## 4   Quine and natural kinds

In order to support induction on the basis of past success in human cognition, it is necessary to postulate some sort of continuity between ordinary experiences and scientific activity. In 'Natural Kinds' Quine provides a naturalistic account of some fundamental notions necessary for any scientific thought. For him the notions of kind and similarity, both of which are inherently part of our psychological makeup, are crucial concepts upon which all scientific knowledge can be built. His criticism of Popper is that knowledge cannot be built on a lack of counterexamples; 'it is negative support: the mere absence of refutation' (Quine 1974, p. 218). For Quine, the object of knowledge must be something positive, or using Goodman's word, projectible. He suggests that we 'equate the projectibility of predicates to the naturalness of kinds' (ibidem, p. 219), so that we avoid the non-projectible predicates such as those that cause Hempel's paradox (for example, unblack, non-raven). The point of bringing up Hempel's paradox is to present the possible problems that arise from an inductive account (which he will later support). If our theory is that all ravens are black then the evidence that confirms the theory would be any black raven, but (at least logically) any *unblack non-raven* would also confirm the theory.[1] The solution to the paradox is that *unblack* and *non-raven* are not projectible because they do not denote a natural kind and thus they need not be considered as evidential.

This notion of natural kinds was characterized in his article *Natural Kinds*, in which he asserts 'how fundamental the notion of similarity is to our thinking, and how alien to logic and set theory' (Quine 1993, p. 162). Actually, the majority of the article shows us how problematic the idea of natural kinds is,[2] yet Quine's point is to show us how we manage successfully to navigate the world in spite of this non-logical system. It is hard to imagine how science could have come this far since 'some similarity of sense was seen to be crucial to all learning, and central in particular to the processes of inductive generalization and prediction which are the very life of science' (ibidem, p. 167). Despite these rotten foundations that were the result of induction, Quine asserts that 'science reveals hidden mysteries, predicts successfully, and works technological wonders. If this is the way of rot, then rot is rather to be praised

---

[1] This point is made in both Quine (1974) and Quine (1969/1993).

[2] Briefly, Quine shows us how relativistic and unruly the notion of *kind* is. This can range from the problem of how we learn language to questions of how we manage to focus on one universal term at a time (such as pick out all the red things from a grouping including red rubber balls, yellow rubber balls, red wooden cubes, and yellow wooden cubes) to the different types of universals (such as mass terms versus terms of divided reference). Providing us with a naturalist solution, Quine suggests that the currently underdeveloped concept of *kind* can evolve into science.

than patronized', and these inductive tendencies may have even been 'an evolutionary product of natural selection' (ibidem). In other words, not only has induction shown itself to be fruitful in scientific pursuits, it may have actually been chosen for due to its capacity for success in our species. Even if it does not seem to correspond seamlessly with our logical system, induction has managed to remain a part of our scientific methodology because of its positive results.

Quine argues that induction signifies a continuum from human psychology to science. Unlike Popper, he sees no point of demarcation between human cognition and scientific methodology; rather, one could conceivably talk about them in terms of levels of complexity. 'A standard of similarity is in some sense innate. This is not a point against empiricism; it is a commonplace of behavioral psychology' (ibidem, p. 163). The capacity to think inductively is innate. 'Not only is ostensive learning a case of induction, it is a curiously comfortable case of induction, a game with loaded dice' (ibidem, p. 164), which our species cannot help but play. Moreover, Quine seems to be suggesting that this is the foundation for all thought. Since our perspective of the world is inevitably from within the world, we cannot take tools like induction for granted. 'There is no vantage point, no first philosophy. All scientific findings, all scientific conjectures that are at present plausible, are therefore in my view welcome for use in philosophy as elsewhere. . . . the problem of induction is a problem about the world' (ibidem, pp. 164f.). Still, Quine must address the puzzle of how we, with our rigid conformity to similarity standards, manage to get things right every once and a while.

## 5  Arbitrary categories and inductive thought

In reality, there is nothing intrinsic about the way we have carved up our world. Although it would probably be to our detriment, Quine acknowledges that 'we can rig sets arbitrarily' (ibidem, p. 167) and therefore have the potential to have a system of representation of the world that is as useless as we perceive ours to be useful. Given the potentially disastrous results for science, it would seem that induction offers no solace at all. Moreover, there seems to be some intimation that the way we think will make good science. Implying that our brains were selected for their potential to do good science sounds far fetched but it is not far off from what Quine is saying.

It is one thing to say that we are inherently disposed to recognize similarities and organize our world accordingly, but this does not necessarily make good science. Quine is not in opposition to this, but his solution is not to discredit induction entirely. Instead, his approach advocates the use of induction for the purposes of progression. Once we have reached a sufficient level of development, induction can be discarded. Induction may not be good science but it may very well get us there; 'in general we can take it as a very special mark of the maturity of a branch of science that it no longer needs an irreducible notion of similarity and kind' (ibidem, p. 170).

One question arises: how can something be worthy of the process of developing a science, but unworthy of being part of its methodology? Using induction as a sort of ladder to elevate one to a final science then kicking it away as obsolete is strategically problematic. If something is not good enough to count as methodology, then how could it possibly help us achieve our goals? Quine appeals to an argument not unlike Putnam's: given that induction does manage to serve a genuine purpose, we can validate it as an activity (but, for Quine, only in the meantime). In looking at science as continuous with all other cognitive capacities, one would reduce merely to levels of complexity the difference between the highest levels of science and the anticipation of the sun rising.

Speaking of projectible predicates, Quine defers to the success of induction. 'We newly establish the projectibility of some predicate, to our satisfaction, by successfully trying to project it. In induction, nothing succeeds like success' (ibidem, p. 196). Like Putnam, Quine appeals to the apparent fertility of induction in his defence of it. In Popper's *negative* project, there is no *thing* that we can project, successfully or not. Yet what Quine and Putnam are saying is hardly different from saying that induction is successful because it succeeds. We still do not have an answer to the question of what justifies induction. Instead we have what looks more like a guideline to establish when we can say that induction is successful. Why choose it in the first place; and having done so, why discard it afterwards? Quine still needs to explain why we should choose *this* methodology over another and more importantly, what we should choose to replace it once we have arrived at a final science.

## 6 The demarcation between laws of science and lawlike statements

'On Popper's Negative Methodology' is a direct look at Popper's project of falsification. Quine concentrates on Popper's methodology and speculates what might draw him to universal statements. In consideration of this, Quine suggests 'the answer is clear: the universal ones are the interesting ones, being lawlike ones' (Quine 1974, p. 219). Popper's interest in searching out lawlike statements is directly related to the project of falsification, since these are precisely the kinds of statements that basic statements falsify. As for the project itself, for Quine, Popper's system suffers from a lack of complexity. Falsification might work on simple universal statements that are easily and obviously falsified by basic statements, but Quine insists that most of our universal statements do not afford us this luxury. If the statement, *all ravens are black* is a simple universal statement, Quine sees it as logically different from a statement such as *all men are mortal* wherein 'the problem of spotting and certifying an immortal man is a problem of a different order from that of spotting and certifying an unblack raven' (ibidem). What complicates things and serves as a problem for Popper is that universal statements are not as simple as he thought. 'Our laws or hypotheses are neither simply universal nor simply existential, but multiply quantified; and we are considering

what observable consequences these laws imply not law by law but conjointly'
(ibidem, p. 220). If this were the case, then falsificationism would seem to
be subject to the same sort of criticism that Popper made against induction.
There would be no determinate way of establishing the truth or falsity of these
lawlike statements. This does not, however, get induction off the hook either.
There is no basic statement that manages to serve as a falsifier for statements
such as *all men are mortal*, but there is no way for induction to account for
this either.

Furthermore, calling a statement such as *all men are mortal* lawlike certainly does not mean that it is a law, much less that it should be a law. To
call a statement law*like* is only a description, and does not justify our promoting it to the status of a law or theory. Quine's attack fails to recognize
an essential characteristic of Popper's project: Popper is committed to the
demarcation between science and non-science. Thus this attack is hardly an
issue for Popper, since he need not call a statement of this sort a law. Falsificationism not only serves the purpose of eliminating false theories, but it
reveals to us the kind of statements that could count as theories or laws. In
falsificationism, universal statements have as their falsifiers singular (basic)
statements. This is not a description; it is a normative rule for the method
of falsificationism. Therefore, if a lawlike statement does not imply any basic
statements as potential falsifiers, then it remains law*like*; it is not a scientific
theory it just looks like one.

## 7 Psychological foundations for induction

From the start, Popper is very clear about the role that psychology plays
in the scientific process. While it may be instrumental to discovery, it must
be entirely absent from testing and the establishment of a theory as a law.
Even if induction is inherently part of our psychological makeup, this does not
give it a place in science. For Popper, induction is the name of a particular
process. 'It is usual to call an inference "inductive" if it passes from *singular
statements* (sometimes also called "particular" statements), such as accounts
of the results of observations or experiments, to *universal statements*, such
as hypotheses or theories' (Popper 1959, § 1). This may be something we do,
but it has no place in science. 'Now it is far from obvious, from a logical point
of view, that we are justified in inferring universal statements from singular
ones, no matter how numerous; for any conclusion drawn in this way may
always turn out to be false' (ibidem). The problem is that induction has more
to do with the connections we make in our head than it does with the world.
Moreover, there is no reason to expect our inductive tendencies to be helpful
for science.

In essence, Quine was partially right; we *can* rig the sets arbitrarily. Yet
given that this is the case, induction would say more about how we carve up
the world than it would about the world. '[w]e can, with a little ingenuity, find
always points of view such that all things belonging to that set are similar

(or partially equal) if considered from one of these points of view; which means that anything can be ... a "repetition" of anything, if only we adopt the appropriate point of view' (ibidem, Appendix *x, (1)). The way in which we interpret the world is a question of how our minds work. To make an observation about the inductive process teaches us not about the world, but about what tends to satisfy us as evidence, a concept that is most definitely psychological.

## 8 Methodology and normativity

As undeniably powerful the force of discovery may be, Popper has made it clear that it is not a part of his project. 'The question of how ... a new idea occurs to a man ... may be of great interest to empirical psychology; but it is irrelevant to the logical analysis of scientific knowledge. This latter is not concerned with *questions of fact* ..., but only with questions of ... *validity*' (ibidem, § 2). Popper's project is a normative one; he is not interested in observing what scientists are doing, but in analysing the validity of a methodology. Consequently, the arguments he offers in *The Logic of Scientific Discovery* 'are quite independent of this problem', and rather his view 'is that there is no such thing as a logical method of having new ideas, or a logical reconstruction of the process' (ibidem).

What is apparent from the outset of this book is that Popper has made a particular decision, a luxury afforded to you if your project is non-empirical. As a metatheoretical program designed to regulate the empirical sciences, falsificationism is itself exempt from their restrictions. Rather than being subject to these rules, it is creating them. Thus, Popper suggests we 'adopt such rules as will ensure the testability of scientific statements; which is to say, their falsifiability' (Popper 1959, proem to Chapter 2). As empirical statements are the subjects of falsificationism, they are a decidedly different sort of statement from those that make up the doctrine of falsificationism. '[T]he distinguishing characteristic of empirical statements (is) their susceptibility to revision — in the fact that they can be criticized, and superseded by other ones.' (ibidem, § 9) What determines the fate of an empirical statement is partially its relation to the world (whether or not it is in accord with the facts), but equally important is the theoretical framework within which it is being evaluated. This is the crucial difference between the object of a science (the corpus of empirical statements) and the scientific theory itself.

In the end, what determines methodology is not the set of scientific statements; scientists determine methodology. '[w]hat it is to be called a "science" and who is to be called a "scientist" must always remain a matter of convention or decision' (ibidem, § 10). Decisions of this sort are also entirely different from decisions made within a given science, as metatheoretical statements about a system have as their subject not only a different body of knowledge, but an entirely different *kind* of knowledge. Hence, 'questions of this kind should be treated in a different way' (ibidem). Since induction was deemed successful based on its successes (at least for Putnam and Quine), we see only one type of statement: empirical statements. It could be argued that the statement *induction is successful when it succeeds* is metatheoretical, and to some extent it is. However, it is metatheoretical only to the extent that the dictionary definition of "successful" is; and that seems hardly sufficient to count as a scientific theory. While it may be metatheoretical to some extent, it is certainly not normative as well, but a description of what is taking place when we call an induction successful. Inevitably, we are faced with the circularity of the argument, an instance of empirical statements justifying empirical statements.

For Popper, this is quite simply insufficient. Without normative metatheoretical statements, you do not have a scientific theory, you have only a collection of data: '[f]rom a logical point of view, the testing of a theory depends upon basic statements whose acceptance or rejection, in its turn, depends upon our *decisions*. Thus it is *decisions* which settle the fate of theories' (ibidem, § 30). It could be argued that an assertion of this sort is a form of conventionalism. If it is, this is as conventionalistic as Popper allows himself to be. Despite the fact that the tentative decision to hold on to a theory is ours, the rigorous method that precedes that decision as well as the conditional support of that theory is far from being conventionalistic. Furthermore, Popper sees conventionalism as a flaw in the naturalistic (inductive) view. 'Its upholders fail to notice that whenever they believe themselves to have discovered a fact, they have only proposed a convention. Hence the convention is liable to turn into dogma' (ibidem, § 10). The inductivist convention is the same one that Hume criticized, namely, that the future will be like the past. If it is the case that our minds really work this way and that this is a convention we cannot avoid, then let it stay out of science. 'Such processes are the concern of empirical psychology but hardly of logic' (Popper 1959, § 2).

## 9  Logical necessity and normativity

Universal statements are based on contingent facts about the world, *this* world, not all possible worlds. Hence the necessity derived from these statements is a kind of physical necessity, which Popper separates from logical necessity: '[i]t is a mistake to underrate the differences between this natural or physical necessity, and other kinds of necessity, for example, logical necessity. We may, roughly, describe as logically necessary what would hold in any conceivable world' (Popper 1959, appendix ∗x, (8)). Not only do empirical statements have an entirely different logical status from the scientific theories that they are supposed to support (that is to say, singular versus universal statements), but both have a different status from the methodology that determines science (for example, falsificationism).

The problem with induction is that it does not make this distinction, rather it supports a continuity between empirical and theoretical statements, resting on the assumption that the descriptive and normative are continuous as well. What would be required would be an account of what exactly bridges the gap between the normative and the descriptive. What is required is a metatheoretical statement that is itself normative. To say that the success of induction serves as its own defence is to say nothing at all. To justify induction we must use inductive inferences (a concept Putnam not only admits to, but embraces). 'Thus the attempt to base the principle of induction on experience breaks down, since it must lead to an infinite regress' (Popper 1959, § 1). For all of Putnam's assertions, an entirely circular argument is simply not acceptable for the basis of a scientific theory. Whether induction works or not (or simply appears to work — it is possible that it could prove to be wrong at a future date), it does not make good theory.

Quine offers a solution that appeals to some higher order of truth in the universe. 'Similarity itself, what [a] man's judgements purport to be judgements of, purports to be an objective relation in the world. It belongs to subject matter not of our theory of theorizing about the world, but our theory of the world itself. Such would be the acceptable and reputable sort of similarity concept, if it could be defined' (Quine 1993, p. 168). This would suggest that notions of similarity and kind exist independently of our recognition, and that success in induction signifies our successful perception of these external relations. This would solve the problem of the infinite regress since there would be a concrete foundation for inductive knowledge. It would not, however, solve the re-occurring problem of synthetic a priori truths. To postulate an independent and necessary system in nature would be giving physical necessity the same status as logical necessity, which we have already seen as an unproductive pursuit.

Empirical data are crucial to science because they provide the evidence that both proves (or for Popper corroborates) and falsifies theories. On their own, however, these data has no use; they are not even data. To suppose that they have some intrinsic scientific value independent of us makes no sense whatsoever. '[t]here is no such thing as "pure experience", but only experience interpreted in the light of expectations or theories which are "transcendent"' (Popper 1959, Appendix *x, (4)). Without a normative methodological perspective, empirical science is uncritical and without direction. Moreover, empirical science would be forced to appeal to synthetic a priori truths or submit to an infinite regress.

We have seen both Putnam and Quine attack Popper's project from the premise that it neither surpasses induction nor represents what is natural for our species to do. Their arguments predominantly circle around the past successes of induction and its naturalness. We have seen also that all of their arguments hinge on two key premises: that there is a continuity between the psychological and the scientific and that the descriptive justifies the prescriptive. Given that neither of these premises can be supported, it becomes apparent that induction, while inevitably a part of our cognitive capabilities, does not provide a valuable methodology of science.

# Bibliography

Boyd, R., Gasper, P., & Trout, J. D (1993). *The Philosophy of Science*. Cambridge MA: MIT Press.

Popper, K. R. (1959). *The Logic of Scientific Discovery*. London: George Routledge & Sons. Revised edition, 1992. London & New York: Routledge.

Putnam, H. (1974). 'The "Corroboration" of Theories'. In Schilpp (1974), pp. 221-240. Reprinted in Boyd, Gasper, & Trout (1993), pp. 121-137.

Quine, W. V. O. (1969). 'Natural Kinds'. In W. V. O. Quine, *Ontological Relativity and Other Essays*. New York: Columbia University Press. Page references are to the reprint in Boyd, Gasper, & Trout (1993), pp. 159-170.

——— (1974), 'On Popper's Negative Methodology'. In Schilpp (1974), pp. 218-220.

Schilpp, P. A., editor (1974). *The Philosophy of Karl Popper*. La Salle IL: Open Court Publishing Company.

# 38

# The Pragmatic Problem of Induction

Ingemar Nordin

## 1 Introduction

An inductive argument, or 'proof', is an argument that goes from the particular to the general. In the philosophy of science the problem of justifying (or avoiding) this kind of invalid reasoning is known as 'the problem of induction', or, with reference to the philosopher who first took it seriously, as 'Hume's problem'.[1] There have been numerous suggestions as to how to solve this problem in the case of science, but less has been said about it in a pragmatic context. In this paper I shall point out some important characteristics of the practical, or pragmatic, choice situation. It will be argued that in technology, and in practical action, it is, *ceteris paribus*, rational to prefer a technique that has some positive support rather than one that does not. This is so even if we fully accept a fallibilistic view of knowledge and reject inductivism.

There is always a risk of ridicule in treating induction as problematic since most people take it to be a self-evident hallmark of all empirical research. But as has been pointed out by Karl Popper, this is wrong on two counts. Firstly, the problem has by no means any self-evident solution. Secondly, there is much to say for the claim that induction is not even practised in pure science. Instead Popper offers a purely falsificationist methodology of science. But what about technology and practical action? The pragmatic methods in technological research seem to be concerned with positive solutions rather than problems, with confirmation rather than criticism, with what works rather than with what does not. Let us have a look at some of the characteristics of technology and see what they may imply for the problem of induction.

A demarcation between pure science and technology could be based on the distinction between truth (for explanations) and usefulness (with respect to solving practical problems). A scientific theory may be true without being useful (a theory of cosmology for example), and it may be useful without being true (like Newtonian mechanics). Techniques are of course neither true nor false. They are (more or less) useful or useless. And they may be functional or non-functional in obtaining desired results. Pure science aims at producing true and explanatory theories about nature, society, and man. Technology aims at producing functional and useful techniques.

---

[1] For the distinction between this problem and other problems that have been attributed to Hume, see Popper (1972), Chapter 1, § 2, note 7.

Functionality (with respect to a desired result) is a precondition for usefulness. Not everything that effectively produces a certain result is useful. But since the technological problem of induction is about functionality, it only indirectly concerns usefulness. Let me suggest a definition of functionality.

> *A technique $T(E)$ functions (with respect to an intended result $E$) to a degree $r$ in situations of type $S$ if, and only if, (a) $T(E)$ produces $E$ with at least the frequency (efficiency) $r$ in $S$, and (b) $r$ is greater than zero or what nature/chance is doing by itself.*

If $T(E)$ is to be useful as well, the number $r$ has to be determined from case to case, and even from user to user, depending on the demands put on $T(E)$'s efficiency.[2] But given an $r$ that the user estimates to be necessary for $T(E)$ in order that it shall be useful to him or her, it is an objective matter whether $T(E)$ measures up to $r$ or not. If so, we simply say that $T(E)$ works or functions. Note also that efficiency is one thing and that evidence (which may come in degrees, some of it positive and some of it negative) of a given efficiency is another.

A first version of the technological problem of induction can then be formulated as: *Is it legitimate to draw the conclusion that a technique functions (or will function in the future) from the fact that it has produced the desired result a finite number of times in the past?*

## 2   What does positive evidence prove?

In science, positive evidence (that is, observed new confirmations of a theory) plays virtually no role according to the falsificationist view. At most the corroboration of a theory could give a psychological boost to the scientists involved.[3] The fact that all tests of a theory so far have corroborated it to the last decimal provides not a shred of evidence for its truth. It does not even increase the probability of its being true. However, when we talk about the functionality of a technique instead of the truth of an explanatory theory, the situation is slightly different. Positive evidence concerning a technique shows at least one thing. It shows that the technique in question may well have worked in the past. And that is still the case even if, under slightly different circumstances, the technique works no longer.

Does this in any way alter the situation? Could it perhaps explain why positive evidence is considered of vital importance in technology? Because in technology, it seems that positive evidence is much more important than negative evidence. The latter is seldom considered to be a definite disproof of a technique. On the contrary, given the not too unusual situation where we have both positive and negative evidence concerning the functionality of a new technique it is the positive evidence that is of most interest. It is important, it seems, because it shows that it might be possible to produce $E$ in

---

[2]The distinction between functionality and usefulness is elaborated in Nordin (1989).
[3]See further the discussion in Popper (1963), Chapter 10, § XXII.

that way. And it seems to give a promise that with further refinement of the technique it could be brought to an acceptable level of efficiency. That a novel technique does not work in a reliable manner is not very surprising and it is not considered to speak seriously against it. Positive evidence, on the other hand, shows that a functional technique is *possible*.

One condition for having positive evidence of the functionality of a technique $T(E)$ is that $E$ is obtained when $T(E)$ is applied. Another is that it is $T(E)$ that gives rise to $E$ and not something else. Hence, when testing a new drug, for example, one does so in a double blind test. This testing process is not, however, sufficient for actually proving that $T(E)$ works, or that it will work to a sufficient degree. (The situation may differ from the test situation; the patient in question may differ from the patients in the test, and so on.) But it certainly shows that $T(E)$ is possibly working.

Could one perhaps be more specific about the way in which $T(E)$ has shown its 'possibility'? After all, given that we know nothing at all about $T(E)$, anything is possible from a logical point of view. But a tested technique proves more than just a logical possibility. It also shows that in the test situation $S$, $E$ was obtained when $T(E)$ was applied, while $E$ was not obtained in $S$ when $T(E)$ was not applied. If $T(E)$ works, then there should be situations such that $E$ is obtained (to a sufficient degree) if, and only if, $T(E)$ is applied. If the result of the test is positive, that is, if $E$ is obtained precisely when $T(E)$ is applied, then we cannot draw the conclusion that it will work every time (or to a sufficient degree). But we have at least *corroborated* the assumption that $T(E)$ works.[4] In spite of a serious test, we have failed to show that $T(E)$ does not work. It seems that $T(E)$ in that sense has proved a worthy candidate for further trials and, possibly, also for use. So, an empirical test may show that it is possible (in a non-trivial sense) that a technique works. Such a test corroborates the technique in the sense that the test fails to prove that it does not work in the test situation. Let me call this the *corroborated possibility* of a technique.

Let us consider a totally different kind of test for comparison. Suppose that a medical scientist did not do empirical tests of his new drugs, but simply asked the Oracle in Delphi. 'Will this drug work and cure the disease?' he asks. The Oracle contemplates the question for an hour behind hallucinogenic clouds of smoke and then delivers her prophetic answer. A yes-answer is then taken as a proof of the functionality of the drug. — From a rational point of view, what is the difference between this kind of oracular evidence and the empirical kind?

If Hume is right, there is no real difference here, since neither the Oracle's answer nor the inductive evidence gives logical support to the hypothesis that the drug will work. Perhaps our preference for the double blind testing is just a consequence of cultural convention and nothing else. Perhaps if we had been

---

[4]Strictly speaking, a positive correlation between the application of $T(E)$ and the event $E$ does not show that $T(E)$ *caused* $E$ in that test. The correlation could arise in other ways. But what matters here is that the test fails to falsify the assumption that $T(E)$ causes $E$.

born and raised in pre-Socratic Greece every sensible person would definitely have trusted the Oracle more than the empirical testing?

Still, this possibility does not seem to be entirely convincing. If the people in Greece trusted the Oracle this would be so because the tales about her told them that she had been correct in her past predictions. That is, even oracles seem to obtain their worthiness through some kind of positive support. And if oracles did not have that support then it would simply be illegitimate to prefer them to empirical testing. But the problem is to show why this is so.

## 3 A reformulation of the problem

There are some important aspects of the pragmatic choice situation that should be considered. In science we do not have to decide which theory is true in order to make progress, whereas in the practical situation we usually *have to* act. According to falsificationism, the rationality of science can be upheld solely by falsifying theories. Progress is made when we have disproved one theory and found a better one. But we do not have to 'trust', or 'rely on', any theory, claiming that we, at last, have found the truth. Instead, we can lean back in a sceptical mood without ever taking any theory as true or probable and focus instead on a forever ongoing critical scrutiny of possible explanations. In the practical situation, however, it is unavoidable to act on the basis of some *positive* decision concerning desired goals, efficiency and usability of techniques.

What we are dealing with here is not a logical necessity. We are forced to do things only if we want to achieve something. If I want to achieve health it is necessary to choose an action that cures the illness. If I am hungry I have to choose a method (go to a restaurant or cook the food myself) in order to get food. And so on. Let me call this condition the *practical necessity* of acting.

However, besides being driven by a practical necessity our choice should preferably be a rational (legitimate) one. In a falsificationist context it is natural to ask whether not the process of eliminating non-functional techniques would be sufficient. For example, if there are two techniques, $T_1$ and $T_2$, where $T_2$ has failed to produce the expected result in all tests, would it not be rational to choose $T_1$? Well, that depends on the status of $T_1$. If $T_1$ has been tested and corroborated, that would be a good choice I think. But if $T_1$ has not been tested at all, and if we know nothing about its practical possibilities, then there seems to be no rational choice that can be made.

Now let me try to reformulate the problem of induction. According to the sceptical view on induction (which I fully agree with) it is clear that the original pragmatic problem cannot be solved. We cannot prove that any given technique is working. We cannot ever obtain any certainty about a technique. It may fail us at any level of efficiency. But the condition of practical necessity forces us to make a choice even under total uncertainty. And in my view, we have to make a choice based on positive, or corroborating, evidence since purely negative trials are clearly insufficient for making legitimate choices of action. The question is, can such non-inductive but corroborated choices be legitimate?

To make it simple, let us assume that there are two alternatives $T_1(E)$ and $T_2(E)$. Our only concern is to achieve $E$ (that is to say, they are equally useful if they work) and these two techniques are the options conveniently at hand. $T_1(E)$ is empirically tested in the way described above and found corroborated. That is, in $S$ the event $E$ occurred sufficiently often when $T_1(E)$ was applied, and only then. The alternative $T_2(E)$ has not been tested at all, or it has perhaps just been supported by an oracle test or some other such non-empirical test. The reformulation of the problem is now: *In this situation, what makes it rational (legitimate) to prefer $T_1(E)$ to $T_2(E)$?*

If there is no answer to this question the situation will be awkward, to say the least. If there is no 'justification' for preferring $T_1(E)$ to $T_2(E)$ then there is no positive guidance for acting other than social conventions or psychological preferences. 'Falsifying' one technique does not say anything about the other, or help us to make a positive choice. If our choice is not rational, our obsession with empirical tests is just a cultural or psychological phenomenon that has nothing to do with what are good or bad strategies in general. The conclusion would be in accord with Hume's when he says that it is not rationality but 'custom, then, [which] is the great guide of human life'.

## 4 A solution

When faced with two unreliable options it might be tempting to say that there cannot be any rational choice at all. But given a practical choice situation — where there is no practical possibility but to choose, where no alternative is excluded, and where one technique has been tried and found satisfactory in that test — it is not at all clear that a choice is necessarily non-rational. Since a choice has to be made anyway it is not unreasonable to make the best of the situation even though the outcome is very uncertain.

But the outcomes *are* uncertain, and there is always room for scepticism. It is rational to be sceptical about the reliability of any technique. It is not just that we know that all techniques are imperfect and never work with 100% efficiency and in all circumstances. We have also reason to be sceptical about whether a technique will work at all, in any situation or at any level of efficiency. The key to the solution is to note that we are comparing two techniques here, and that there is a difference between them involving our *reasons for scepticism*.

Our reasonable doubt about the reliability of a technique could be of two kinds. Firstly, we may doubt that the technique works at all. Secondly, we may doubt that the technique will work sufficiently well in the present situation. Of course, if we have reason to believe that it does not work at all, then there is reason to believe that it will not work in the present situation either. On the other hand, if our reason to believe that the technique does not work at all is weakened, then our reason to doubt that it will work in the present situation is weakened as well. Now, if we compare the reasons for doubt behind $T_1(E)$ and $T_2(E)$ it is quite clear that there is less reason to doubt that $T_1(E)$ works at all than there is to doubt that $T_2(E)$ works at all. Hence, there is less reason to doubt that $T_1(E)$ will work in the present situation (and in the future) than there is to doubt that $T_2(E)$ will do so. I do not say that there is no reason to doubt $T_1(E)$, but there is less. And in a situation where we *have to* choose, and where only functionality is at stake, it is obviously more rational to prefer $T_1(E)$ to $T_2(E)$ than the other way around.

Let us take it really slowly here. Why is there less reason to doubt $T_1(E)$ than $T_2(E)$? The answer is that we have tested $T_1(E)$ empirically but not $T_2(E)$. And the result of the test was such that we failed to show that $T_1(E)$ did not work in the test situation. The functionality of $T_1(E)$ is a corroborated possibility. Hence, we have somewhat less reason than before to believe that $T_1(E)$ does not work in any situation, including the present situation. But our reason for doubting $T_2(E)$ is just as strong as before.

There is still good reason to doubt that either of the techniques will work. That the application of $T_1(E)$ happened to coincide with $E$ in the test situation gives no guarantee that they will coincide in future situations. We have not *added* any reason, or justification, in favour of the conjecture (or belief) that $T_1(E)$ will work. Any choice of action, and any use of a technique, is risky. That is something we cannot do much about. But since we have to choose an action anyway, we should seek to avoid the technique whose functionality we have the most reason to doubt. It would certainly be more irrational to prefer $T_2(E)$ to $T_1(E)$ in this choice. Or, in other words, it is less irrational to prefer $T_1(E)$ to $T_2(E)$. And given the conditions that we have to act it follows that it is not only less irrational but just plain rational to make this choice. Yes, it is rational, and not just a question of custom, culture, or psychology, to prefer $T_1(E)$ to $T_2(E)$ if only functionality (and not usefulness) is at stake.

The case may of course easily be generalized to other cases where the testing of $T_2(E)$ has simply been less severe than the testing of $T_1(E)$, or where $T_2(E)$ has been tested with negative outcomes. As long as the choice concerns only the functionality of the techniques, we should prefer the one that has been most corroborated.

This solution to the problem of induction avoids proving too much. There cannot be a solution that proves that empirically tested techniques are always reliable. (Who has ever heard of such a technique?) There cannot be a solution that proves that an empirically tested technique will work the next time it is used. (There is a first time for everything, and who knows, the darned thing might stop working just when you need it!) There cannot even be a solution that proves that tested techniques are reliable in the long run, that is, that they are more likely to work. (From past rates of success we cannot draw any logically valid conclusions about future relative frequencies.)

Actually, this solution has nothing to do with induction at all. Rather, it is an attempt to give a rational explanation of the role of positive evidence in technology; to explain why empirical evidence may put one technique ahead of others and why it is rational to act positively on that technique. My explanation here makes no attempt to employ the positive evidence in question as a support for the future reliability of techniques. The point is that such positive evidence still makes a difference. Positive evidence work as a basis for critical evaluation and comparison of our *scepticism* against different techniques. The practical necessity to act — and therefore to make a choice between alternatives — in spite of total uncertainty makes such an evaluation appropriate. To Hume there is no real difference between the Oracle's positive verdict and the positive verdict of an empirical test. And that is true in a sense. There is no difference between these authorities with respect to predictions about the future. However, the difference between oracle tests and empirical corroboration is that only the latter is capable of eliminating certain sceptical claims about functionality.

It explains why corroborating data are so important in technology in the sense that they guide future investments, research, and use. Technology aims at producing useful techniques for practical action. In acting, the user does not really have to *rely on* a technique in the sense that he has to *believe* that it will work. In fact, there is no reason to trust it at all. But he will in any case have to *base* his action partly on it (and even use it without any hesitation if that is the appropriate way to apply it). Therefore technology will primarily aim for corroborating data that could make a difference to the user's choice of technique. Negative evidence is not all that interesting, at least in a developing phase. To show that a technique does not work in a particular situation does not prove that it will not work in another. In pure science, on the other hand, the situation is almost the reverse. Here negative evidence shows that a theory is false and that new avenues will have to be tried, while corroborating data only give a record of past failures to falsify it. The goal in science is not to find reliable or useful theories, but to find theories with a high empirical content and with a high explanatory value. Science therefore aims at finding falsifying data that could function as a guide to further research.

## 5   The role of science

The above solution is intended as a contribution to a falsificationist, noninductivist standpoint when applied to technology. In a critical paper[5] on the falsificationist view of practical choice Wesley Salmon complains that Popper and his allies really do not answer the question why we should choose a corroborated predictive theory. Popper says for example, 'My *solution* of the logical problem of induction was that we may have *preferences* for certain of the competing conjectures; that is, for those which are highly informative and which so far have stood up to eliminative criticism.'[6] In another place he says:[7]

---

[5] Salmon (1981).
[6] Popper (1974), p. 1024.
[7] Popper (1972), Chapter 1, § 11.

> ... *a pragmatic belief in the results of science* is not irrational, because there is nothing more 'rational' than the method of critical discussion, which is the method of science. And although it would be irrational to accept any of its results as certain, there is nothing 'better' when it comes to practical action; there is no alternative method which might be said to be more rational.

At the same time Popper of course emphasizes that no theory can have any certain predictive power whatsoever.

Salmon has some ground for his complaint that this is a weak argument as to why it is rational to prefer a corroborated prediction to a prediction that is not corroborated. After all, the non-corroborated prediction may have the support of an oracle, and exactly why should empirical support be better than the support of an oracle when neither of them can enhance certainty concerning the future?[8]

> The position of the Humean sceptic would be, I should think, that neither of these methods can be shown to be either more or less rational than any of the others. But if every method is equally lacking in rational justification, then there is no method which can be said to furnish a rational basis for prediction, for any prediction will be just as unfounded rationally as any other.

To claim, as Popper does, that we should prefer empirical corroboration because there is nothing 'better' that we can do, is a bit question-begging, and calls for further explanation.[9]

We have such an explanation if we focus on the choice of techniques instead of 'highly informative' theories. Given the scepticism against induction, we cannot justify our choice of a scientific theory by the back door so to speak. We have to aim at eliminating false theories. But making a choice between different techniques in order to solve a practical problem is something else. Here we may justify a positive choice, but not in terms of boldness, explanatory power, or falsifiability. It calls for making the best choice given that we have to act even if there is legitimate doubt that it will work. And such a choice is to prefer the alternative concerning which there is the least reason for doubt; or, in other words, not to choose an alternative concerning which there is more reason for doubt. This is the non-inductivist notion of 'justification' that I believe is necessary for a proper interpretation of the falsificationist position here.

Furthermore, not all techniques are based on scientific theories. But some are, and this fact is sometimes taken to be a justification of the functionality of the technique. That is, it is assumed that the fact that a technique (or more precisely, a prediction that a technique will work) is 'embedded' in a system of scientific, informative theories somehow increases its credibility. Popper's formulations above could perhaps be interpreted in this way. However, I am a bit sceptical about this hypothesis about embedded techniques. Why would

---

[8]Salmon (1981), p. 121.

[9]For a fuller account of the debate here, see Miller (1994), pp. 20f.

scientific theories help justifying techniques when there is no way of justifying the truth of the theories themselves? Why, for example, would bloodletting be more justified as a medical method against the influenza when it became in accord with Galen's theories? And since falsified theories sometimes are preferred to corroborated ones in practical matters (Newtonian mechanics is usually preferred to the theory of relativity when constructing cars and aeroplanes), how can this lend credibility to a technique?

In an inductivist discourse, these questions are awkward, especially the last one. A falsificationist may simply deny that scientific theories give a higher credibility (other than from a purely psychological point of view) to those techniques that happen to be based on them. A better — or perhaps a complementary — answer is that although scientific theories do not make those techniques more certain, they do make them a rational choice compared to techniques that lack both scientific support and direct empirical corroboration. The reason for this is that established scientific theories usually have been tested already. They are considered 'established' precisely because they have managed to survive several critical tests. I propose that from a pragmatic point of view the important thing is that the predictions of the theory have been confirmed *within the range of practical interest*. Whether the theories have been falsified at other places — that is, that they are false — is of less importance. An approximately true theory, such as Newtonian mechanics, will do just as well as (or even better than) a non-falsified one as long as it is 'true' within its range of application.

My claim, then, is that it is the empirical support of scientific theories that does most of the work in their 'justifying' of techniques. It is not the truth value, or the imbedding capacity, of scientific theories that makes scientifically based techniques a rational choice.[10] This explains why even falsified theories may be helpful in constructing working techniques. And it explains why a tested technique, such as the use of acupuncture to mitigate pain, may be a rational choice even though it is not quite embedded in a scientific structure.[11]

## 6  Why not be content with negative evidence?

One objection to my proposal concerning the role of positive evidence in a situation of practical action could be that negative evidence is all we need. In his paper, 'Induction: A Problem Solved', David Miller writes: 'What must not be admitted is the suggestion that a proposal that has been subjected to critical scrutiny, and has survived it, thereby qualifies as a better proposal than one that has not been subjected to critical scrutiny.'[12] And later in the

---

[10] David Miller and Karl Popper suggest that the function of scientific theory is to criticize alternative technologies, in Popper (1974), p. 1025. This suggestion, however, does not explain the positive role of false theories in technology. Nor does it explain the rationality of choosing the corroborated alternative where this evidence is all we have.

[11] The role of science in technology is much more complex than the simple-minded notion of 'applied science' suggests. For an elaboration of this point, see Nordin (1989) and (1999).

[12] Miller (2002), p. 95; (2006), p. 124.

same paragraph: 'The correct advice is, as usual, negative: *Refrain from any practical proposal that does not survive critical scrutiny as well as others do.*'

The problem with just focusing on negative choice (that is, do not choose a $T$ that didn't make it through the test) is that it leaves us with no legitimate positive guidance. In every practical choice situation there are not just one or two options. There are an infinite number of possibilities; perhaps some that have been negatively tested, perhaps one or two that have been corroborated and always an infinite number that have not been tested at all. Suppose you get a sickness that you are unfamiliar with. You are alone in the jungle. Since you do not have any doctor or hospital conveniently at hand, you try your own methods: berries of different colours, roots and whatnot. Some of these techniques make you sicker, but the bright red berries make you feel better. So you decide to keep on eating the bright red berries and stop eating the other stuff. But you have not tried *all* alternative stuff. Would it not be just as rational to start eating new things: black berries, herbs, insects, and other things? Or why not try a variant of the red berries: eating red berries and having bloodletting at the same time? Or, eating red berries and praying? Or, eating red berries and standing on just one leg? Anything that has not been tried is possible. But this leads us to inaction instead of action. That is not rational.

I agree that it need not be a mistake to prefer to 'adopt' a technique that is untried, at least not in certain situations. But I think that we have to distinguish between the situation where the goal is to invent and try out new techniques from the practical situation I have in mind in this paper, that is, the situation where the goal is to solve a practical problem outside technological research itself. In the inventive situation, where the task is to try out *new* techniques, choosing well-known and corroborated techniques would, of course, not be a good idea. But if our goal is to solve the problem, irrespectively of how it is solved (like the one in the jungle), then I find it less rational (although perhaps not completely irrational) to refrain from choosing the best corroborated technique.

## 7  Guarantees

One important consequence of the analysis of the role of positive evidence in technology is that no technique can be proven reliable, even to a certain degree. Instead the central role of corroborating data is to show the possible functionality of the technique and thereby set forth a rational option for the agent. Therefore it is also rational to take into account, and be prepared for, the possibility that the technique will malfunction.

Of course, in practice this is not big news. The existence of basic uncertainty does not make it unnecessary, or irrational, to plan for the future. Action is necessary and we have to act on assumptions of what will happen. But, depending on the importance of the action, we also give some thought to alternative plans.

Insurance and guarantees have a role to play in that job. When a new car is bought, the company states that the price includes guarantees. When premiums are paid to an insurance company it gives us certain guarantees concerning the consequences of accidents and sickness. Obviously, no one can guarantee that certain events will, or will not, occur. Instead of buying certainty, we buy alternatives. If the car breaks down — in spite of all the tests, and in spite of what it is reasonable to expect — the car company will repair it and compensate the buyer. If we do fall ill, the insurance company will pay us money and pay our hospital bills.

The car company and the insurance company, in turn, base their prices and premiums on recorded frequencies of accidents and disease. Is that rational? Yes, though not because past experience proves what frequencies will occur in the future but because, given the goal of selling cars or selling insurance (implying a necessity to offer their customers an alternative option in an unpredictable world), they have less reason to doubt strategies based on past experience than other strategies. A strategy based on past experience is a corroborated possibility and therefore a better alternative than one that has not been corroborated. This is so even though there is no reason whatsoever to believe that the one will work better than another. Insurance companies are simply skilled gamblers and make their living out of that. We — their customers — prefer to do less gambling in our lives and are prepared to pay for the possibility of being compensated if things go wrong.

This answer differs from, or perhaps complements, the answer given by Joseph Agassi concerning the question of the role of positive evidence in technology.[13] In his view the role of positive evidence is primarily social. The reason that technology is occupied with empirical testing so much is that insurance companies and government institutions demand a certain amount of corroboration before they are ready to give any guarantee against failure. In the case of such technology as may lead to catastrophic results, either for the individual or for society at large, the national institutions have the power to stop techniques that are too dangerous. Therefore techniques such as medical drugs, nuclear power, and aeroplanes have to prove their mettle before being allowed on the market. And since proof equals a given amount of positive evidence in the eyes of the social institutions, all technological work has to provide such evidential support for its techniques. Now Agassi, being a falsificationist, does not for a moment propose that such evidence is a guarantee of the reliability and security of the techniques. Catastrophes may happen no matter how well corroborated the techniques are. No, the role of this evidence is simply to persuade the social institutions to offer guarantees, that is, to take the responsibility if and when these techniques fail.

In many cases, such as medical drugs, it is true of course that the immediate controller is a public institution and that the amount of positive evidence needed is regulated according to law in a sweeping and sometimes rather ad

---

[13]See Agassi (1975), especially Chapter 14.

hoc way. It has an air of being nothing but a social convention. When the medical industry has gone through the rituals of testing (first animal testing, then a certain amount of testing on humans), the drug in question has fulfilled the requirements for getting a safety stamp from the authorities. It has proved its mettle and the public can be safe. In the unlikely event that something should go wrong — the industry may have cheated or the authorities may have been a bit too slack — society will of course do what it can to compensate for any damage. So, by playing the game we do get a kind of safety within a society. But if the rules of the game were nothing but social conventions, the same thing would have been achieved if the rules had demanded that the drug should pass an oracle test. In that case medical technology would focus, not on double blind test on animals and humans, but on persuading the oracle to get the right vision concerning the power and future performance of the drug. Not accepting this conclusion, I suggest that political authorities and insurance companies sell us 'safety' in the form of guaranteeing compensation in the case of things going wrong, not in guaranteeing anything about the future. But they do so on as rational grounds as possible.

The sceptical idea that the sole purpose of positive evidence is to give psychological comfort according to social conventions is here rejected. So is the justificationist idea that past experience gives guarantees about what will happen in the future. As was argued above, a third alternative is possible, namely that positive evidence gives a basis for a rational choice of practical action. It is used for corroborating the possibility that a technique will work, thereby discriminating between our reasons for doubt.

## 8   Conclusions

My purpose in this paper has been to clarify the role of positive evidence in technology, and for practical action in general. If positive evidence cannot be used for justifying a belief in the functionality of a technique, the big question is what other role it may have. If we cannot prove or make probable that a given technique works, then why is technology so preoccupied with testing in the hope of obtaining corroboration? My own suggestion follows a falsificationist line of thought. Technology values positive evidence because we have less reason to doubt those that are well corroborated compared to other alternatives. The role of positive evidence is not to give guarantees or certainty but to make a difference with respect to other competitors.

But this result has, as I see it, important consequences. For example, it changes the traditional way of analysing the rationality of making practical choices. Given that there cannot be any certainty concerning the reliability of techniques, we should concentrate much more on thinking about options in the case that the preferred technique does *not* work. We should be making plans about such things as possible alternatives and insurance. The empirical investigation of past performance is just an initial step in the process. After that other things will have to be considered. Will the technique preferred according to past performance endanger the possibility of making other choices if it does not work? If so, then perhaps one should not choose that technique after all. What alternative techniques are there? How can the situation be mitigated if nothing works? And in the larger perspective: how can one increase the rationality of technology in general by having a greater pluralism with respect to technical methods?

Answering questions such as these is the real challenge for making rational decisions in practical choice situations. Traditional decision theory cannot give us any guarantees about the wisdom of our choices for the future.

# Bibliography

Agassi, J. (1975). *Science in Flux*. Dordrecht: D. Reidel Publishing Company.

Miller, D. W. (1994). *Critical Rationalism. A Restatement and Defence*. Chicago & La Salle IL: Open Court Publishing Company.

———— (2002). 'Induction: A Problem Solved'. In J. M. Böhm, H. Holweg, & C. Hoock, editors (2002), pp. 81-106. *Karl Poppers kritischer Rationalismus heute*. Tübingen: Mohr Siebeck. Reprinted as Chapter 5 of D. W. Miller (2006). *Out of Error*. Aldershot: Ashgate.

Nordin, I. (1989). 'The Rationality of Technology'. *Science Studies* **2**, pp. 3-10.

———— (1999). 'The Role of Science in Medicine'. *Theoretical Medicine and Bioethics* **20**, pp. 229-244.

Popper, K. R. (1963). *Conjectures and Refutations*. London: Routledge and Kegan Paul. 5th edition 1989. London: Routledge.

———— (1972). *Objective Knowledge*. Oxford: Clarendon Press. 2nd edition 1979.

———— (1974). 'Replies to My Critics'. In P. A. Schilpp, editor (1974), pp. 961-1197. *The Philosophy of Karl Popper*. La Salle IL: Open Court Publishing Company.

Salmon, W. C. (1981). 'Rational Prediction'. *The British Journal for the Philosophy of Science* **32**, pp. 115-125.

# 39

# Methodological Objectivism and Critical Rationalist 'Induction'

## Alfred Schramm

This paper constitutes one extended argument, which touches on various topics of Critical Rationalism as it was initiated by Karl Popper and further developed (although into different directions) in his aftermath. The result of the argument will be that critical rationalism either offers *no solution to the problem of induction at all*, or that it amounts, in the last resort, to a kind of *Critical Rationalist Inductivism* as it were, a version of what I call *Good Old Induction*. One may think of David Miller as a contemporary representative of what I consider as the 'no solution' version of critical rationalism, while Alan Musgrave stands for the version of 'critical rationalist induction'. Popper's own writings admit of either interpretation.[1]

## 1 Objectivism

Popper states as one of his[2]

(P₁) ... principal methods of approach, whenever *logical* problems are at stake ... to translate all the subjective or psychological terms, especially 'belief', etc., into *objective* terms. Thus, instead of speaking of a 'belief', I speak, say, of a 'statement' or of an 'explanatory theory'; and instead of an 'impression', I speak of an 'observation statement' or of a 'test statement'; and instead of the 'justification of a belief', I speak of 'justification of the claim that a theory is true', etc.

Even though it is not difficult to recognize what Popper is driving at with this meta-philosophical principle, it is not difficult either to see that he simply does not get it right: why should, for instance, a '*claim* that a theory is true' be less 'subjective' than a '*belief* that a theory is true? Does a *claim* not presuppose a *claiming subject*, just as a *belief* presupposes a *believing subject*? Concerning these questions it is not of much help either that Popper distinguishes[3]

---

[1]This depends on whether we look at his position up to the mid-1950s, which is covertly inductivistic (notwithstanding his clamours to the contrary), or whether we think of his later views, which belong to the 'no solution' kind (notwithstanding ...).

[2]Popper (1972), Chapter 1, § 4.

[3]Ibidem, Chapter 3, § 1.

(P$_2$)  ... two different senses of knowledge or of thought: (1) *knowledge or thought in the subjective sense*, consisting of a state of mind or of consciousness or a disposition to behave or to react, and (2) *knowledge or thought in an objective sense*, consisting of problems, theories, and arguments as such. Knowledge in this objective sense is totally independent of anybody's claim to know; it is also independent of anybody's belief, or disposition to assent; or to assert, or to act. Knowledge in the objective sense is *knowledge without a knower*: it is *knowledge without a knowing subject*.

The unquestionable part of this distinction is that it differentiates between *attitudes* of persons towards statements (or, as I would prefer, towards propositions) on the one hand, and the *statements* (propositions) *themselves* on the other. Either is sometimes referred to as 'knowledge'. But the same goes for 'claims', 'assertions', 'beliefs', and so on, because *all* such terms are ambiguous in this respect. They sometimes refer to *propositional attitudes* (which Popper deems 'subjective' or 'psychological') and sometimes to the *contents* of such attitudes, that is, *statements* or *propositions* (which Popper calls 'objective'). The distinction is one between *knowing* and *the known, claiming* and *the claimed, asserting* and *the asserted, accepting* and *the accepted, believing* and *the believed*, and many more of these. On the one side there are *subject-related*, that is, *pragmatic*,[4] notions involving *persons* who know, claim, assert, accept, or believe certain propositions, while on the other side there are *objective*, that is, *semantic*, notions involving just *propositions* and, as we shall see, their truth values, their truth conditions, and such objective properties as can, in essence, be explicated in terms of truth conditions. All this has been made entirely clear by Carnap as early as 1950.[5] Thus, it is not a question of the *terms* being 'subjective' or 'objective' (cp. P$_1$), but a question of their *meanings* which may be ascertained from the respective occasions on which these terms are used.

That it is important to distinguish between the objective semantic and the subject-related pragmatic meanings of such terms can be demonstrated by the following simple consideration: It is *logically possible* that there exists some person $X$ who believes (or claims seriously the truth of) both $h$ and $\neg h$ at the same time[6] (or, at least, that $X$ believes inconsistent propositions). But it is *logically impossible* that both $h$ and $\neg h$ are true, that is, that such *contents* of $X$'s beliefs or claims — what *is* believ*ed* or *is* claim*ed* by $X$ — can 'occur', as it were, at the same time.

This example should also illustrate that the distinction between the semantics and the pragmatics of the involved terms carries over to the *attributes* going with them: restricting ourselves to purely objective logical and/or

---

[4] For the distinction of pragmatics, semantics, and syntax as parts of semiotic, cp. Carnap (1948), pp. 8ff.

[5] Cp. Carnap (1950), especially §§ 11f.

[6] This is so at least as long as we do not *define* the notions of believing and of seriously claiming in such a way that only consistent beliefs are beliefs. This, however, would not be advisable, because most people hold at least *some* inconsistent beliefs.

semantic considerations, we may delimit the *truth conditions* of propositions, characterize, say, a proposition *q* as being a *logical consequence* of some proposition *p*, or *contradicting* some other proposition *v*, or, if we have some appropriate *logical weight function*, we may say, for instance, that the logical probability (or the logical support, or the corroboration, or any other weight) of *p*, given *q*, has some value *r*. For all these attributions we don't need *any* reference to persons or attributes of persons at all.[7] They are *objective* in the sense that they obtain quite *independently of whether or not there exist any persons* who consider, believe, deny, or even like or detest the involved propositions. And all such attributions can be characterized in *purely logical and/or semantic terms* in virtue of their objective semantic properties. As long as we remain in the realm of semantic considerations, no reference to persons or properties of persons is needed or called for.

However, as soon as we introduce pragmatic considerations, we are dealing with entirely different matters. For instance: Given any two *propositions p* and *q*, where *p* is 'knowledge' or a 'belief' in Popper's *objective* sense, that is, is a known (or believed, or otherwise entertained) proposition, while *q* is *not* 'knowledge' or a 'belief' in the objective sense (is *not* a known or believed, or otherwise entertained, proposition) — which *purely semantic* characterization can be given in order to delimit one from the other *in this respect*? Obviously none. There is no other way than to move on to *pragmatic* considerations, involving persons and/or their attributes (such as, for instance, their propositional attitudes): the *known* (or *believed*) proposition is the one where there exists at least one person who knows (or believes) it, while there is no such person for the other proposition. As not every proposition is known or believed, we simply *cannot distinguish purely semantically* (that is, without reference to persons) such propositions which do constitute knowledge in Popper's objective sense, from those which do not. And this is also the case with all other notions of the discussed kind, such as 'belief', 'claim', and so on.

So, can we then pose the *problem of induction* and/or a possible *solution* of it in a purely objective manner? Popper proposes to restate Hume's logical problem '...in an objective or logical mode of speech'. Here is one of the many versions he gives of what he considers to constitute the *logical problem of induction*:[8]

(P₃)  Can the claim that an explanatory theory is true or that it is false be justified by 'empirical reasons'; that is, can the assumption of the truth of test statements justify either the claim that a universal theory is true or the claim that it is false?

Note that Popper asks expressly (in a shortened version, taking only the second half of P₃ after 'that is') whether the *assumption* that some singular

---

[7]Nor do we need any reference to 'science as an institution', in which Jarvie (2001) is interested.

[8]Popper (1972), Chapter 1, §5.

propositions (test statements) are true can justify either the *claim* that some general proposition (universal theory) is true or the *claim* that it is false.

This, however, indicates a fatal confusion: depending on which way we understand the involved terms, we have either (a) an objective logical problem *but not the problem of induction*, or we have (b) a (subject-related, or 'subjective', as Popper calls it) version of the problem of induction *but not a logical problem*.[9]

If we start with case (a) where we understand 'claim' and 'assumption' *objectively*, that is, as *propositions*, then we get:

(oP₃)   Can the *proposition* that some singular propositions (test statements) are true *justify* either the *proposition* that some general proposition (universal theory) is true or the *proposition* that it is false?

As in this case the 'justifying' relation takes propositions as arguments and, thus, must be an objective semantic relation, it would be better not to speak (misleadingly) of justification, but, rather, of logical consequence, logical implication, or some other suitable and semantically explicable relation (such as logical probability, for instance). And indeed, even though it may sound somewhat exaggerated to call it a logical *problem*, this is, after all, a purely logical question to which there is a trivial answer: yes, true singular propositions can prompt the logical consequence (and, thus, 'justify' in some far-fetched sense) that some general proposition is false. Furthermore, it is also the case that no general proposition can be a valid consequence of (and, thus, be 'justified' by) a consistent set of singular propositions. However, I don't know of *any* relevant philosopher of the past century who would have denied *this*. In particular, none of the Logical Empiricists, Popper's prime targets in his anti-inductivist crusade, would have claimed anything to the contrary. As far as this *logical* question is concerned, there has always been full unanimity. Thus, if the 'solution' of the problem of induction consists in nothing more than in the mere recognition of the asymmetry of falsifiability and verifiability, then this would constitute neither an original nor a particularly specific achievement of Karl Popper, but, rather, a commonplace hardly deserving any further discussion.

And, finally, this was not, and is no version of, Hume's Problem of Induction: Hume did not ask for a logical triviality (whether certain propositions follow, or do not follow, from certain others, or whether there exist any other logical relations among propositions), nor was he sceptical about the validity of some logical relations (such as entailment), but he asked whether we (humans) can reasonably believe (or know), that is, can be *justified in our believing*, some general propositions, given (or granted) that we have nothing more than justified belief (or knowledge) of some singular propositions to start with. Even though this way to put it is not exactly Hume's,[10] the decisive point should be clear: Hume did not ask for the reasonableness of certain *logical relations* (whatever it should mean to talk about the 'reasonableness'

---

[9]This dilemma is discussed in my (1998).

[10]I had to make some terminological adaptations for a clearer fit with the present context.

of *objective* matters) but for the reasonableness of certain *propositional attitudes*. Thus, by 'objectivizing' the matter, Popper lost track of the very *problem* that he claimed to have 'solved', or, as Musgrave aptly puts it on several occasions, he simply *changed the subject*.[11]

This leads us to case (b): Let us then take the terms 'assumption' and 'claim' at their face values as denoting *propositional attitudes* of persons and adapt P₃ accordingly:

(sP₃)   Can the *assumption* (of some person *X*) that some singular propositions (test statements) are true *justify* either the *claim* (of person *X*) that some general proposition (universal theory) is true or the *claim* (of person *X*) that it is false?

In this case the 'justifying' relation takes *propositional attitudes* ('assumption' in the sense of *assuming* and 'claim' in the sense of *claiming*) as arguments, as demanded by Hume's problem, but this is *not a logical relation*. What we are asked for is to explicate 'justification' or, what amounts to the same, 'reasonableness' and 'rationality' as *attributes of, or relations among, propositional attitudes*, and we can easily see why this must be the case. If we tried to explicate these terms in a purely semantic manner, nothing of any interest would come up, indeed, any such notion would remain totally superfluous: we might as well get on without it and speak of the truth, or some truth relations, of propositions. Nothing of any interest would be added, if we called them 'rational' or 'reasonable' or 'justified' in excess to what we can say about them anyway in purely semantic terms. Thus, given the proposed analysis, we should be careful in each individual case to consider what is meant by 'belief', or 'knowledge', or the like: it is *propositional attitudes* to which we properly ought to attribute *rationality*, or *reasonableness*, or *justification*, and it is *propositions* to which we ought to properly attribute *truth*, *falsity*, or any other attributes or relations definable in terms of truth conditions. It means simply committing category mistakes to call the propositional attitudes true or false, or to call the propositions justified, or reasonable, or rational.[12] Thus, a person *X*'s *belief* may be *reasonable* or *unreasonable*, a proposition *h* may be *true* or *false* — all four resulting combinations are possible (*X* may believe un/reasonably the true/false proposition *h* to be true).

There is much more which can be said about this, but I shall restrict my remarks to what will be needed for the understanding of some issues still to be dealt with.[13] My model or paradigmatic case of a propositional attitude is that of a belief. By a *belief* I understand a *disposition* of some person *X* to '*affirm*' some proposition *h*. An *affirmation* is a *mental event* which occurs (is aroused) *more or less intensely* as an *actualization* of the belief disposition under appropriate conditions (for instance, if *X* considers seriously

---

[11] Musgrave (2004).

[12] This is, incidentally, my reason for thinking that Alan Musgrave is right in his insistence that it is the believ*ing* and not the believ*ed* for which we can have 'good reasons'. Cp. among others, his (1993).

[13] Cp. below, p. 260. For details see my (1996a) and also my (1996b) and (2002).

the proposition $h$ in respect to its truth). Proportional to the intensity of the affirmation, a belief is more or less *firm* ('stronger' or 'weaker'). There are analogous properties for *disbelief*, which is a disposition to '*negate*' some proposition $h$, and where *negation* is a more or less intense actualization of the disbelief disposition. There are two kinds of unbelief of $h$, either *disbelief*, where $h$ is negated and $\neg h$ is affirmed, or *being agnostic*, where neither $h$ and $\neg h$ is affirmed nor negated.[14]   As both belief and disbelief can be more or less firm, we can use appropriate *metric concepts* (dis/belief of firmness $r$) for the formulation of rationality principles such as (roughly): a person $X$ has a rational attitude of belief or unbelief concerning a proposition $h$ if and only if $X$ believes $h$ with that firmness $r$ that is proportional to the degree of support that $X$'s empirical evidence $\mathcal{E}$ lends to $h$ (all at time $t$).

Now, does all this mean subjectivism, or psychologism, or the like? Not at all. It *would*, indeed, be subjectivistic to bind the validity of logical or semantic properties of propositions and their relations in any way to the involved persons or their attitudes. For instance, it would be subjectivistic to demand that, say, the relation of logical consequence ought to 'obey the laws of thought', or, even worse, that the truth value of some proposition depended on the propositional attitudes of eventually involved persons. But nothing of this kind is demanded by the simple distinctions we have drawn above. The objective semantic properties of, and/or relations among, propositions remain untouched by our eventual attitudes towards them.

As an incidental aside we may note that all that talk about the '*rationality of science*', which is so dear to many critical rationalists, is in great danger of subjectivism, or, better, sociologism: *either* 'science' is meant here as a collection of propositions (which ones, by the way, — those from the textbooks, those from the journals, those to which *all* scientists would agree, those to which *at least one* scientist agrees, or what?), then this collection is neither 'justified' nor 'rational' but simply and objectively a (consistent or inconsistent) set of *true* or *false propositions*. Or 'science' refers to a social institution, for which one may define yet another concept of rationality. But this concept will always and unfailingly be of such kind that any talk of the rationality of science becomes sociological, that is, empirical science. The mixup of these two spheres (collection of propositions and social institution) will then constitute sociologism.

Popper seems to have simply overreacted in his fight against subjectivism: he eliminated (or tried, unsuccessfully in the end, to eliminate) *any* explicit or implicit reference to persons and their propositional attitudes. But, as already observed above, by doing so he lost sight of the very problem which he claimed to have solved. Hume's problem, or the problem of induction, can neither be adequately stated, nor can it be solved, under the restrictions of a Popperian 'objectivist' programme. This does not mean, however, that the *distinction* between objective (logical/semantic) and subject-related

---

[14]This gives rise to my claim that *beliefs* cannot be (formal) probabilities, because probabilities do not allow us to distinguish between disbelief and agnosticism. Cp. my (1996a).

(pragmatic) considerations is not important — quite to the contrary, we must remain careful to observe it in all relevant contexts, which can sometimes, due to the ambiguity of the discussed epistemic terms, become a tricky task.

Most of this, however, will be disputed by many contemporary followers of Popper, because in their view I have as yet hardly scratched the surface of the true controversy. So, we may leave this matter here as it stands and turn back to it later.

## 2 Methodological rules and rational belief

As can be gathered from the foregoing, in particular from $sP_3$, I have come to claim that justification or rationality pertains to propositional attitudes and, thus, to attributes of persons. (I shall argue later that we must further subdivide this into questions of pure or *theoretical rationality* and questions concerning the *rationality of decisions*.) Critical rationalists, however, like to talk about the 'rationality' of *science*, or of scientific progress, procedures, discussions, criticism, preference, methods, and so on. This inflationary proliferation of ascriptions of rationality can be reduced to the focal point of Popper's *methodological* outlook, as it was initiated already in *Logik der Forschung* (Chapter II) and combined with the idea of *objective truth* (which Popper added after it had become respectable) as the *aim of science*. I shall argue that the whole enterprise is seriously flawed.

Let us start by considering the status of methodology and methodological rules.

Whether we regard the rules of scientific method ('methodological rules') as introduced by *decision* (convention) or by *proposal* (convention, again),[15] it is in either case inappropriate to liken them straightforwardly to rules of games, for instance to those of chess, as Popper and, following him, David Miller[16] and others do. Rules of games in the straightforward sense (call them *constitutive rules*) define the framing conditions under which a game is to be played. Constitutive rules are purely conventional; we may change them any time or invent new ones and then play, given such different rules, a different game. In chess, they define the number of squares, kinds and numbers of pieces, and their permitted moves, checking positions, mating the opponent's king as the goal of the game, and so on. But by merely obeying *such* rules one will hardly ever *achieve the goal* of the game, that is, *win it*, and even *if* that should happen nevertheless, it would happen only by mere coincidence. It is not in order to *win* the game that one obeys these rules, but in order to *play* it. If one does not comply with the constitutive rules, one may either be said to play a different game or no game at all, but as long as the rules are obeyed, it is a game of chess by definition (or, rather, by convention).

---

[15]This fine distinction was stressed by David Miller (1998), p. 78. Heaven knows what it should be good for.

[16]Cp. especially Miller (1998).

An entirely different matter is whether one plays the game *well* or *badly*. Sometimes strategic and/or tactical *advice* is also based on *a kind of* rules. Such rules, call them *strategic rules*, tell, for instance, whether a move is a 'good' or a 'bad' one *in respect to attaining or approximating the aim of the game*. They are not obligatory in the strict sense like the constitutive rules are, because they fulfil tasks that are analogous to those of so-called rules of prudence: if a player does not comply with them, we will not say that he 'retires from the game', but, instead, that he plays the game badly or foolishly. Strategic rules are based on *hypotheses* about the strengths and weaknesses of moves, positions, and the like, *given* the constitutive rules of the game, in particular its respective aim. They are *not* conventional, but, instead, shaped according to the *underlying hypotheses* about how to increase the chances of success (that is, attaining the aim of the game). The quality of the advice that we can get from strategic rules depends, thus, on the quality of the hypotheses forming their background or basis.

Now, of which kind shall we understand the rules of scientific method to consist of? Are they *constitutive rules* to tell us merely *how* the 'game of science' is to be played, or are they *strategic rules* to tell us how it is to be played *well*?

Popper seems to have not even considered this or any other distinction to this effect and remains thoroughly ambiguous in this respect. His insistence that, for instance, his 'supreme rule'[17] is to be adopted by *decision*, that is, by *convention*, would indicate that it is meant as a *constitutive rule*. This, however, would leave it without any rationale for *why* we should adopt it (we might as well adopt some other rule) and *why* the 'game of science' should be directed by it. More plausibly, and taking into account Popper's explicit reference to the demarcation criterion in this connection (and the further reference to truth or 'getting nearer to the truth' as the aim of science and of 'rational discussion'[18]), we may well assume that he meant it as a *strategic rule*. But then this rule (and all the other 'subsidiary' ones[19]) cannot be reasonably or rationally adopted by a simple decision without backing it up by the *hypothesis* that it is *good* (helpful, supportive, and so on) for doing science *well*, that it is *conducive* (even if fallibly and not unfailingly) *to attaining truth* (or to increasing verisimilitude) as the aim of science. This step, however, leads us full circle back to where we started from: the *hypothesis* that by obeying certain methodological rules we are more likely to approximate the aim of science than we are without obeying them can itself be rationally held only if we have good reasons for believing so, that is, if we are *justified in our (more or less firm) believing* that this hypothesis is true.

---

[17]Popper (1935), § 11: '...that the other rules of scientific procedure must be designed in such a way that they do not protect any statement in science against falsification'.

[18]Cp. Popper (1972), Chapter 1, § 7. 'The methodological rules ...may be regarded as subject to the general *aim of rational discussion, which is to get nearer to the truth.*'

[19]Jarvie (2001) counts 14 of them.

This last point may as well be substantiated in the following way:[20] by a *method* we must always understand a method *to some effect* or *for pursuing some aim*.[21] In order to be 'good' for pursuing an aim $A$, a method $M$ need not be 'safe', that is, lead unfailingly to the realization of $A$. Let us call a method $M$ 'basically good' if the employment of $M$ raises the tendency for the realization of $A$ as compared to the non-employment of $M$, and let us call $M$ 'optimal' if $M$ is basically good and there is no other method $M'$ that prompts a stronger tendency for the realization of $A$ than $M$ does; then we may say that a method is 'good' just in case it is either basically good or optimal. This is an *objective* characterization of the 'goodness' of a method: a method $M$ is good, just in case it fulfils these conditions, irrespective of whether or not there exist any persons who believe or know that $M$, indeed, fulfils them.

Now let us apply this to Popper's *critical method* (CM) *of conjectures and refutations*, and let us, for the sake of the argument, assume that CM were, indeed, objectively good in the explained sense. Let us furthermore assume that scientists were busily occupied with inventing daring hypotheses, testing them severely, and preferring best-corroborated hypotheses for further testing, in short: let it be a critical rationalist's picture book world where scientists take their decisions according to the methodological rules, for example, never to protect their hypotheses against falsification, never to stop testing them severely, never to allow them to drop out without 'good reason', and whatever else CM has in stock for its model scientists. May we then say that these scientists are *rationally pursuing the truth*? Not quite, because *even if* they were, indeed, *objectively* approaching the truth (which nobody could ever find out), they might still be deciding and acting in the described manner because, say, the fortune teller has told them to do so, or for some other insane reason, *or for no reason at all*, thus acting, at best, as the unwitting tools (or fools) of a Hegelian 'cunning of reason'. In other words, neither their actual behaviour nor their *success*, if indeed there is any (objectively speaking), ought to be mistaken for *rationality*.[22]

The same point must apply if one (rashly) were to call it rational if a person *merely believed* that the employed method is a good one, even if it were, indeed, (objectively) good, because such believing might as well be based on a madman's or on no reasoning at all.

There is, thus, no other way left than to postulate that a person must, in order to *pursue an aim rationally*, employ a method of which she *rationally believes* that it is a good method. I have come to call this the *thesis of the primacy of theoretical rationality*: there is, and there can be, *no rational acting or deciding without rational believing*.[23]

---

[20] For a more detailed account of this see my (2002).

[21] It would be nonsensical to claim to be in possession of a method without, at the same time, being able to specify what it should be good for.

[22] That the proverbial dog has its day does not make its actions rational.

[23] This thesis was first introduced in my (1998).

This thesis allows for the fallibility of human reason and of human rationality. It is *quite possible* that CM is a good, even an optimal method. But who knows — it may just as well be not better than throwing coins in order to 'decide' which hypothesis to prefer from a given collection of alternative ones. But if we have *good reasons for believing* that CM is good or optimal, that is, if we *rationally believe* that CM is (objectively) good, then we *decide rationally* if we make our decisions in accordance with the rules of CM, *whether or not* CM *is in fact (objectively) a good method*. We *have* nothing better than our justified beliefs to get on with.

We may summarize this section by observing that Popper's methodological view cannot overcome the force of the primacy of *theoretical* rationality, of the rationality of our *beliefs*, without which none of our actions or decisions can gain themselves the status of being reasonable or (*practically*) rational. This does not amount to the claim that CM is not *objectively* a good method. My claim is only that we cannot get on *without* good reasons, *without* justifications for our beliefs, *including* beliefs of such hypotheses that constitute the background of our methodological convictions.

This, however, will be repudiated as a 'subjectivistic' and 'justificationistic' (and, possibly, 'inductivistic') prejudice by all critical rationalists who agree with David Miller's (and William Bartley's) position of *methodological objectivism* (as I call it).

## 3 Methodological objectivism

Miller's position of methodological objectivism is diametrically opposed to both main points which I have put forward so far: it is *objectivistic* in Popper's sense of objectivism, of which I have argued that it fails even to state the problem of induction adequately, let alone to solve it. And it is *methodological*, of which I have argued that it fails to provide us with an appropriate conception of rationality, let alone to show us why it should be rational to obey the rules of the critical method (or why the critical method should be taken for a 'rational method'[24]). Thus, if my analysis is correct, then Miller's methodological proposals must be useless and his ascriptions of rationality must be empty.

We may skip Miller's reproduction of all the verbal twists and turns that Popper has produced in support of his claim that we may have (good) '*critical*' *reasons* for '*defending*' a *preference* for a theory, in contradistinction to (useless and unavailable) '*positive*' *reasons* for '*justifying*' such a preference (or a theory).[25] Instead, we may deal straight on with Miller's own account of theory preference, or, rather, non-preference, of which he gives a dense version,

---

[24]According to Miller (2002), p. 81 (2006, p. 111) 'rationality' in a primary sense ought to be attributed to procedures or methods.

[25]Popper (1983), Part I, § 2, admits that '[g]iving reasons for one's preferences can of course be *called* a justification (in ordinary language). But [so he continues] it is not a justification in the sense criticized here.' I gather from this that the notion of justification 'criticized here' must be some *technical term* of Popper's private making. I must confess

thereby restricting 'attention to the simplest case, where only truth and falsity are at issue, not comparisons of verisimilitude':[26]

(M₁) ...it is not hard to give an impeccably deductivist account of what is going on ...A theory $T_1$ that is refuted is definitely false (given the truth of the test statements involved), while an unrefuted theory $T_2$ may be true. ...All that may be derived from the empirical report that $T_1$ is refuted and $T_2$ is not refuted (together with a statement of our preference for truth over falsehood) is ...that $T_1$ *should not be preferred to* $T_2$. No attempt to justify this ...claim is made, but manifestly no justification is needed. Anyone who denies it exposes himself at once to deadly criticism.

I shall risk such deadly criticism and argue that this allegedly 'impeccably deductivist account' is inconclusive and that not even the weak methodological advice

C      $T_1$ should not be preferred to $T_2$

follows as a conclusion from the proposed premises.
    Obviously C cannot follow from

P₁      $T_1$ is refuted.

P₂      $T_2$ is not refuted.

P₃      Truth has preference over falsehood.

because P₁ is still compatible with $T_1$ being true and P₂ is compatible with $T_2$ being false. But we may attempt to add further premises, as contained in the paragraph quoted:

P₄      A theory $T_1$ that is refuted is definitely false (given the truth of the test statements involved).

P₅      An unrefuted theory $T_2$ may be true.

---

that this specific Popperian concept of justification, as 'criticized here' and at so many other places, is beyond my comprehension.

[26]Miller (2002), p. 99; (2006), p. 127. This is a more detailed version of Miller (1994), pp. 113f.

The (quite sensible) basic idea (though still in 'subjective' terms) can be found already in Popper (1963), Chapter 1, § x: 'Another question sometimes asked is this: why is it reasonable to prefer non-falsified statements to falsified ones? ...The only correct answer is the straightforward one: because we search for truth (even though we can never *be sure* we have found it), and because the falsified theories are *known* or *believed* to be false, while the non-falsified theories may still be true' (my emphases).

Even though Popper tried already in his (1963), Chapter 1 (originally a lecture given in 1953), to correct the true history of his intellectual development (something which later seems to have become his most favoured preoccupation), this piece contains his last sensible (and important) word on induction. However, it was written in a vein that he himself later denounced as 'subjectivistic' and 'inductivistic': in his (1972), in particular Chapters 1 and 3, and in his nearly unbearable (1983), Part I, § 2 (with the footnote: 'partly rewritten in 1979', but really rewritten in 1980 under the harmful influence of W. W. Bartley III) he tried to make us believe that he never meant it that way.

Now, what can we get from $P_1, \ldots, P_5$? Again not C, which Miller claims to deduce, but, instead:

C'     $T_1$ should not be preferred to $T_2$ (*given the truth of the test statements in-volved*).

But *such* advice is *no* advice. To advise somebody to do $p$, given that condition $q$ is fulfilled, is of no use at all for actually making a decision if, at the same time, $q$ is of such kind that its truth *can never be found out*. The decisive point here is that $P_4$ imposes an *objective* condition under which $T_1$ is '*definitely*' false. And we cannot skip this condition, because without it the refuted theory $T_1$ would *not* be 'definitely' false but might (even though 'refuted') still be true, which would render $P_4$ itself 'definitely false'. Nor can we weaken the condition and put in instead, say, 'given the test statements involved are cor-roborated', or 'given the test statements involved are provisionally accepted', or similar conditions. They all would allow that the refuted theory $T_1$ might still be true, in which case an according reformulation of $P_4$ would, again, be false, in short, $T_1$ is 'definitely' false *only* if the test statements are *simply and objectively true*. Consequently, it remains for ever unresolved and unascertain-able whether the refuted theory $T_1$ is 'definitely' false. This must carry over to the conclusion, such that from $P_1, \ldots, P_5$ no advice in the sense of C (not to prefer $T_1$ to $T_2$) can follow, but only C', the mocking 'advice' not to prefer $T_1$ to $T_2$ *if an absolutely unrevealable condition is fulfilled*. But a 'methodology' that does not allow, if needed, to derive *usable* advice is itself useless. Take *any* (contingent) statement $q$ and then give somebody the advice: 'Do $p$, if $q$ is true — not, if you *believe* or *think* or *provisionally accept* that $q$ is true, but only if $q$ is plainly and objectively true.' Whoever understands the difference between *objective truth* and *belief* or *acceptance of truth* (and is a fallibilist) will also understand that one will *never* find out whether $p$ should be done or not. But then — what's the advice?[27]

From this and the foregoing I draw the conclusion that Miller's and any other objectivistic programme, in the sense of Popper's objectivism, is incap-able of solving the problem of induction or even to give sound methodological advice, because it comes to grief over the primacy of theoretical rationality.

But there is still hope left for *critical fallibilism*.

## 4  Musgrave and good reasons

Alan Musgrave has taken the right step in holding that '[t]hough there are no justified beliefs (belief-contents), there are justified and hence rational believings'.[28]   That he proposes an 'act-theory' of belief while I prefer a 'disposition-theory' (as well as some other differences in this respect) is of minor importance here. Suffice to say that he holds that it is the believings,

---

[27] For further remarks on this issue see my (2002).
[28] Musgrave (1991), p. 20. Similarly at various other places.

the propositional attitudes (as explained above), that are the proper subject of any attribution of rationality.

But when (under which conditions) can we claim of a belief of some hypothesis to be rational or reasonable? In order to answer this question, Musgrave gives an explanation (with which I agree, subject to some provisos) and an 'epistemic principle' (which I find to be wanting). The explanation is this:[29]

> At the heart of critical rationalism ... is the positive contention that the failure of our best efforts to show some potential belief or hypothesis to be false *is* a good cognitive reason for us tentatively to adopt that hypothesis as true, that is, to believe it. And if we have a good reason of this kind ... then our belief ... is a reasonable belief.

Leaving aside the fact that this formulation might be misunderstood because it mixes up 'potential belief' with 'hypothesis' as possible bearers of truth values, it contains nicely the basic intuition that, for instance, also any software programmer will recognize: in order to validate an item of software it ought to be *tested*, and testing means to try out the most vicious and aggressive tricks in order to let the software produce mistakes. The harder one tries without 'success' (that is, without producing a false or 'unwanted' output) the more one can be satisfied that the software is 'good'. Of course, by this procedure one can never *prove*, that is *verify*, that the software contains no mistakes, but it is the best one can do.

Even though scientific hypotheses are not computer software, we can see that the analogy is telling: produce 'trust' or belief by trying to show a hypothesis to be wrong. If you can't show it wrong then you are right (justified) to trust it *up to a certain point*. This is my first proviso: *how firmly you may believe* a hypothesis in order for this belief to be a *justified* one must be proportional in some way to *how hard you have tried to falsify* it. Thus, it is not a simple matter of belief or not belief, but a matter of belief *of a certain firmness* or *strength* that determines whether it is justified or unjustified, rational or irrational.

My second proviso is that all this must be combined with what Joseph Agassi has aptly put in a nutshell: 'Empirical support is failed refutation'.[30] In other words, our 'best efforts to show some ... hypothesis to be false' ought to be attempts at *empirical* refutations as long as we are dealing with contingent, that is, non-analytic (and, of course, consistent) propositions. Metaphysical hypotheses (which are also contingent) do not belong to this category; they are not refutable on an empirical basis. They may clash only with *other* metaphysical propositions. Such efforts towards 'showing' one metaphysical hypothesis to be 'false' by insisting on the truth of another one (and there is no other way of criticizing consistent metaphysical claims), however, cannot lead to any *sound reasons* for believing it. It is true that metaphysical

---

[29] Ibidem, p. 21; cp. also Musgrave (2002), p. 30.
[30] See this volume, p. 7.

musings, like many other kinds of idle tinkering with thoughts, may sometimes *lead* to, or get *transformed* into, interesting, that is *empirically testable* hypotheses. But then they, or, rather, their empirically testable substitutes, are not metaphysical anymore. *Belief* in metaphysical theses, though of no cognitive value, is open to anybody who has a taste for them, *rational* belief in them is impossible. The appropriate, that is *rational*, attitude towards untested because untestable propositions must always be to *remain agnostic*.

But now for Musgrave's epistemic principle, which in one version (in terms of corroboration) reads:[31]

> CR* It is reasonable to adopt as true or to believe (at time *t*) that hypothesis from a group of competing hypotheses which has (at time *t*) been best corroborated.

Before dealing with this, a few procedural remarks should be appropriate.

Musgrave calls this principle 'epistemic' and claims that it is synthetic, which would mean that it expresses a contingent truth (or falsity). But then it ought to be empirically testable, otherwise it is metaphysical.

Hans Albert,[32] Volker Gadenne,[33] and, I believe, also Gunnar Andersson, adopt the policy of treating principles like this as metaphysical. But then I cannot see what they should be good for. As a *justified belief* in metaphysical theses is not possible (as explained above), Albert, Gadenne, and Andersson may believe them or not — it will not add, nor take away, anything from what they may be justified in believing anyway (which latter, however, will be very little indeed for lack of an adequate and *rationally* believed principle as a *presupposition* for so many other beliefs).

Musgrave himself tries to wriggle out of this predicament by simply inventing a third category: '...the things usually called "inductive principles" ...were *metaphysical* principles ..., whereas CR* is an epistemic principle.'[34] Unfortunately he never explains wherein this difference between 'metaphysical' and 'epistemic' should lie. Furthermore, his insistence that CR* is synthetic gets him into a vicious circle which he fails to get rid of in a convincing manner.[35]

My view of this matter is that principles like CR* should be taken as *proposed explications*, and, thus, as *provisionally acceptable 'analytical hypotheses'*. This contention affords some explanation, which I shall try to give by utilizing an accordingly adapted Popperian terminology.

We may understand the task of explicating a concept as a process that can be arranged in analogy to the empirical method of conjectures and refutations in the following way: The conjecture is, that the proposed principle provides

---

[31] Musgrave (1991), p. 26; cp. also Musgrave (2002), p. 36.
[32] Albert (2002), p. 5 and p. 21.
[33] Gadenne (2002), p. 76 and p. 286.
[34] Musgrave (1991), p. 26; cp. also Musgrave (2002), p. 37.
[35] Cp. the critique in Miller (1994), pp. 121-125.

an adequate *concept of rationality*. Such a conjecture can be tested against our pre-explicative conceptual intuitions by describing (as 'test statements'), and agreeing upon, particular cases that (to our pre-explicative conceptual intuition) are obvious cases of rational belief or of irrational belief. Then, if such a particular case is, according to our agreed opinion, one of *rational* belief, while the principle does *not* cover it, or if such a particular case is, according to our agreed opinion, one of *irrational* belief, while the principle covers it as rational, the principle is 'refuted', that is, it has been shown to be faulty in respect to our purpose of finding a suitable concept of rationality as an explicatum. Otherwise, as long as no such 'falsifying' example comes up, we may use the concept of rationality in exactly the sense in which it is explicated by the principle.

Before we try this procedure of 'analytic conjectures and refutations' on Musgrave's principle CR*, a possible objection must be dealt with, which runs as follows: CR*, or other principles of such kind, cannot be analytic, because they are 'ampliative' in the sense, as Musgrave claims, '...that they enable you to obtain conclusions which do not follow from ...other premises of ...deductive arguments in which they figure. ...To be ampliative in this sense is simply to be non-analytic.'[36] This he claims to show by the following argument in which CR* occurs as a non-redundant premise:

CR*
Hypothesis $h$ is the best corroborated hypothesis at time $t$.
_____
Therefore, it is reasonable to adopt hypothesis $h$ as true at time $t$.

But in my opinion, all that is shown by this is merely that CR* is *inadequate* as a *principle of rational belief* (or of 'reasonable adoption').

Consider a conclusion such as: 'Therefore, Peter Jones is a bachelor.' We may derive this validly from 'Peter Jones is an unmarried male person', which would render the additional *analytic* premise 'All unmarried male persons are bachelors' redundant. But we may as well arrive at the same conclusion from 'Peter Jones is a male person' and an *inadequate and non-analytic* 'principle' to the effect that 'All male persons are bachelors'. Thus, what we should be looking for is a principle on which we can agree that it gives the *meaning* of rational belief such that it would be rendered redundant if we have a premise stating that in some individual case the conditions of that principle are fulfilled. To such purpose we shall apply the method of explication, or of 'analytic conjectures and refutations', as I have called it.

Suppose now that there exists a group of competing hypotheses $\{h_1, \ldots, h_n\}$, of which $h_i$ has (at time $t$) been best corroborated, and suppose that there is a person $X$ who, at time $t$, adopts $h_i$. According to CR* this would be reasonable of $X$. But suppose further that $X$ doesn't know at all that $h_i$ is best corroborated. In this case, I submit, $X$'s adoption of $h_i$ ought not be rated as reasonable. *Objectively* speaking, it *would* be reasonable for $X$ to adopt $h_i$,

_____
[36]Musgrave (1991), p. 27; cp. also Musgrave (2002), p. 38.

but without knowing this it may as well be by mere coincidence that $X$ has adopted $h_i$, which should not earn him or her the epistemic 'praise' of being reasonable. But then CR* is inadequate, since it rates a case as reasonable that obviously ought to be rated as unreasonable. So, let us try to improve a little on CR* and call this CR$^1$.

CR$^1$   A person $X$ has a *reasonable* belief in some hypothesis $h_i$ from a collection of hypotheses $\{h_1, \ldots, h_n\}$ just in case $h_i$ is best corroborated, $X$ knows that $h_i$ is best corroborated, and $X$ believes $h_i$ (all at time $t$).

This does away with the awkward counterexample, but, as can be expected, CR$^1$ can also easily be refuted.

Let us assume that $h_i$ is best corroborated as before, $X$ knows of this, and $X$ believes $h_i$, so that, according to CR$^1$, $X$ would believe $h_i$ reasonably. However, let us furthermore assume that the empirical record (that is, all the empirical evidence gained so far, in particular the evidence gained from all the attempts to falsify the hypotheses under consideration) is still pretty meagre. Even though the evidence corroborates $h_i$ best, everybody working in the field knows that further corroboration will be needed, or that some runner-up $h_j$ is in for corroborations that might even turn the tables. Now suppose further that our person $X$ simply and plainly *believes* $h_i$, maybe even believes beyond nearly any reasonable doubt. This case would still be covered by CR$^1$ as a reasonable belief, while I would call it plainly irrational. Obviously we shall have to construct yet another version CR$^2$, making allowance for beliefs (and disbeliefs) to be graded with respect to their firmness and for *proportioning this firmness of belief according to the degree of corroboration that the involved hypotheses gain from the evidence.*

Whichever formulation of such a principle we shall ever propose as adequate in the end,[37] it should be clear by now, that it conforms with a scheme that can be called the '*Principle of Good Old Induction*' because it served also as the basic idea for both Keynes's[38] and Carnap's[39] theories of induction. And whatever else Carnap changed in later years, there was never any need to change the basic model, as can be seen from a clear restatement of it in his posthumously published 'Inductive Logic and Rational Decisions'.[40]

---

[37]For a principle that can cope with all the counterexamples to which Musgrave's CR* falls prey cp. my (2002). For a previous version of it see also my (1996b), which, however, was unfortunately badly mutilated by the printers.

[38]Keynes (1921), p. 17: 'In order that we may have rational belief in $p$ of a lower degree of probability than certainty, it is necessary that we know a set of propositions $h$, and also know some secondary proposition $q$ asserting a probability-relation between $p$ and $h$.'

[39]Carnap (1962), p. 181: 'Our conception of the nature of inductive inference ... enables us to regard the inductive method as valid without abandoning empiricism. ... Any inductive statement (that is, not the hypothesis involved, but the statement of the inductive relation between the hypothesis and the evidence) is purely logical. Any statement of probability$_1$ ... is, if true, analytic.'

[40]Cp. Carnap (1971), especially p. 30.

The decisive point is, that this principle links the *firmness of belief* with the *degree of support* that the believed hypothesis gains from the evidence. It is true that Keynes and Carnap took *probability* for measuring that support, while we take *corroboration*. But this is of minor relevance, because a fitting concept of corroboration that does justice to the basic intuition as contained in Agassi's slogan 'empirical support is failed refutation' is still wanting anyway.

# Bibliography

Albert, H. (2002). 'Varianten des kritischen Rationalismus'. In Böhm, Holweg, & Hoock (2002), pp. 3-22.

Böhm, J. M., Holweg, H., & Hoock, C., editors (2002). *Karl Poppers kritischer Rationalismus heute*. Tübingen: Mohr Siebeck.

Carnap, R. (1948). *Introduction to Semantics*. Cambridge MA: Harvard University Press.

——— (1950). *Logical Foundations of Probability*. Chicago: The University of Chicago Press. 2nd edition 1962.

——— (1971). 'Inductive Logic and Rational Decisions'. In: R. Carnap & R. C. Jeffrey, editors (1971), pp. 5-31. *Studies in Inductive Logic and Probability*, Volume I. Berkeley & Los Angeles CA: University of California Press.

Gadenne, V. (2002). 'Hat der kritische Rationalismus noch etwas zu lehren?' In Böhm, Holweg, & Hoock (2002), pp. 58-78.

Jarvie, I. C. (2001). *The Republic of Science: The Emergence of Popper's Social View of Science 1935-1945*. Amsterdam & Atlanta: Editions Rodopi B.V.

Keynes, J. M. (1921). *A Treatise on Probability*. London and New York: Macmillan. 3rd edition 1973. London and Basingstoke: Macmillan.

Miller, D. W. (1994). *Critical Rationalism. A Restatement and Defence*. Chicago and La Salle IL: Open Court.

——— (1998). 'On Methodological Proposals'. In H. Keuth, editor (1998), pp. 67-81. *Karl Popper, Logik der Forschung*. Berlin: Akademie Verlag.

——— (2002). 'Induction: a Problem Solved'. In Böhm, Holweg, & Hoock (2002), pp. 81-106. Reprinted as Chapter 5 of D. W. Miller (2006). *Out of Error*. Aldershot: Ashgate.

Musgrave, A. E. (1991). 'What is Critical Rationalism?' In A. Bohnen & A. E. Musgrave, editors (1991), pp. 17-30. *Wege der Vernunft: Festschrift zum siebzigsten Geburtstag von Hans Albert*. Tübingen: J. C. B. Mohr (Paul Siebeck).

——— (1993). *Alltagswissen, Wissenschaft und Skeptizismus*. Tübingen: J. C. B. Mohr (Paul Siebeck).

——— (2002). 'Karl Poppers kritischer Rationalismus'. In Böhm, Holweg, & Hoock (2002), pp. 25-42.

——— (2004). 'How Popper (Might Have) Solved the Problem of Induction'. In P. Catton & G. Macdonald, editors (2004), pp. 16-27. *Karl Popper. Critical Appraisals*. London: Routledge.

Popper, K. R. (1935). *Logik der Forschung*. Vienna: Julius Springer Verlag.

———— (1963). *Conjectures and Refutations*. London: Routledge & Kegan Paul. 5th edition 1989. London: Routledge.

———— (1972). *Objective Knowledge*. Oxford: Clarendon Press. 2nd edition 1979.

———— (1983). *Realism and the Aim of Science*. London: Hutchinson.

Schramm, A. (1996a). 'Bejahung und Verneinung: Drei $J/N$-Kalküle'. In A. Schramm, editor (1996), pp. 51-66. *Philosophie in Österreich 1996*. Wien: Hölder-Pichler-Tempsky.

———— (1996b). 'Inductive Knowledge'. In K. Lehrer & J. C. Marek, editors (1996), pp. 221-235. *Austrian Philosophy Past and Present*. Dordrecht, Boston, & London: Kluwer.

———— (1998). 'Vermutungswissen: Keine Lösung des Induktionsproblems'. In V. Gadenne, editor (1998), pp. 77-88. *Kritischer Rationalismus und Pragmatismus*. Amsterdam & Atlanta: Editions Rodopi B.V.

———— (2002). 'Rationalitätsbegriffe und Begründungsurteile'. In Böhm, Holweg, & Hoock (2002), pp. 107-125.

# 40

# Artificial Intelligence and Popper's Solution to the Problem of Induction[*]

## Guglielmo Tamburrini

## 1 Introduction

Popper maintained that induction plays no role in scientific inquiry, practical action, or belief formation processes. Developments in artificial intelligence (AI) and closely related fields of investigation, such as machine learning, have been claimed to undermine this view. I shall raise some difficulties for this particular challenge to Popper's anti-inductivism. AI research, no matter how significant for understanding or attaining mechanical intelligence, has not bolstered the inductivist case. Moreover, significant AI achievements in the way of so-called inductive learning can be informatively redescribed in purely falsificationist terms.

In attempting to bring AI to bear on discussions of induction in scientific inquiry one is confronted with a pervasive difficulty: current investigations of the learning and generalization capacities of computing agents, even the more theoretically oriented ones, provide impoverished frameworks for descriptive or normative analyses of scientists' work. To the extent that reasonable connections are found, however, no tensions arise between AI achievements and Popper's view of what he called the *logical* problem of induction (Popper 1972, Chapter 1).

I explore first the connection between some mathematical limitations of computational learning agents and Popper's ideas on induction and scientific method. These unlearnability results — concerning idealized agents having access to unbounded computational resources — show that substantive background information is needed to ensure convergence on correct learning hypotheses on the basis of finite input data. Popperian scepticism about

---

[*]I am greatly indebted to Alberto Mura for many invaluable suggestions and comments. I wish to thank David Miller for his friendly support and helpful comments on an earlier draft. For stimulating discussions on the issues addressed here my thanks are due too to Victor Finn. I benefited from engaging and broad-ranging discussions with the late Giovanni Del Giudice and with the other participants in the 2001-2002 Epistemology Seminar at the University of Pisa — in particular Giovanni Casini, Andrea Colombini, Hykel Hosni, Federico Lazzerini, and Daniele Romano.

induction is coherent with these findings, whereas those who look for computational rules of induction in AI are urged to turn their attention towards AI
systems operating on the basis of domain-specific background knowledge.

Accordingly, I consider next machine learning from examples, achieved by
systems drawing on background hypotheses about the concepts and rules to
be learnt. These systems are meaningfully related to the problem of induction
in scientific inquiry, insofar as scientific laws are special kinds of rules, and
conceptual change is a major component of scientific discovery. But clearly,
concept and rule learning from examples bear on the broader epistemological
issue of the role of induction, if any, in commonsense knowledge acquisition.

A sweeping problem in learning from examples jeopardizes the idea that
genuinely inductive processes are at work there. This is the overfitting of training data, which reminds one that a good approximation to the target concept
or rule on training data is not, in itself, diagnostic of a good approximation
over the whole instance space of that concept or rule. And the successful
performances of learning systems are of no avail either: a familiar regress in
epistemological discussions of induction arises as soon as one appeals to past
performances of these systems in order to conclude that good showings are to
be expected in their future outings as well.

The difficulties surrounding inductivist construals of computational learning from examples reveal the conjectural character of the background hypotheses embedded in learning algorithms, and suggest the opportunity of changing
perspective: learning procedures that are usually called inductive are appropriately viewed as hypothesize-and-test procedures, framed into more comprehensive trial and error-correction processes.

Methodological issues wane, and psychological considerations about induction progressively wax as one turns towards more cognitively oriented AI.
The systems for scientific hypothesis formation that inherit distinctive traits
of Newell and Simon's information processing psychology do not perform inductive inference in any of the senses licensed by epistemological discussions of
induction. And AI models of perceptual capacities are coherent with Popper's
anti-inductivism in psychology: similarity judgments presuppose theoretical
assumptions and defeasible expectations.

## 2 AI, computational learning, and induction

AI is concerned with the computational investigation of intelligent behaviours:
it aims at constructing machines capable of exhibiting such behaviours; and
it also aims at modelling and explaining how a wide variety of intelligent behaviours arise in human beings, other animals, and machines (Nilsson 1999,
pp. 1f.). It is usually agreed that AI pursues its engineering and more properly scientific goals by computational means: computing machines are to be
suitably organized to exhibit intelligent behaviours; the underlying capacities

of both machines and biological systems (perceiving, reasoning, learning, and so on) are to be explained in purely computational terms.[1]

AI research on learning draws on computational analyses developed in such fields as machine learning, evolutionary and neural computing, and computational learning theory. Learning algorithms have been studied in each of these fields, often making their way into AI systems. These developments, Howson recently suggested, provide new material for philosophical and logical reflections on induction (Howson 2000, p. 3):

> ... the problem of induction, considered as the problem of characterizing soundness for inductive inferences, has recently become hot (so to speak). People are now for the first time allocating ... substantial intellectual and material resources to the design of intelligent machinery, and in particular machinery that will learn from data ... What is clear is that some logical basis for learning will certainly have to be built into any successful system.

What is not so clear, however, is whether successful AI learning systems impel a real turn in epistemological discussions of induction. Craig was careful to observe that the AI and philosophical communities use the term 'induction' in rather different ways (Craig 1989). Philosophers have been chiefly concerned with the problem of whether and what sorts of constraints can be imposed on inductive patterns of inference, so that their conclusions *be reasonable to believe*. According to Popper, such constraints can be found neither in scientific inquiry nor in psychological belief formation processes (Popper 1972, Chapter 1). AI researchers are often less demanding in the way of epistemic justification, as they are primarily concerned with effective procedures enabling one to find parsimonious hypotheses that are consistent with available data. The additional problem of justifying the plausibility of such hypotheses, which is crucial for philosophical discussions of induction, is either deferred to a different stage of inquiry or simply dismissed by many AI researchers.[2] Even though the AI and philosophical communities use the term 'induction' in rather different ways, several attempts to establish significant connections have been made. Gillies claimed that Popper's scepticism towards induction, though unaffected by work on BACON and related AI systems for scientific discovery, is no longer tenable in the light of recent advances in concept and rule learning (Gillies 1996). Michalski made a similar suggestion in the early 1980s, at a time when machine learning was just beginning to be recognized as an independent field of investigation (Michalski 1983, pp. 87f.):

---

[1] See Tamburrini (1997) for a discussion of this broad constraint on AI theorizing, and its relationship to the Church–Turing thesis.

[2] As an example of the former attitude, see the quotation from Michalski (1983) later in this section. An example of the latter attitude is examined in §4 below: in the work of Langley, Simon, Bradshaw and Zytkow on the mechanization of scientific discovery by means of BACON and related AI systems, the justification problem is dismissed as a philosophical misconception about the nature of scientific inquiry. A more abstract, formal setting for much work on the mechanization of hypothesis formation processes is presented in Hájek and Havranek (1978), which builds on both logical and statistical concepts.

> ... There was even doubt whether it would ever be possible to formalize inductive inference and perform it on a machine. For example, philosopher Karl Popper believed that inductive inference requires an irrational element .... The above pessimistic prospects are now being revised. With the development of modern computers and subsequent advances in artificial intelligence research, it is now possible to provide a machine with a significant amount of background information. Also the problem of automating inductive inference can be simplified by concentrating on the subject of hypothesis generation, while ascribing to humans the question of how to adequately validate them.

The doubts that Michalski intended to dispel are not even mentioned in a more recent, systematic presentation of learning-theoretic results, where the idea that computational learning systems have the competence for inductive inference is simply taken for granted (Jain et al. 1999, pp. 28 and 61):

> The Theory of Machine Inductive Inference (or 'Computational Learning Theory', etc.) attempts to clarify the process by which a child or adult discovers systematic generalizations about her environment.

> The focus of our book is the inductive competence of scientists whose behavior can be simulated by computer.

In contrast with most of the above claims and presuppositions, I maintain here that AI investigations on learning systems do not compel one to relinquish Popper's radical scepticism towards induction. A proper understanding of both learning-theoretic and machine learning results does not require any appeal to alleged principles of induction, which are supposed to provide partial justification for hypotheses that are effectively generated on the basis of available data by computational agents. And the intelligent behaviour exhibited by learning systems can be properly accounted for in terms of trial and error-correction processes.

To begin with, let us examine the idea that learning-theoretic paradigms provide a suitable framework for studying the inductive competence of what one may appropriately call *effective idealized* scientists.

## 3  Learning theory and inductive incompetence

Effective idealized scientists are computational agents (whence effective) who draw on unbounded computational resources (whence idealized) in their search for empirically adequate theories and laws. These agents, however, can entertain only scientific hypotheses that take the form of some computable function. More important for our present concerns, the effective idealized scientists investigated within this conceptual framework possess no genuinely inductive competence. In fact, the information that computational learning paradigms provide us with is mostly proscriptive rather than prescriptive: unlearnability results point to computational approaches that we do well to avoid if our aim is to model inductively competent agents.

To set the stage for a discussion of these critical points, let us briefly recall how learning is construed within learning-theoretic frameworks.

A learning paradigm is any precise construal of the following concepts:[3]

(1) a learner;

(2) something to be learnt;

(3) an environment that provides the learner with information about what is to be learnt;

(4) the hypotheses that the learner can entertain about what is to be learnt;

(5) criteria of successful learning.

We are presently interested in those computational learning paradigms that were originally proposed to model a child's language learning capacity (Gold 1967): children are viewed as computational agents producing grammars that account for the stream of sentences they are exposed to, discard previously hypothesized grammars that turn out to be inadequate with respect to new incoming sentences, and successfully learn the language if they converge in finite time on a grammar they are no longer forced to abandon in the face of additional input sentences.

Extensions of this particular approach to language learning were framed to cover scientific inquiry. Computational agents (now called effective idealized scientists) advance a scientific hypothesis (theory, law, and so on) accounting for the finite stream of data they have examined so far, can change the selected hypothesis any number of times upon examining more experimental data, and successfully complete the assigned 'learning' task if they converge in finite time on a hypothesis they are not forced to relinquish in the face of new incoming data.

Additional constraints on effective scientists and their environment concern admissible hypotheses and sets of data: these are usually represented as number-theoretic functions and sets of natural numbers, respectively (Jain et al. 1999, p. 48, emphasis mine).

> Scientists often investigate physical systems that implement functions on a suitably chosen domain. The volume of a gas, for example, varies functionally with its temperature and pressure, and the electrical response of a photoreceptor depends functionally on the incident light. Such functions can be approximated with arbitrary precision using rational numbers, which may in turn be coded as natural numbers. In this way, scientific inquiry may be often represented as an attempt to discover which numerical function is actually represented by Nature. To simplify our discussion we assume that the functions in question are total recursive mappings from $N$ to $N$ ... the class of all such functions is denoted by $R$ ... restricting our attention to $R$ represents *the non-trivial assumption* that many natural phenomena can be construed as computational processes.

---

[3]Cp. Osherson, Stob, & Weinstein (1986), p. 7.

Let us focus on the 'non-trivial assumption' mentioned above: any hypothesis that a computational agent can conjecture in response to observed data is expressible as a total computable function. The hypothesis space (HS) of any effective scientist is thereby restricted to theories and laws that are representable as elements of the set $R$ of recursive functions (or of their numerical indices). Call this condition $R_{HS}$.

$R_{HS}$ appears to be overly restrictive when compared to another notion of computational (physical) theory that emerged in discussions of Gödel's views about human and mechanical intelligence. Gödel regarded mind as separate from matter. He also suggested that the immaterial human mind may transcend the mathematical limitations of computational agents revealed by the undecidability and incompleteness theorems.[4] Kreisel noted that the hypothesis of an immaterial mind is not needed to envisage the possibility of an agent surpassing the mathematical powers of computing machines: a physical system harnessed by non-computational laws of matter might as well do. Kreisel's remark presupposes a relatively clear idea of what a non-computational law of matter can possibly be; accordingly, he introduced a definition of computational physical theory, and asked whether physical theories such as classical or quantum mechanics satisfy the definition.[5] A physical theory is computational, according to Kreisel (1974, p. 11)

> (K): if every sequence of natural numbers or every real number which is well defined (observable) according to the theory [is] recursive or, more generally, recursive in the data (which, according to the theory, determine the observations considered).

Later attempts to circumscribe the idea of algorithmic physical theory (by Wang or Penrose, for example) essentially agree with definition (K).[6] Unlike $R_{HS}$, these various attempts accommodate the fact that observable (physical)

---

[4]See Gödel (1990), pp. 266-269 and pp. 305-307, and Gödel (1995), pp. 309f.

[5]Cp. Kreisel (1980), p. 216:

The question above expresses an objection: for if some laws of ordinary matter are non-mechanical, then the notion of machine is not adequate 'in principle' to separate mind and matter. Gödel was at first tempted to dismiss the question, by the familiar petitio principii of supposing that only mechanical laws are precise (for the non-mechanical mind?), but he stopped himself in the middle of the sentence, I believe, the only time in all our conversations. Afterwards, he took an active interest in the search for non-mechanical laws both in physics and in the part of logic which studies specifically mental constructions.

[6]In connection with 'the question whether physical laws are algorithmic' Wang remarks: 'the best sense which can be made of this question is ... to ask whether the predictions of the theory under consideration preserve computability. That is to say, to ask whether the predictions are always computable when the input data are computable.' (Wang 1993, p. 110.) Penrose asks a similar question about Newtonian mechanics: 'Newtonian mechanics is, as we all know, deterministic, but is it computable? Suppose initial data for some physical situation is given in terms of computable numbers (all constants involved being also computable numbers), and we wait for a computable time. Is the state at that time computable from the initial data?' Penrose (1990), p. 649. For discussion, see Guccione et al. (1998).

magnitudes take their values in the real field. Thus, in particular, (K) associates with each computational physical theory $T$ a class of Turing machines: for each one of the real numbers $r$ that are observable according to $T$ there is a Turing machine $M_r$ that generates $r$ (in the data). $R_{HS}$ does not allow for a multiplicity of such machines, as it associates a scientific theory or law $T$ with a single Turing machine $M_T$ computing a total function, and the rational numbers generated by $M_T$ with the values of the magnitudes that are observable according to $T$. The restriction to discrete-valued data, enforced through $R_{HS}$, is not equally problematic in the linguistic domain that computational learning paradigms were originally set to investigate, for the hypotheses entertained by language learners must account for finite strings of symbols from some finite alphabet.

The comparatively narrow requirement on computational theories expressed by $R_{HS}$ could be justified if it turned out that each hypothesis in $R$ can be inductively learnt. This is not the case, however. There are no good reasons to believe that an effective scientist operating on an HS as vast as the set of recursive functions will converge on an empirically adequate hypothesis in finite time. To prepare the ground for a discussion of this claim, let us consider more closely the criteria for successful computational learning.

An effective idealized scientist is allowed to examine arbitrary finite segments of the graph of a recursive function $f$. Without loss of generality, one can suppose that this effective scientist examines only progressively more inclusive, initial (rather than arbitrary) finite segments of the function graph.[7] These segments can be coded by natural numbers, to form an infinite class $I_f$ of inputs for the effective scientist. The latter, in its turn, is modelled as a (partial) recursive function $g$ on the natural numbers. The learning task is successfully completed (the correct hypothesis is *identified* by effective scientist $g$) if $g$ converges to a limit value[8] on $I_f$, and this value is a code of (a program for computing) $f$. In other words, $f$ is identified by $g$ if $g$ takes on a fixed value $m$ for all but a finite number of elements of $I_f$ and $m$ is an index of $f$. This criterion of success reflects the intuitive idea that one is allowed to advance a hypothesis and change one's mind any finite number of times, provided that one eventually conjectures and holds on to (a numerical index for) the function $f$.

A hypothesis $f$ is said to be *identifiable* in the limit by effective idealized scientists if there is at least an effective idealized scientist which identifies (converges in the limit to) an index of $f$. More generally, a class of hypotheses $C \subseteq R$ is identifiable if there is an effective idealized scientist that identifies every $f \in C$. Identification by effective idealized scientist $s$ does not entail that there is any moment at which $s$ can come to know that a correct hypothesis has been identified.

---

[7] See proposition 4.21 in Jain et al. (1999), p. 70.
[8] For precise definitions, see Odifreddi (1989), Chapter IV.1.

We are now in the position to state some uncomputability results that are readily interpreted as theoretical learning limitations of effective idealized scientists.

(1) There is no partial recursive function that identifies $R$ in the limit. Thus, for each effective idealized scientist $s$ there is an $f \in R$ such that $s$ does not identify $f$ (Jain et al 1999, p. 72). The unlearnability of $R$ does not exclude that such an $s$ might improve its performance by considering more limited hypothesis spaces. For example, $s$ may draw on background knowledge in order to reduce its search space.

(2) In the framework of computability theory, a natural way of conveying background knowledge to effective scientists is to make assertions of the form: 'The hypothesis that $s$ is looking for is in recursively enumerable set $W_j$.'[9] Furnishing effective scientists with such hints does not systematically improve learnability. The latter can be improved, if the set $W_j$ happens to contain indices of total functions only, for the recursively enumerable sets that meet this condition are identifiable in the limit (Jain et al. 1999, p. 80). However, the problem of deciding whether recursively enumerable sets meet this condition is recursively unsolvable: no computational informant can systematically do the required job.

(3) According to the above definitions, convergence to a limit value $m$ by an effective scientist is not sufficient for identification to occur, for $m$ may not be an index of the function to be identified. The more demanding requirement of *reliable* convergence by an effective scientist was investigated in Minicozzi (1976). A reliable effective scientist converges on the index $i$ of a function in $R$ if and only if $i$ is an index of the correct function to identify. It turns out that reliable scientists can identify only a proper subset of the set of hypotheses that are identifiable by effective scientists. (See Jain et al. 1999, pp. 118f.) Thus, reliable identifiability requires additional background information with respect to plain identifiability.

These various unlearnability results inform us about approaches that we do well to avoid if our aim is to build learning algorithms that are somehow guaranteed to converge in finite time on correct scientific hypotheses. To express the same point in more explicit falsificationist terms: the information that computational learning paradigms provide us with is proscriptive rather than prescriptive.[10] Once $R_{HS}$ is put in place, identifiability and reliable identifiability by an effective scientist — if possible at all — call for additional restrictions on hypothesis spaces. Thus, to the extent that interesting aspects of scientific hypothesis selection can be modelled within learning-theoretic frameworks, unlearnability results point to the opportunity of drawing on

---

[9]A set of natural numbers is said to be recursively enumerable if it is the domain of some partial computable function. See Davis et al. (1994), p. 79.

[10]For a more general discussion of the relationship between science and technology along these lines, see Miller (1994), pp. 39-41, and Miller (2002).

richer background knowledge in order to meet sceptical doubts about alleged principles of computational induction and pursue the quest for genuinely inductive rules in AI. The machine learning algorithms that we are going to examine in the next section bring into play a wealth of such background hypotheses. These systems are commonly — and, in my view, misleadingly — described as systems for the *inductive* learning of concepts and rules.

## 4 Concept learning as a trial and error-correction process

The learning-theoretic paradigms examined above draw on the conceptual tools of computability theory to explore the learning of hypotheses that are represented as numerical indices of recursive functions. In machine learning approaches, hypothesis spaces are described in less austere terms, and the central role of rich background knowledge is recognized from the outset.[11]

A learning agent is, from the broad perspective of machine learning, any algorithmic system that improves through experience its performance at some task. In concept learning from examples, these systems gain their experience by examining concept instances.[12] Hypothesis spaces are often construed as sets of boolean-valued functions over concept instances.[13] In order to learn target concept $h$, the algorithm examines a training set, that is, a finite subset of the whole instance space $X$ formed by positive or negative instances of $h$.

A distinctively inductive assumption is often made about computational systems that learn concepts from examples. Schematically,[14]

(IC): Any hypothesis found to approximate the target function well over a sufficiently large set of training examples will also approximate the target function well over unobserved examples.

A critical examination of this assumption requires an extensive survey of learning systems that goes well beyond the scope of this paper. Here, I will focus on versions of (IC) concerning the decision tree algorithm ID3: decision tree learning is a widely used method in concept learning, and Quinlan's ID3 reflects crucial features of this method (Quinlan 1986, 1993); Popper's anti-inductivism was questioned on the basis of ID3 performances (Gillies 1996);

---

[11]I have chiefly drawn on Mitchell (1997) as a valuable source for the machine learning algorithms examined here. In a section of this book, significantly entitled 'The futility of bias-free learning', on p. 42, it is claimed: 'a learner that makes no a priori assumptions regarding the identity of the target concept has no rational basis for classifying any unseen instances.'

[12]Machine-learning theorizing is mostly oriented towards learning mechanisms for commonsense knowledge concepts and rules. Thus, the problem of induction in scientific method is only indirectly related to these research efforts, insofar as scientific inquiry often involves the acquisition of new concepts, and the category of rule, broadly construed, subsumes scientific law.

[13]If $H$ is a hypothesis space and $X$ is the associated concept instance space, then $h : X \mapsto \{0, 1\}$, for each $h \in H$.

[14]Cp. Mitchell (1997), p. 23.

critical considerations about an allegedly inductive working of ID3 can be readily transferred to a variety of so-called inductive learning algorithms.

Let us then focus on

(IC-ID3): Any hypothesis constructed by ID3 which fits the target function over a sufficiently large set of training examples will approximate the target function well over unobserved examples.

To begin with, let us recall some distinctive features of (the ID3) decision tree learning. Decision trees provide classifications of concept instances in a training set, formed by conjunctions of attribute/value pairs. Each path in the tree represents a classified instance. The terminal node of each path in the tree is labelled with the yes/no classification. The learnt concept description can be read off from the paths which terminate in a 'yes' leaf. Such description can be expressed as a disjunction of conjunctions of attribute/value pairs. Concept descriptions that make essential use of relational predicates (such as 'ancestor') cannot be learnt within this framework.

ID3 uses a top-down strategy for constructing decision trees. Each non-terminal node in the tree stands for a test on some attribute, and each branch descending from that node stands for one of the possible values assumed by that attribute. An instance in the training set is classified by starting at the topmost, root node of the tree, testing the attribute associated with this node, selecting the descending branch associated with the value assumed by this attribute in the instance under examination, repeating the test on the successor node along this branch, and so on until one reaches a leaf. Each concept instance in the training set is associated to a path in a tree, which is labelled 'yes' or 'no' at the terminal node. ID3 places closer to the tree root attributes that better classify positive and negative examples in the training set. This is done by associating to each attribute $P$ mentioned in the training set a measure of how well $P$ alone separates the training examples according to their being positive or negative instances of the target concept. Let us call this preference in tree construction the ID3 '*informational* bias'.

There is another bias characterizing the ID3 construction strategy. ID3 stops expanding a decision tree as soon as a hypothesis accounting for the training data is found. In other words, simpler hypotheses (shorter decision trees) are singled out from the set of hypotheses that are consistent with the training data, and more complicated ones (longer decision trees) are discarded. On account of this *simplicity* bias,[15] longer decision trees that are compatible

---

[15]Simplicity is identified here with the length of decision trees, and the latter is contingent on the choice of primitive attributes. A simplicity bias is introduced in many machine learning algorithms for hypothesis selection. Cp. Michalski (1983), p. 89:

For any given set of facts, a potentially infinite number of hypotheses can be generated that imply these facts. Background knowledge is therefore necessary to provide the constraints and a preference criterion for reducing the infinite choice to one hypothesis or a few preferable ones. A typical way of defining such a criterion is to specify the preferable properties of the hypothesis, for example, to require that the hypothesis is the shortest or the most economical description consistent with all the facts.

with the training set are not even generated, and thus no conflict resolution strategy is needed to choose between competing hypotheses.

We are now in the position to state more precisely inductive claim (IC-ID3), by reference to the main background hypotheses used by ID3 to reduce its hypothesis space:

> (IC-ID3: second version): Any hypothesis constructed by ID3 on the basis of its informational and simplicity biases that fits the target function over a sufficiently large set of training examples will also approximate the target function well over unobserved examples.

Scepticism about this claim is fostered by the overfitting problem. A hypothesis $h \in H$ is said to overfit the training set if another hypothesis $h' \in H$ performs better than $h$ on $X$, even though $h'$ does not fit the training set better than $h$. Overfitting in ID3 trees commonly occurs when the training set contains an attribute $P$, unrelated to the target concept, that happens to separate well the training instances. In view of this 'informational gain' $P$ is placed close to the tree root (Mitchell 1997, p. 68).

> Overfitting is a significant practical difficulty for decision tree learning and many other learning methods. For example, in one experimental study of ID3 involving five different learning tasks with noisy, nondeterministic data, . . . overfitting was found to decrease the accuracy of learned decision trees by 10-25% on most problems.

Unprincipled expansions of the original training set may not prevent the generation of overfitting trees, for a larger training set may bring about additional noise and coincidental regularities. Accordingly, claim (IC-ID3) is to be further qualified: the 'sufficiently large set of training examples' mentioned there must be 'sufficiently representative of the target concept' as well. This means that conjectures about the representativeness of concept instance collections play a central role in successful ID3 learning. Consider, in this connection, the post-pruning of overfitting decision trees (Mitchell 1997, pp. 67-72). In post-pruning, one constructs a 'validation set', which differs from both training and test sets. The validation set can be used to remove a subtree of the learnt decision tree: this is actually done if the pruned tree performs at least as well as the original tree on the validation set. Expectations of a good performance of the pruned tree on as yet unobserved instances rely on the assumption that the validation set is more representative of the target concept than the training set. Thus, the sceptical challenge directed at (IC-ID3) can be iterated after post-pruning, just by noting the conjectural character of this assumption.

In order to counter this sceptical challenge to (IC-ID3), one should look more closely at the criteria used for judging the representativeness of training and validation examples. But additional problems arise here. These criteria may vary over concepts, and are not easily stated in explicit form. In expert systems, for example, the introspective limitation of human experts is a major bottleneck in system development. The process of extracting rules from human experts turns out to be an extremely time consuming and often unrewarding task. These subjects can usually pick out significant examples of rules or concepts, but are often unable to state precisely the criteria underlying these judgements.[16] Accordingly, automatic learning from examples is more likely to be adopted when criteria for selecting significant concept or rule instances are not easily supplied by human experts; and yet an examination of these criteria is just what is needed to support inductive claim (IC-ID3) by appeal to the representativeness of training examples.

Confronted with these various difficulties, which the sceptic consistently interprets as symptoms that inductive claim (IC-ID3) cannot be convincingly argued for, let us try to assume a falsificationist perspective on ID3.

We have already formed a vague picture of ID3 as a component of a trial and error-elimination cycle: ID3 makes predictions about the classification of concept instances that are not included in the training set, on the basis of assumptions guiding both training set construction and the selection of some concept $c$. If predictions about unseen instances are satisfactory, then one is provisionally entitled to retain concept $c$. Otherwise $c$ is discarded, and correction methods (such as post-pruning) come into play, which implicitly modify the original set of assumptions.

To sharpen this description of ID3 processing as a two-layered prediction-test cycle (leading from a falsification of instance classification predictions to a refutation of the conjunction of the various assumptions used to select the falsified hypothesis), let us draw on the above distinction between the *preferences* or biases embedded in ID3 proper (which determine both the language for expressing concepts and the construction of decision trees) on the one hand, and the presuppositions that are used to select training sets on the other hand. If the presuppositions of the first kind (ID3 biases) can be suitably stated in declarative form, then a concept learning algorithm such as ID3 can be redescribed as a theorem prover. This is brought out by the following definition of the *inductive bias* of a concept learning algorithm, see (Mitchell 1997, p. 43):

> *Definition*: Consider a concept learning algorithm $L$ for the set of instances $X$. Let $c$ be an arbitrary concept defined over $X$, and let $D_c = \{\langle x, c(x) \rangle\}$ be an arbitrary set of training examples of $c$. Let $L(x_i, D_c)$ denote the classification assigned to the instance $x_i$ by $L$ after training on the data $D_c$. The **inductive bias** of $L$ is any minimal set of assertions $B$ such that, for any target concept $c$ and corresponding training examples $D_c$,
>
> $$\forall x_i \in X [L(x_i, D_c) \text{ is logically derivable from } (B \wedge D_c \wedge x_i)].$$

It is worth noticing that the deductive premises mentioned in this definition include the training set rather than the underlying selection criteria. This is quite reasonable, in view of the above considerations about the introspective

---

limitations of human experts, and the fact that $D_c$ is not necessarily invariant over concepts $c$. The search biases embedded into the learning algorithm proper are invariant over concepts. If these can be made explicit through a set $B$ of sentences (in the case of ID3, $B$ must capture its informational and simplicity preferences), a theorem prover can be specified that is extensionally equivalent to $L$ in the way of classification predictions over unseen concept instances.

One is provisionally entitled to preserve $B$ and $D_c$ as long as the classifications coming in through $L$ or its equivalent deductive system are satisfactory. Suppose, however, that for some given number of $i$, $L(x_i, D_c)$ is an incorrect prediction. Then the theorem-proving version of $L$ tells us that either $B$ or $D_c$ has to be changed in order to obtain correct classification in those cases. And Popper's methodological precepts can be applied here, to constrain the ways in which the set of premises is to be changed.

Let us note the following remark of Popper in the light of the above connection between so-called inductive learning algorithms, theorem proving and falsificationist methodology.[17]

> ... we proceed by a method of *selecting* anticipations or expectations or theories — by the method of trial and error-elimination, which has often been taken for induction because *it simulates induction*.

The I/O behaviours exhibited by what is commonly described as an inductive concept learning algorithm $L$ are mappings from concept space instances to their classification. Popper tells us that if one looks into this black box device, one will find there 'a framework determining what is relevant or interesting in its world: the machine will have its "inborn" selection principles'.[18] If these built-in principles are expressed in declarative form, one can account for the I/O behaviour of $L$ in terms of purely deductive procedures. It is also possible to redescribe, in terms of theorem-proving procedures, the learning of first-order rules and concepts by inductive logic programs when analogous conditions are verified.[19]

In concluding this section, let me briefly mention the *probably approximately correct* learning processes (pac-learning), and the constraints characterizing this approach to computational learning. Pac-learning introduces quantitative constraints that are meant to ensure that the hypotheses advanced by means of a learning procedure using a reasonable amount of computational resources are most likely correct. In the case of concept acquisition,

---

[17]Popper (1972), Chapter 7, § 2, p. 272. See also ibidem, p. 266:

We learn about our environment not through being instructed by it, but through being challenged by it: our responses (and among them our expectations, or anticipations or conjectures) are evoked by it, and we learn through the elimination of our unsuccessful responses — that is, *we learn from our mistakes*. An evocative method of this kind, however, can *imitate or simulate* instruction: its results may look as if we had obtained our theories by starting from observation and proceeding by induction.

[18]Popper (1963), Chapter 1, § v.

[19]See Mitchell (1997), pp. 106-112 and pp. 291-293.

for example, pac-learning is concerned with the problem of characterizing classes of concepts that one can learn with arbitrarily high probability from randomly drawn training examples using a reasonable amount of computational resources.[20] Conceptually, this is the more satisfactory machine learning explicatum of the intuitive idea of an inductive procedure we have come across so far, as long as the 'arbitrarily high probability' of a hypothesis is regarded as a meaningful indication of its plausibility. Indeed, hypotheses about the representativeness of training examples are not needed here, for the instances are randomly drawn; and unlike the limiting recursion approaches discussed above, a complexity bound is placed on the computational resources available to each learner. It turns out, however, that the classes of concepts that are pac-learnable are severely limited,[21] to the extent that their relevance to broad philosophical discussions of induction in scientific method and the theory of knowledge is no longer evident. For this reason we forgo any further discussion of pac-learning, and move on to consider AI in its relation to what Popper called the psychological problem of induction.

## 5  Cognitively oriented AI and induction

The investigations of scientific discovery conducted by Langley, Simon, Bradshaw, & Zytkow occupy, as it were, a middle ground between machine learning and cognitively oriented AI. Systems developed by these authors, such as BACON, can be *prima facie* taken to vindicate a role for induction in scientific discovery. But various reasons can be adduced to undermine this view.

To begin with, let us notice that BACON and related systems are primarily meant to demonstrate that scientific discovery is not an inscrutable or idiosyncratic process: 'mechanisms of scientific discovery are not peculiar to that activity but can be subsumed as special cases of problem solving' (Langley et al. 1987, p. 5). Problem solving was extensively analysed by Allen Newell and Herbert Simon in the framework of their pioneering work on information processing psychology (IPP).[22] Psychological fidelity, however, is

---

[20]Computational resources must be polynomially bounded in the parameters expressing the relevant measures of the learning problem. Computational complexity constraints can play a significant role in connection with the problem of induction, insofar as the latter is formulated, in connection with a cognitive system operating in the real world and endowed with bounded resources, as the problem of 'specifying processing constraints that will ensure that the inferences drawn by a cognitive system will tend to be plausible *and relevant to the system's goals*' (Holland et al. 1989, p. 5, emphasis mine).

[21]For example, even though conjunctions or disjunctions of boolean formulas are pac-learnable, boolean formulas in disjunctive normal form are not. See Valiant (1994), p. 103, Mitchell (1997), pp. 213f., and references therein.

[22]Newell & Simon developed computer programs to simulate the problem-solving behaviour of human subjects performing particular problem-solving tasks, such as playing chess, proving elementary logic statements, or doing cryptoarithmetic (Newell & Simon 1972). The empirical data for both designing and testing simulation programs were provided by verbal reports of subjects asked to vocalize their conscious thinking activity when performing these problem-solving tasks. Since problem-solving behaviour is not invariant over *individuals* and *tasks*, the range of both parameters had to be suitably restricted to

not sought in this case.[23] The work of Langley and colleagues is rather meant to provide sufficiency demonstrations: some scientific laws *can* be isolated by a computational system endowed with suitable problem-solving strategies.[24] In particular, BACON's problem-solving strategy for finding terms with constant values is used to 'rediscover' Kepler's third law of planetary motion.[25] Applying this procedure to data concerning distance $D$ and period $P$ of Jupiter's satellites from their primary planet, the program eventually produces the term $D^3/P^2$ to account for the observed data.

It has been justly pointed out that severe constraints on the hypothesis space are built into BACON's problem-solving strategy, and that the formulation of analogous constraints is a most significant part of the inquiries leading up to Kepler's discovery. BACON exploits these constraints to carry out a fairly straightforward task of function extrapolation (Gillies 1996, Holland et al. 1986), one that science undergraduates perform rather well.[26] But this extrapolation process does not make it reasonable to believe that the discovered law will withstand future empirical tests. Hence, there is no apparent connection between BACON and the epistemological problem of induction,

---

special classes of human subjects and problem-solving tasks in order to achieve faithful simulations. Each simulation program, Newell & Simon claimed, can be regarded as a restricted empirical theory (or '*microtheory*') expressed as a computer program: it is a microtheory, because its intended domain is limited to narrow classes of subjects and problem-solving tasks; it is empirical, because the program can be used to derive predictions about the processes that human subjects execute, and the problem states they reach along the way. This methodology cannot be routinely transferred to investigations of scientific discovery: the problem-solving environments of scientific discovery are not, in general, clearly delimited, and there are no detailed verbal reports of scientists' thinking to be compared to computer program traces.

[23] Even though similarities have been detected between BACON's heuristic procedure and the verbal protocols of human subjects engaged in the same problem-solving activities (Qin & Simon 1990).

[24] Thus, no appeal to an inscrutable 'intuition black box' is necessary insofar as some particular aspects of scientific discovery are concerned: 'In testing our simulations, we will usually have to be content with a sufficiency criterion: Can a program that contains only these selective heuristics to guide it actually discover significant scientific laws with only a modest amount of computer effort? If an affirmative answer can be given to this question, then we can claim to have driven the mystery out of these kinds of scientific discovery, at least.' (Langley et al. 1987, p. 33).

[25] This procedure can be summarized in the following way (Carbonell & Langley 1989, p. 484):

If term $X$ has near-constant values, formulate a law involving $X$.

Else, if $X$ increases as $Y$ increases, consider the ratio $X/Y$ and start again.

Else, if $X$ increases as $Y$ decreases, consider the product $XY$ and start again.

[26] Kepler's third law was obtained by 4 out of 14 university students asked to find a numeric law fitting the same data given in input to BACON. Just like BACON, the successful students (mostly science majors) ignored what the data represented. And the guesswork used by successful students was found to embody, by an analysis of their thinking aloud protocols, some sort of simplicity ordering of candidate function types. The authors of this experimental work claim: 'The data for the successful subjects reveal no "creative" processes in this kind of a discovery situation different from those that are regularly observed in all kinds of problem-solving settings' (Qin & Simon 1990, p. 281).

as long as the latter is conceived as the problem of specifying processing constraints enabling one to reach hypotheses that are reasonable to believe.

This view of BACON's operation is consistent with the overall view of scientific discovery advanced by Langley and colleagues: finding *any* parsimonious generalization consistent with the data is the problem of scientific discovery, they suggest, whereas the problem of *justifying* the plausibility of universal generalizations is largely dismissed or deferred to a different phase of scientific inquiry (Langley et al. 1987, p. 16).

> It is well-known that no universally quantified generalization can be verified decisively by a finite set of observations. Not only may subsequent observations overthrow the verification, but it will never be the case that the generalization that has been found to fit the observations is unique. Other generalizations, known or not, will describe or explain the data just as well as the one being considered. It is our claim that, in the discovery phase of its work, science solves these problems of certainty and uniqueness largely by ignoring them. The problem of discovery is precisely to find some generalization that is parsimonious and consistent with all the given data (within some criterion of accuracy).

If the generalizations carried out by BACON are nonetheless called inductions, Langley and colleagues are careful to point out, it is only because the term 'induction' acquires a different meaning in the context of their treatment of scientific discovery (Langley et al. 1987, p. 17).

> The concern that the philosophy of science has had for the certainty and uniqueness of inductions stems from a misconception of the nature of science .... The scientist is a lighthearted gambler, making no greater demands on the world for insurance than the world is willing to supply. Laws, or supposed laws, will often be discovered (a happy moment). They will often be refuted by later evidence (a sad moment), and they will sometimes have to contend with rival laws that explain the same data (a perplexing moment). We do not wholly dismiss the problem of induction — of prediction and uniqueness. Rather, we redefine it.

Let us finally turn to consider briefly what is more properly described as cognitively oriented AI, in connection with the psychological problem of induction. Popper's view here is that psychological expectations arise without or before any repetition, because repetition presupposes similarity, and similarity judgments presuppose theoretical assumptions and expectations about the world (Popper 1972, Chapter 1, § 10).

The conjectural character of the hypotheses built into perceptual systems can be brought out by an elementary example about the classification of binary arrays (forming, for example, strictly black and white images of a given size).[27] The selection of a classification algorithm depends on what one is looking for or expects to find in there. To classify a binary array $x$

---

[27] For a discussion of this example in connection with the problem of devising appropriate similarity measures, especially in the context of neural computing, see Aleksander & Morton (1990), Chapter 1.

as an instance of a letter-type, one may compare $x$ with black and white prototypes of each letter, calculate the Hamming distance[28] of $x$ from each prototype, and classify $x$ according to the lower distance. If one wants to discriminate between, say, bald and non-bald (or bearded and non-bearded) drawings of human faces, then using a Hamming distance applied to a whole image will not do. A more 'local' approach may produce better results: select first a region of the whole image (the upper third of the image for detecting baldness, the lower third for beardedness), and then determine the Hamming distance between the selected image and prototypes of each category.

A more notable illustration of the motives that are commonly adduced to introduce theoretical presuppositions and expectations into AI models of perception is Marr's approach to early visual processing (Marr 1982, Chapter 2). The 'raw' input to the visual system, identified by Marr as a two-dimensional array of (grey) intensity values detected by the retina, is insufficient to recover information about the three-dimensional scene in the visual field. Built into the visual system, Marr suggested, are hypotheses about the visual world that constrain the possible interpretation of bidimensional inputs. Accordingly, a crucial task for a computational theory of vision is to isolate a set of hypotheses constraining three-dimensional interpretations of bidimensional inputs.[29]

Expectations and theoretical presuppositions about the perceptual scene are clearly embedded in the more recent behaviour-based robotic systems for reactive sensing and acting cycles (Arkin 1998, Murphy 2000), as well as in the perception machines of the Darwin series, designed by Edelman and co-workers (Edelman 1989) to probe the idea that adaptively valuable perceptual categorization can develop on the basis of early interactions with the world. Edelman was careful to emphasize, however, that categorization presupposes a set of pre-wired internal values,[30] and that 'general information about the kinds of stimuli that will be significant to the system is built in .... Such a choice is akin to the specializations built into the receptor organs of each species during the course of evolution.'

These pre-wired expectations, Popper relentlessly emphasized, can be defeated in any future interaction of the system with its world. More generally, Popper underscored the conjectural character of the generalizations that are

---

[28] The Hamming distance is the number of array positions for which such binary patterns differ from each other.

[29] In particular, Marr & Poggio developed their classical algorithm for stereo vision (Marr 1982, pp. 111-116) exploiting continuity and uniqueness of location hypotheses. *Continuity*: the surfaces of physical objects are usually smooth and opaque, so that from an observer's point of view the variation in depth is generally continuous, with sharp discontinuities only at the boundary of surfaces. *Uniqueness of location*: a given point on a physical surface has only one three-dimensional location at any given time.

[30] 'This categorization proceeds according to internal criteria that emerge because the automaton has biases or values. For example, the value 'seeing is better than not seeing' is expressed in terms of changes in connection strengths in oculomotor repertoires when visual units become more active following eye movements. Note that value does not prespecify categories, but when categories do emerge, it biases the selection of behaviours consequent upon them.' (Edelman 1989, p. 60).

either wired into biological and mechanical agents or consciously formed and entertained by human beings. This radical anti-inductivist stance survives the challenges raised on the basis of the AI systems and models examined here. Some of these systems, moreover, are informatively redescribed in purely falsificationist terms. According to the standards of critical rationalism, one could have hardly anticipated a better outcome from the rational discussion of a philosophical idea.

# Bibliography

Aleksander, I. & Morton, H. (1990). *An Introduction to Neural Computing*. London: Chapman & Hall.

Arkin, R. C. (1998). *Behavior-Based Robotics*. Cambridge MA: MIT Press.

Carbonell, J. & Langley, P. (1989). 'Learning, Machine'. In S. Shapiro, editor (1989), pp. 464-488. *The Encyclopedia of Artificial Intelligence*. New York: Wiley.

Craig, I. D. (1989). 'Machine Learning and Induction'. In H. Mortimer, editor (1989), pp. 154-176. *The Logic of Induction*. Chichester: Ellis Horwood.

Davis, M., Sigal, R., & Weyuker, E. (1994). *Computability, Complexity, and Languages*. 2nd edition. Boston MA: Academic Press.

Edelman, G. M. (1989). *The Remembered Present*. New York: Basic Books.

Gillies, D. A. (1996). *Artificial Intelligence and Scientific Method*. Oxford: Oxford University Press.

Gold, M. (1967). 'Language Identification in the Limit'. *Information and Control* **10**, pp. 447-474.

Gödel, K. (1990). *Collected Works*, Volume II. S. Feferman, J. W. Dawson, Jr., S. C. Kleene, G. H. Moore, R. M. Solovay, & J. van Heijenoort, editors. New York & Oxford: Oxford University Press.

Gödel, K. (1995). *Collected Works*, Volume III. S. Feferman, J. W. Dawson, Jr., W. Goldfarb, C. D. Parsons, & R. N. Solovay, editors. New York & Oxford: Oxford University Press.

Guccione, S., Tamburrini, G., & Termini, S. (1998). 'On physical laws and computability'. *Agora* **17**, pp. 159-166.

Hájek, P. & Havranek, P. (1978). *Mechanizing Hypothesis Formation, Mathematical Foundations for a General Theory*. Berlin: Springer Verlag.

Holland, J. K., Holyoak, K. J., Nisbett, R. E., & Thagard, P. R. (1989). *Induction Processes of Inference, Learning, Discovery*. Cambridge MA: MIT Press.

Howson, C. (2000). *Hume's Problem. Induction and the Justification of Belief*. Oxford: Clarendon Press.

Jain, S., Osherson, D., Royer, J. S., & Sharma, A. (1999). *Systems that Learn. An Introduction to Learning Theory*. Cambridge MA: MIT Press.

Kreisel, G. (1974). 'A notion of mechanistic theory'. *Synthese* **29**, pp. 11-26.

——— (1980). 'Kurt Gödel'. *Biographical Memoirs of Fellows of the Royal Society* **26**, pp. 149-224.

Langley, P., Simon, H. A., Bradshaw, G. L., & Zytkow, J. M. (1987). *Scientific Discovery. Computational Explorations of the Creative Processes*. Cambridge MA: MIT Press.

Marr, D. (1982). *Vision*. San Francisco: Freeman.

Michalski, R. S. (1983). 'A Theory and Methodology of Inductive Learning'. In R. S. Michalski, J. Carbonell, & T. M. Mitchell, editors (1983), pp. 83-134. *Machine Learning, An Artificial Intelligence Approach*. Berlin: Springer Verlag.

Miller, D. W. (1994). *Critical Rationalism. A Restatement and Defence*. Chicago & La Salle IL: Open Court.

––––––– (2002). 'Induction: a Problem Solved'. In J. M. Böhm, H. Holweg, & C. Hoock, editors (2002), pp. 81-106. *Karl Poppers kritischer Rationalismus heute*. Tübingen: Mohr Siebeck. Reprinted as Chapter 5 of D. W. Miller (2006). *Out of Error*. Aldershot: Ashgate.

Minicozzi, E. (1976). 'Some Natural Properties of Strong Identification in Inductive Inference'. *Theoretical Computer Science* **2**, pp. 345-360.

Mitchell, T. M. (1997). 'Machine Learning'. New York: McGraw Hill.

Murphy, R. R. (2000). *Introduction to AI Robotics*. Cambridge MA: MIT Press.

Newell, A. & Simon, H. A. (1972). *Human Problem Solving*. Englewood Cliffs: Prentice Hall.

Nilsson, N. J. (1999). *Artificial Intelligence: A New Synthesis*. San Francisco: Morgan Kaufmann.

Odifreddi, P. G. (1989). *Classical Recursion Theory*. Amsterdam: North-Holland Publishing Company.

Osherson, D. N., Stob, M., & Weinstein, S. (1986). *Systems that Learn. An Introduction to Learning Theory for Cognitive and Computer Scientists*. Cambridge MA: MIT Press.

Penrose, R. (1990). Précis of *The Emperor's New Mind*. *Behavioral and Brain Sciences* **13**, pp. 643-705.

Popper, K. R. (1963). *Conjectures and Refutations*. London: Routledge & Kegan Paul. 5th edition 1989. London: Routledge.

––––––– (1972). *Objective Knowledge*. Oxford: Clarendon Press. 2nd edition 1979.

Puppe, F. (1993). *A Systematic Introduction to Expert Systems*. Berlin: Springer Verlag.

Qin, Y. & Simon, H. A. (1990). 'Laboratory Replication of Scientific Discovery Processes'. *Cognitive Science* **14**, pp. 281-312.

Quinlan, J. R. (1986). 'Induction of Decision Trees'. *Machine Learning* **1**, pp. 81-106.

––––––– (1993). *C4.5: Programs for Machine Learning*. San Mateo CA: Morgan Kaufmann.

Tamburrini, G. (1997). 'Mechanistic Theories in Cognitive Science: The Import of Turing's Thesis'. In M. L. Dalla Chiara, K. Doets, D. Mundici, & J. van Benthem, editors, pp. 239-257. *Logic and Scientific Methods*. Dordrecht: Kluwer.

Valiant, L. G. (1994). *Circuits of the Mind*. Oxford: Oxford University Press.

Wang, H. (1993). 'On Physicalism and Algorithmism: Can Machines Think?' *Philosophia Mathematica* **1**, pp. 97-138.

# Index

Lightning Source UK Ltd.
Milton Keynes UK
UKOW05f0604190417

299439UK00007B/260/P

9 781848 901919